A History of ILLUMINATED MANUSCRIPTS

Miserationis diuine indagatoris Eximij. Datis
Allegherij prelibati. Secunda pars ipsius Comedie
que Purgatorium dicitur. ipsiusque secute partis
Feliciter incipit Cantus Primus

ER CORRER MI

ghor acque alça le uele
omai la nauicella del mio igegno
che lascia dietro ase mar si crudele.
Et cantero di quel secondo regno
doue lumano spirito si purgha
et di salir al ciel diuenta degno.
Ma qui la morta poesi risurga
o sancte muse poi che uostro sono
et qui Calliope alquanto surga.
Seguitando el mio canto con quel suono
di chui le piche misere sentiro
lo colpo tal che disperar perdono.
Dolce color dorientali gaffiro
che saccoglieua nel sereno aspecto
dellaire puro in sin al primo giro

A History of Illuminated Manuscripts

CHRISTOPHER DE HAMEL

DAVID R. GODINE · PUBLISHER · BOSTON

ACKNOWLEDGEMENTS

The publishers have endeavoured to credit all known persons holding copyright or reproduction rights for illustrations in this book, and wish to thank all the public and private owners, and institutions concerned, and the photographers and librarians.

57, 136, 143 MAS, Barcelona; 89 The Estelle Doheny Collection, St. John's Seminary, Camarillo, California; 4, 7, 80, 91 The Master and Fellows of Corpus Christi College, Cambridge; 3 The Master and Fellows of Trinity Hall, Cambridge; 72, 99 The Master and Fellows of Trinity College, Cambridge; 2 Michael de Hamel; 16, 22, 30 The Board of Trinity College, Dublin; 13, 82, 104 The Dean and Chapter of Durham; 79 Reproduced by permission of the Provost and Fellows of Eton College; 11 The Bankes Collection, National Trust, Kingston Lacy; 86 The Dean and Chapter of Lincoln; 112 and 165 The Estate of the late Major J. R. Abbey; 74, 219 His Grace the Archbishop of Canterbury and the Trustees of Lambeth Palace Library; 162, 241 Christie's Colour Library; 250 The Courtauld Institute; 182 Trustees of Sir John Soane's Museum. Photo: Godfrey New Photographics Ltd, Sidcup; 46, 70, 71, 109, 140, 144, 148, 160, 161, 176, 181, 194, 196, 197, 200, 201, 204, 205, 210, 211, 214, 217, 226, 233, 245, Sotheby's, London; 44, 162, 225 By Courtesy of the Board of Trustees of the Victoria and Albert Museum, London; 245 Reproduced by permission of the Marquess of Bath, Longleat House, Warminster, Wilts.; 28 The Beinecke Rare Book and Manuscript Library, Yale University; 164 All rights reserved, The Metropolitan Museum of Art; frontispiece H. P. Kraus, New York; 112, 120, 129, 223 Photo: Bodleian Library; 85 The Governing Body of Christ Church, Oxford. Photo: Bodleian Library; 115 The President and Fellows of Corpus Christi College, Oxford. Photo: Bodleian Library; 83, 84, 87, 102 The Principal and Fellows of Jesus College, Oxford. Photos: Bodleian Library; 184 Paris, École Nationale Supérieure des Beaux-Arts; 59, 139, 154, 156, 157 Giraudon, Paris; 16, 41, 45, 144, 143, 144 Foto Biblioteca Vaticana; 100, 101 The Dean and Chapter of Winchester.

First U.S. edition published in 1986 by
David R. Godine, Publisher, Inc.
Horticultural Hall
300 Massachusetts Avenue
Boston, Massachusetts 02115

First published in the U.K. by Phaidon Press Limited

Library of Congress Cataloging in Publication Data
De Hamel, Christopher, 1950–
A history of illuminated manuscripts.
Bibliography: p.
Includes index.
1. Illumination of books and manuscripts—History.
I. Title
ND2900.D36 1986 745.6′7′09 85–82310
ISBN 0–87923–631–0
First Printing

Designed by Tim Higgins

Typeset by Keyspools Ltd., Golborne, Lancashire, in 'Monophoto' Poliphilus and Blado italic with titles in VGC Zapf Chancery Demi-Bold

Printed by The Bath Press, Avon, England

(FRONTISPIECE) New York, H. P. Kraus manuscript, f.95r; Dante, Divina Commedia, Florence, written by Paolo di Duccio Tosi, 1412.

Contents

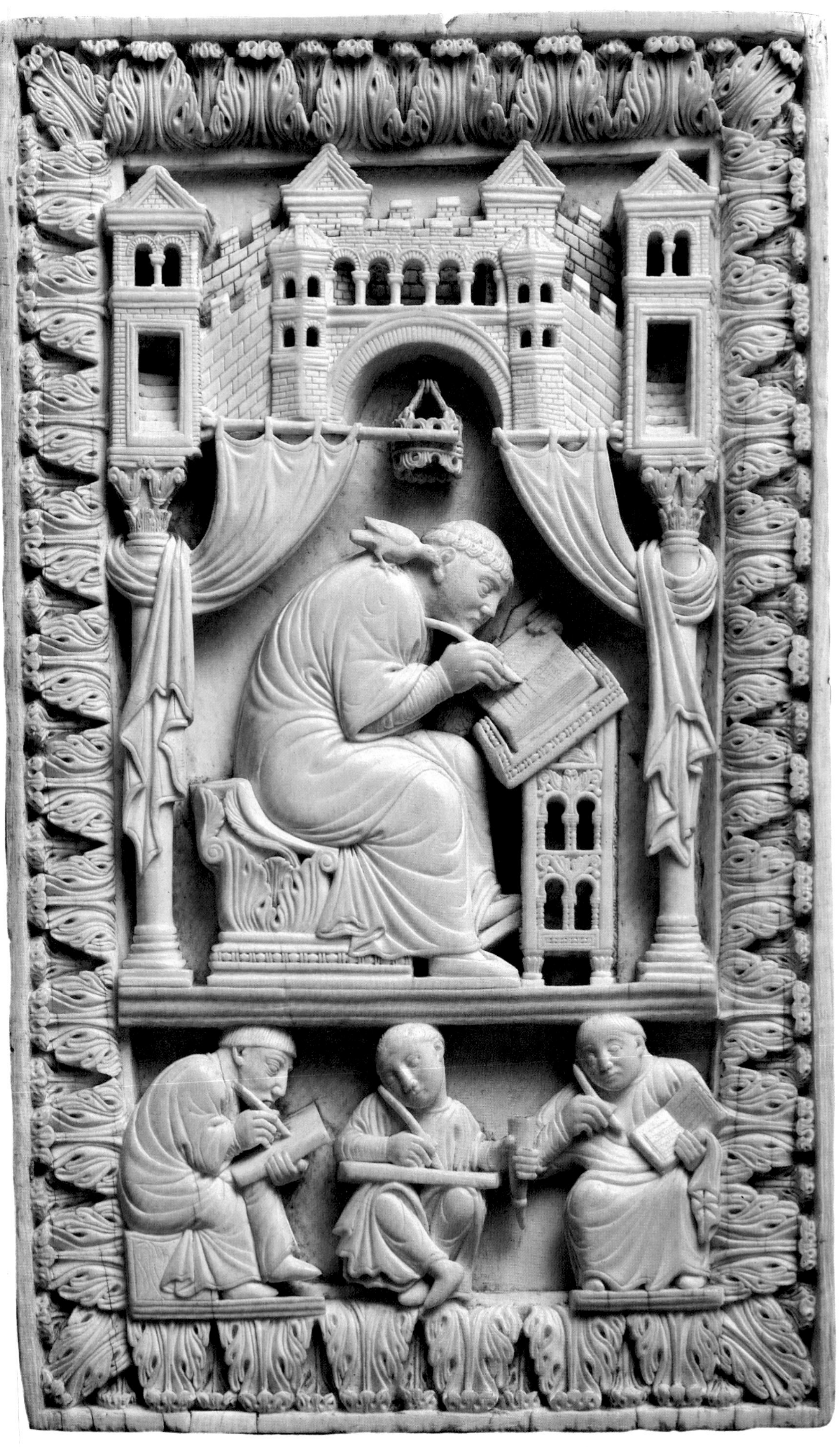

1 Vienna, Kunsthistorisches Museum; Ivory book cover, tenth century. *St. Gregory the Great is composing a text and three scribes are copying it.*

Introduction

The word 'manuscript' literally means 'written by hand'. When we talk about medieval manuscripts we usually mean the books produced by hand in Europe between about the fifth century and the Renaissance of the late fifteenth century. The books are all written by hand and are sometimes beautifully decorated. It happens that the Middle Ages form a neatly defined historical period, but the outside limits for medieval manuscripts are determined by two crucial changes in the methods of book production. The first was the invention of the book as a more or less rectangular object with pages. There had been various forms of writing from the earliest periods of recorded history: scratched impressions in clay, chiselled stone inscriptions, ephemeral wax tablets, and the long-lasting papyrus scroll. Most ancient Roman literature was first written down on scrolls. The great change took place in the first centuries AD. The scroll gradually gave way to the book, or *codex*, in the modern sense with separate pages that can be turned and read one after the other. Scribes began to use prepared animal skin (parchment or vellum – the terms are interchangeable) rather than papyrus because vellum leaves are less likely to break off if they are frequently turned. Scrolls are practical for reciting a continuous literary text and are convenient to store (and are perhaps enjoying a revival in the modern microfilm), but they are difficult to handle for works such as the Bible or law books in which the reader often needs to refer backwards and forwards. As Christianity overtook classical culture from the fourth century and as the old Roman law was finally collected and codified (a word which refers directly to the new type of book), so the scroll evolved into the vellum *codex* in the last years of the Roman empire. This development coincides with the beginning of what are called the Middle Ages. It marks the opening of our story.

The end of our period is indicated by the invention of printing. This began with experiments in the Rhineland in the 1440s, and sophisticated printing with movable type was introduced from Germany into Italy (1465) and France (1470), followed rapidly by the Low Countries, Spain, and England. By about 1510 most European books were being made on printing presses. The invention had an enormous impact on literature and on the written word, as has often been stressed; it represents the end of the production of illuminated manuscripts and coincides with the close of the medieval period. Not all scribes regretted the passing of the handwritten book. Many welcomed printing. At last books could be made more quickly and with greater accuracy than ever before. We shall see how scribes had tried to devise methods of doing this centuries before. Printing was a tremendous boon, and many scribes themselves became printers, doing what they had always done but with greater efficiency and profit. Book production was a very practical business.

We are concerned therefore with the books made in the Middle Ages – manuscripts because (in the absence of other methods) they were made by hand. The period covered is vast, more than a thousand years (twice as long as the history of the printed book), and it covers all countries of western Europe. Manuscripts are the medium for the entirety of the Scriptures, liturgy, history, literature, law, philosophy, and science from the classical and medieval ages. They preserve the major portion of medieval painting and all the arts of handwriting, bookbinding, and publishing. If the field is huge, the number of surviving books is enormous. Illuminated manuscripts are often included in that general (and pleasantly deceptive) category of 'rare books'. Rarity is not their most obvious characteristic, and there is no doubt that more books survive than any other artefact from the Middle Ages. Books have a knack of surviving. In a limited way we can see this survival against all odds reflected in our own households today: the items we still possess from childhood are not the long-gone toy aeroplanes and tricycles, but the books, battered perhaps and often repaired, but still with us. Books from the distant past can survive in the same way, just because they were never thrown out. St. Augustine's Abbey in Canterbury, the first monastery in England, has been an utter ruin for centuries, but over 250 of its medieval books have passed from owner to owner and still exist today. We shall be meeting some of them in chapters I and 3. What private possessions still survive from the great figures of European history, such as St. Boniface, Charlemagne, Otto III, Thomas Becket, St. Louis, Boccaccio, and Erasmus? Their books survive, handled and read by all of them.

Medieval books are now preserved in all parts of the world. Hundreds of thousands exist, and energetic collectors can still acquire them. Many are concentrated in the great national collections such as the British Library in London, the Bibliothèque Nationale in Paris, and the Bayerische Staatsbibliothek in Munich, but there are great holdings of medieval books in universities, museums, and libraries in many cities and countries. I cannot resist mentioning that I began to look at them in Dunedin, New Zealand. Most people live somewhere near at least a few medieval manuscripts. Almost anyone, with a little patience and tactful persuasion, can get to handle one. It can be a fascinating experience.

The breadth of the subject makes it very difficult to synthesize into a single volume. Manuscripts are so different from each other. A small grammatical treatise written out by a priest in Verona in the seventh century, for instance, has little in common with an illustrated Book of Hours ordered by a Parisian cloth merchant's wife around 1480, except that they are both manuscripts. A Carolingian imperial Gospel Book, to take another example, not only looks quite different from a fourteenth-century Bohemian song book, but its original purpose was quite different and the circumstances of its production share almost nothing except that scribes were involved. Even in the same period, the mechanics of illuminating a Livy for Cosimo de' Medici, for example, are altogether unlike the methods used the same year by a student at Erfurt University to make his own commentary on the Psalms. This should surprise nobody. The function of the student's book was quite different. To try to account for all kinds of medieval book in a single all-embracing narrative would not only be impractical but infinitely confusing, as one style and category of book would run parallel with countless others and diverge and rejoin and cross the main threads in a tangled web of copies and influences as wide and diverse as the whole of medieval culture.

2 Dunedin, Public Library, Reed Collection MS.8, f.36v; Book of Hours, northern France, *c.*1500.
The miniature shows the Coronation of the Virgin and illustrates the Office of Compline.

There are several ways of coming to terms with the vast mass of historical information and artefact. The traditional method is to take the high spots only and to consider the very famous manuscripts on their own. We would jump from one masterpiece to another, but, to re-use a famous metaphor, we cannot explore a mountain range by looking only at the peaks. The *Très Riches Heures* of the Duc de Berry is great because it is so exceptional, and even if we knew everything about it (which we do not), it would add little to our understanding of the fifteenth-century book trade. It would be like writing a social history entirely by means of biographies of kings.

A second method would be to follow right through certain characteristics of manuscripts, such as handwriting and illumination. This approach is often successful over a short period or limited geographical area. However, many manuscripts are not illuminated at all, and are no less valuable. All manuscripts include handwriting, of course, but script does not evolve with a fixed and universal regularity. Nor does the reader now want eighty thousand words on the shape of the letter 'g' (a subject I rather recommend, incidentally). The brilliant attempts by Belgian manuscript historians to classify medieval script with the precision of botanists are fascinating in the classroom but are difficult to apply in the library. Medieval scribes were human too. A bad scribe followed few rules. A skilful one could produce a dozen different kinds of handwriting according to the kind of book he was making.

If one were really faced with contrasting the Book of Kells and the *Très Riches Heures* of the Duc de Berry, the difference would not be in the text (by chance, parts are identical) or even in the decorative style (of course that is not the same – the books are six hundred years apart) but in the purpose in making the book. Monks in a tiny Northumbro-Irish island monastery had a reason for making the Book of Kells that was completely different from that of the rich, secular Limbourg brothers who undertook a prestigious commission in the court of the king's brother in the early fifteenth century. This difference of purpose is reflected in the material, size, colour, layout, decoration, and binding of the two manuscripts. Only when we can see what they were trying to do can we stand back and try to judge the work of art in its own right.

Therefore it seems appropriate to try to isolate some of the principal reasons for making books in the Middle Ages. Each forms a separate chapter. Each is only part of the whole subject of medieval manuscripts. If we can look at certain groups of books from the point of view of the people who needed them, we can conveniently cover a much wider range and can jump centuries and styles without losing track of the theme. By examining a few manuscripts we may be able to apply general observations to others sharing the same purpose. Of course no classification can be exact and one theme overlaps another, but some chronological sequence emerges and one angle of inquiry represents each period. Briefly, we can take the subjects in turn.

The first theme is the need for books for missionaries. Christianity is the religion of written revelation. As early parties of missionaries moved across northern Europe preaching to heathen tribes, they offered literacy and a civilization founded in Judea and polished in Rome. Their books were the tangible proof of their message. They exhibited them, read the services from them, and taught civilization from them. We shall see something of how this must have been done. The missionary movement chosen to illustrate the theme took place in Britain and among the British missions to Germany. This is a useful choice. England and Ireland were never really engulfed in the Dark Ages and, while tribes were ravaging seventh-century Europe, monks in Northumberland and Ireland were producing Latin manuscripts of an extraordinary sophistication. It was from Britain that Christianity was re-exported to the Low Countries and to Germany. Britain produced two of the world's great works of art, the Lindisfarne Gospels and the Book of Kells. But it must be stressed that this is only a sample of what was going on in the *scriptoria* of Europe between about AD 650 and the ninth century. There was literacy in Italy and in North Africa and in great parts of Spain and southern France. It is convenient for us, in asking the question of where Benedict Biscop of Northumbria obtained his books, to say that he got them in Italy, but that only puts the problem back one stage. The reader must take for granted the vast cultural legacy of ancient Rome. If we have to exclude such celebrated monuments as the two fifth-century Virgil manuscripts now in the Vatican or the classical texts from Bobbio and Verona, this is because it is simpler to plot the advance of literacy (and Roman literacy too, expressed in the Roman script known as uncial) as it moves with the missionaries across pagan countries far from the Mediterranean.

The court of Charlemagne brings us into a fascinating blend of the rough free-for-all Germanic traditions of the north and the newly imported southern civilization of Rome where Charlemagne was crowned by the pope in AD 800. The new Holy Roman Emperor deliberately imitated classical culture and used the imperial purple for the pages of manuscripts. But his subjects were brought up in the traditions of warfare rewarded by booty and of allegiance rewarded by protection. Now, however, golden manuscripts replaced barbarian loot. Books were treasure. They were deliberately valuable. They were almost part of the fiscal resources of the empire. Again this is a specific theme which can carry us for four centuries through the imperial treasuries of France and Germany to admire the manuscripts of Charlemagne, Otto III, Henry II, and Henry the Lion. These books are some of the very grandest ever produced, and that is why they were made.

It is stating the obvious to stress again that of course imperial manuscripts are not the only books written during those centuries. They are merely one very remarkable type. At the same time books were being made all over Europe. The greatest contribution comes from the monasteries. This will be no surprise: the association of monks and old manuscripts comes easily to mind. What is less well known is that the great period of monastic book production came to an end around 1200 and that for the last three hundred years of the Middle Ages manuscripts were usually made by professionals rather than by monks. For this reason, the theme of making books for monastic libraries focuses here on the twelfth century. We can watch the change from the old to the new methods of supplying books for the needs of monks. The country chosen to illustrate this phenomenon is England. The choice could perfectly well have been France, but Germany or Italy would probably have furnished fewer really great monastic books. Craftsmanship and the monastic life are commonly linked and probably never again were such fine books made in England. It is in the monastic context that we can follow through most simply the general aspects of making vellum, ruling, writing, mixing paints, and applying gold. In this chapter we see the unhurried book production of the cloister.

The phenomenon which marked the end of the monks' monopoly of learning was the dramatic rise of the universities. Students need books, and universities need a great number of books. We must look primarily at Paris. Here from the early thirteenth century there were organized professional stationers who devised and marketed textbooks. The university book trade gives a fascinating insight into the needs of scholarship and into the mechanics of publishing. There were clear rules about the purpose of books in a university, and this is directly reflected in the manuscripts made and decorated for students. It is a subject curiously neglected in general studies of medieval manuscripts, but it takes us right back to the beginning of the profession of making books for sale.

When I was at school, two neat explanations for any historical event always seemed available: one was the rise of nationalism (probably they do not teach this one any more) and the other was the rise of the middle classes. One or other was cited to explain almost everything from the Peloponnesian War to the Weimar Republic. Both themes emerge in the fifth chapter. Secular literature is the most enduring monument of the Middle Ages. The great national epics of the Trojan War, King Arthur, Roland, and the Nibelungenlied, and the works of the first modern authors, Dante, Jean de Meun, and Chaucer, all come into prominence with the emergence of a wealthy literate laity (or nearly literate, as we shall see, helped by pictures). There was now a market for simple vernacular stories, and books were produced for this purpose. The theme is most striking in the fourteenth century, but it goes back to the twelfth century and forwards indefinitely, since it is still a feature of book production.

By the fifteenth century the number of people wanting and

using books seems almost unlimited. While we must not neglect the famous patronage of such collectors as the French and Burgundian royal families, it is the extreme popularization of books which forms so distinctive a feature of the end of the Middle Ages and which eventually gave way to printing with little change in the book trade. The most popular text of all was the Book of Hours. These are by far the most common surviving manuscripts, and one might sometimes imagine that everyone in the fifteenth century owned a copy. It is a standard series of prayers and psalms intended for recitation at the eight canonical 'hours' of the day, from Matins to Compline. How much they were actually used is a different question altogether. The need for quite unprecedented numbers of copies led to many new methods of mass-producing and selling Books of Hours. The examples must be mainly French, but they take us through the wealthy bourgeois towns of Flanders and the Low Countries. Books of Hours were rare in Germany and usually of poor quality in England. If the image of a virtual production line in cheap Books of Hours is distressing to those of us who liked to dream of old monks painstakingly labouring in ivy-clad cloisters, it is an important historical fact with significance not only for the study of art but also of popular education. Most people learned to read from Books of Hours. The word 'primer' reflects the office of Prime which they read in a Book of Hours each morning.

Although a Book of Hours was a prayerbook, it was intended for use at home rather than in a church. Priests had their own manuscripts for use during Mass and for the daily round of services which took place in parish churches all across Europe. The Reformation had not yet taken place, and all countries of western Europe belonged to the Catholic church. Priests used Missals and Breviaries as well as Graduals, Antiphoners, Psalters, Manuals, Processionals, model sermons and handbooks on parish duties. A great many such manuscripts still survive. They are not all beautifully decorated as many were utilitarian copies. The function of the books would have been very familiar in the late Middle Ages but those who handle them today often find the texts difficult to distinguish. Nineteenth-century owners used to call all these manuscripts 'Missals', a title which is often far from correct. Chapter 7 examines the books which a priest would have used in his church in the fifteenth century.

The Middle Ages came to an end with the Renaissance. This started in southern Europe. While Parisian workshops were still undertaking thoroughly gothic Books of Hours for contemporaries of the Duc de Berry, the scribes of Florence and Rome were already producing elegant classical texts in what they thought was the ancient Roman manner. They devised neat round scripts and pretty vinestem initials. A whole new generation of humanistic collectors was swept into the excitement of rediscovering the classics (and the booksellers neatly met this demand, enriching themselves in the process). By the time that printing offered a more accurate alternative to manuscripts, there was an efficient and professional network of decorators, binders, and booksellers. The change was straightforward. The first printers in Italy copied the small round script (which, for this reason, we still call 'Roman' type). Classical culture was re-exported from Italy all over again, taking us back to what the missionaries had started a thousand years before. Printing was here to stay. Books were no longer manuscripts.

•1•

Books for Missionaries

When St. Augustine and his fellow missionaries landed in south-east England in AD 597, they asked for an interview with King Ethelberht of Kent, saying they had important news of eternal life to announce. Bede recounts that an audience was arranged in the open air and that, as the missionaries approached the king, they held up a silver cross and the image of the Saviour painted on a board. A few days later the monks reached Canterbury, where Ethelberht had assigned a house to them, and once again it is related by Bede that, according to their custom, they came for the first time towards the city bearing aloft the cross and the image of Christ. It was evidently very important that right from the outset the monks should exhibit a visual image of the new religion which could be seen and wondered over even before they began explaining the message of Scripture.

After Augustine had reported his successes back to Rome, a further delegation of missionaries was sent out to consolidate the newly founded church. In 601 the party arrived, led by Mellitus, and brought with them, Bede says, 'all such things as were generally necessary for the worship and ministry of the Church, such as sacred vessels, altar cloths and church ornaments, vestment for priests and clerks, relics of the holy apostles and martyrs, and very many books' ('codices plurimos', in his words). It is these books which are of interest. Christianity is the religion of the book and its message goes with literacy, a concept new to many of its British converts. Missionaries, then as now, could face sceptical audiences with the Gospels under their arms – a specific manual for salvation in debate against a religion based on oral tradition – and the scarcely literate are quite rightly impressed by the written word.

We do not know exactly what manuscripts were brought in 601. Alfred the Great says that St. Augustine owned a copy of the *Pastoral Rule* of Gregory the Great, the pope who sent the mission, and this is more than likely. Bede calls it a remarkable book, and it was of great value for missionaries. The late medieval library catalogue of St. Augustine's Abbey in Canterbury recorded ten copies of the *Pastoral Rule* and many other texts by Gregory the Great, some described as old, imperfect and worn out through use. St. Augustine's copy, sent to him by the author, would have been an exciting relic if it had survived. It would have looked something like the ancient copy now in Troyes (Bibliothèque Municipale MS. 504), written probably in Rome about AD 600 in splendid uncial script in twenty-five long lines to a page without division between words and with penwork initials in dark red, dark green, and brownish yellow. The volume has been cruelly repaired with modern gauze but is still impressive, though it is not (as far as anyone knows) from the English mission.

The late medieval monks of St. Augustine's Abbey believed they had some books acquired from St. Augustine himself, and these were carefully examined by Thomas of Elmham between 1414 and 1418. He drew a sketch of the high altar in the abbey church showing that the books were kept there propped up in two rows among other relics of saints (Pl. 3). He describes a two-volume Bible with inserted purple leaves, a Psalter and hymnal, a Gospel Book (known as the Text of St. Mildrid – Elmham says a certain peasant in Thanet swore falsely on it and was said to have been struck blind), and another Psalter with a silver binding showing Christ and the Evangelists. Elmham quotes the exact contents of this last book, and it still survives. It is now MS. Cotton Vespasian A. I in the British Library (Pl. 6). The book had passed after the suppression of St. Augustine's Abbey to William Cecil, Lord Burghley (1520–98), and from him to Sir Robert Cotton (1571–1631), whose magnificent library entered the newly founded British Museum in 1753. It is disappointing to find that the ancient tradition does not stand up to investigation. The manuscript is of superb quality, in uncial script rather like that of the Troyes St. Gregory, but it is English in execution and must be assigned to a decade or so around 730. St. Augustine himself had died in 604. The Vespasian Psalter, as it is called, is almost certainly based on some Italian models, but it is a local production. The important point is that the monks remembered St. Augustine as bringing books to Britain and they associated this square uncial manuscript with the earliest mission. We need not blame them because after eight hundred years they were venerating the wrong volume.

There may be an actual candidate, however, for one of St. Augustine's books. This is a Gospel Book which belonged to Matthew Parker (1504–75), Archbishop of Canterbury, and which is still in the library that Parker gave to Corpus Christi College in Cambridge (MS. 286). It too comes from

3 Cambridge, Trinity Hall MS. I, detail of f. 77r; Thomas of Elmham, Chronicles of St. Augustine's Abbey, Canterbury, *c.* 1414–18. *This is an early fifteenth-century drawing of the High Altar in the abbey church at St. Augustine's. Behind little battlements and on either side of the relics of St. Ethelberht, first Christian king of Kent, are the six manuscripts said to have been sent by Pope Gregory to St. Augustine in 601.*

4 (BELOW) Cambridge, Corpus Christi College MS. 286, detail of f. 58v; Gospels, Italy, sixth century. *This manuscript, which was certainly in England by the early eighth century, was very possibly one of the actual books brought by St. Augustine's mission.*

St. Augustine's Abbey. It is Italian work of the sixth century, quite consistent with the first missions (Pls. 4 and 7). It was certainly in England by the late seventh or early eighth century when numerous corrections were made to the text, and it was demonstrably at Canterbury from the early tenth century. The book has been much used, and it is not complete. It does, however, preserve two full-page miniatures of which the first shows twelve scenes from the life of Christ and the second depicts St. Luke holding an open book and surrounded by six further scenes from Christ's life. If all the miniatures had survived (indeed there are faint offsets from at least four others) there would have been a very extensive cycle of pictures from the story of Christ. Those that survive are simple and dramatically explicit in their message. It was the custom of St. Augustine's missionaries, as we have just seen, to exhibit the painted image of Christ as a prelude to preaching and no doubt the technique was very effective. He could have held up this book too. The illustrations had a very simple and very practical function.

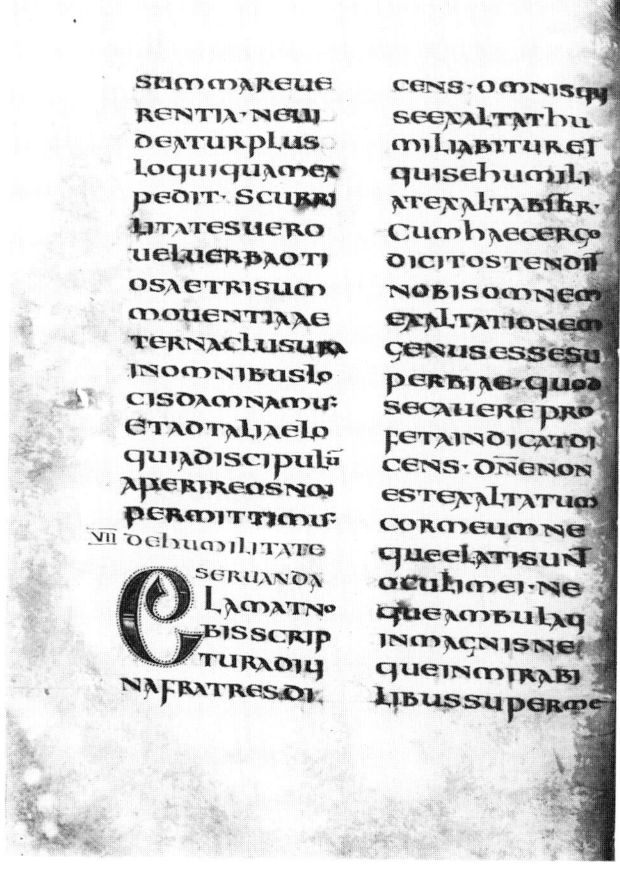

5 Oxford, Bodleian Library, MS. Hatton 48, f. 17v; Rule of St. Benedict, England, early eighth century. *St. Benedict (c. 480–c. 547) was the founding father of western monastic life. This manuscript, which was written in England, is the oldest surviving copy of his book of rules for monks. It is written in uncial script on the model of Italian manuscripts and must have belonged to one of the earliest communities of Roman monks in England.*

The 'very many books' which arrived with St. Augustine's mission were certainly not the only Italian manuscripts brought to Britain in the early generations of Christianity. A similar phrase, 'innumerabilem librorum omnis generis copiam', is used by Bede to describe the acquisitions in Northumbria at Wearmouth and at Hexham. Both Bede and an anonymous monk wrote lives of abbots of Wearmouth and Jarrow, and we are well informed about Benedict Biscop and his successor Ceolfrith, two exceptional Northumbrian administrators and bibliophiles. Benedict (*c.* 628–90) travelled to Rome five times. On his third visit, Bede says, he acquired 'no inconsiderable number of books'. In 674 he was given land by Egfrith, King of Northumbria, for a monastery to be built at Wearmouth, in the extreme north-eastern corner of England. His library, temporarily on deposit at Vienne in France, now went to form the nucleus of the Wearmouth collection. Once again Benedict set off for Rome in the company of Ceolfrith in 678. They returned with relics and pictures for the new abbey, including panel paintings of Christ, perhaps something like the one held aloft by St. Augustine, and above all they seem to have brought back manuscripts. We have a few clues about these forays into the book collections of Italy. Bede recounts that many books were acquired on one of Benedict Biscop's visits to Italy, 'and these he had either bought at a price, or received as presents from his friends'. This is important. The reference to purchasing at a price is tantalizing, as it suggests there was a market for books in Italy. It would be fascinating to have details of how this worked in practice. Were there still some kinds of bookshops as there had been in late classical Rome? However it was achieved, Benedict Biscop and Ceolfrith may actually have brought off one of the greatest book-collecting *coups* of all time. It seems very possible that they purchased second-hand the library of Cassiodorus (*c.* 485–*c.* 580), the great Roman patristic author and scholar. When he retired from public life, Cassiodorus had set up two monastic communities at Vivarium in the far south of Italy and he had formed there a kind of academy for the promotion of both religious and secular learning. Cassiodorus mentions in his *Institutiones Divinarum et Saecularium Litterarum* that he furnished the foundation with different kinds of scriptural manuscripts which he describes in some detail. These included what was known as the Codex Grandior, a huge one-volume 'pandect' (that is, a Bible in a single volume) in the old Latin or pre-Jerome version. This actual book, Cassiodorus's copy, was certainly in Northumbria in the time of Bede.

Probably Ceolfrith and Benedict acquired all or some of Cassiodorus's Bible in nine volumes (the *Novem Codices*), which we know to have been at Vivarium too, and they may have obtained a third Bible which Cassiodorus described as being in tiny script. Not impossibly the purchase included copies of Cassiodorus's own commentaries (of which Durham Cathedral MS. B. II. 30 may be some echo) and perhaps even the old Latin version of Josephus and other classical texts. We know that, one way or another, the resources of Wearmouth and of Benedict's second foundation of Jarrow became exceptionally rich.

Bede himself, working in Jarrow *c.* 690–*c.* 735 and never travelling out of the north of England, cites some eighty different authors whose works he must have seen. The importance of the Christian missions to Britain cannot be overstated, but it is not insignificant either that the learning which went hand in hand with Christianity brought patristic and classical literature to the very edge of the known world.

Once furnished with exemplars to copy, monks began making their own books (Pl. 5). An important documented record of book production occurs also in the lives of the abbots of Wearmouth and Jarrow. The biography of Ceolfrith (642–716) ends with an account of his works and says that he commissioned three huge Bible manuscripts ('tres pandectes novae translationis'), one each for use in the churches at Wearmouth and Jarrow, and one which Ceolfrith eventually announced was to be offered as a present to the pope. One could imagine that Ceolfrith wished to demonstrate to the Roman see (through whom Cassiodorus's Codex Grandior and its fellow volumes had possibly come)

6 London, British Library, Cotton MS. Vespasian A. I, f. 30v, Psalter, England (probably Canterbury), *c.*730.
This Psalter, which the monks of St. Augustine's Abbey erroneously believed had belonged to St. Augustine himself, is an eighth-century copy of an Italian original which may well have been contemporary with Augustine. This miniature shows King David with his court musicians.

7 (OPPOSITE) Cambridge, Corpus Christi College MS. 286, f. 125r; Gospels, Italy, sixth century.
Two full-page paintings remain in the Gospel Book which may well have come to England with St. Augustine's mission. This one shows twelve little scenes illustrating the Passion of Christ from the Entry into Jerusalem until the Carrying of the Cross. It is the kind of picture which St. Augustine would have exhibited to his pagan and illiterate audiences to explain the Gospel story.

that even remote England was now able to reproduce great books and was worthy of housing the exemplars. He may even have been fulfilling a business arrangement: perhaps the Cassiodoran library was released only on the understanding that a copy of the great pandect was returned to Rome for reference. The chronicle quotes a dedication inscription added to the presentation manuscript, naming Abbot Ceolfrith as offering the book in token of faith from the furthest ends of the earth, as indeed it then was ('extremis de finibus'). Abbot Ceolfrith himself accompanied the expedition to carry the manuscript to the pope. They set out on 4 June 716. This is the earliest date known to us for the export of a book made in England. Unfortunately Ceolfrith never arrived. He died on the road at Langres on 25 September. The book is not known to have reached Rome, and that, until a hundred years ago, was the end of the story.

In the Biblioteca Laurenziana in Florence is a celebrated Latin Bible of the very early eighth century – in fact, the oldest complete Latin Bible known – which was used for the revision of the Vulgate published in 1590. It had come to Florence from the abbey of Monte Amiata, and is known as the Codex Amiatinus. It has a presentation inscription from

8 Florence, Biblioteca Medicea-Laurenziana, MS. Am. 1, f. Vr; Bible, Northumberland, c.700–716.
The frontispiece of the huge Bible intended by Ceolfrith to be a present to the pope shows a saintly figure, presumably the Old Testament prophet Ezra, writing a manuscript on his lap and seated before an open book cupboard which contains a Bible in nine volumes, like that owned by Cassiodorus and probably brought to England by Ceolfrith.

a 'Petrus Langobardorum' (Pl. 9) and the volume was always thought to be Italian work. In 1886, however, G. B. de Rossi observed that several names in the inscription had been tampered with and were written over erasures and, without at first linking this with Wearmouth/Jarrow, he pieced out the original donor's name as 'Ceolfridus Anglorum'. The next year, F. J. A. Hort noted that this newly recovered dedication exactly matched the one quoted in the life of Ceolfrith. The Codex Amiatinus is quite simply the actual volume written at Wearmouth or Jarrow by English scribes in imitation of the Codex Grandior. As Ceolfrith died on the journey, the book never reached Rome. The diagrammatic illustrations reproduce precisely those described by Cassiodorus in the Codex Grandior itself. The strange frontispiece shows the aged prophet Ezra (or Cassiodorus or, more probably, both as the same man) seated before an open cupboard containing the carefully labelled nine volumes of the Novem Codices which Cassiodorus gave to the Vivarium community (Pl. 8). This picture too is no doubt copied from the sixth-century Italian original.

The identification of the Codex Amiatinus as Ceolfrith's copy created great excitement in the late nineteenth century,

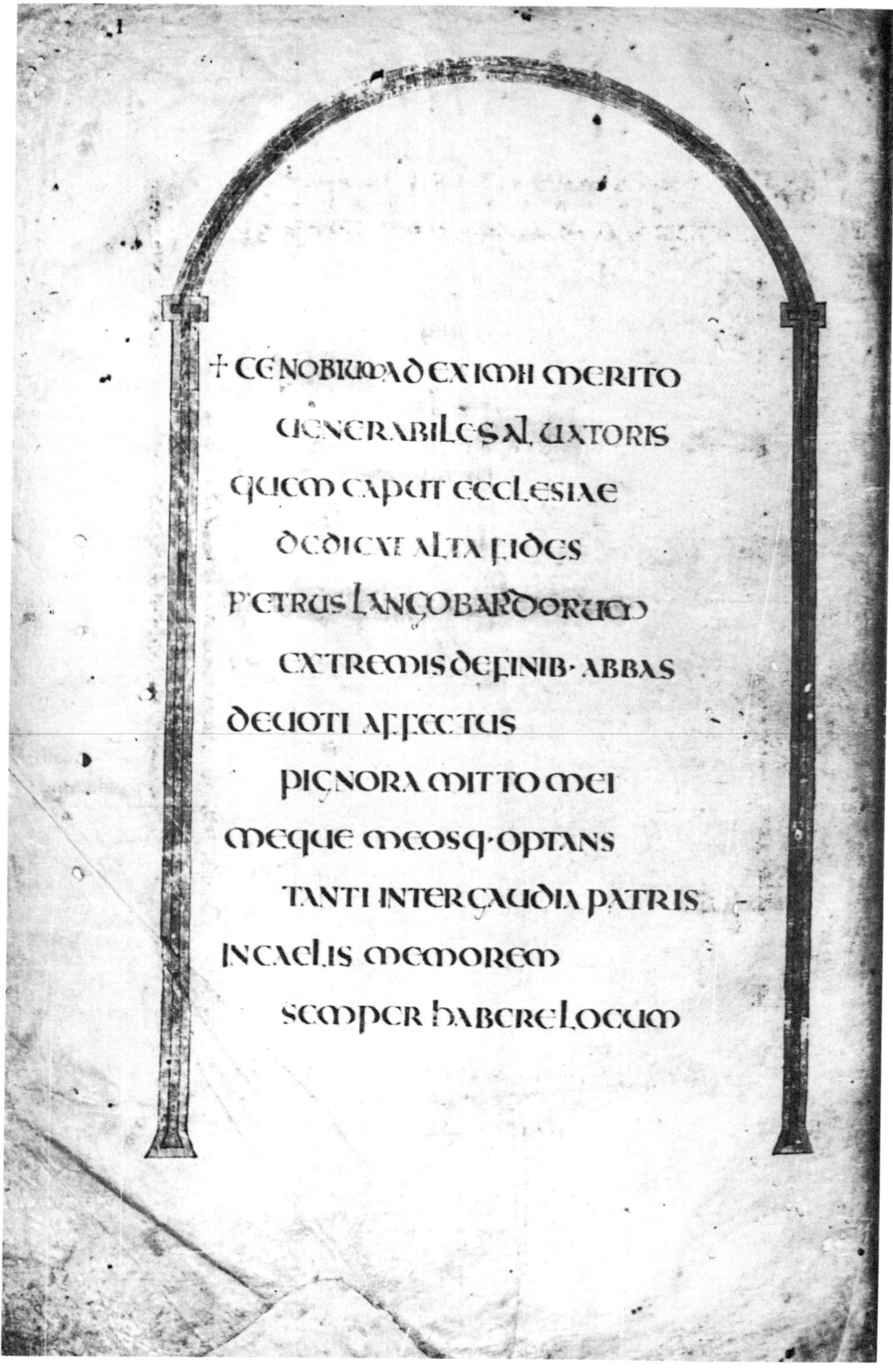
+ CENOBIUMAD EXIMII MERITO
UENERABILE SAL UATORIS
QUEM CAPUT ECCLESIAE
DEDICAT ALTA FIDES
PETRUS LANGOBARDORUM
EXTREMIS DE FINIB· ABBAS
DEUOTI AFFECTUS
PIGNORA MITTO MEI
MEQUE MEOSQ· OPTANS
TANTI INTER GAUDIA PATRIS
IN CAELIS MEMOREM
SEMPER HABERE LOCUM

9 Florence, Biblioteca Medicea-Laurenziana, MS. Am. 1, f. 1v; Bible, Northumberland, c. 700–716. *This is the dedication page of the Codex Amiatinus. There are erasures in the first and second lines and in the fifth line where the name of Ceolfrith has been carefully written over to make it seem as though the book was a present from a certain Peter of the Lombards. The original names were first deciphered in 1886.*

especially among patriotic antiquarians glad to learn that the earliest known complete Latin Bible was made in England. In 1889 Canon William Greenwell of Durham bought an old register from a bookseller in Newcastle and found that its binding was made up of an ancient leaf of vellum with part of the Latin Book of Kings in script almost identical to that of the Codex Amiatinus. He gave his find to the British Museum (now B. L., Add. MS. 37777) (Pl. 10). Soon afterwards, ten leaves (and scraps of an eleventh) were sorted out from among the archives of Lord Middleton. On the publication of the Greenwell leaf in 1909 it became quite clear that they came from the same dismembered manuscript. They were acquired by the British Museum in 1937 (now B.L., Add. MS. 45025). Quite recently, in July 1982, yet another leaf was found forming a binding at Kingston Lacy House, then just acquired by the National Trust (Pl. 11).

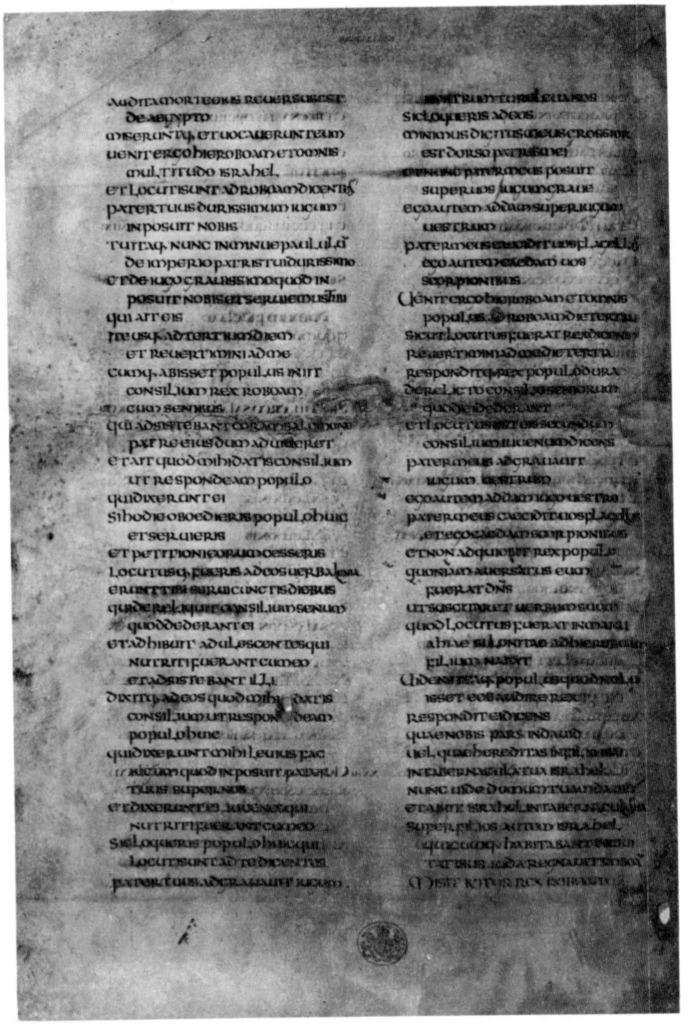

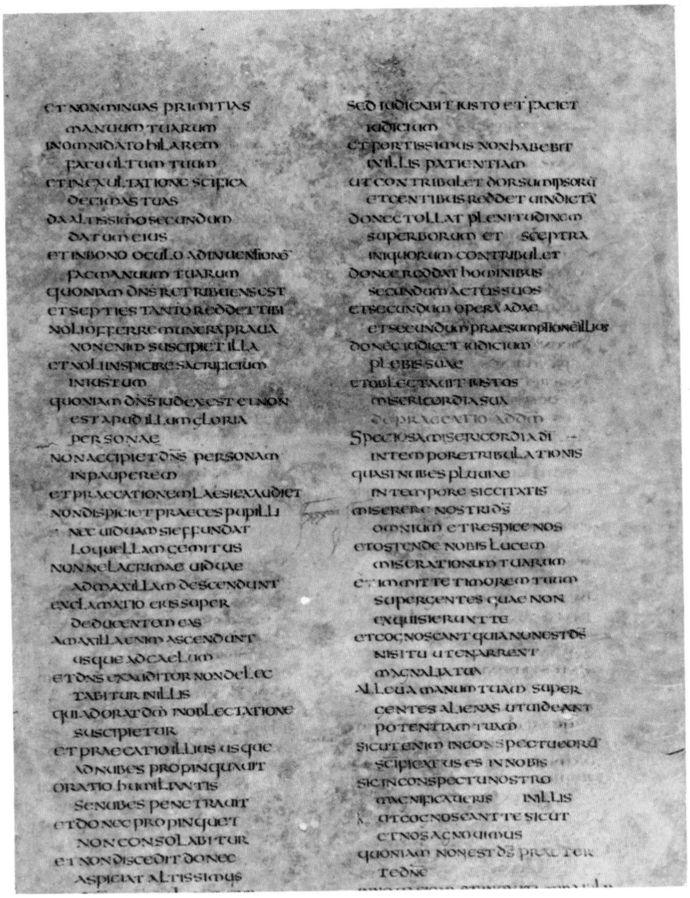

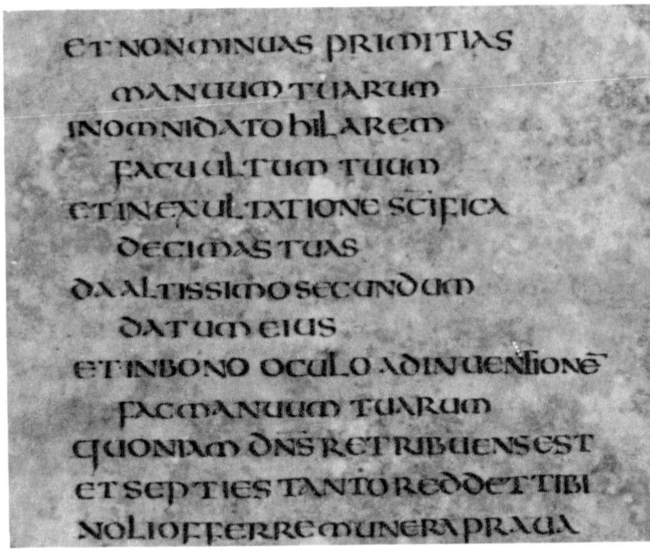
ET NONMINUAS PRIMITIAS
MANUUM TUARUM
INOMNIDATO hILAREM
FACUULTUM TUUM
ETINEXULTATIONE SCIFICA
DECIMAS TUAS
DA ALTISSIMO SECUNDUM
DATUM EIUS
ET INBONO OCULO ADINUENTIONE̅
FACMANUUM TUARUM
QUONIAM DN̅S RETRIBUENS EST
ET SEPTIES TANTO REDDET TIBI
NOLI OFFERRE MUNERA PRAUA

10 (ABOVE, LEFT) London, British Library, Add. MS. 37777, single leaf, verso; Bible, Northumberland, c. 700–716.
In 1889 this leaf was discovered in a bookshop in Newcastle. It comes from one of the two other huge Bibles written out by order of Ceolfrith before he set out for Rome with the Codex Amiatinus in June 716.

11 (ABOVE, RIGHT) Kingston Lacy House, National Trust, Bankes Collection, single leaf, recto; Bible, Northumberland, c. 700–716.
This is a leaf from the same manuscript found in 1982. It is not impossible that there exist other leaves somewhere, still unrecognized.

12 (RIGHT) *Detail of pl. 11.*

Possibly there are others still to be discovered and it is not silly for any of us to search bookshops with hopeful dreams. The significance of these leaves is that they must be from one of the other two matching Bibles ordered by Ceolfrith and assigned by him to the use of Wearmouth and Jarrow. Both monasteries were destroyed by the Vikings in the late ninth century and remained as ruins for two hundred years. Relics from the sites were rescued for Durham Cathedral whose monks later claimed to own several manuscripts 'de manu Bede' (in fact, an over-optimistic attribution). After the Reformation at least one Durham Cathedral manuscript Bible migrated into the library of the Willoughby family, later Lords Middleton, and very probably the Willoughbys owned a substantial portion of the Ceolfrith manuscript and used its huge pages centuries ago for binding their books at Wollaton Hall, near Nottingham, or Middleton Hall, near Tamworth.

An even smaller fragment, still in Durham Cathedral, links in with the story too. There is a tiny scrap of part of the Bible (bits of I Maccabees 6–7) reused as a flyleaf in Durham MS.B.IV.6 (Pl. 13). It is only $8\frac{1}{2} \times 5$ inches (217 by 127mm), about the size of a postcard, but is certainly Italian work of the sixth century. Could it be a relic from Cassiodorus's nine-volume Bible? It shares two extremely rare readings – one of them unique, in fact – with the Codex Amiatinus, and was doubtless the model used by Ceolfrith's scribes. These copyists used both the Codex Grandior and the Novem Codices at least. By calculating the amount of text that the scribe of the Durham fragment could have fitted onto a single page, one can conclude that the whole Bible, if indeed it was a whole Bible, would have been well over two thousand leaves thick. If divided into nine volumes, on the other hand, each part would have averaged about 240 leaves, which would be quite manageable. Beyond that, we hardly dare speculate.

All the manuscripts mentioned so far in this chapter, whether British or Italian, are written in uncial script. This is the late classical handwriting made up of capital letters formed with graceful curved strokes. The dependence of the Kentish missionaries on their Roman origins and the fierce allegiance of the Wearmouth/Jarrow communities to the papacy are demonstrated not only by historical record but, most graphically, by the use of this handwriting. It is a script specifically associated with Rome. The very earliest library catalogues describe uncial manuscripts as 'Romana litera scriptum'.

We must now introduce a whole new element into the story. To the embarrassment and confusion of the Roman-based apostles in England, theirs was not the only or even the first Christian mission to Britain. Christianity had flourished in Ireland since the mid-fifth century, led by St. Patrick and others, and in 563, more than thirty years before St. Augustine landed, St. Columba founded the famous island monastery at Iona off the west coast of Scotland. It was the beginning of a great missionary movement. By 635 St. Aidan had brought this Celtic Christianity right across the country to another offshore foundation at Lindisfarne on the east coast of Northumbria. The Irish liked islands. Ceolfrith, dedicating his Bible to the pope, thought he lived in a remote

13 Durham Cathedral MS.B.IV.6, flyleaf; Bible, Italy, sixth century.
This small fragment was preserved among the books and relics moved from Wearmouth and Jarrow to Durham in the wake of the Viking invasions. It was almost certainly part of one of the original manuscripts used by Ceolfrith's scribes as a model for the Codex Amiatinus.

place, but it was nothing to the extreme and literal insularity of the tiny primitive Irish communities. The image of Benedict Biscop thoughtfully purchasing classical texts in Rome sounds supremely civilized. It contrasts dramatically with the legends of the earliest Irish books. St. Columba (*c.*521–97) is said to have borrowed a manuscript from St. Finnian (*c.*495–579) and stayed on in the church at night illegally copying it while his fingers shone like candles and filled the church with light. Finnian's messenger, interrupting this scene, had his eyes pecked out by St. Columba's pet crane, we are told. The feuding saints appealed to the local king who declared against Columba ('to every cow her offspring, and to every book its transcript'), who then marshalled the king's enemies against him and defeated him at the Battle of Cul Dremhe in 561. The actual manuscript of the legend used to be identified with the so-called Cathach of St. Columba, a seventh-century manuscript now kept at the Royal Irish Academy (Pl. 14). It is as different from the Codex Amiatinus as one can imagine. It is small and decorated with spiralling penwork initials, and it survived in the early medieval shrine or *cumdach* in which its owners took it into battle shouting for victory. Even the name 'Cathach' means 'battler' in Old Irish. We are in a different world.

Historians from the time of Bede onwards have described the distressing rivalry and differing emphases of the early Irish Christians and the first Roman missionaries, and the disputes were made no easier by the absolute sincerity of the protagonists. A major difference of tradition was represented by contrasting methods for calculating the date of Easter, and no doubt the arguments were watched with sly amusement by any still pagan British, a race famous for carefully regulated festivals and seasons. Finally in 664 the Christians came together for their great synod at Whitby in Yorkshire when

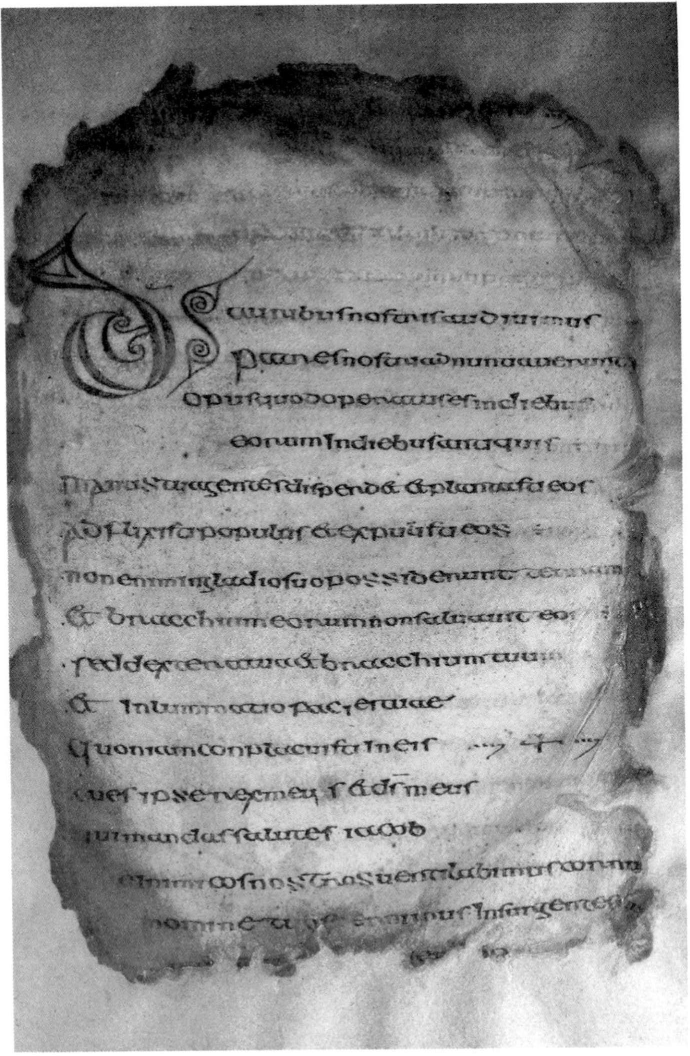

14 Dublin, Royal Irish Academy, s.n., f.12v; Gospels, Ireland, first half of the seventh century.
This is the Cathach of St. Columba, one of the earliest and most primitive surviving Irish manuscripts.

King Oswy chaired the debate between Colman for the Irish and Wilfrid for Rome. In the event, the argument came to hinge on whether St. Peter or St. Columba had greater authority in heaven, and the claims of the Roman Church triumphed. Almost all adherents of the Irish cause, including the king, now declared their new allegiance to the universal church, but Colman himself, with a few dissenting followers, returned unconvinced to Ireland.

Literacy and a belief in written revelation were the most fundamental tenets of both Irish and Roman Christians, and they all owned books. We see something of their politics reflected in the surviving manuscripts. The Irish – isolated, holy, ascetic, independent of Rome – produced no uncial manuscripts at all, and wrote entirely in their eccentric Irish majuscule and minuscule scripts. Their books were at first generally cramped and irregular and on poor quality vellum, consistent with the primitive nature of the communities. The Cathach of St. Columba is Irish work dating from well before the Synod of Whitby. The leaves are crooked and the lines uneven, but there is something deeply venerable about this relic. The Bangor Antiphonary (Milan, Bibl. Ambros., MS.C.5.inf.) was written at Bangor in northern Ireland during the abbacy of Colman (680–91) and is an unorthodox volume full of original holes (Pl.15). The same ascetic roughness can still be seen in the eighth-century Irish pocket-sized Gospel Books like the Book of Dimma, probably made in County Tipperary (Dublin, Trinity College, MS.A.IV.23), and in the Book of Mulling which has a colophon associating it with the name of St. Moling (d.692–7) and which was probably made by his eighth-century successors at the monastery of Tech-Moling in County Carlow (Dublin, Trinity College, MS.A.I.15). Somewhere in this misty early period too belongs the controversial Book of Durrow (Pl.16). The manuscript, now in Trinity College, Dublin (MS.A.IV.5), is tall and narrow, about 9½ by 5½ inches (245 by 145 mm.) and includes twelve interlaced initials, five full-page emblematic figures symbolizing the Evangelists, and six 'carpet' pages, an evocative term used to describe those entire sheets of multicoloured abstract interlace patterns so characteristic of early Irish art. Anyone can see that it is a fine manuscript and it has attracted much speculation. It ends with an invocation asking that whoever holds this book in his hands should remember Columba its scribe, but the inscription has been altered and rewritten and if it actually refers to St. Columba himself, founder of Iona, it is at best a copy made a century later from one made by the missionary saint. It is very possible that the book comes from one of St. Columba's foundations (of which Durrow is one) some time in the second half of the seventh century. Students have argued for origins in Ireland (*c.*650), Iona itself (*c.*665), or even right across at Lindisfarne (*c.*680). The size of the book suggests it could easily slip into a traveller's saddle-pack, and perhaps it was used in several missionary outposts. It was back in Ireland when King Flan (d.916) commissioned a *cumdach* for it, and it seems to have been at Durrow, about fifty miles west of Dublin, from at least the eleventh century.

After 664 and the merging of Irish and Roman interests, many manuscripts graphically reflect their double pedigree. The term 'insular manuscripts' is used to describe books made in the British Isles (as distinct from the Continent), but whether in England or Ireland may not be clear. Another general term is 'Northumbro-Irish'. We have already mentioned the Vespasian Psalter from St. Augustine's Abbey in Canterbury, written in uncials so Roman in type that the late medieval monks kept it on the high altar as St. Augustine's own copy. It is true that its miniature of King David and his musicians must be copied, perhaps directly, from a sixth-century Italian original but the broad arched top of the picture is thoroughly Irish with its delicate swirling interlaced patterns (Pl.6). It is very closely related to a Gospel Book now in Stockholm (Royal Library MS.A.135), known as the Codex Aureus (Pl.17). This manuscript is also in uncial script and is ascribed to the mid-eighth century. It too has delicate Irish interlaced and animal-filled initials.

Like the Vespasian Psalter, it was almost certainly made in Canterbury, right in the centre of the Roman tradition. There were clearly Northumbro-Irish models there by the eighth century. Indeed the Codex Aureus itself nearly disappeared, carrying the style far away, in a most dramatic manner. In the mid-eighth century the volume was stolen in a raid by the pagan Norsemen. It was then ransomed for gold by Aldorman Aelfred and his wife Werburg and presented to Christ Church, Canterbury, probably between 871 and 889, a famous donation recorded in Anglo-Saxon on the upper and lower margins on f. 11. By the sixteenth century the book was in Spain, belonging in turn to the historian Jerónimo Zurita (1512–80), the Carthusians of Aula Dei near Saragossa, and members of the Guzmán family. In 1690 it was bought in Madrid by John Gabriel Sparwenfeldt for the Swedish royal collections. After eight hundred years, therefore, it fell back into Scandinavian hands, now duly Christian and bibliographically minded.

But if Celtic decoration edged its way quietly into uncial manuscripts, the losing faction at Whitby achieved a far more enduring monument in the victory of their script. This is the period of the great insular Gospel Books. They are all written in Irish half uncial script, like the Book of Durrow, and Irish minuscule, like the Book of Armagh. The most famous is certainly the Book of Kells, but this is really the last in a long line and was preceded by such outstanding manuscripts as the Lindisfarne Gospels (*c.*698), the Echternach Gospels, the Durham Gospels (both *c.*700 and probably Northumbrian), the Book of St. Chad or Lichfield Gospels (eighth century, possibly Welsh), the Hereford Cathedral Gospel Book (perhaps the west of England or Wales, late eighth century), the Book of Armagh (Ireland, *c.*807), and a good many other splendid books of this class.

The Book of Kells is a problem. No study of manuscripts can exclude it, a giant among giants (Trinity College, Dublin, MS. A. I. 6). Its decoration is of extreme lavishness and the imaginative quality of its workmanship is quite exceptional (Pls. 22 and 30). It was probably this book which Giraldus Cambrensis in about 1185 called 'the work of an angel, not of a man'. But in the general history of medieval book production the Book of Kells has an uncomfortable position because (despite much investigation, not all of it free from hysterical patriotism) really very little is known about its origin or date. It may be Irish or Scottish or English. It has been assigned to various dates between the early eighth and the early ninth century, quite late (in any case) in the story of insular manuscripts. It is sometimes suggested that it was made at Iona and that the monks fled with it back to Ireland when in 806 Iona was sacked by the Vikings and sixty-eight members of the community were killed. The survivors escaped to Kells, about thirty miles north-west of Dublin, and the abbot of Iona, Cellach, was buried there in 815. All that is known for certain is that the Book of Kells was there by the twelfth century.

In the case of the Lindisfarne Gospels (B. L., Cotton MS. Nero, D. IV) which may be up to a hundred years earlier, the documentation is, by contrast, almost embarrassingly rich. We know where it was made, who wrote it, why, who bound it, who decorated the binding, and who glossed the text. We know enough about the craftsmen to be able to date the manuscript fairly closely. Although the colophon was added in the tenth century by the priest who filled in an Anglo-Saxon gloss long after the volume was first made, there is no reason to doubt the accuracy of his information. In translation, it reads:

> Eadfrith, bishop of the Lindisfarne Church, originally wrote this book, for God and for St. Cuthbert and – jointly – for all the saints whose relics are in the island. And Ethelwald, bishop of the Lindisfarne islanders, impressed it on the outside and covered it – as well he knew how to do. And Billfrith, the anchorite, forged the ornaments which are on the outside and adorned it with gold and with gems and also with gilded-over silver – pure metal. And Aldred, unworthy and most miserable priest, glossed it in English between the lines with the help of God and St. Cuthbert . . .

Eadfrith, said to be the scribe, became bishop in 698 and was succeeded in 721 by Ethelwald who (according to the colophon) first bound the book. Ethelwald himself was a novice at Lindisfarne, but between about 699/705 and his return as bishop in 721 he held office as prior and then abbot at Melrose Abbey. Therefore if the two men worked together at Lindisfarne, a date around 698 must be about right for the manuscript. The book was intended to be a showpiece (Pls. 21 and 29). In 698 the monks of Lindisfarne reburied the body of St. Cuthbert in an elaborate wooden shrine, an

15 Milan, Biblioteca Ambrosiana MS. Ambros. C. 5. inf., f. 30v; Antiphonary, Northern Ireland (Bangor), *c.*680–91.

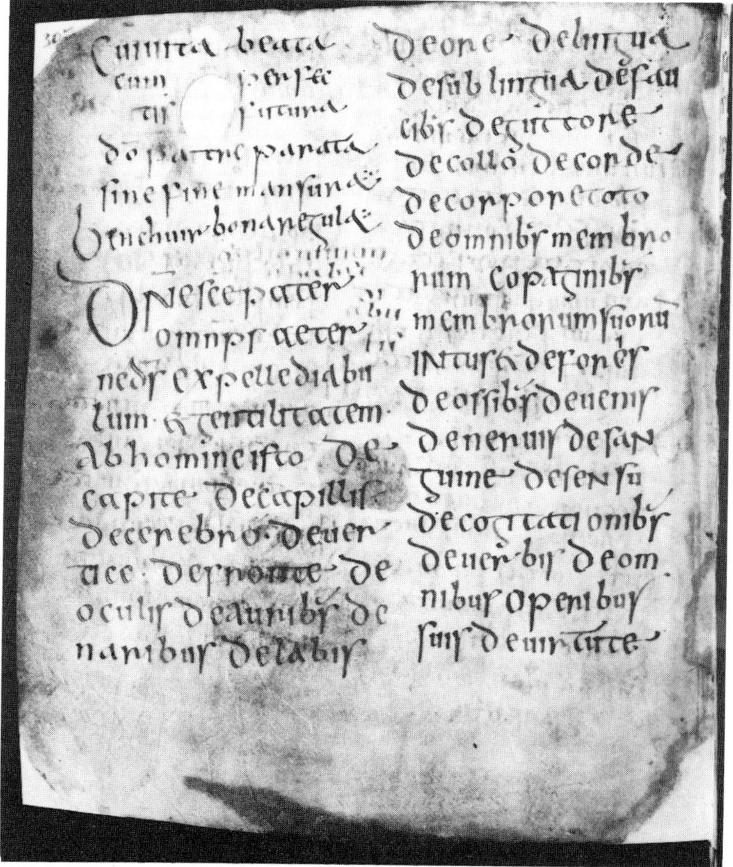

16 (LEFT) Dublin, Trinity College MS. A. IV. 5, f.125v; Gospels, Ireland or the north of Britain, second half of the seventh century.
This is the Book of Durrow which has six of these elaborate interlaced 'carpet' pages. It may have been painted in Ireland or perhaps in an Irish foundation in Scotland, such as the island of Iona.

17 (RIGHT) Stockholm, Royal Library MS. A. 135, f. 11r; Gospels, southern England (probably Canterbury), mid-eighth century.
This is the Codex Aureus with an inscription in Anglo-Saxon recording that it was looted by the Vikings and ransomed (probably in the 870s or 880s) by Aldorman Aelfred.

+ In nomine dni nri ihv xpi. Ic aelfred aldormon 7 werburg min gefera begetan ðas bec æt hæðnum herge
mid uncre clæne feo ðæt ðonne wæs mid clæne golde. 7 ðæt wit deodan for godes lufan 7 for uncre saule ðearf[e]

Ond forðon ðe wit noldan ðæt ðas halgan beoc lencg in ðære hæðenesse wunaden, 7 nu willað heo gesellan inn to
cristes circan gode to lofe 7 to wuldre 7 to weorðunga 7 his ðrowunga to ðoncunga, 7 ðæm godcundan geferscipe to brucen[ne]
ðe in cristes circan dæghwæmlice godes lof rærað, to ðæm gerade ðæt heo mon arede eghwelce monaðe for aelfred
7 for werburge 7 for alhðryðe heora saulum to ecum læcedome, ða hwile ðe god gesegen hæbbe ðæt fulwiht æt
ðeosse stowe beon mote. Ec swelce ic aelfred dux 7 werburg biddað 7 halsiað on godes almaehtiges noman 7 on allra
his haligra ðæt nænig mon seo to ðon gedyrstig ðætte ðas halgan beoc aselle oððe aðeode from cristes circan ða hwile

event which brought many pilgrims to the monastery. The manuscript belongs exactly to this period and the colophon names St. Cuthbert as co-patron. The volume was probably on display for about a hundred years. But, at about the time of the raids on Iona, Lindisfarne too came under attack from the Vikings. In 793 the island community was sacked by the invaders and eventually in 875 the monks fled to the mainland taking with them their most precious possessions, including the relics of St. Cuthbert and the Lindisfarne Gospels. There is a tale recorded in the early twelfth century by Symeon of Durham that the refugees intended to cross to Ireland (as the Iona monks had done), but that, as they put out to sea, a terrible storm arose and a copy of the four Gospels, richly bound in gold and jewels, was swept overboard and lost. The monks quickly abandoned their voyage and, through the miraculous intervention of St. Cuthbert, their precious manuscript was restored to them at low tide, still perfectly preserved. This story very probably refers to the Lindisfarne Gospels. If there had been no storm and the refugees had brought the book safely to Ireland, of course, Aldred would never have been there to add his detailed colophon and we might never have known the Lindisfarne provenance. In that case, students could still be debating whether the book was English or Irish.

The attempted export of the Lindisfarne Gospels to Ireland contrasts dramatically with the movement of the British missionaries and their manuscripts eastwards across the North Sea. No storms interrupted them now. One of the great achievements of the insular Church was to carry the Word of God to the Continent. After the Synod of Whitby, Colman had retreated to Ireland but the champion Wilfrid had turned his zeal to Frisia in 677 and Wihtberht preached there in 690. The missions gained momentum at the extreme end of the seventh century. While the Lindisfarne islanders

18 London, English Province of the Society of Jesus, on loan to the British Library, s.n., upper cover of binding; Gospel of St. John, Northumbria, late seventh century.
The Saint Cuthbert Gospel, also known as the Stonyhurst Gospel, survives in its remarkably decorated original binding, the oldest extant decorated European bookbinding known. The manuscript seems to have been buried with St. Cuthbert in 698 and was carried around Northumbria inside St. Cuthbert's coffin for 400 years. In 1104, when the relics of St. Cuthbert were installed in Durham Cathedral, the coffin was opened and the tiny Gospel Book found miraculously preserved. It has been kept as a relic ever since.

19 The Saint Cuthbert Gospel, f. 27r.
The manuscript is written in a very fine uncial script, but this page is annotated in an insular minuscule, 'pro defunctis' ('for the dead'), a heading which may allude to use of the manuscript in the ceremonies for the enshrinement of St. Cuthbert's relics in 698.

Dixit autem eis ihs
ego sum panis uitae
qui uenit ad me non esuriet
et qui credit in me
non sitiet umquam
sed dixi uobis quia et uidistis me
et non credidistis
Omne quod dat mihi pater
ad me ueniet
et eum qui uenit ad me
non eiciam foras
Quia descendi de caelo non
ut faciam uoluntatem meam
sed uoluntatem eius
qui misit me
Haec est autem uoluntas eius
qui misit me patris
ut omne quod dedit mihi
non perdam ex eo

20 Paris, Bibliothèque Nationale MS. lat. 9389, f. 18v; Gospels, Northumbria, late seventh or early eighth century. *The Echternach Gospel Book was probably one of the books brought from England to Echternach Abbey in Luxembourg by St. Willibrord (658–739) and his fellow missionaries. The painting here is inscribed 'Imago hominis' ('picture of a man'). and prefixed the Gospel of St. Matthew whose symbol in art is a man or an angel. Like the missionaries themselves, the man is exhibiting an open book.*

21 (OVERLEAF, LEFT) London, British Library, Cotton MS. Nero D. IV, f. 211r; Gospels, Lindisfarne, c. 698. *The opening page of St. John in the Lindisfarne Gospels shows elaborate initials filled with animals and faces.*

22 (OVERLEAF, RIGHT) Dublin, Trinity College MS. A. I. 6, f. 34r; Gospels, Ireland or the north of Britain (possibly Iona), probably late eighth century. *The great Book of Kells is one of the most famous of all manuscripts. This illustration shows one of the opening pages of St. Matthew's Gospel.*

were making their Gospel Book at home, St. Willibrord (658–739) and his younger contemporary St. Boniface (680–754) set forth from Britain across Germany. Willibrord founded the famous monastery at Echternach in 698. Before 742 the missionaries had established dioceses at Utrecht, Würzburg, Erfurt, Eichstätt, and elsewhere; in 744 Boniface founded the great abbey of Fulda and in 747 he adopted Mainz as his cathedral. With St. Willibald and others, they evangelized most of Frisia, Saxony, Thuringia, Bavaria, and part of Denmark. To return to the theme of this chapter, Christian missionaries need books. These are essential tools for impressing the pagans and educating the converts. It is hardly possible to think of a more striking way of illustrating the impact of the Anglo-Saxon missionaries on German cultural life than by looking at their books. Even today, twelve hundred years and many wars later, Northumbro-Irish manuscripts are scattered right across northern Europe. For instance, the magnificent Echternach Gospel Book (Paris, B. N., MS. lat. 9389) was written probably in Northumberland, perhaps even at Lindisfarne, as the same scribe seems to have written another great Gospel manuscript, Durham Cathedral MS. A. II. 17. It is not at all unlikely that the Paris volume came to Echternach in the mission of its founder, St. Willibrord (Pl. 20). But it is only one of a huge cache of insular manuscripts from Echternach which, after the secularization of the abbey in the French

+ Iohannis aquila

Incipit euangelium secundum Iohan[nem].

IN PRINCIPIO ERAT UERBUM ET UERBUM ERAT APUD D[EU]M ET D[EU]S

h generatio

Revolution, passed in about 1802 to the Bibliothèque Nationale (MSS.lat.9527, 9529, 9538, 10399, 10837, etc.). There are similar substantial runs of insular books from the libraries of the Anglo-Saxon foundations of Fulda (many now in Basel University Library (Pl.24) and in the Cassel Landesbibliothek), Würzburg Cathedral (now in the Würzburg University Library (Pls.25 and 31)) and at St. Gall (still in the old abbey library). Many books survive on their own. Often there is no clue as to how they reached Europe except that they have been there from time immemorial. Examples, among many, are Leipzig Universitätsbibliothek MSS.Rep.I.58[a] and Rep.II.35[a] (perhaps from Niederaltaich in Bavaria but 'written presumably in Northumbria', according to E. A. Lowe), parts of two manuscripts in the church of St. Catherine, Maeseyck (Pl.23), the lovely Vatican MS.Barberini Lat.570 which has a scribal invocation 'Ora pro uuigbaldo' – conceivably Hygebeald, bishop of Lindisfarne 781–802 (Pl.26), Leningrad Public Library Cod.F.v.I.8 (another splendid manuscript with textual similarities with the Lindisfarne Gospels), and St. Gall Cod.51 (written in Ireland but certainly at St. Gall in the Middle Ages). All these are Gospel Books, expensively made and exported by missionaries.

If we look back at the catalogue of missionary equipment sent by Gregory the Great to St. Augustine in 601 with 'all such things as were generally necessary for the worship and ministry of the church', we see that books are put on a par with sacred vessels, vestments, and relics of the apostles and martyrs. When Benedict Biscop was furnishing his new Northumbrian monasteries, he too acquired liturgical objects and relics along with the books. Manuscripts were part of the paraphernalia of Christianity. They were regarded as essential

23 Maeseyck, Church of St. Catherine, Trésor, s.n., f.1r; Gospels, Northern England (possibly York), early eighth century.
This full-page miniature shows St. Matthew writing his Gospel.

accessories, like relics and vestments. The fact that insular Gospel Books are preserved today in libraries, not in vestry cupboards or high altars (or even museums), should not prejudice our view of these artefacts as liturgical equipment. The books survive (because later generations preserved libraries) but it would be fascinating to know what else came with them in the wagons which trundled across Europe in the wake of the Anglo-Saxon missionaries. An evocative hint of this is given by a tiny ribbon of vellum about 4½ inches long (114mm.) still kept in the abbey of St-Maurice in Switzerland. It was once wrapped around a relic and it is itself a label inscribed in an eighth-century insular minuscule 'de terra aeclisiae in qua sepultus est petrus primo'. It accompanied, therefore, a crumb of the earth from St. Peter's first tomb in Rome. Benedict Biscop specifically fetched relics from Rome; it was the pre-eminence of St. Peter himself which swayed the Synod of Whitby. This little relic, no doubt fraught with emotive value, must have come from Rome to the insular missionaries by whom it was labelled and lodged in a continental church.

In several manuscripts too there are traces of this line of supply from Italy to England to northern Europe. A Gospel Harmony in the Fulda Landesbibliothek (Cod. Bonifatianius 1) was written in south Italy for Victor, bishop of Capua, in the mid-sixth century but it has insular annotations in a minuscule hand which some students identify with that of St. Boniface himself, founder of Fulda Abbey in 747. Two manuscripts from the Anglo-Saxon cathedral of Würzburg seem to have been brought from Italy to England before re-export to Germany: one had missing leaves replaced in Northumberland and the other has a signature of an abbess associated with Worcester in *c.* 700 (Pl. 25).

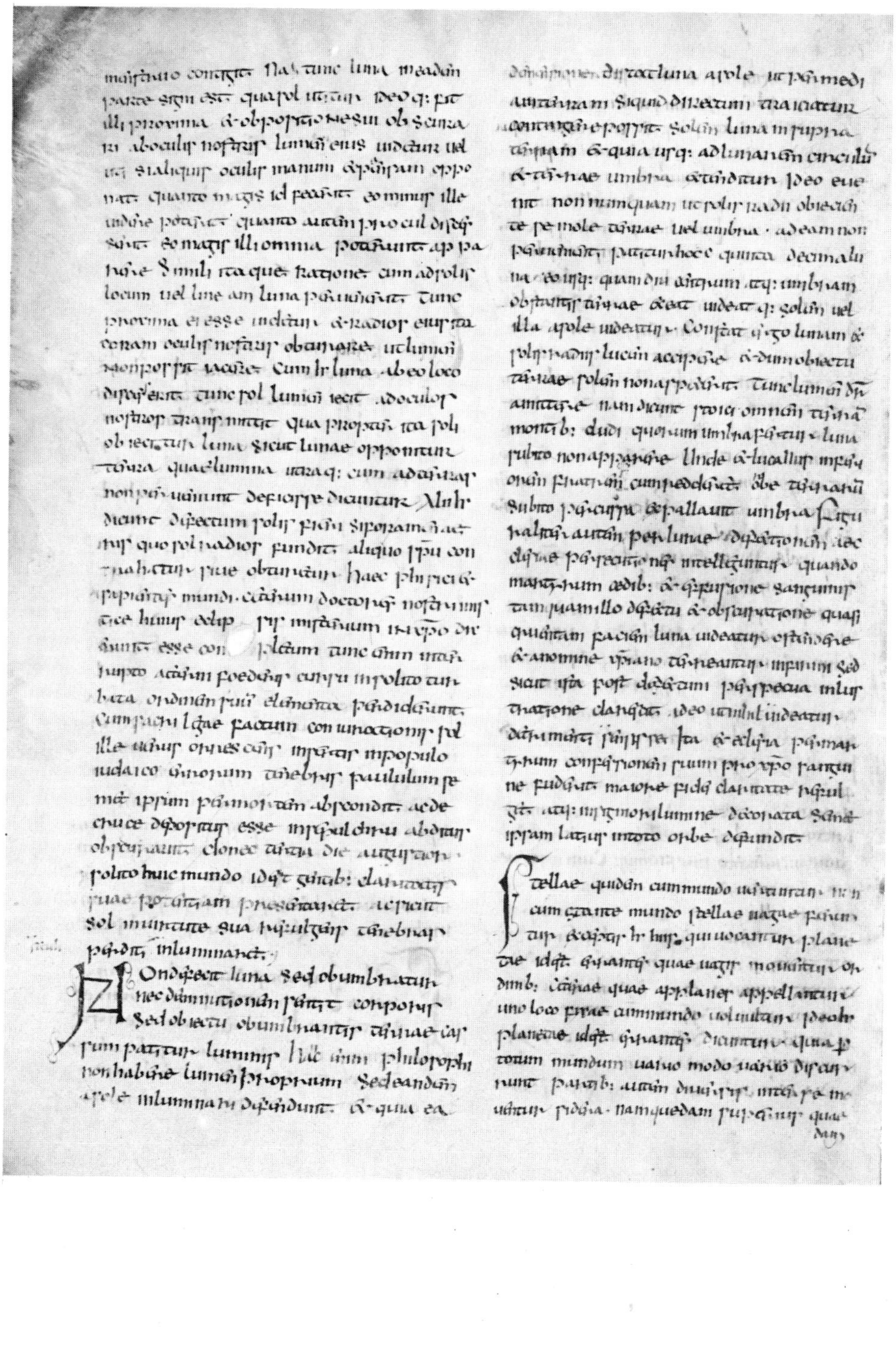

24 Basel, Universitätsbibliothek MS. F. III. f, f. 7v; Isidore, De Natura Rerum, England, eighth century.
By an early date this scientific treatise had reached the library of the Anglo-Saxon missionaries at Fulda.

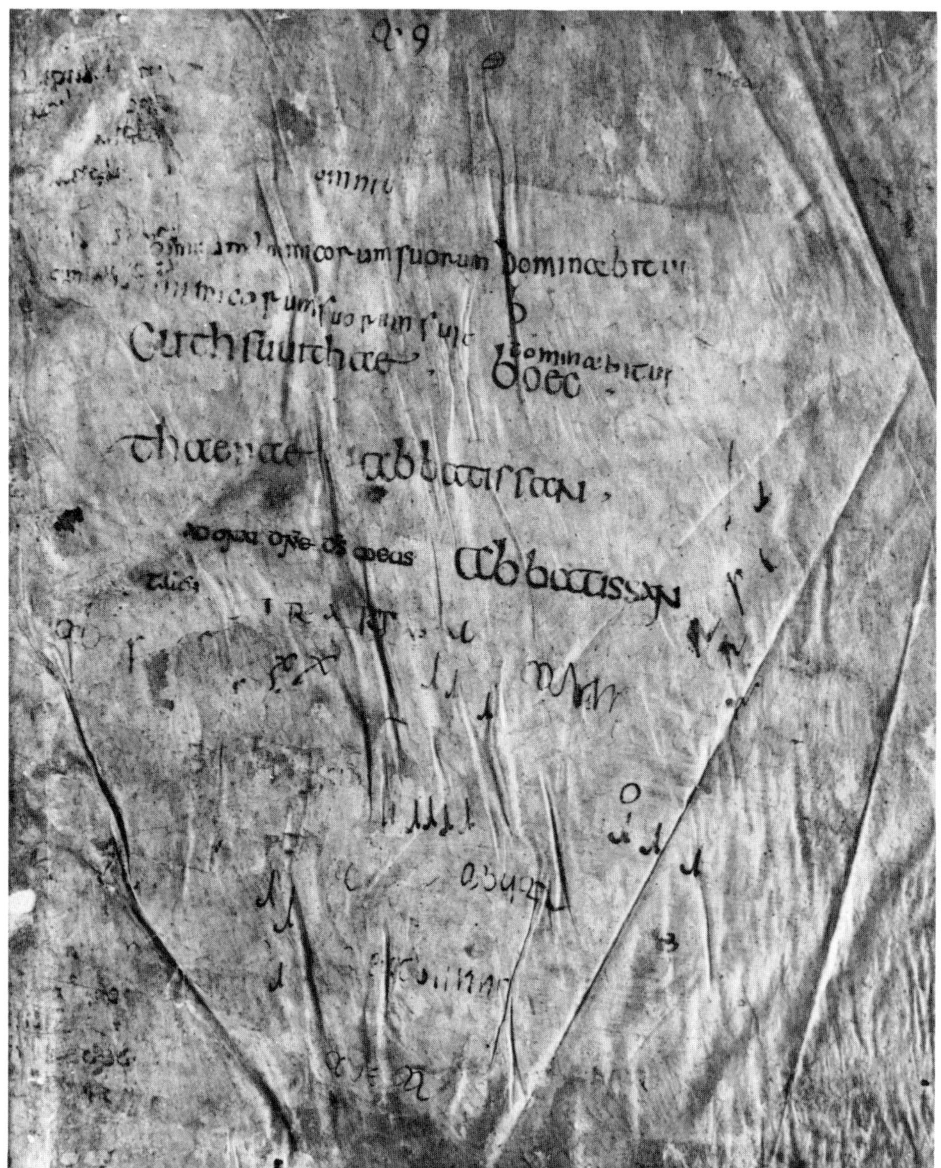

25 Würzburg, Universitätsbibliothek MS.M.p.th.q.2, f.1r; St. Jerome, Commentary on Ecclesiastes, Italy, fifth century; Anglo-Saxon flyleaf of *c.*700, inscribed in England with the name of the abbess Cuthswith.
The manuscript had very possibly reached Würzburg by the eighth century.

26 (OPPOSITE) Vatican, Barberini MS. Lat. 570, f. 125r; Gospels, Northumbria, late eighth century.
This manuscript is signed by its English scribe Wigbald.

There were probably three ways that an Anglo-Saxon community on the Continent could acquire books. It could receive them from the effects of its founder or from the luggage of a visiting Anglo-Saxon missionary. It could write its own manuscripts. It could send to Britain for manuscripts. The second method was easily done, if the monks had exemplars, and there are many 'insular' manuscripts copied out by Anglo-Saxons while on the Continent. It requires delicate tact to assign nationality to a book like Vienna MS. 1224, a late eighth-century Gospel Book written out by Cutbercht, probably an insular scribe, while he was in Salzburg. The third method is the most interesting, if only because it implies the existence of some kind of cottage industry for the export of manuscripts from Britain. There survive several fascinating letters to and from St. Boniface and his successor as archbishop of Mainz, Lul, who both wrote from Germany between the 740s and 760s to the archbishop of York and to the abbot of Wearmouth/Jarrow trying to obtain copies of the works of Bede. The missionaries in Germany explained that they much regretted any trouble involved but none the less bluntly itemized books which 'we request you will kindly have copied out and sent to us', as Boniface wrote. One such book prepared for export around 746 was no doubt the Leningrad Bede (Public Library MS. lat. Q. v. I. 18) (Pl. 32). Perhaps we can evoke something of the spirit of these monks busily supplying manuscripts for missionaries if we try to imagine whoever wrapped up the relics from St. Peter's tomb cited above: perhaps he or she divided up a pile of crumbs into many packages and labelled each one for wider distribution. So also St. Boniface asked for manuscripts of Bede 'so that we also may benefit from that candle which the Lord bestowed on you.' The abbot of Wearmouth/Jarrow wrote almost in desperation to Lul in 763–4 saying they had dispatched all they could but that the terrible winter had hampered the scribes' progress and that they would still try to supply all the needed books, adding 'si vixerimus' ('if we

live'). 'We can almost see him wringing his hands,' writes Dr M. B. Parkes.

The most enduring victory of Irish Christianity can now be seen. The early and slow uncial script was abandoned, even in Canterbury and Wearmouth/Jarrow, and the insular script became standard both for the grand Gospel Books and for the simple missionary texts. In Ireland today it more or less still survives, the longest lasting European handwriting, far more than a millennium after the last Roman uncial was used. The script was so intimately linked with its Celtic origins that the ninth-century library catalogue of St. Gall listed together a whole group of missionary books as 'libri scottice scripti' (Pl. 27).

27 St. Gall MS. 728, p. 4; library catalogue, St. Gall, ninth century.
This is a list of thirty books which the monks of St. Gall described as being in Irish script ('Libri Scottice scripti') and which must have been brought over by the missionaries or written by insular scribes at St. Gall in Switzerland.

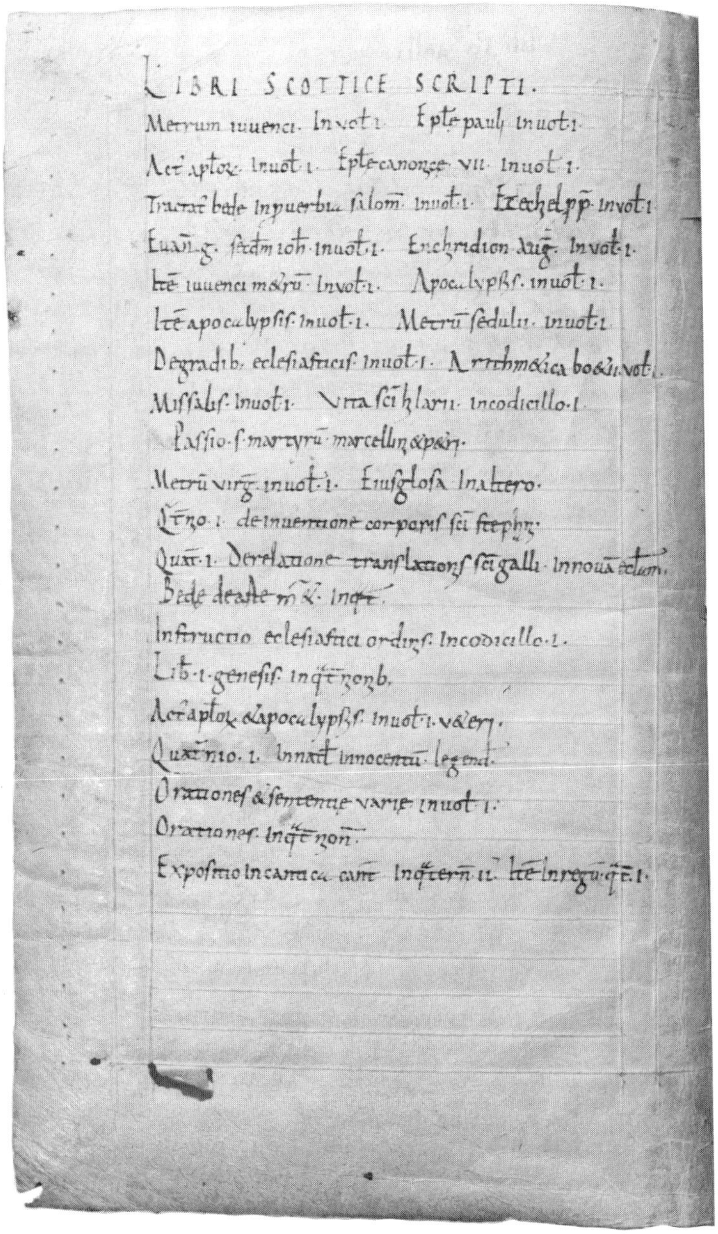

We are now in a position to look back over the writing of manuscripts for missionaries and to ask several questions which will recur in subsequent chapters but with different answers. Who made books? What use were books? Why were they decorated? On a superficial level, we know a surprising amount about the scribes of insular manuscripts, even many of their names. There are books signed by Sigbert, Eadfrith, Burginda, Edilbericht son of Berichtfrid, Wigbald, Cadmug, Cutbercht, Diarmait, Ferdomnach, MacRegol, Dubtach, and many others; we could probably not name so many scribes for surviving fifteenth-century French Books of Hours. The fact that so many scribal invocations appear, with and without names, is some evidence that the duplication of books was not a mere mechanical function, like building a wall, but was a human and individual activity. No one in the later Middle Ages cared who had written out their manuscripts, but the insular monks did. Even the fact that Giraldus Cambrensis imagined that the Book of Kells was the work of an angel, not of a man, shows that he was considering the question.

Whether insular scribes worked in a scriptorium, or special place set aside for writing, is quite unknown. Several of the known scribes were themselves bishops, indicating (if nothing else) that they were not full-time copyists, though a seventh-century bishop was not exclusively an administrative official, as so often later, but a man chosen as a spiritual leader, a role which need not exclude practical labour. Billfrith, maker of the metal binding of the Lindisfarne Gospels, was an anchorite: he at least, presumably, did not work in a communal scriptorium. In fact, there is no proof that scribes even worked at desks, and some insular pictures of Evangelists show them as scribes writing open books on their laps: one is in the Lindisfarne Gospels, f. 25v (derived from the similar Ezra picture in the Codex Amiatinus), and others are in the Maeseyck and Barberini Gospel Books (Pl. 23). The Wearmouth/Jarrow scribes were held up by cold weather in 763–4. The Irish annotator of a St. Gall Priscian of the ninth century poetically claimed to be writing under the greenwood tree as the clear-voiced cuckoo sang from bush to bush. A few slight clues from insular manuscripts themselves do not preclude a scribe writing a small book on his knees.

When a medieval scribe ruled his vellum, he needed to multiply the page ruling throughout the book. He would measure the first page in a stack of unwritten leaves and then with a sharp instrument he would prick holes at the ends of the lines and push these right through the pile of vellum. When he turned to each page, therefore, he had only to join up the prickings to duplicate the ruling pattern from page to page. This is well known and applies throughout the Middle Ages. What is curious about insular manuscripts, however, unlike their continental counterparts, is that the prickings occur in both margins of a page instead of just in the outer margin. The explanation is easy. It means that insular scribes

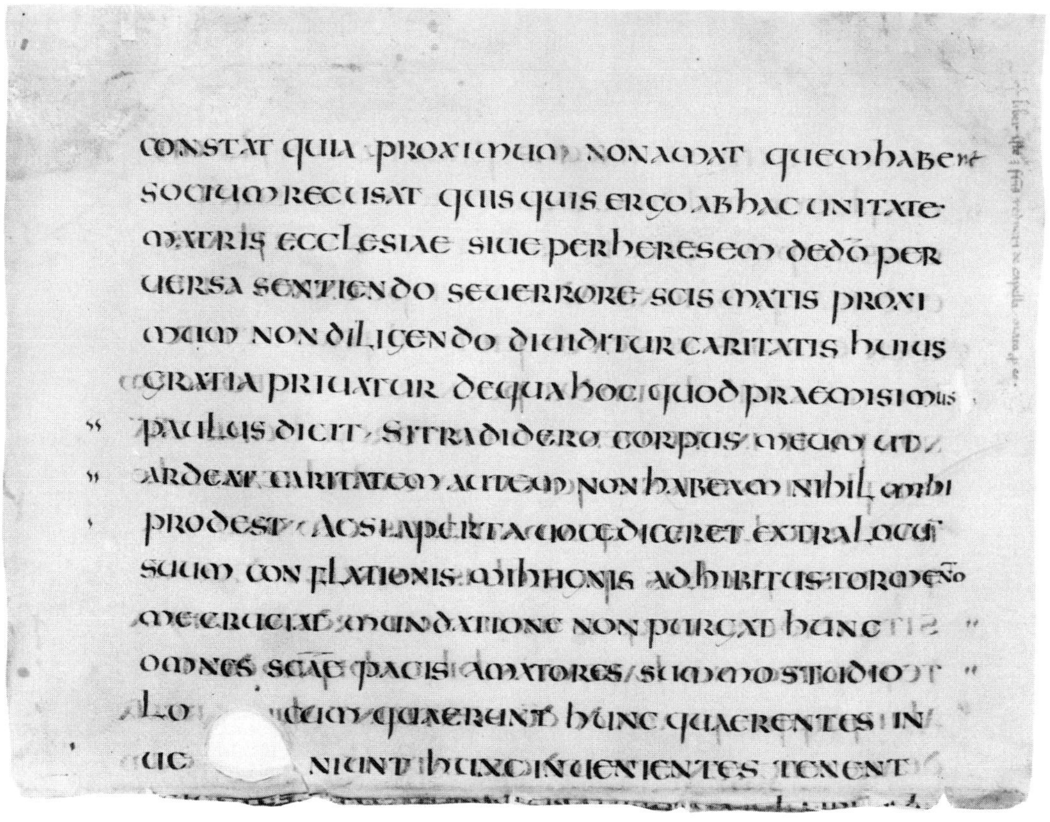

28 New Haven, Yale University, Beinecke Library MS. 516; St. Gregory, Moralia, Northumbria, late seventh or early eighth century.
This fragment was recovered from use as a flyleaf in a German bookbinding and was probably sent out to Germany by the missionaries from Wearmouth or Jarrow in Northumbria.

folded their leaves before they ruled them; continental scribes, by contrast, probably wrote on large oblong bifolia. We can go further than that. The little St. Cuthbert Gospel of St. John (the so-called 'Stonyhurst Gospel') is the only insular book still in its original binding (Pl. 18), and it has evidence of having been loosely stitched in gatherings before the proper binding was made. Similar little stitching holes can be detected in the Lindisfarne and Lichfield Gospels. Temporary sewing would hold the volume in shape while it was being written. A small book folded into secure gatherings can be written almost anywhere. Sometimes insular books must have remained in these *ad hoc* bundles of folded gatherings. The eighth-century legend of St. Boisil (d. *c*. 664) tells that he and St. Cuthbert read through the Gospel of St. John one gathering a day, strongly implying that the quires were quite distinct units. Books carried across Europe by missionaries would have been lighter without heavily fitted bindings. Nearly a third of the 'libri scottice scripti' at St. Gall were described as 'quaterno' or 'in quaternionibus' – stitched (perhaps) in quires, but unbound. We must never forget the informality of these early books.

Just as there is no surviving scriptorium from early Anglo-Saxon England, so there are certainly no library fittings, and almost nothing is known about how books were kept. The Ezra picture in the Codex Amiatinus includes a painted cupboard with hinged doors and shelves on which books are lying flat with their spines outwards (Pl. 8). A seventh-century Jerome in Irish style but probably made at Bobbio has a contemporary inscription 'Liber de arca domno atalani' (Milan, Bibl. Ambrosiana MS. S. 45. sup.) and the word 'arca' suggests a chest or box with possessions of Atalanus, abbot 615–22. A Gospel Book, however, may have been kept on an altar or with other liturgical apparatus rather than in a library (the association with vestments and relics has already been stressed). Especially in Ireland, a Gospel Book might have a *cumdach*, or portable shrine, made for it. Examples were on the Cathach of St. Columba and the Books of Durrow and Mulling. It must be remembered that a Gospel Book was itself a holy object to be venerated and to be saved from the pagan. A Durham monk suffered terrible swellings when he impiously tampered with the Stonyhurst Gospel in 1104. There is a legend of the Irish scribe Ultan whose finger bones, having written out Gospels in Ultan's lifetime, performed a miracle after his death. It seems to have been especially in Ireland that Gospel Books had these near-magical talismanic qualities. Bede, in praising Ireland, says he had heard of victims of snake-bite being cured by drinking a solution of water and scrapings from the leaves of Irish manuscripts. As late as the seventeenth century, the Book of Durrow was still being immersed in water to provide a cure for sick cattle.

Gospel Books were obviously the volumes most needed by missionaries. The next most popular authors were Isidore of Seville (Pls. 24 and 31), Bede (Pl. 32), and Gregory the Great (Pl. 28), to judge from the numbers of surviving copies. All these had a practical evangelical function too. Isidore and Bede provide simple science and a careful explanation of the Church calendar. This must have had great value in

imago aequilae

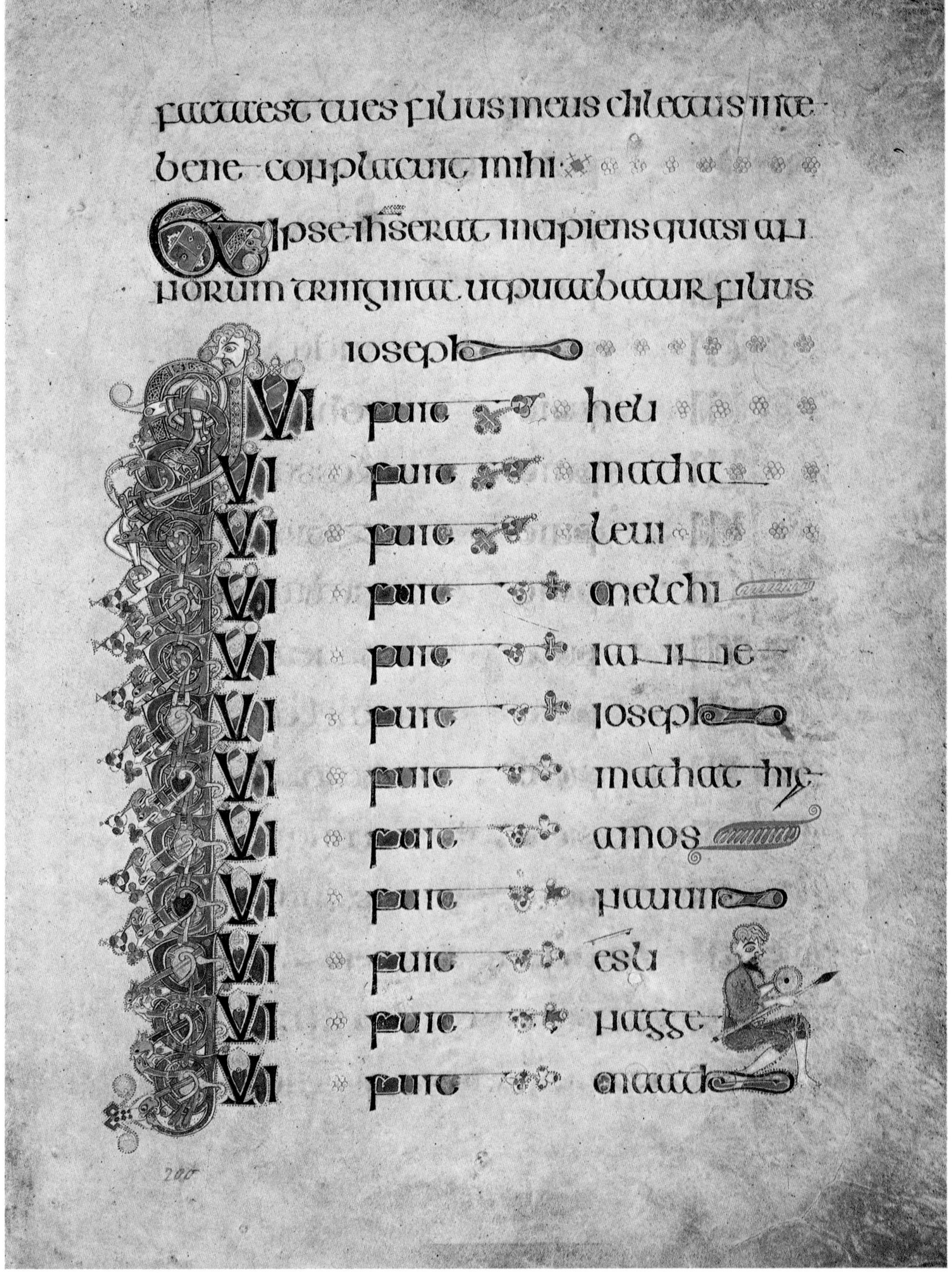

29 (OPPOSITE) London, British Library, Cotton MS. Nero D. IV, f. 209v; Gospels, Lindisfarne, *c.* 698.
The full-page portrait of St. John in the Lindisfarne Gospels is simple and dramatic in its impact and is probably intended to be viewed at a distance.

30 (ABOVE) Dublin, Trinity College MS. A. I. 6, f. 200r; Gospels, Ireland or the north of England (possibly Iona), probably late eighth century.
The page shows the delicate microscopic ornament in the Book of Kells.

31 (LEFT) Würzburg, Universitätsbibliothek MS. M. p.th. q. 28b, f. 43v; Isidore, Synonyma, possibly Würzburg, *c.* 800. *This manuscript is written in an Anglo-Saxon script but it belonged to the library of Würzburg Cathedral and is likely to have been written there.*

32 (RIGHT) Leningrad, State Public Library MS. Q. V. I. 18, detail of f. 26v; Bede, Historia Ecclesiastica, Northumbria, eighth century. *Though a much later hand has added the name 'Augustinus' to this little portrait, it evidently shows St. Gregory holding a cross and a manuscript.*

presenting Christianity to the British pagan whose sense of natural order and (especially) of chronology was so strong that even now we still use their pre-Christian names for the days of the week and for the major festivals such as 'Yule' and 'Eostre'. We can hardly imagine how embarrassing to the Christians the squabbles over calculating Easter must have been, and how comforting a textbook would be. Bede's *Ecclesiastical History* too has value as a manual for the conversion of pagans and it was very popular among the missionaries on the Continent. Gregory the Great was very highly regarded. It was he who sent Augustine to England. His *Pastoral Rule* is the most fundamental missionary handbook. The Leningrad Bede (f. 26v) shows what is sometimes regarded as the earliest historiated initial in western art (Pl. 32): the humble little drawing shows St. Gregory half-length holding up a cross and clasping a book. No one would forget that St. Gregory's initiative had brought both Christianity and book learning to Britain.

It is, however, in the Gospel Books that the most famous and most elaborate decoration occurs. With hindsight we look back on medieval manuscripts as if their illumination was a matter of course, but we must ask why these specific books (for the first time) were so elaborately ornamented. There is virtually no decoration in other texts. There must be several answers. The first and most practical function was as a means to find one's way about the Gospels. The text was used

for reference. There were no chapter numbers or running titles in the eighth century. Even now, as one thumbs through a manuscript, the bright carpet pages on the versos of leaves provide the quickest possible indicator of the beginning of each Gospel, and the initials of varying size have a convenience in separating the text into visually recognizable sections. Secondly, there is the theological reason. Gospel Books were decorated precisely because they contained the revealed word of God, which was being honoured by being ornamented and whose mystery and complexity were being praised by the amazingly elaborate illumination. Thirdly, there was probably a protective function in depicting crosses and the Evangelist symbols on the opening pages of a Gospel, as a talisman to ward off evil from the treasure in the book.

The final reason, however, takes us right back to the function of the books as missionary equipment. We can notice that there are really two kinds of decoration in an insular Gospel Book: the huge heavily outlined and brightly painted pictures, and the extremely delicate and endlessly varied plantlike interlace. Anyone can try a simple experiment. Prop up the facsimile of the Lindisfarne Gospels or the Book of Kells and walk backwards. At a few feet the initials lose their clarity, but at twenty paces the Evangelist portraits are magnificient (Pl. 29). We remember now that on arrival in England, St. Augustine held up in the open air religious paintings. Bede describes the effect of pictures in the church at Wearmouth 'to the intent that all ... even if ignorant of letters, might be able to contemplate ... the ever-gracious countenance of Christ and his saints.' These big books belonged to a missionary society. Their purpose was to show the word of God to ill-educated audiences. No doubt the big pictures did exactly that. But to the convert and to the priest, allowed close access to the manuscript, the effect was altogether different (Pl. 30). 'Look more keenly at it and you will penetrate to the very shrine of art. You will make out intricacies, so delicate and subtle, so exact and compact, so full of knots and links, with colours so fresh and vivid ... For my part, the oftener I see the book, the more carefully I study it, the more I am lost in ever-fresh amazement, and I see more wonders in the book.' The writer is Giraldus Cambrensis in 1185; his is the intellectual response of the priest and it is no less valid; it is very probably that of the art historian today.

Insular Gospel Books were made for missionaries. Once conversion was assured, the books become quite different. The last great Irish Gospel Book is the Macdurnan Gospels (Lambeth Palace MS. 1370) made well into the ninth century. It was given to Christ Church, Canterbury, in the tenth century not by a missionary but by a king, Athelstan (925–40), King of Wessex and Mercia. We have moved beyond the world of Saints Augustine, Columba, Wilfrid, Ceolfrith, and Boniface, and are now in the age of kings and politics.

·2·

Books for Emperors

The legend recounts that in the year AD 1000 the Emperor Otto III, then an unbelievably rich young man of about twenty, ordered the opening of the tomb of Charlemagne at Aachen. His great predecessor had died in 814, nearly two hundred years earlier. It is said that they found the body of Charlemagne almost intact and fully clothed, seated on a chair, holding a sceptre and with a gold chain about his neck, and on his lap (the story claims) there was a splendid illuminated manuscript. Otto III removed these treasures, together with one of Charlemagne's teeth as a relic. The fact that a manuscript was among the symbols of state is important in the history of books. This was not a missionary text but part of the regalia of the Christian emperor.

The manuscript from Charlemagne's tomb was kept. It is traditionally identified with the so-called Vienna Coronation Gospels in the Vienna Schatzkammer (Pls. 34–5). It is a big square volume decorated with rather blotchy vibrant impressionistic paintings in heavy colours, totally unlike the intricately controlled mathematical designs of the Gospel Books we met in the western islands. The miniatures look more like wall-paintings and the vellum leaves are stained in purple. The style derives from Byzantine art and thus ultimately from classical antiquity. In fact, the Vienna Gospels includes the Greek name 'Demetrius presbyter' in gold capitals in the outer margin of the first page of the Gospel of St. Luke and it is not impossible that there were artists from Byzantium itself at the court of Charlemagne. At least three other manuscripts were painted in this Greek style in western Europe in the late eighth or early ninth century. They are the Xanten Gospels in Brussels (MS. 18723), a Gospel Book in Brescia (Bibl. Civ. Queriniana cod. E. II. 9) and the Aachen Gospels (Pl. 36) which is still in the cathedral treasury in Charlemagne's capital. The books were perhaps all decorated in Aachen, or at least at the imperial court which (in its primitive Frankish way) followed Charlemagne on his endless journeys around the royal residences over much of Europe. When the emperor travelled, he was followed by imperial wagons of gold, treasure, archives, and manuscripts.

33 Paris, Bibliothèque Nationale MS. lat. 266, f. 1v, Gospels, Tours, mid-ninth century.
The Gospel Book of the Emperor Lothaire, grandson of Charlemagne, opens with a frontispiece of Lothaire enthroned between two members of the imperial guard.

Charlemagne's empire was vast and it eventually extended from the pleasant villas and orange groves of southern Europe, where classical learning and literacy had never completely disappeared, to the enormous wastelands of northern Germany where wolves roamed the forests and where Roman culture was symbolized only by the ruins of abandoned garrisons. Without doubt, Charlemagne himself was a quite exceptionally brilliant man. He was literate and cultured; his favourite reading (we are told) was St. Augustine's *City of God*; he understood some Greek; he was on intimate terms with popes and saints; he gathered around him the most cultured men of Europe, including Peter of Pisa, Paul the Deacon, Theodulf the Visigoth, and the great Alcuin; he himself was admitted to sainthood in 1165. At the same time Charlemagne was primarily a man of the north. His capital Aachen is in Germany today. He was a descendant of the Frankish tribesmen who ruled by extravagant displays of military arms and of personal wealth, by appalling double-dealing and thuggery, and who regarded a kingdom as the private property of a ruler who could use it entirely according to whim. The ancient tribal leaders had held together their precarious kingdoms by military retinues whom they rewarded with gold and with the spoils of war. Charlemagne, for all his elegant classical dinner parties, was above all a Germanic military leader and his strategic success in warfare is literally legendary.

Charlemagne's own ancestors acquired the Merovingian kingdom by outmanoeuvring competitors. From the early seventh century they had been officials in the household of the Frankish kings. The family became mayors of the royal palace and effective power was seized by Charles Martel in the 720s. In 751 his son Pepin the Short managed to get himself anointed king by St. Boniface and in 754, after skilful diplomatic appeals, Pope Stephen II crossed the Alps and at the abbey of St-Denis crowned Pepin and consecrated him and his two sons, Charles (the future Charlemagne, then aged about ten) and Carloman. Pepin died in 768 and Carloman in 771, leaving Charlemagne as sole king of the Franks.

One of the first really great manuscripts produced in Charlemagne's reign must have been the so-called Maurd-

34–35 (ABOVE AND RIGHT) Vienna, Kunsthistorisches Museum, Weltliche Schatzkammer, ff. 76v–77r; Gospels, probably Aachen, late eighth century.
The Vienna Coronation Gospels is traditionally said to have been the manuscript found in the tomb of Charlemagne by Otto III. It is written in gold on purple vellum.

INCIPIT EUANGELIUM SECUNDUM MARCUM

INITIUM
EUANGELII IHU XPI FILII DI SIC
UT SCRIPTUM EST IN ESAIA PRO
PHETA ECCE MITTO ANGELUM
MEUM ANTE FA[illegible] TUAM
QUI PRAEPARABIT UIAM TUAM
VOX CLAMANTIS IN DESERTO PARATE UI
AM DNI RECTAS FACITE SEMITAS EIUS
FUIT IOHANNES IN DESERTO BAPTIZANS
ET PRAEDICANS BAPTISMUM PAENITEN
TIAE IN REMISSIONEM PECCATORUM
ET EGREDIEBATUR AD ILLUM OMNIS
IUDEAE REGIO ET HIEROSOLYMITAE
UNIUERSI ET BAPTIZABANTUR AB ILLO
IN IORDANE FLUMINE CONFITENTES
PECCATA SUA
ET ERAT IOHANNES UESTITUS PILIS CAME
LI ET ZONA PELLICIA CIRCA LUMBOS EIUS
ET LOCUSTAS ET MEL SILUESTRE EDE
BAT ET PRAEDICABAT DICENS UENIT FOR
TIOR ME POST ME CUIUS NON SUM DIGNUS
PROCUMBENS SOLUERE CORRIGIAM CAL
CIAMENTORUM EIUS EGO BAPTIZAUI UOS

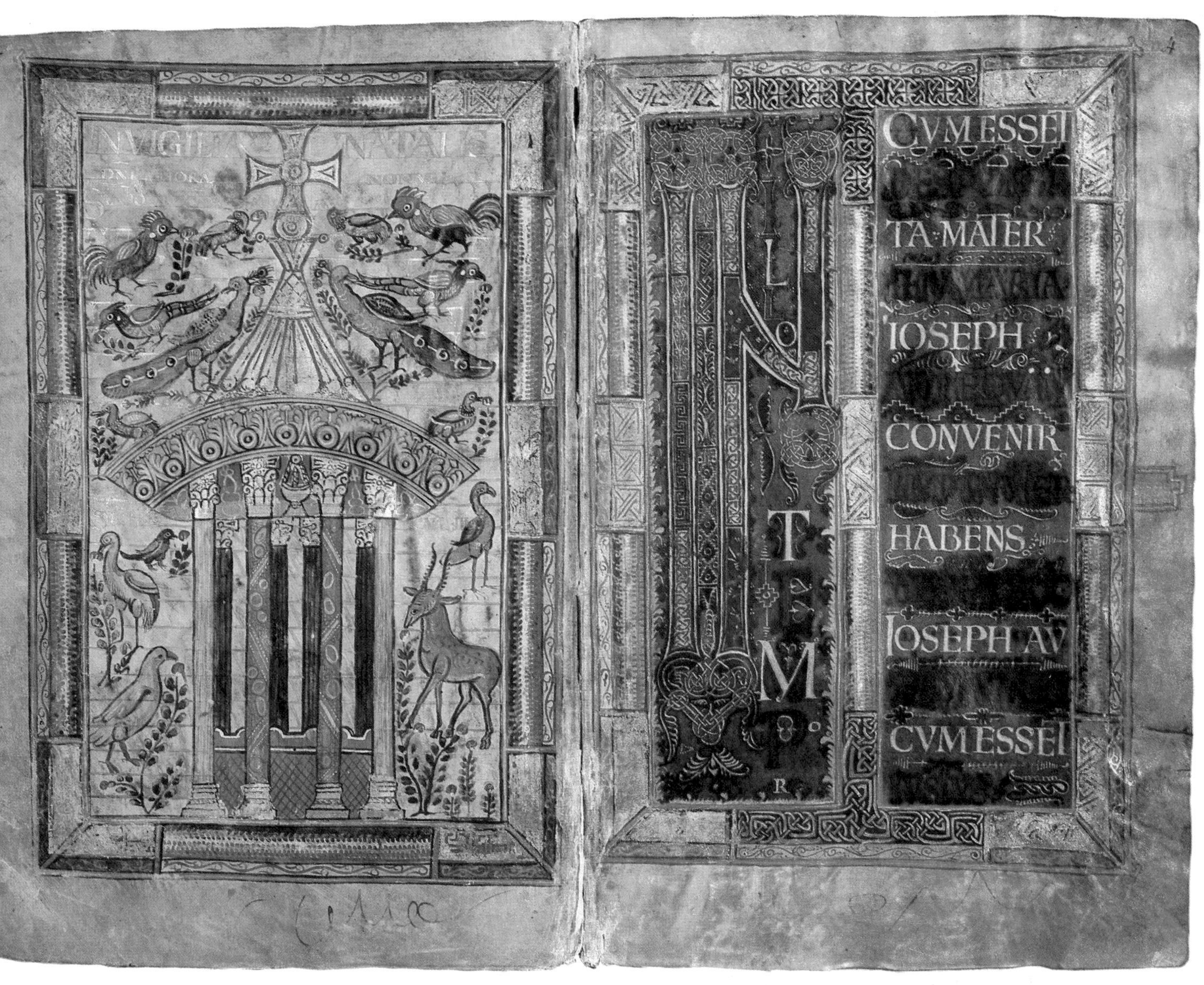

36 (OPPOSITE) Aachen, Cathedral Treasury s.n., f. 13r; Gospels, probably Aachen, late eighth century.
The miniature shows the four Evangelists writing their Gospels. The style of painting is inspired by classical art.

37 (ABOVE) Paris, Bibliothèque Nationale MS. nouv. acq. lat. 1203, ff. r–v; Gospels, Rhineland, *c.* 781–3.
This manuscript was written by the scribe Godescalc for Charlemagne and his wife Hildegard. The miniature on the left commemorates the baptism of Charlemagne's son Pepin at the Lateran church in Rome.

38 (LEFT) Paris, Bibliothèque Nationale MS. lat. 8850, f. 6v; Gospels, Rhineland, *c.* 827.
This miniature, which is derived from the picture in the Godescalc Gospels (pl. 37), illustrates the Fountain of Life in the St.-Médard Gospel Book which was given in 827 by Louis the Pious to Angilbert, abbot of St.-Médard in Soissons.

39 (RIGHT) Vienna, Österreichisches Nationalbibliothek MS. 1861, f. 4v, Psalter, probably Aachen, *c.* 783–95.
This is the dedication inscription in gold in the Psalter ordered by Charlemagne from the scribe Dagulf for presentation to the pope.

ramnus Bible, a huge book in many volumes now divided between the Bibliothèque Municipale in Amiens (MSS. 6–7, 9, 11–12) and the Bibliothèque Nationale in Paris (MS. lat. 13174). It was made at Corbie Abbey near Amiens during the abbacy of Maurdramnus (772–81). It is a monumental volume intended for display at one of the greatest eighth-century monasteries, and it is sometimes suggested that a project of this size and expense would have needed the patronage of the royal treasury. The Maurdramnus Bible comprises the Old Testament only, and it is the Old Testament that contains the politically appropriate themes of the election of kings, maintenance of authority by warfare, the anointing of kings by patriarchs to confer legitimacy on their titles, and the vision of a tribal society invincible under the special protection of God. These were favourite subjects for the Carolingian propagandists of the eighth century.

King David's seizure of power over the Israelites must have been comforting to Charlemagne. There is no doubt that he identified himself with the Old Testament king and psalmist. Charlemagne's companions had a kind of private joke among themselves in which they pretended to be their heroes from classical antiquity: Alcuin was 'Flaccus' (that is, Horace), Angilbert, abbot of St-Riquier, was 'Homer', Charlemagne's son Pepin was 'Julius', but Charlemagne himself, to his friends, was 'King David'. Alcuin called him David in public and the nickname became known. It was later applied to Louis the Pious and Charles the Bald. One enchanting early Carolingian manuscript is a little Psalter (Pl. 39) written out at the order of Charlemagne himself for presentation to Pope Hadrian I (772–95). The book is now in Vienna (ÖNB MS. 1861). It begins with an opening dedication (f. 4r), written in gold and saying that the psalms are the golden words of King David and that Charlemagne is his golden successor. There is as much politics as politeness in Charlemagne choosing this volume for the papacy, or at least in having it known that he had ordered it (for there is no evidence that it actually left Germany), and Charlemagne ruthlessly manipulated papal support for himself, his kingdom, and (after his coronation in St. Peter's on Christmas Day 800) for the new Holy Roman Empire. The Psalter for Pope Hadrian is signed by the scribe Dagulf (f. 4v). The name appears in several contemporary documents; in a letter of Alcuin written between 789 and 796 he is called 'Dagulfus scrinarius', which means a kind of archivist. He was in the royal household. The book is beautifully decorated with

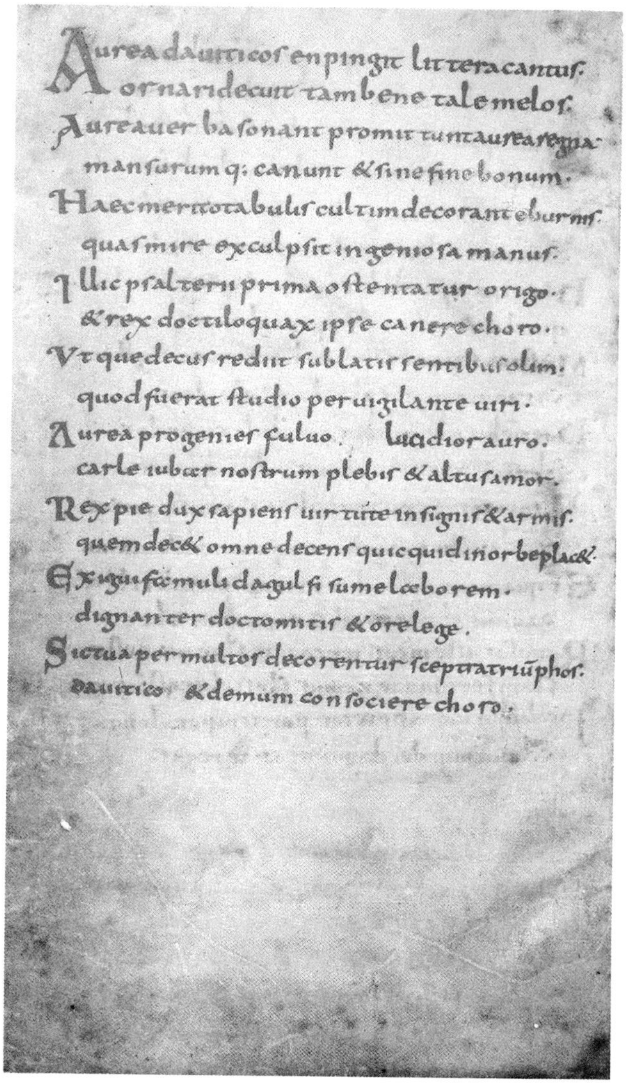
Aurea dauiticos en pingit litteracantus.
ornari decuit tam bene tale melos.
Aurea uerba sonant promitt unt aurea regna
mansurumq; canunt & sine fine bonum.
Haec merito tabulis cultim decorant eburnis
quas mire exculpsit ingeniosa manus.
Illic psalterii prima ostentatur origo.
& rex doctiloquax ipse canere choro.
Utque decus redit sublatis sentibus olim.
quod fuerat studio peruigilante uiri.
Aurea progenies fuluo lucidior auro.
carle iubar nostrum plebis & altus amor.
Rex pie dux sapiens uirtute insignis & armis.
quem dec& omne decens quicquid in orbe plac&.
Exigui famuli dagulfi sume laborem.
dignanter docto mitis & ore lege.
Sic tua per multos decorentur sceptra triumphos.
dauitico & demum consociere choro.

majestic initials and headings in gold and silver, often on purple grounds (the imperial colour, deliberately chosen), and the script by Dagulf is an elegant minuscule.

This introduces a fundamental theme in Carolingian book production – the reform of handwriting and the adoption of minuscule script. Historians of manuscripts love to argue endlessly over exactly how and why this occurred. There had been many kinds of script used for writing books in Merovingian France, derived from various forms of Roman writing. Sometimes these were so bizarre that one can localize eighth-century manuscripts fairly closely from the use of a local script such as the 'Corbie a/b' script or the 'Luxeuil minuscule', which were employed in particular monasteries and their surrounding regions. In keeping with Charlemagne's carefully planned campaign to reform education, grammar, and liturgy, a new and very simple script was introduced with extreme efficiency and in all parts of the Carolingian dominions. It is known as Carolingian (or Caroline) minuscule. It is small and very round and has tall vertical ascenders and descenders, and was compact and no doubt quick to write and easy to read, and it was phenomenally successful. Virtually all Carolingian manuscripts were written in this famous minuscule.

At the risk of anticipating chapter 8, we can glance ahead and foresee that the majority of manuscripts of classical texts that were rediscovered by the humanists in the fifteenth century were Carolingian in date and therefore in this writing. The humanists wrongly convinced themselves that these represented original Roman manuscripts. They began to imitate Carolingian minuscule, abandoning the gothic script of the period. At that time (and we are still looking ahead by seven hundred years) the art of printing was introduced into Italy and the first Italian printers also adopted this neat round writing: it was called 'Roman' type. Printing had the remarkable effect of stabilizing letter forms and they have remained substantially unchanged ever since. We still use Charlemagne's script. It is probably the most long-lasting achievement of Carolingian civilization. Through a mistake in the dating of eighth- and ninth-century manuscripts, Carolingian minuscule is used (for example) for the printing of this book.

The manuscript usually regarded as the first to contain the new Carolingian minuscule writing is the Godescalc Gospels, as it is called, which is now B.N. MS. nouv. acq. lat. 1203. It was commissioned by Charlemagne and his queen Hildegard on 7 October 781 and completed on 30 April 783. It was written by the scribe Godescalc and (as the dedication verses explain) commemorates Charlemagne's fourteenth anniversary as king of the Franks and the baptism of his son Pepin by Pope Hadrian in Rome. One suspects Charlemagne was especially proud of this baptism: the manuscript includes a miniature of the baptistery of the Lateran church in Rome (Pl. 37), and this image entered Carolingian art as a symbol of the Fountain of Life (Pl. 38). The Godescalc Gospel Book is illuminated in the same style as the Dagulf Psalter. They both belong to a whole group of closely related ceremonial manuscripts usually known as the 'Ada' group of books because one of them (now Trier Cod.

22) includes a dedication to Ada, the servant of God, who is said to have been Charlemagne's sister. Some leaves of Ada's book seem to be in the hand of Godescalc also. Other manuscripts in this style include the St-Riquier Gospels (Abbeville MS.4) which was apparently given by Charlemagne to Angilbert, abbot of St-Riquier (790–814), the so-called Golden Gospels of Charlemagne from the abbey of St-Martin-des-Champs in Paris (Arsenal MS.599), the Harley Golden Gospels (B.L. Harley MS.2788), the Lorsch Gospels (divided between Vatican MS.Pal.Lat.50 (Pl.41) and the library in Alba Julia in Romania, and the St-Médard Gospels (B.N. MS.lat.8850) which was given by Louis the Pious in 827 to Angilbert, abbot of St-Médard in Soissons.

These are all extremely grand manuscripts. Some of their interlaced initials reflect Celtic styles, but the whole appearance of these books is Mediterranean with medallions like Roman coins and with classical pediments and marbled columns. Most of them are at least in part written in gold script on a purple-coloured ground, a device which (as Charlemagne's scribes certainly knew) went back to imperial antiquity. It is a very distinctive feature. Suetonius mentions a poem by Nero which had been written in gold; the emperor Maximinus (235–38) is said to have had a Homer written in gold on purple vellum; St. Jerome in his prologue to the Book of Job criticizes those who like ancient books written out in gold or silver on purple leaves. It is a practice which probably survived into Charlemagne's time through its use in Constantinople. One can understand how important it was to Charlemagne, who was rebuilding his dominions on the model of classical antiquity, to propagate the image of the cultured emperor, and displays of books were (and are) among the accepted trappings of the cultured. Manuscripts written in gold on purple had a promotional value in symbolizing imperial culture. That is one reason why these spectacular manuscripts were made for distribution by Charlemagne's family to communities in his Christian empire, as it was called.

There may be a cruder, more barbarian, reason too. These books are heavy in gold. This was really quite a new development in Frankish manuscript production. Charlemagne's books look expensive. The dedication verses in the Godescalc Gospel Book begin with the word 'gold' ('Aurea purpureis pinguntur . . .'). Those in the Dagulf Psalter start 'Aurea daviticos . . .': the text is not only golden but the volume is to be interpreted as comprising gold. It was the ancient Germanic custom for tribal leaders to reward their retinues in gold. Charlemagne regularly summoned his secular armies and in return for military service he gave lands and booty. The soldiers understood this. But the cohorts of religion – the monks of Corbie, Lorsch, and other imperial abbeys – were rewarded for spiritual service in the same way. In the most primitive sense, a Frankish prince distributed gold, and books were gold.

Charlemagne himself seems to have had a personal interest in manuscripts if one can judge from remarks by his biographer Einhard who mentions a great quantity of books that he had collected in his library or from the observation that he liked to read St. Augustine, histories, and tales of the ancients. One fragmentary library catalogue survives from about 790 and it was at one time supposed that it might record part of the holdings of Corbie Abbey (Berlin Deutsche Staatsbibl. MS. Diez B. Sant. 66, f.218r). However, Professor Bernhard Bischoff has demonstrated that it is very probably a list of the texts belonging to the private library of the court of

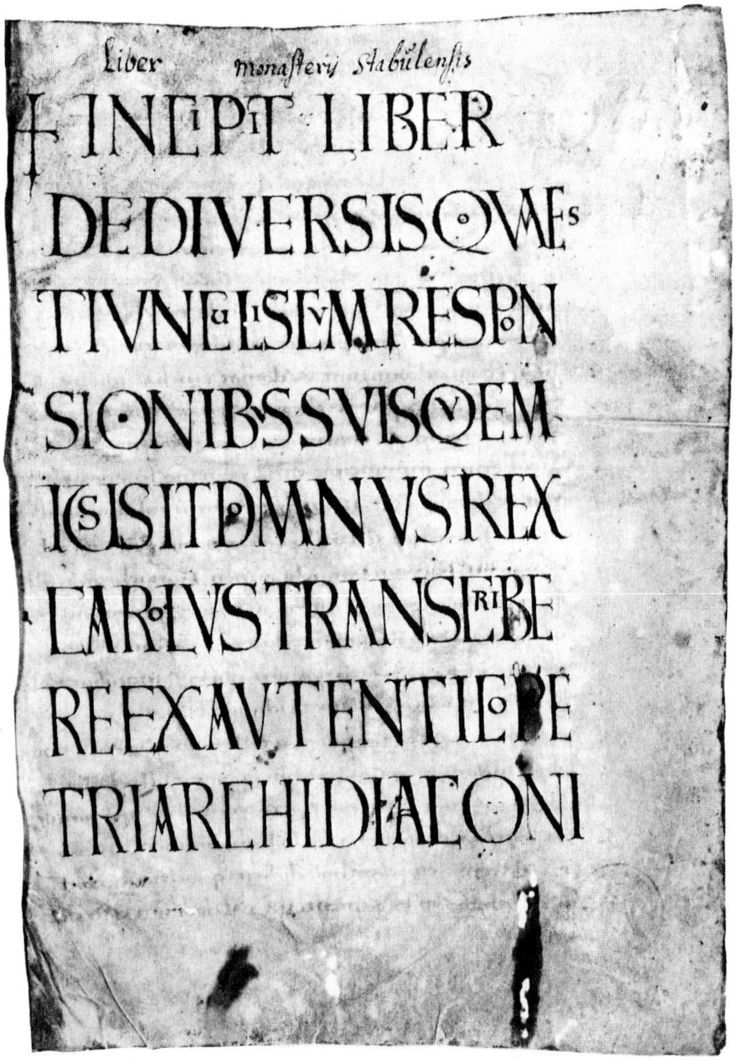

40 (LEFT) Brussels, Bibliothèque Royale MS.II.2572, f. 1r; Peter the Archdeacon, Liber de Diversis Quaestiunculis, early ninth century.
This title leaf from a manuscript later at Stavelot Abbey in Flanders records that the lord king Charles ordered this book to be copied from the original.

41 (RIGHT) Vatican MS.Pal.Lat.50, f.71r; Gospels, perhaps Aachen, early ninth century.
The Lorsch Gospels is one of the last and most splendid golden manuscripts illuminated in the court of Charlemagne. It was recorded at Lorsch Abbey by about 830, described as 'scriptum cum auro', and passed at the dissolution of Lorsch into the collections of the Elector Palatine at Heidelberg. In 1623, the Palatine Library was ceded to the papacy and the books are now in the Vatican, still with their Palatine shelfmarks.

INPRINCIPIO
ERATVERBUM
ETVERBUME
RATAPUDD̄M̄.
ETD̄SERATVER
BUM·HOCERAT
INPRINCIPIO
APUDD̄M̄·

Charlemagne. It is an impressive roll-call of classical works, including books by Lucan, Statius, Terence, Juvenal, Tibullus, Horace, Claudian, Martial, Servius, Cicero, and Sallust. The Tibullus is especially tantalizing, as the earliest-known surviving manuscript is no older than the late fourteenth century. The list itself occurs in a volume of little treatises on Latin grammar – works by Donatus, Pompeius, and others – and one can imagine Charlemagne reading up classical grammar with the anxiety of a modern self-made millionaire furtively studying books of etiquette.

Another grammatical manuscript probably from the court scriptorium of around the year 800 (Brussels B.R.II.2572) has a spectacular opening page comprising eight lines of capitals recording that the lord King Charles commanded it to be transcribed from the original book by Peter the Archdeacon (Pl.40). We are told Charlemagne was so anxious to learn to write that he slept with writing materials under his pillow. It is rather touching to catch these glimpses of the great king trying to keep up with the cultural renewal that he had initiated, and perhaps he was trying to practise the new minuscule in the middle of the night. The decree of 789 commanding liturgical reform ordered that only skilful or mature scribes should be entrusted with the most solemn books and 'if the work is a Gospel Book, Psalter, or Missal, the scribes should be of the perfect age for writing diligently.'

Part of Charlemagne's promotion of education and book learning included the importation of the world's most distinguished scholars into his court. One of these was Alcuin (*c.*735–804), who had been born at York in England and who was related to St. Willibrord, the missionary bishop. He was already head of the cathedral schools in York when, during an embassy to Italy in 780, he met Charlemagne, who tempted him with two great abbacies and persuaded him to come to France. For upwards of ten years Alcuin then directed and inspired the revival of classical culture around the figure of Charlemagne. In 796 he retired to Tours, where he became abbot of St. Martin's Abbey, and set in motion there a campaign of manuscript production which lasted far into the ninth century and made Tours the world centre for Bibles and for Carolingian minuscule script.

The making of manuscripts in the Frankish empire in the early ninth century slipped effectively from the court scriptorium into the great royal monasteries such as Chelles and St-Denis, near Paris, and Fleury, Rheims, Tours, Lorsch, St-Médard at Soissons, and elsewhere. The finest manuscripts were expensive and richly decorated. The best-known centre for book production in the early ninth century is Rheims, where manuscripts of really imperial quality were made in the time of Ebbo who had been Charlemagne's librarian and who was appointed archbishop of Rheims in 816. The most extraordinary of the surviving Rheims manuscripts is the famous Utrecht Psalter which is illustrated throughout with incredibly lively, vigorous, sketchy little drawings. The style seems to point straight back to the classical and Byzantine art which the court artists at Aachen introduced into Charlemagne's own books. One early ninth-century manuscript from the abbey of St-Denis can be partially dated from a curious feature in its decoration. B.N. MS.lat.2195 is a copy of Cassiodorus' commentary on the Psalms made at St-Denis in the style associated with Abbot Fardulphus (793–806). One of its big initials includes several imaginary monsters and a surprisingly accurate sketch of the head of an Indian elephant. Medieval artists knew about ivory but not many had seen elephants. This illuminator probably knew the elephant which was presented to Charlemagne by caliph Haroun-al-Rachid in the year 802

42 (OPPOSITE, LEFT) Paris, Bibliothèque Nationale MS. lat. 2195, detail of f. 9v; Cassiodorus of the Psalms, St.-Denis, *c.* 802–10. *This ornamental initial* 'B' *includes the head of an elephant with long tusks. It may represent Charlemagne's elephant Abulabaz.*

43 (OPPOSITE, RIGHT) Paris, Bibliothèque Nationale MS. lat. 1, detail of f. 328v; Bible, Tours, *c.* 845. *This is a detail of an elephant from one of the canon tables in the First Bible of Charles the Bald. The artist had probably never seen a live elephant and knew of the animals only by reputation.*

44 (RIGHT) London, Victoria and Albert Museum Inv. no. 138–1866. *This is one of the Carolingian ivory covers from the Lorsch Gospels* (PL. 41).

(Pl. 42). The elephant's name was Abulabaz and he lived until 810. Therefore the Cassiodorus manuscript cannot be earlier than 802. For all we know, Abulabaz's tusks survive in some of the really magnificent Carolingian ivory book-covers (Pls. 1 and 44) which decorated the grandest Gospel Books.

Charlemagne died at Aachen on 28 January 814. Among various bequests he directed that three-quarters of the gold and silver in his treasury should be distributed among the twenty-one metropolitan churches of the empire and (probably the first time that anyone left this instruction) that his library should be sold and the proceeds given to the needy. This confirms again that it was part of the attribute of a Frankish ruler to distribute treasure, and it shows that books had a monetary value. Despite his fascination with King David and Augustus, Charlemagne planned no dynastic empire. He was enough of a barbarian and a politician to let his empire be subdivided among his heirs, and it was subdivided again and again on their own deaths, until it was unrecognizable a century later.

The custom of commissioning treasure manuscripts continued among some of Charlemagne's descendants. His illegitimate son Drogo, bishop of Metz 826–55, owned at least two Gospel Books written entirely in gold (B.N.

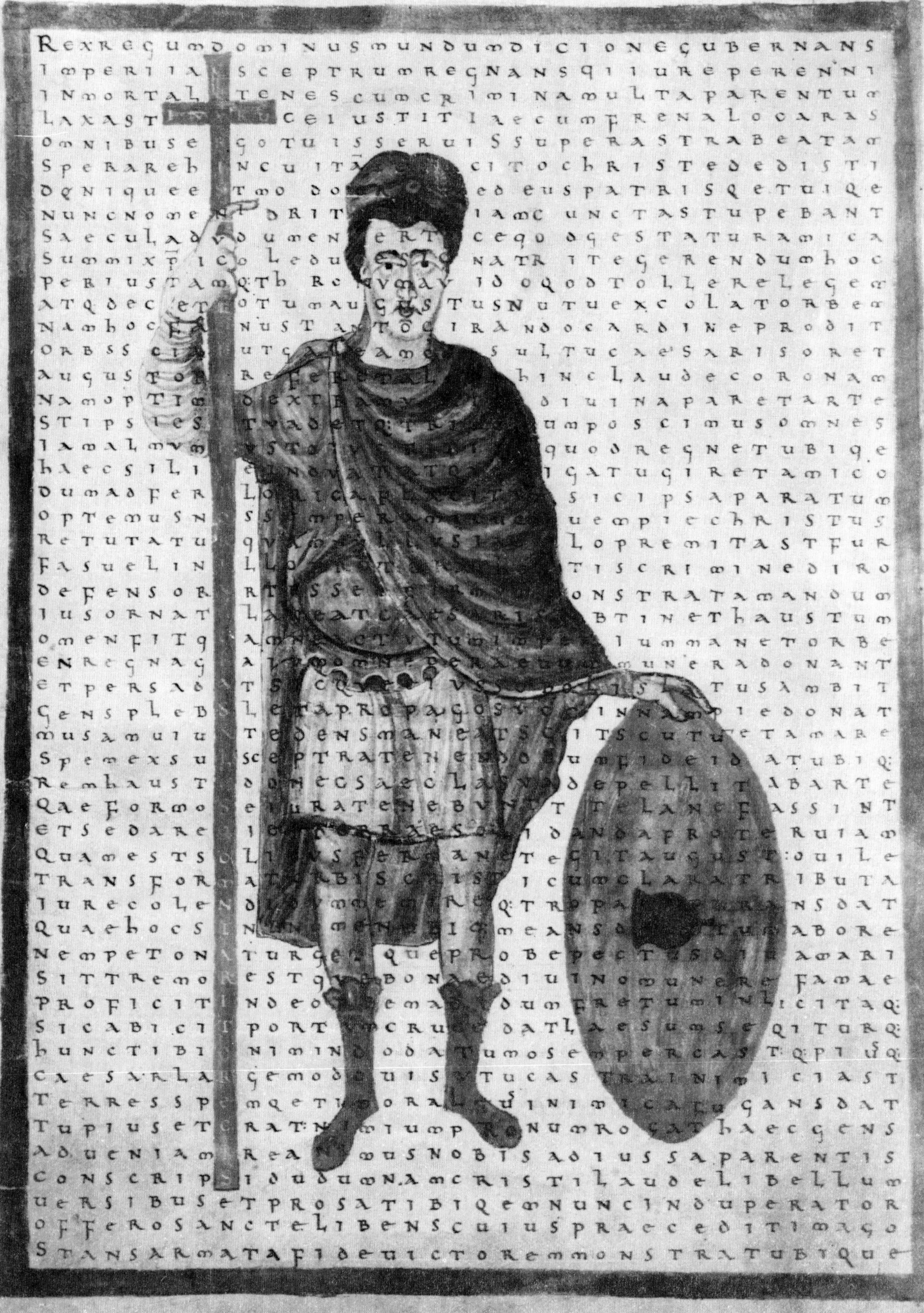

45 Vatican MS. Reg. Lat. 124, f. 4v; Rabanus Maurus, De Laudibus Sancte Crucis, probably Fulda, early ninth century. *This portrait of Louis the Pious, son of Charlemagne, is the earliest picture of a Carolingian emperor in a manuscript. The letters in the background spell out different messages where they cross the image.*

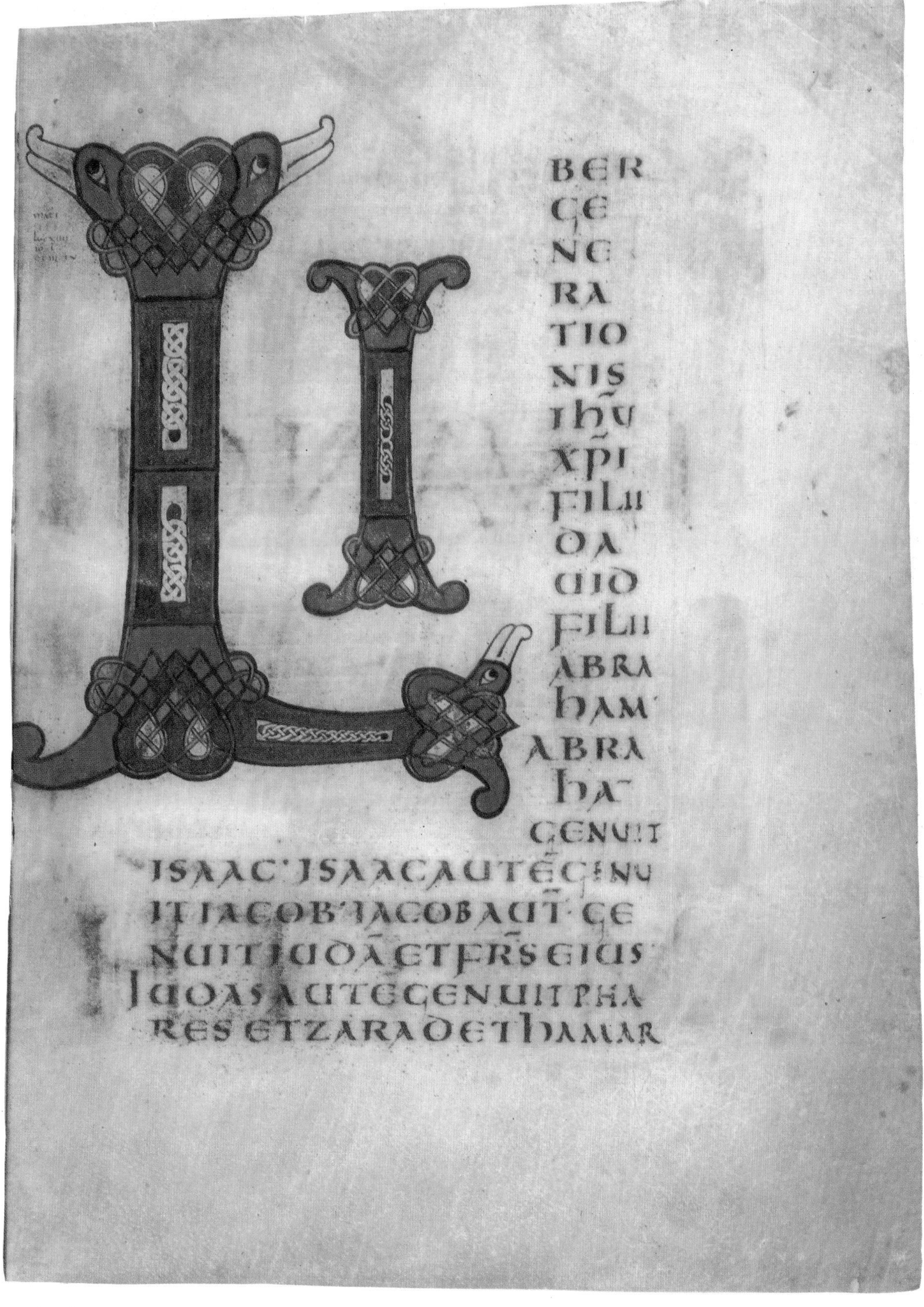
BER
GE
NE
RA
TIO
NIS
IHU
XPI
FILII
DA
UID
FILII
ABRA
HAM
ABRA
HA
GENUIT
ISAAC ISAAC AUTE GENU
IT IACOB IACOB AUT GE
NUIT IUDA ET FRS EIUS
IUDAS AUTE GENUIT PHA
RES ET ZARA DE THAMAR

46 London, Sotheby's, 26 November 1985, lot 93, f. 12r; Gospels, probably St.-Amand, *c.* 870.
This manuscript belonged by the Abbey of St. Hubert near Liège and from at least the early twelfth century it was erroneously said to have belonged to Louis the Pious. It shows Franco-Saxon illumination of the period of Charles the Bald.

47–48 (LEFT AND RIGHT) Paris, Bibliothèque Nationale MS. lat. 1152, ff. 3v–4r; Psalter, possibly St.-Denis, *c.* 850–69.
The Psalter of Charles the Bald was written by the scribe Luithard. The miniatures here show the emperor himself, crowned on a jewel-studded throne, and St. Jerome as a scribe translating the Psalms.

MSS. lat. 9383 and 9388) and the amazing Drogo Sacramentary (MS. lat. 9428) which has forty-one huge historiated initials of classical foliage filled with bustling little figures and scenes. The nearest, however, to a palace school of book production was that of Charles the Bald, grandson of Charlemagne and son of Louis the Pious (Pl. 45), who, after fierce warfare with his half-brothers, held the kingdom of the western Franks from the treaty of Verdun in 843 and who finally obtained the imperial crown in 875 and died less than two years later. His life reflects the same kind of desperate tribal struggle for leadership which marked the less civilized aspect of the Carolingian royal family. We find Charles the Bald preparing treasure manuscripts for his ecclesiastical vassals, like an old chieftain distributing gold bullion.

The grand manuscripts illuminated for the use of Charles the Bald include a prayerbook (now in the Munich Schatzkammer) and a Psalter (now B. N. MS. lat. 1152; Pls. 47–8), both datable to before 869, and probably the famous Bible of San Paolo fuori le Mura (which belongs now to the abbey of that name in Rome). This is a massive manuscript with 336 leaves about $17\frac{1}{2}$ by $14\frac{1}{4}$ inches (443 by 362 mm.). It has twenty-four full-page paintings; at least seven of them include scenes showing biblical kings. The figure of Solomon looks remarkably like Charles the Bald himself. The manuscript concludes with a portrait of Charles enthroned as king, holding in his left hand a golden disc inscribed with a

monogram in red which has been interpreted as 'Charles king [and] caesar, save Charles and Richildis, this [is] king Solomon of the new Rome'. Probably it commemorates Charles' marriage to Richildis on 22 January 870.

But this spectacular manuscript is eclipsed by an even richer volume, made for the treasury of Charles the Bald. It is the Codex Aureus (or Book of Gold – the name is a valid one) of St. Emmeram, now Munich, CLM. 14000. This is really a volume of phenomenal luxury, still (by extreme good fortune) in its original golden binding profusely encrusted with jewels and pearls and gold repoussé pictures. If Charles the Bald identified himself with Solomon, he must have known the text of 1 Kings 6:21–22 describing Solomon's work on the temple at Jerusalem: 'So Solomon overlaid the house within with pure gold . . . And the whole house he overlaid with gold, until he had finished all the house.' On f. 5v of the Codex Aureus is a portrait of Charles the Bald on a jewel-studded throne within a domed temple with angels and the hand of God above (Pl. 66). On either side are armed soldiers and allegorical figures, representing Francia and Gotica, and on panels along the top and bottom of the page are gold inscriptions identifying this rich king as Charles, son of Louis, heir of Charlemagne, David (it calls him) and Solomon, by whose provision this book shines with gold. The manuscript has page after page of paintings, canon tables, and huge illuminated initials, all brilliantly illumi-

49 Paris, Bibliothèque Nationale MS. lat. I, f. 423r; Bible, Tours, *c.* 846, *This is the dedication miniature in the First Bible of Charles the Bald, sometimes known as the Vivian Bible. The scene shows a delegation of monks led by Vivian (abbot of Tours 845–851) presenting their Bible, wrapped in cloth, to the emperor, who is attended by an armed guard.*

50 Paris, Bibliothèque Nationale MS. lat. 8851, f. 16r;
Gospels, Trier, *c.* 983.
This Gospel Book is one of the earliest great Ottonian manuscripts and is illustrated here with gold coins of Otto II. In 1379 it was given by Charles V of France to the Sainte-Chapelle in Paris.

nated. Charles himself presumably provided the gold for the artists who may have been working in the abbey of St-Denis which the king retained as his own possession after the death of one of its abbots in 867. The Codex Aureus is signed by the scribes Beringar and Liuthard and is dated 870. There is a contemporary reference to Charles the Bald's manuscripts kept in his treasury. Certainly the Codex Aureus of St. Emmeram was not for daily use, but was a dazzling display of the king's fiscal assets. After the death of Charles the Bald in 877, it came into the hands of his distant cousin King Arnulf of Bavaria who, soon after 893, passed it on to the abbey of St. Emmeram in Regensburg. Thus its name comes from the monastery where it was finally received as a royal gift.

Sometimes the tremendous financial value of these imperial manuscripts worked the other way round: the king also received manuscripts as well as presenting them. Again it was part of a king's function to accept tribute and to dispense wealth. Several such manuscripts were made for the royal family at Tours. We mentioned earlier that Charlemagne's adviser Alcuin had retired to the abbey of St. Martin at Tours. Here a great programme of manuscript production had been set in motion by Alcuin and his successors, Fridugisus (804–34), Adalhard (834–43), and Vivian (843–51). These abbots were royal appointments: Adalhard had been seneschal to Louis the Pious, and Vivian was a count and court official of Charles the Bald. Manuscripts produced under royal patronage at Tours were exported from there all over the Carolingian kingdoms. Probably two of them were presented to Emperor Lothair (d.855), half-brother of Charles the Bald and king of the Italian part of Charlemagne's empire. These are a Gospel Book (B.N. MS. lat.266; Pl.33) and a Psalter (B.L. Add.MS.37768; Pls.54–5). E. K. Rand, the historian of the scriptorium of Tours, described the former as 'Perfected. The *ne plus ultra* of excellence . . . The unsurpassed model of perfection in script and ornament among the books of Tours.' The monks were determined to impress King Lothair.

A better-known presentation from Tours is the famous First Bible of Charles the Bald, sometimes called the Vivian Bible (B. N. MS.lat.1; Pl.49). It was commissioned by the abbot to present to the king in *c.*846. It opens with an unusual miniature in three horizontal rows showing scenes from the life of St. Jerome, translator of the Latin Bible. In the centre is Jerome dictating to a group of scribes and at the bottom Jerome distributes copies of his new translation. This probably has an allegorical allusion to Alcuin correcting the text of the Bible and having copies made and disseminated from his abbey in Tours. It is worth looking closely at the boxes from which St. Jerome is shown handing out manuscripts: they are typical treasure chests, with wooden bands and massive metal locks. Books were equated with extreme wealth. The recipients are shown furtively hurrying away with the treasured gifts. The association between the manuscript and secular wealth is reflected again in its dedicatory verses which are illustrated with two imperial coins, one inscribed 'David rex imperator' and the other 'Carolus rex Francorum'. Thus the biblical King David is linked with Charles, king of the Franks. It is important that this is represented by gold coins. That is how many would have understood this copy of the Bible. In the Gospels, when Christ was shown an imperial coin, he asked whose portrait and inscription it bore, and when they replied 'Caesar's', he instructed his listeners to render unto Caesar the things that were Caesar's. The dedication miniature in the First Bible of Charles the Bald shows the king exactly like a tax gatherer receiving tribute. He is seated between administrative officials and armed soldiers fingering their weapons. From the left a delegation of nervous monks bring in the huge Bible partly wrapped in white cloth and the king holds out his right hand to accept this addition to his treasury.

Charles the Bald died in 877, while marching across the Alps in one of the seemingly endless Carolingian dynastic feuds, this time against Carloman, king of Bavaria and Italy and great-grandson of Charlemagne. It was, in fact, Carloman's son and heir, Arnulf, who inherited the Codex Aureus of St. Emmeram and perhaps other manuscripts from the library of Charles the Bald. Arnulf's own son, Louis the Child, king of the Franks 900–11, was the last direct descendant of Charlemagne to rule the German part of his great-great-great-grandfather's vast empire. When Louis the Child died without issue, Conrad, duke of Franconia, was elected king, and Conrad (who died in 918) nominated Henry the Fowler as his own successor. This sounds complicated, and indeed the thread of inheritance from Charlemagne is remarkably fragile and one generation succeeded another with great rapidity. Henry the Fowler's son was the Emperor Otto the Great. Now at last the line of succession becomes clear again. Historians grasp willingly at this recognizable figure and call this the 'Ottonian' age. The tenth century was certainly a great period in imperial history. It brought the nearest possible revival of the golden days of Charlemagne, with a fervour of political and religious reform, and it is often known as the Ottonian renaissance. It also produced a great many illuminated manuscripts.

Otto the Great was anointed king in 936 in Charlemagne's palace chapel at Aachen. After a turbulent military life and careful marriages, he brought great portions of Germany and Italy under his control. Even the pope eventually became his vassal, a shrewd political move which did much to stabilize imperial power. Otto was crowned emperor in Rome on 2 February 962. He lived until 973.

As Otto the Great consolidated his position and began to merge the state and Church into a powerful new administration, so the Ottonians looked back wistfully at the cultivated empire of the past. Bruno (925–65), Otto's brother, was appointed royal chancellor, arch-chaplain, and later archbishop of Cologne, and inspired a renewed interest in

51 Paris, Bibliothèque Nationale MS.lat.1141, f.2v; Sacramentary, Metz, *c.*869.
Charles the Bald was crowned king of Lorraine in 869 and a series of miniatures survives from a Coronation Sacramentary made for the occasion. This one shows Charles receiving his crown from God as he stands between two bishops. All three are depicted with haloes.

52–53 (ABOVE AND OPPOSITE) Munich, Bayerische Staatsbibliothek CLM.4453, ff.23v–24r; Gospels, probably Reichenau, *c*.998.
The Gospel Book of Otto III shows, on facing pages, the four provinces of the empire paying homage to Otto himself, flanked by ecclesiastical and military officials.

24.

classical texts (he had learned Greek from the monks of Reichenau) and in grammar, rhetoric, geometry, music, astronomy, commerce, and the other refinements of civilization. Education again became a royal priority. There is an account in Ekkehard's chronicle of the abbey of St. Gall in Switzerland of a visit to that monastery in the year 972 by Otto the Great with his son (the future Otto II, then aged about 17). They spent several days there. The boy discovered a locked chest in the monastic treasury and demanded that it be opened for him. It proved to be full of manuscripts. Young Otto helped himself to the best, as the monks stood by, unable to refuse. Later (following a diplomatic request from the monastery) some of the books were returned, but one which was never sent back was probably a Psalter (now Bamberg MS. A. I. 14) with parallel texts in two versions of Latin and in Hebrew and Greek, which had been made for Salomo III, abbot of St. Gall, in 909. It says something about Ottonian court education that a Germanic prince would bother to seek out a manuscript in three ancient languages.

In the same year that they visited St. Gall, Otto the Great arranged a marriage for his son. It was a political triumph. The bride was Theofanu, a princess of Byzantium. Throughout the whole Carolingian and Ottonian period, the Byzantine empire was regarded as the ultimate symbol of sophistication, and for a daughter of the eastern imperial house to marry the heir apparent of the German ruler conferred immense prestige on the west. (How the poor girl felt in northern Europe, twelve hundred miles from home, would not have been considered.) The original marriage charter of Theofanu and Otto still survives, and it is displayed

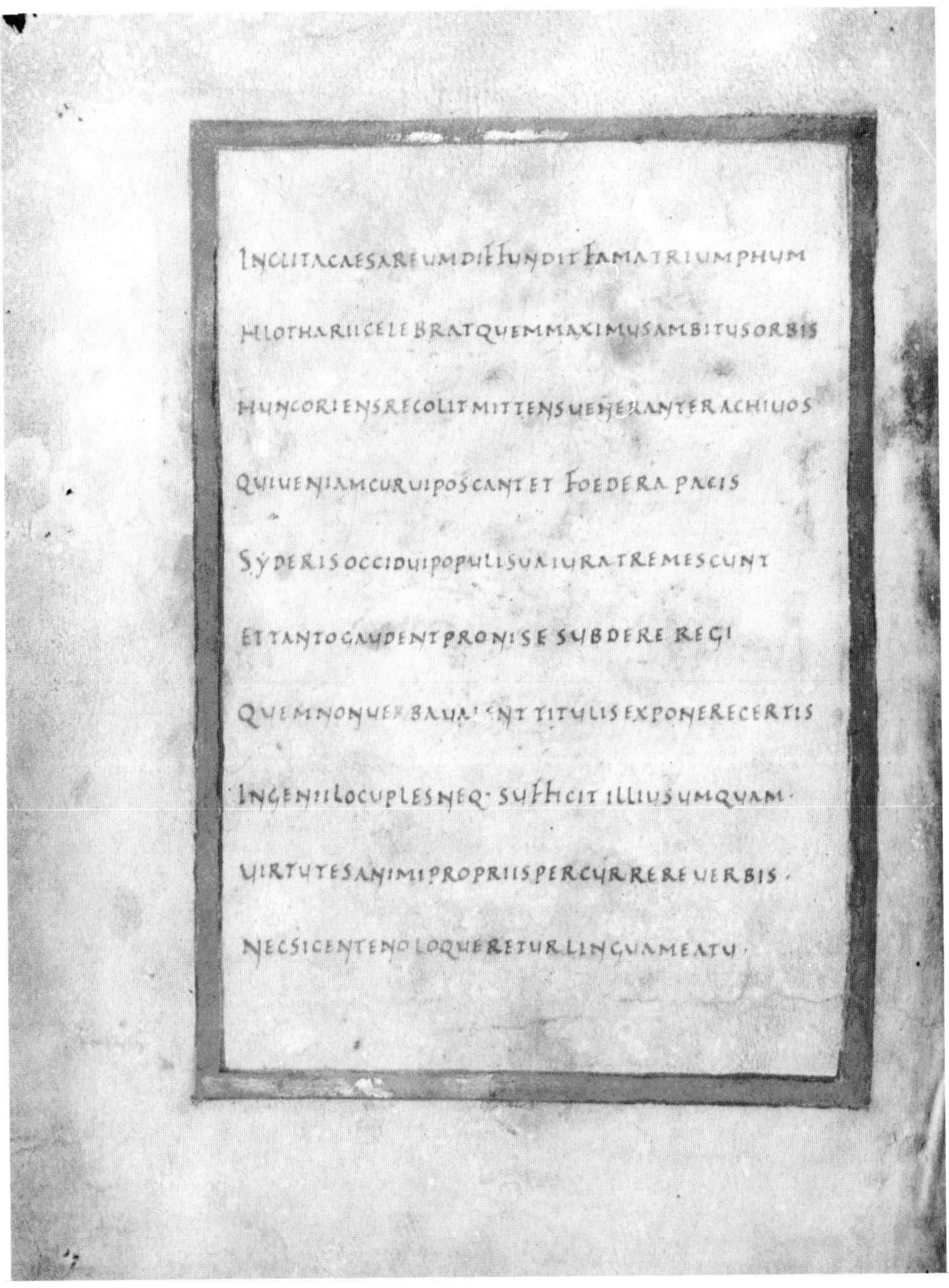
INCLITACAESAREUMDIFFUNDITFAMATRIUMPHUM
HLOTHARIICELEBRATQUEMMAXIMUSAMBITUSORBIS
HUNCORIENSRECOLITMITTENSUENERANTERACHIUOS
QUIUENIAMCURUIPOSCANTETFOEDERAPACIS
SYDERISOCCIDUIPOPULISUAIURATREMESCUNT
ETTANTOGAUDENTPRONISESUBDEREREGI
QUEMNONUERBAUALENTTITULISEXPONERECERTIS
INGENIILOCUPLESNEQ·SUFFICITILLIUSUMQUAM·
UIRTUTESANIMIPROPRIISPERCURREREUERBIS·
NECSICENTENOLOQUERETURLINGUAMEATU·

54–55 (RIGHT AND OPPOSITE) London, British Library Add. MS. 37768, ff. 3v–4r; Psalter, possibly Tours, mid-ninth century.
The Emperor Lothair (795–855), eldest son of Louis the Pious and half-brother of Charles the Bald, received this Psalter from the monks at Tours and passed it to the Abbey of St. Hubert near Liège where it was kept with the Gospel Book illustrated in pl. 47.

in a special room in the state archives of Lower Saxony in Wolfenbüttel. This document of 14 April 972 is an ultimate imperial manuscript, a huge scroll written in gold in uncial and minuscule on purple vellum and decorated with great medallions of classical and mythological designs of animals infilled with ornamental scrollwork. It is a magnificent object. At last the tribal rulers of Europe glimpsed their own names in an inheritance which went back to the Emperor Augustus.

Otto II succeeded to the Holy Roman Empire in May 973, but he lived for only another ten years. He died in Rome and is buried in the crypt of St. Peter's. The revival of manuscript illumination in his reign is partly due to Egbert, who was appointed to the archbishopric of Trier in 977 and was both a churchman and a member of the imperial chancery. He owned a Gospel Lectionary, the Codex Egberti (Trier MS.24), which is signed by two monks Kerald and Heribert of Reichenau Abbey, the wealthy island monastery on Lake Constance. He also almost certainly employed one of the very greatest medieval illuminators, the Master of the Registrum Gregorii, who was probably working at Trier from about 980 until at least 996. About half a dozen surviving manuscripts were painted or refurbished by this artist. One of them, a Gospel Book datable to before the death of Otto II, was given four hundred years later by the king of France to the Sainte-Chapelle in Paris (B.N. MS.lat.8851). The same artist also painted two detached miniatures, one still in Trier and the other now in the Musée Conde at Chantilly, from a volume of the Registrum Gregorii (hence the artist's name) which Egbert gave to Trier Cathedral (Pls. 58 and 59). The

56 Bamberg, Staatsbibliothek MS. Msc. Bibl. 84; St. Gregory, Moralia, south Germany (Seeon Abbey), *c.* 1020.
The scribe Bebo of Seeon Abbey is shown presenting Henry II with a copy of St. Gregory's commentary on the book of Job which the emperor had expressed an interest in owning. The author appears in the upper part of the miniature, writing under divine inspiration. Henry II gave the manuscript to Bamberg and it is still there.

57 (RIGHT) El Escorial, Real Biblioteca, Cod. Vitrinas 17, f. 3r; Gospels, Echternach, *c.* 1043–46.
The Golden Gospels of Henry III is one of the last great imperial manuscripts. It shows Henry as king, not emperor (and therefore dates from before his imperial coronation in 1046), with his wife Agnes whom he married in 1043.

REGEM SPERNERE NOLI
ME TIBI COMMENDO
PRAESENTIA DONA FERENDO
SPIRA FIT INSIGNIS
HEINRICI MUNERE REGIS
SCA MARIA
HEIN RICUS REX
AGNES REGINA

58 Trier, Stadtbibliothek MS. 1171/626; single leaf from St. Gregory, Epistles (Registrum Gregorii), Trier, *c.*983.
This and the facing miniature are fragments from what must have been a magnificent manuscript which was presented to Trier Cathedral by Otto II's counsellor Egbert, archbishop of Trier 977–993. The first miniature shows St. Gregory dictating, while a monk writes down his holy words on a wax tablet.

59 Chantilly, Musée Condé MS. 14 *bis*; single leaf from St. Gregory, Epistles (Registrum Gregorii), Trier, *c.*983. *The emperor is receiving homage from the four provinces of his empire. The miniature commemorates the death of Otto II in 983 and since his successor, Otto III, was then only 3 or 4 years old, it presumably shows his late father, who died at the age of 28 on 7 December 983.*

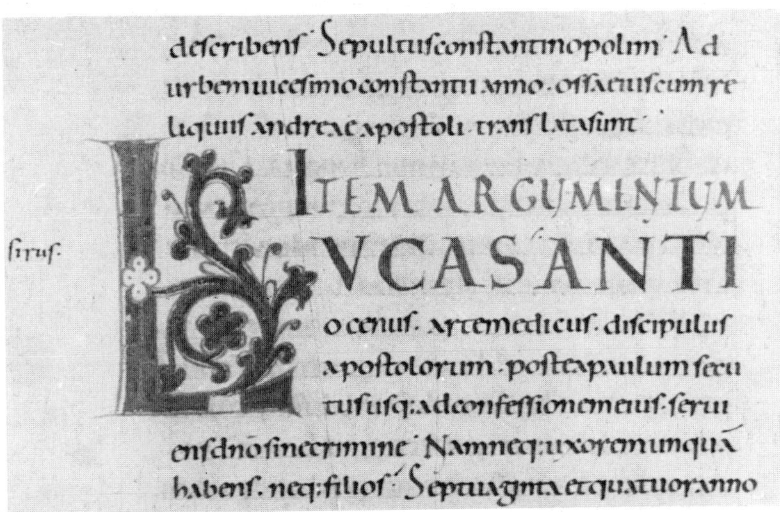

60 (LEFT) Manchester, Rylands Library MS.98, detail of f.95; Gospels, Trier, *c.*1000.
This manuscript includes pictures of gold coins showing Otto III as emperor and therefore dates from after his imperial coronation in 996.

62 (RIGHT) Munich, Bayerische Staatsbibliothek CLM.4453, upper cover of binding.
This is the contemporary golden binding of the Gospels of Otto III, inset with a Byzantine ivory and jewels and classical intaglios.

61 Munich, Bayerische Staatsbibliothek CLM.4453, f.139r; Gospels, probably Reichenau, *c.*998.
The Gospels of Otto III is one of the world's greatest manuscripts. St. Luke appears here, holding five richly bound books on his lap and triumphantly exalting the Old Testament prophets.

surviving fragment includes a poem bewailing the death of Otto II in 983, and the Chantilly miniature of a crowned emperor with his staff and orb no doubt commemorates Egbert's late patron. It shows Otto enthroned under a tiled roof supported by classical columns, and from either side he receives gifts of homage from personifications of Germania, Francia, Italia, and Alemannia. It is a marvellous image.

It was under Otto III, emperor from 983 until his early death in 1002, that Ottonian book production reached its high point. We began this chapter with the account of Otto III opening the tomb of Charlemagne and finding a Gospel Book among the imperial regalia. Otto III considered himself doubly imperial, both through his Byzantine mother and his German father. He was extremely rich and powerful, and young enough to be almost blasphemously arrogant (he was less than five when his father died, and still only eleven on the death of his mother Theofanu in 991). Unlimited wealth is not good for young men. In 996 he promoted his twenty-nine-year-old cousin, Bruno, to the papacy; he took the title of Gregory V, the first German pope, and then promptly crowned Otto III as emperor. When the cousin died, Otto installed as pope his former tutor, Gerbert of Aurillac, who assumed the name of Sylvester II. Even the popes were under the power of Otto III. In his manuscripts the emperor was represented almost on a level with God himself. Otto's Gospel Book now in Aachen, made by the monk Liuthar, shows the emperor seated within a mandorla in heaven with his arms outspread like Christ in glory and with the emblems of the four Evangelists hovering on either side of him. It is amazing that a monk could paint such an image. Another Gospel Book in the Rylands Library in Manchester (Pl.60) includes Otto's portrait four times on the first page of St. Matthew's Gospel (MS.98, f.16r), inscribed with the name of Otto, emperor of the Christian religion and of the Roman people. This illumination occurs on the page which recounts the descent of Christ from David and Abraham.

The grandest manuscript of all is the extraordinary Gospels of Otto III in Munich (CLM.4453). In modern monetary terms this must be a candidate for the most valuable

book in the world. It was made for Otto around 998, probably at Reichenau. It is in its original golden binding set with jewels and with a Byzantine ivory panel (Pls.61 and 62). It is a totally imperial manuscript with full-page illuminated initials, Evangelist portraits, twenty-nine full-page miniatures from the life of Christ, and dominating all these, it has a pair of facing paintings showing the peoples of the world adoring Otto III (Pls.52–3). The worshippers resemble the Magi bringing offerings to the infant Christ. They are four women bearing gold and jewels and their names are written above in capitals: Sclavinia, the eastern European with dark red hair, Germania, a fair-skinned girl with long wispy blonde hair, Gallia, the black-haired French girl, and the curly-headed Roma, who is bowing lowest of all before the ruler of the empire. Otto himself is shown on the opposite page, seated disdainfully on his majestic throne, flanked by two priests with books (possibly to be identified as Heribert, chancellor of Italy (d.1021), and Leo, future bishop of Vercelli (d.*c.*1026)) and by two armed soldiers, one of them perhaps Gerard, count of the Sabine, the guard of the emperor. Otto III had built himself a palace on the Aventine Hill in Rome. His library included (amazingly) a fifth-century manuscript of Livy's history of Rome, probably given to him by the archbishop of Piacenza in about 996; the transcript of it that he had made still survives in Bamberg. His seal had the legend 'Renovatio Imperii Romanorum', the

63 Bamberg, Staatsbibliothek MS.Msc.Bibl.95, f.7v; Gospels, south Germany (Seeon Abbey), *c.*1020. *Henry II is shown holding a Gospel Book in a jewelled binding.*

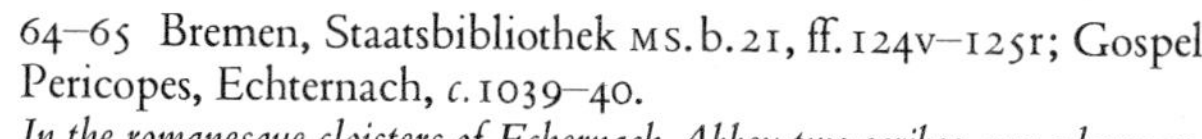

64–65 Bremen, Staatsbibliothek MS. b. 21, ff. 124v–125r; Gospel Pericopes, Echternach, *c.* 1039–40.
In the romanesque cloisters of Echernach Abbey two scribes, one a layman and the other a monk, are writing out a Gospel Lectionary for Henry III. On the facing page the abbot of Echternach, accompanied by the monk, brings the volume to the palace and presents it to Henry.

restoration of the empire of the Romans. He thought himself at least as great as Caesar Augustus.

It is interesting to try to compare the Ottonian imperial manuscripts with those of Charlemagne and Charles the Bald. Sometimes it is quite clear that the later illuminators were actually imitating known Carolingian manuscripts. One example is the Gospel Book made for Gero shortly before he became archbishop of Cologne in 969 (Darmstadt, Landesbibl. MS. 1948): its Evangelist portraits and the miniature of Christ blessing are literally copied from the Lorsch Gospels which was illuminated in the court school of Charlemagne in the early ninth century.

Even more remarkable is the use made of the Codex Aureus of St. Emmeram. We have already described this famous ninth-century manuscript which in the Ottonian period belonged to the abbey of St. Emmeram in Regensburg. First of all, two monks at St. Emmeram's, Aripo and Adalpertus, tried to update the manuscript by adding a frontispiece illustrating the Ottonian abbot Ramwold (975–1001). Then the emperor Henry II had the volume copied for his own use. Henry was a fairly remote cousin of Otto III but, since Otto died without an heir, Henry was able to secure the throne in 1002; he was crowned emperor in 1014, and died in 1024. His imitation of the Codex Aureus of St. Emmeram was painted not long before 1021 and it still survives in Munich (CLM. 4456): many of its illuminations are almost exact reproductions, and the dedication miniature shows Henry on the throne of Charles the Bald (Pls. 66 and 67). The text, however, has become a Sacramentary rather than a Gospel Book. This is a book for use at Mass, and perhaps represents a shift of royal taste from biblical narrative to involvement in the most solemn and impressive Christian display. The reform of the liturgy under the Ottonians resulted in a fashion for Sacramentaries and Gospel Lectionaries, and this happened to be consistent with the emperors' concepts of religious solemnity and of themselves as high priests and mighty kings. Henry II was proud to be depicted in a Missal; Charlemagne would probably have been rather frightened.

Another difference between manuscript production of the Carolingians and of the Ottonians is that there seems to have been no court school of illumination under the Ottonian emperors. Charlemagne employed scribes and artists in his household. Otto III and Henry II sent out to the monasteries. They chiefly used Trier, and then very probably Reichenau, and later Regensburg and Echternach. Nothing seems to have been made for them in Italy. The use of monasteries does not necessarily mean that the artists were always monks, but

66 Munich, Bayerische Staatsbibliothek CLM. 14000, f. 5v; Gospels, probably St.-Denis, 870.
This is the great Codex Aureus of St. Emmeram, illuminated in the ninth century for Charles the Bald who is shown here enthroned and attended by soldiers, personifications of Francia and Gotica, and angels in heaven. In the eleventh century this manuscript was in Regensburg and was much admired by the Ottonians.

67 Munich, Bayerische Staatsbibliothek CLM.4456, f. 11v; Sacramentary, Regensburg, *c.* 1010.
This is an almost exact copy of the miniature shown in pl. 66, but painted 140 years later for the Ottonian emperor Henry II who has had his own portrait inserted in place of that of his Carolingian predecessor Charles the Bald. The text is a Sacramentary and it must have been made for Henry at Regensburg where the ninth-century Codex Aureus was preserved.

68 Munich, Bayerische Staatsbibliothek CLM.4452, f.17v; Gospel Pericopes, probably Reichenau, early eleventh century.
This is one of the books commissioned by Henry II for his foundation at Bamberg Cathedral. The miniature shows the Adoration of the Magi.

that they worked within a monastic community. A Gospel Lectionary now in Bremen actually illustrates this happening (Stadtbibl.MS.b.21, ff.124v–125r; Pls.64–5). It shows the cloisters at Echternach Abbey and busy working on the manuscripts are two men, one a layman and the other a monk, and on the facing page they are shown presenting their book to Henry III in about 1039–40. The nearest to an imperial court scriptorium was the special relationship which Henry II seems to have had with the monks at Seeon Abbey near Bamberg. One scribe there, Bebo, sent to the emperor a copy of St. Gregory's *Moralia on Job*, adding that he asked only for Henry's affection in return for his labour (Bamberg MS.Msc.Bibl.84;Pl.56).

Henry II had a particular reason for wanting manuscripts. Unlike other emperors, who probably built up libraries mainly because books were treasure and partly because they conferred a suitable image of culture, Henry II planned to set up a religious foundation at Bamberg and to furnish it with manuscripts which he had collected. His bequest included not only ancient books (such as the fifth-century Livy from the library of Otto III and Charles the Bald's copy of Boethius on Arithmetic (Pl.69), which had perhaps survived, like the Codex Aureus, in the monastery of St. Emmeram) but also books from his father's library like the great Gospel Book and commentaries on Isaiah and the Song of Songs (Bamberg MSS.A.I.43 and A.I.47) and manuscripts made especially for himself. The very grandest are the Bamberg Apocalypse (Bamberg MS.A.II.42) and a Gospel Lectionary (Munich, CLM.4452; Pl.68), both related in style to the Gospels of Otto III and probably from

Reichenau. Once again, they are magnificently illuminated, with very many pages of miniatures painted on highly burnished gold backgrounds which really flash as the leaves are turned. The Apocalypse is a great illustrated guide to the end of the world which some predicted in the year 1000. The Lectionary opens with a miniature of Henry II and his queen Cunegund receiving crowns from Christ himself. Perhaps after all there was political propaganda here too. Henry was canonized in 1146 and Cunegund in 1200. They are the patron saints of Bamberg.

Nothing so clearly demonstrates the Ottonians' imperial wealth and grandeur as the manuscripts they commissioned. These are their most lasting monument. The Carolingians were ultimately Frankish chieftains who needed books as fiscal assets and who melted down for bullion the gold planisphere owned by Charlemagne; the Ottonians, by contrast, were founders of an empire whose symbols of prestige are now already a thousand years old and still deeply impressive. Charlemagne's luxury manuscripts were made to influence his contemporaries; it may not be unfair to Henry II to suggest that his thoughts were for audiences of the future. In a theological sense, his illustrated Apocalypse will only come into its true use on the day the world ends. One cannot plan further ahead than that.

No survey of the very expensive imperial manuscripts is complete without a reference to the eleventh-century Ottonian books made for Henry III, emperor from 1039 to 1056. The first were produced at Echternach Abbey and probably included the celebrated Codex Aureus of Echternach (Nuremberg, Germanisches Nationalmuseum, MS. 2°.156.142) of about 1053–56, and certainly the Golden Gospels of Henry III (El Escorial, Codex Vitrinus 17) of about 1043–46 (Pl. 57). This manuscript includes a fine miniature of Henry and his wife Agnes kneeling before the Virgin Mary (f. 3r). Curiously, however, this is not an imperial image. Henry is not shown as master of the world, as Otto III would have required, but as a human being like the rest of us before the Mother of God.

The last truly Ottonian manuscript comes from a century later again and it is certainly consciously archaic in function. It is the Gospel Book illuminated about 1180 by the monk Herimann at Helmarshausen Abbey for Henry the Lion (*c.* 1129–95), duke of Saxony and Bavaria and founder of Munich (Pl. 70). It is the final expression of a deliberately arrogant political claim. Henry the Lion, like his Ottonian ancestors, spent most of his life in desperate warfare to maintain his dominions, not least in his struggle with his cousin, the Emperor Frederick Barbarossa. He had married the daughter of the king of England, he had travelled to Byzantium and further, and had taken armies into Scandinavia, Russia, and Lombardy. Yet, despite all this, he was not yet emperor. The Gospel Book seems to be an incredibly

69 Bamberg, Staatsbibliothek MS. Msc. Class. 5, detail of f. 90r; Boethius, Arithmetica, Tours, *c.* 835.
This is a Carolingian mathematical manuscript made in France for Charles the Bald but acquired nearly 200 years later by Henry II for his library at Bamberg.

QVI VULT VENIRE POST ME ABNEG
SEMETIPSV ET TOLLAT CRVCE SVA
IMPERATRIX RICHENZE
IMPERATOR LOTHARIVS
DVCISSA GERTRVDIS
DVX HEINRICVS
DVX HEINRICVS
DVCISSA MATHILDA
REGIS ANGLICI FILIA HEINRICI
REGINA MATHILDA

70 (LEFT) London, Sotheby's, 6 December 1983, lot 50, f. 171v; Gospels, Helmarshausen, *c.* 1180.
The Gospels of Henry the Lion ends with this scene of the coronation of Henry and his wife Matilda, daughter of Henry II of England, who are attended by their imperial and royal ancestors and by the saints in heaven including the newly canonized Thomas Becket.

71 (RIGHT) London, Sotheby's, 6 December 1983, lot 50, f. 4v; Gospels, Helmarshausen, *c.* 1180.
The gold dedication inscription in the Gospels of Henry the Lion reflects Carolingian models such as that in the Dagulf Psalter of the eighth century (pl. 39).

expensive fanfare for the claims of Henry the Lion. It opens, like an early Carolingian manuscript, with a dedication leaf in burnished gold capitals (Pl. 71) beginning 'Aurea testatur' ('it is witnessed in gold' – as if gold alone adds credibility) referring to Henry as descendant of Charlemagne. It is illustrated with seventeen canon pages and twenty-four elaborate full-page miniatures, including one (f. 171v) showing Henry the Lion and his wife Matilda being crowned by God in the presence of their imperial and royal ancestors and the court of Heaven. This is pure Ottonian conceit. It is a book flashing with gold (the dedication refers to 'fulgens auro liber iste') and it was intended to symbolize extreme wealth and power.

Perhaps an author may be forgiven one brief reminiscence. The Gospels of Henry the Lion disappeared from sight in the 1930s (when it was still privately owned by descendants of the last king of Hanover) and I had the opportunity of being involved in its rediscovery. I saw it first in a wooden box on the back seat of a car on 23 August 1983 and flew back to London that night with the Gospel Book in my luggage. Later my wife carried it to America. The manuscript was sold by auction at Sotheby's in London on 6 December 1983 for £8,140,000, over ten times more than any illuminated manuscript had realized before and then the most expensive work of art ever sold at auction. The book was bought by a banking consortium on behalf of the German government. The huge price is irrelevant to the history of manuscript production except as a vigorous reminder that even today imperial treasure manuscripts are still very, very expensive. That is the reason why they were made.

•3•

Books for Monks

There is something altogether fascinating and rather impertinent about rummaging through other people's private belongings. We all know how revealing it can be to look along the bookshelves in an acquaintance's house and to realize what a lot we can tell about the owner's tastes and interests, his background, and his weaknesses and buying impulses. Social manners may prevent us taking the books out and leafing through private letters and notes enclosed between the pages. No such inhibitions need worry the historian of medieval manuscripts. It is hardly possible to recommend too strongly the tremendous fascination of medieval inventories. Imagine how much we could learn about medieval monks if we could spend an hour or so in some cloister in the twelfth century browsing through all the monks' manuscripts, opening up one after another, discovering what titles they owned, where they got them from, and which books looked well used, and if we could ransack their cupboards and wardrobes, pulling out works of art for our own curiosity. We would discover in a few minutes far more than an archaeologist would find in years with a trowel and brush on the earthy site where the monastery had once been. Something of this treasure-hunt experience can be captured by reading medieval library catalogues. A considerable number of them survive, from enigmatic lists of cryptic titles (like the one mentioned in the previous chapter, written at the court of Charlemagne in the late eighth century) to detailed and indexed shelf catalogues like that of St. Augustine's Abbey, Canterbury, compiled in the mid-1490s. If we combine our reading of these catalogues with trying to identify surviving manuscripts from known libraries, we shall learn a great deal about the cultural life of the Middle Ages. It is also fascinating simply to rummage about in someone else's library of eight hundred years ago.

English monasteries reached their peak in the twelfth century. Probably all of them had books of some sort. By no means all monasteries compiled inventories of their libraries, and no doubt some catalogues have not survived. There are reasonably complete twelfth-century library catalogues for Peterborough Abbey, Durham Cathedral, Lincoln Cathedral, Whitby Abbey, Reading Abbey, Burton-on-Trent Abbey, and Rochester Cathedral. There are at least partial twelfth-century catalogues for Abingdon, Christ Church in Canterbury, Waltham, Worcester, and several other houses. Let us examine one catalogue. It is a typical example from the late twelfth century. The one chosen was compiled at Reading Abbey in Berkshire. The site of the monastery itself is now sandwiched between Reading gaol and a noisy car park, and one can just glimpse pieces of its massive battered ruins of flint rubble from the train on the line through Reading between London and Oxford. There is a monument on one wall of the ruined chapter house there to commemorate the fact that the unique thirteenth-century manuscript of 'Sumer is icumen in', the best-known early English song, probably came from Reading Abbey. Otherwise the monastery ruins do not conjure up images of contemplative life and scholarship.

The catalogue of the library of Reading Abbey survived in a curious way. It is one of the texts in the Reading cartulary, or book of charters, which was discovered about 1790 by a bricklayer who was taking down part of a wall in Shinefield House, near Reading. It was published in 1888 when the volume still belonged to the family of Lord Fingall, owner of Shinefield. The book is now in the British Library (Egerton MS. 3031; Pl. 73).

The catalogue opens with four Bibles, in two or three volumes each. It goes without saying that the Latin Bible was the fundamental text of every medieval monastery. An important point (and one which will recur in the next chapter) is that old monastic Bibles were usually extremely large. We have discussed earlier huge books like the Codex Amiatinus of around 700 and the Bible of San Paolo fuori le mura of around 870. Twelfth-century Bibles were gigantic too. The labour in making them was immense. The most famous surviving examples are the Bury Bible (only one volume still exists now (Pl. 91)) and the Dover (Pl. 80), Lambeth (Pl. 74), Winchester (Pls. 100–1), and 'Auct' Bibles, all of which are in two volumes and at least 20 by 14 inches (505 by 350mm.). The Durham copy was in four volumes. These are monumental Bibles intended for use on a

72 Cambridge, Trinity College MS. R. 17. 1, f. 283v; tripartite Psalter with Gloss, Canterbury, *c.* 1150.
This portrait of the monk Eadwine shows a scribe at work on a manuscript with his penknife and curved pen. Around the edge is a Latin inscription in which Eadwine is made to say that he is the prince of all scribes and that his fame will never die.

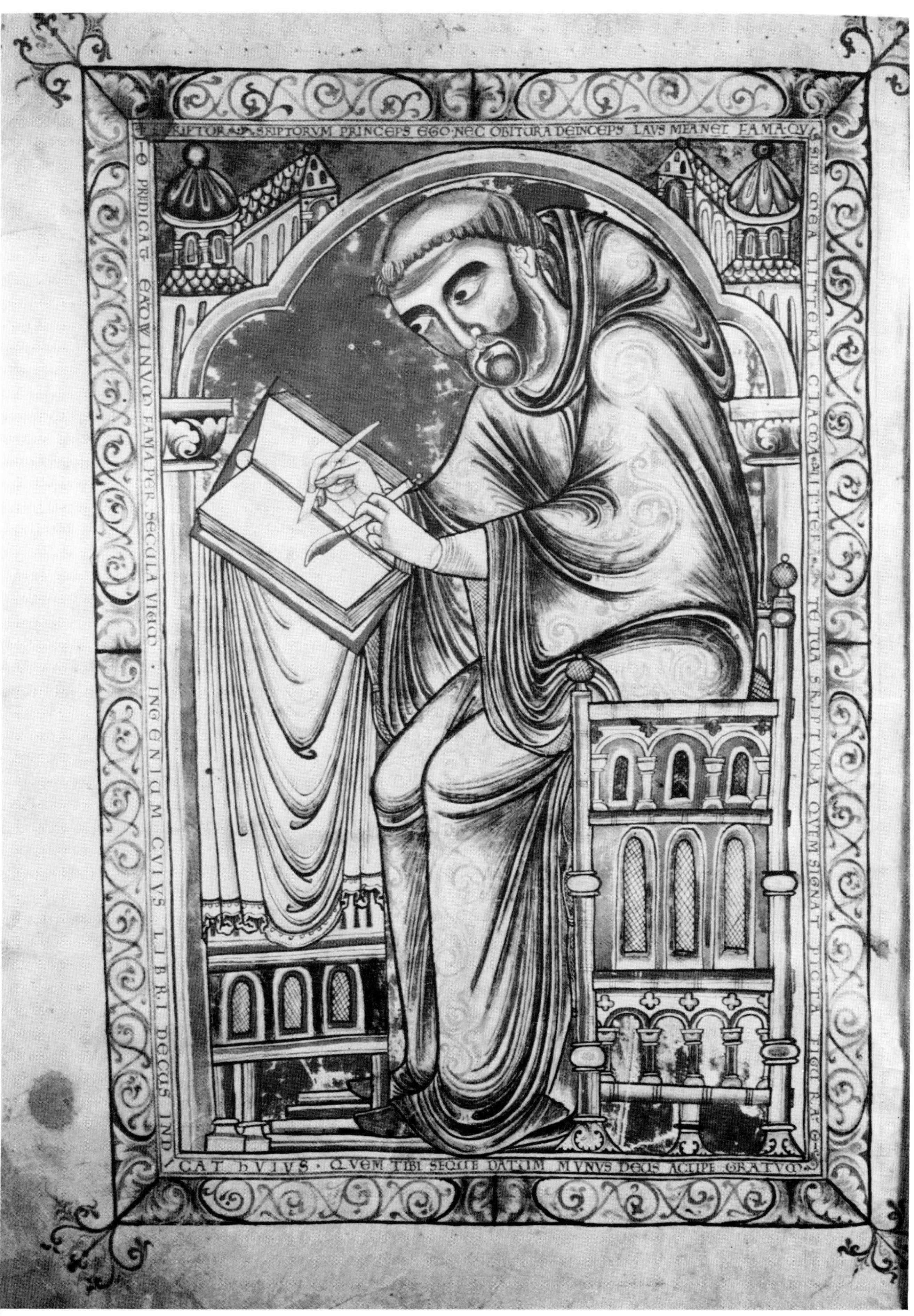
SCRIPTORUM PRINCEPS EGO NEC OBITURA DEINCEPS LAUS MEA NEC FAMA
PREDICAT EADWINUM FAMA PER SECULA VIVUM · INGENIUM CUIUS LIBRI DECUS INDI
CAT HUIUS · QUEM TIBI SEQUE DATUM MUNUS DEUS ACCIPE GRATUM

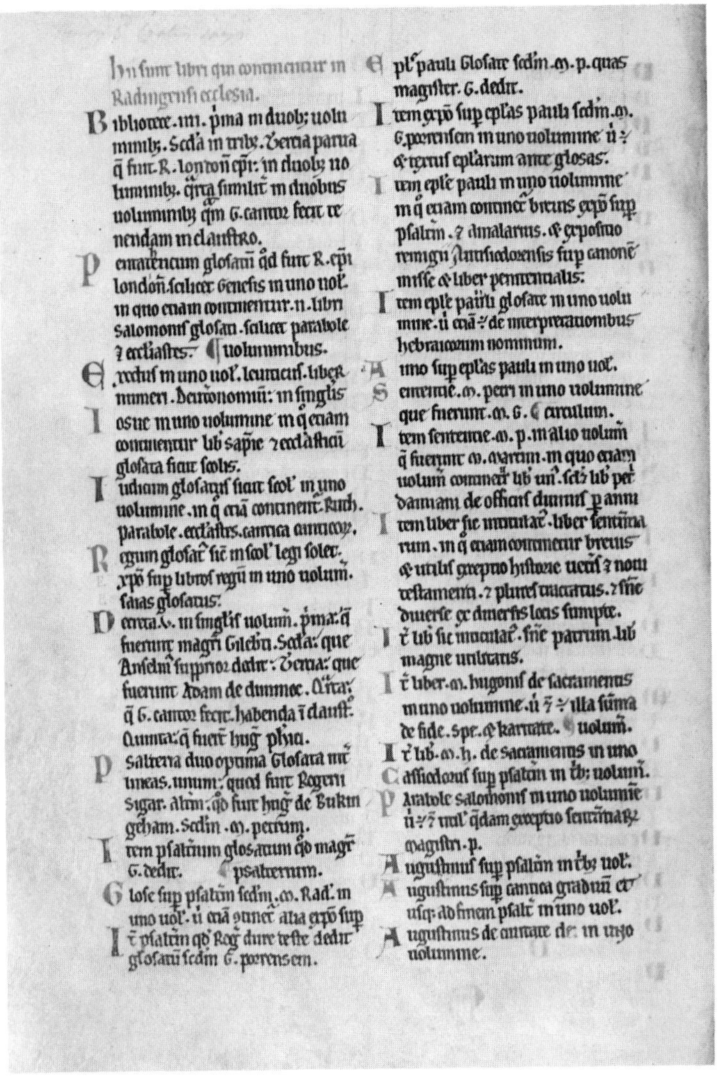

lectern rather than for private study. They are usually in handsome black script, and are sometimes marked up with accents so that they can easily be read aloud. The Reading Abbey catalogue is quite explicit. Three of their copies were in two volumes each and one was in three volumes. This three-volume Bible is mentioned again at Reading two hundred years later when it was described as being kept in the monks' dormitory as a spare to be used for reading out at mealtimes in the refectory. Perhaps it was getting too battered by then to serve as the daily copy. The twelfth-century catalogue records that the smallest of the two-volumed Bibles had belonged to R., bishop of London. There are several candidates for this donor, the most likely being Richard de Belmais (1152–2) or Richard FitzNeal (1189–98). Episcopal donations are typical of the period too. There was a custom for bishops to give Bible manuscripts. Hugh de Puiset gave a lectern Bible to Durham where he was bishop from 1153 to 1195. It is very likely that the Reading copy was elegantly decorated at a bishop's expense. It was probably not for everyday use. A final Bible at Reading Abbey brings us down to the level of the common monk. 'A fourth, likewise in two volumes,' says the catalogue, 'which G. the cantor ordered to be kept in the cloister.' The cloister was where the monks walked and meditated. The cantor (or chanter – he was primarily in charge of education) had the fourth copy put out for the monks.

The Reading Abbey library catalogue then continues with various glossed books of a Bible. This, in fact, is the way that the Bible was usually studied in the twelfth century: in separate books, each with a marginal gloss or commentary written down either side of the page in a smaller script. It was a standard text, usually called the Gloss (with a capital 'G'). Here we find titles of Leviticus, Numbers, Deuteronomy, Joshua, Judges, Kings, Matthew, Mark, Luke, John, and so on, mostly bound in separate volumes. Several of the actual Reading copies described here still exist. The Leviticus is Bodleian MS. Auct.D.3.12, the Books of Kings are Bodleian MS. Auct.D.3.15, the St. Luke is Queen's College, Oxford, MS. 323, and the copy of Judges with other texts may be B.L. Add.MS.54230, which was purchased in 1916 for £12. It is still in its original binding. If one checks against the books of the whole Bible one finds that the Reading monks had all but about seven volumes to complete a full set of the Gloss on all the Bible. Medieval cataloguers used to count up glossed books too to see how far short they were of a complete run. When St. Augustine's Abbey in Canterbury received a set of twenty-one glossed books from an uncle of Abbot Roger (1176–1216), they described the benefaction as a complete Bible 'except Chronicles, Maccabees, and the Apocalypse'. These glossed books greatly appealed to twelfth-century monks. The Peterborough Abbey library catalogue records copies acquired in the time of Abbot Benedict (1177–94), and the St. Albans chronicle says that when a set was obtained in the time of Abbot Simon (1167–83) the monks said they had never seen more noble books. We shall be meeting glossed books again in the next chapter as they were very popular among students in the early universities. The Reading catalogue actually describes several of them as 'glossed, as in the Schools'. The latest additions to the Gloss

were edited by Gilbert de la Porrée (d.1154) and by Peter Lombard (d.1160). Reading Abbey had copies of both. This was a very up-to-date library. One, a Psalter with the Gloss of Gilbert de la Porrée, is described as having been given by Roger, who is perhaps the abbot from 1158 to 1164. The volume itself has been identified as Bodleian MS. Auct. D. 4. 6, a Psalter with Gilbert's gloss, medieval annotations referring to Reading, and a remarkable initial signed with the artist's name, 'Johannes me fecit Rogerio' ('John made me for Roger') (Pl.78).

A very large part of the twelfth-century Reading monastic library evidently comprised works of the Church Fathers. The catalogue lists eighteen volumes of texts by St. Augustine, ten by St. Ambrose, seven by St. Gregory the Great (Pl.79), eight by Bede (his biblical commentaries, not his history which we quoted in chapter 1), and good runs of St. Jerome and Origen. These authors formed the central core of any twelfth-century monastic library. It is worth stressing this. These were very old, basic, fundamental texts which any self-respecting romanesque library had an obligation to own: Augustine on the Psalms (Pl.86) in three volumes, Gregory's *Moralia* on Job in two volumes, Ambrose's *De Officiis* bound up with his *Enchiridion*. They were all at Reading and in most other libraries at the time. Yet this passion for owning the old theological classics was comparatively new in England. A monastery before the Conquest

73 (OPPOSITE, TOP) London, British Library, Egerton MS. 3031, f. 8v; the opening page of the library catalogue of Reading Abbey, late twelfth century.

74 (OPPOSITE, BELOW) London, Lambeth Palace MS. 3, detail of f. 258v; Bible, probably Canterbury or possibly St. Albans, mid-twelfth century.
The Lambeth Bible is one of several surviving twelfth-century English monumental monastic Bibles. The initial here shows Ezechiel receiving a prophecy from God and then, as a scribe with inkpot and pen, planning to write his book.

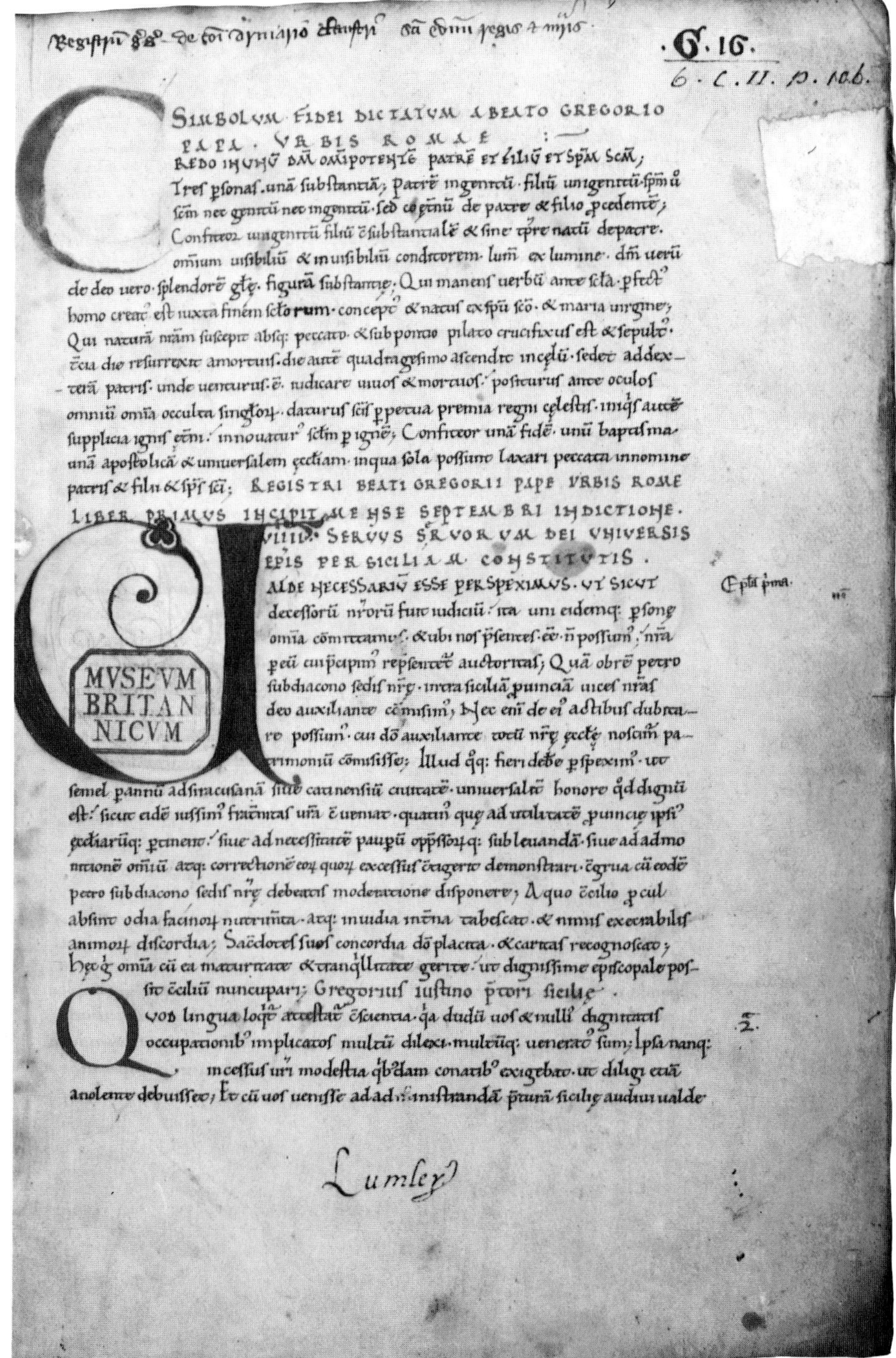

75 London, British Library, Royal MS. 6. C. II, f. 1r; Epistles of St. Gregory, Bury St. Edmunds, first half of the twelfth century.
This manuscript belonged to the monks of the Benedictine Abbey of Bury St. Edmunds in Suffolk. It has the abbey's pressmark 'G.16' in the top right-hand corner (the 'G' stands for Gregory) and the ownership inscription recording that it was kept in the common chest in the cloister. At the foot is the signature of John, Lord Lumley (d.1609), whose library was purchased by James I and given with the Royal Library in 1757 to the British Museum. The Museum's stamp is across the elegant decorated initial.

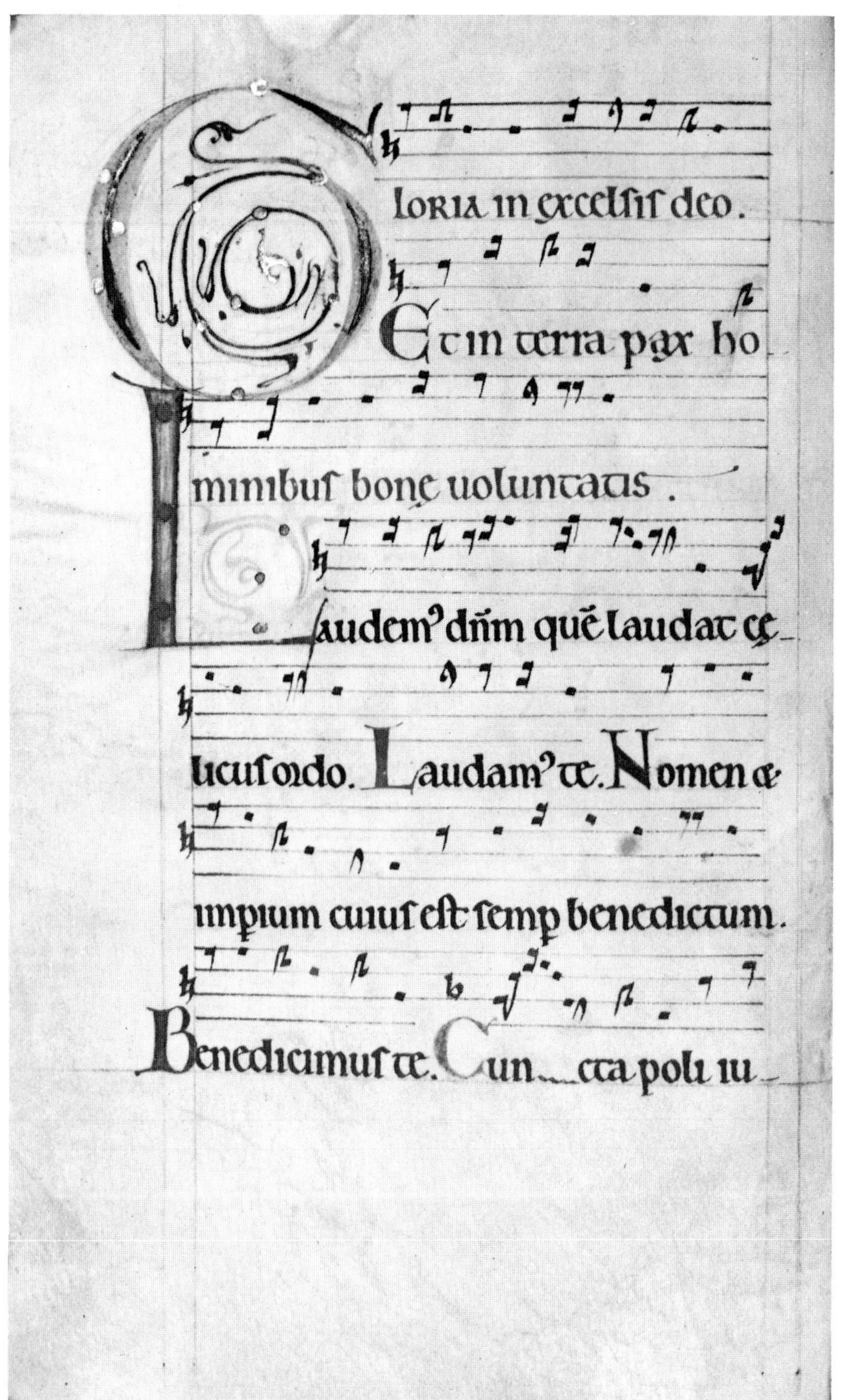

76 London, British Library, Royal MS.2.B.IV, f.24v; Gradual, St. Albans Abbey, mid-twelfth century.
The text shows part of the Christmas Mass.

of 1066 might own a few volumes by chance, but a Norman abbey systematically set about building up its holdings. They often wrote them together, and they stored them as great sets. By curious chance, seven of the twelfth-century manuscripts of St. Augustine's works recorded in the Reading Abbey catalogue passed after the Reformation to one Reynoldes and remained together in the collections of James Bowen (1748) and Sir Thomas Phillipps (1792–1872) and were still a group when purchased in 1937 by the Newberry Library in Chicago (MS.Ry.24). Three of them have the medieval ownership inscription of Reading Abbey and a curse against anyone who takes them away: 'liber sancte Marie Radyngensis, quem qui alienaverit Anathema.'

The Church Fathers make up many bulky volumes, not easy to read. The ones in Chicago amount to 762 leaves of closely written Latin. Were they used much by the monks? If not, the cynic will ask, why own them? There is something in the concept of a monastery as a repository for religious knowledge, especially long-respected religious knowledge in an age troubled (almost for the first time in England) by a fear of heresy. Furthermore, in the twelfth century, and probably never since, it was still possible to think of human knowledge as finite. The biblical scholar Gilbert (who taught in Auxerre and became bishop of London from 1128 to 1134) was known as 'The Universal', because it was thought he knew everything. There was no sarcasm in the nickname. Reading Abbey owned a copy of St. Jerome's *De Viris Illustribus*, which amounts to an encyclopaedia of famous authors and their works. It would be a most useful bibliographical handbook for a twelfth-century librarian outfitting his collection (Pl. 77). The smattering of classical texts at Reading perhaps reflects this vague ideal of comprehensiveness: Seneca, Virgil, Horace, and Juvenal. Whether all these books were used often may be revealed by the chance use of an adjective here and there in the catalogue: four times in the list of nearly three hundred volumes the cataloguer throws in the comment 'utilis' or 'magne utilitatis', a 'useful' work. He applies the term to a collection of excerpts from biblical history, a volume of quotations from the Fathers, an excerpt from Peter Lombard's *Sentences*, and a book of saints' lives. These are all secondary works. There is something rather touching about the fact that it was the summaries and quotations which the monks at Reading mention in their catalogue as useful while they accept without comment the multi-volumed patristics with which the library was handsomely stocked.

The Reading Abbey catalogue is comparatively unusual among library lists in that it includes liturgical manuscripts. These were kept in the abbey vestries and chapels rather than with other library books. Looking through the Reading catalogue, however, one gains the impression that the compiler had systematically searched for books in all corners of the abbey. Obviously he began in the main library. We do not know where this was. It would not have been a special room in the twelfth century. Perhaps the books were stored in chests in the cloister or in the slype (passage-way) which at Reading ran off the south-east corner of the cloister beside the church. With a little imagination, and a plan of the ruins of Reading Abbey, one can see the cataloguer moving from room to room. He lists the principal books first. Then he describes a two-volume Breviary in a chapel off the cloister (he has not moved far), then walking clockwise round the cloister he went up the passage (its ruins can still be seen) to the guest house, infirmary, and the abbot's lodging (four more Breviaries recorded), back into the cloister and through the refectory on the south side (three books for reading at meals, including a two-volume Lectionary) and on again right round to the door into the abbey church. He found three great Missals (two in precious bindings and one for the early morning service) and seventeen smaller Missals for everyday use by the monks in church and in the chapels. He counted fifteen Graduals – that is, music for the Mass (Pl. 76) – including two in the abbot's private chapel. There were six full Processionals and seven smaller copies for specific occasions (they would be easier to carry as the line of monks walked chanting round the cloister) and there were seven Antiphoners, big volumes of church music for the daily round of services. There were three Psalters for the novices (they probably learned to read from them) and four more copies chained in the church and the infirmary, a very early reference to the practice of chaining up manuscripts. With Lectionaries, Tropers, Collectars, and other specialized liturgical texts listed, we gain an impression of a great many books in daily use at Reading Abbey. The information is all the more valuable because minor liturgical books have seldom survived from the twelfth century: constant use, obsolescence, and religious reformation have caused the loss of all but a few precious scraps of English romanesque liturgy. In considering the history of medieval book production, it is too easy to overlook whole categories of manuscripts, just because they no longer exist. No complete liturgical books survive from Reading Abbey. A small four-leaf fragment, now at Douai Abbey in Berkshire (MS. 11), may be from Reading. It dates from the first half of the twelfth century and includes responses for the Sundays after Trinity. It was recovered from re-use inside a sixteenth-century bookbinding and its possible origin is suggested both by the script and by its text which is distinctively Cluniac, the reformed Benedictine order to which Reading belonged.

Both the keeping of books and the making of them in the twelfth century were essentially monastic. Monks need books. They needed service-books in large quantities, if we can judge from the Reading Abbey lists. But more than that, monasteries were the focal points of intellectual and artistic life in the twelfth century. Very few manuscripts were produced entirely independently of a monastic or religious context. It is difficult for us, so long afterwards, to comprehend the tremendous pull of the monastic life in the twelfth century. The flourishing of the monasteries is one of the remarkable features of romanesque Europe. At the time of the Norman Conquest there were about thirty-five monasteries in England. They included the uniquely English institution of cathedral priories (places like Winchester, Durham, and Christ Church in Canterbury), which were cathedrals staffed with Benedictine monks instead of priests and canons, and which figure prominently in the history of book illumination in the twelfth century. Soon they were all swept into a vast programme of monastic reform and recommitment and the establishment of new religious orders and the building of new monasteries and abbeys on an extraordinary scale. Many old monasteries were rebuilt, like Winchester, Durham and Canterbury, or even transferred to new sites, like Tewkesbury. The Cluniacs arrived in England about 1077; their houses included Reading Abbey itself, founded by Henry II in 1121. The Augustinians came to Britain in 1105, the Cistercians in 1128, the Gilbertines (an entirely English order) in 1131, and the Carthusians in 1180. They took their recruits from the local population and many people joined. However we explain it away now, there was quite clearly a whole movement of spiritual dedication. By 1200 there were over five hundred monasteries and priories in England, almost all constructed within the previous century. The old Anglo-Saxon way of life gave way to internationalism. 'With their arrival', William of Malmesbury recollected in the twelfth century, 'the Normans breathed new

77 London, British Library, Royal MS. 5. B. VIII, ff. 15v–16r; St. Jerome, De Viris Illustribus, Westminster Abbey, mid-twelfth century.
Jerome's Lives of Famous Men listed brief biographies and the principal writings of the early Christian fathers. Its text provided monastic librarians with a bibliography of early patristic books which they might hope to acquire.

78 (RIGHT) Oxford, Bodleian Library MS. Auct. D. 4. 6, f. 91r; Psalter with Gloss, Reading Abbey, *c.* 1160.
This is possibly the Psalter glossed by Gilbert de la Porrée which is recorded in the Reading Abbey library catalogue as given by 'Rogerus dure teste' (perhaps the same man as Roger, abbot of Reading 1158–64). This initial is signed by the artist 'Iohannes me fecit Rogerio' ('John made me for Roger').

Supbo oclo & isaciabili corde: cu hoc n
edebā. Oculi mei ad fideles t̄re ut se
deāt mecū: ambulās i uia imaculata
hic m ministrabat. Non habitabit in
medio dom mee q facit supbiā: q loqt
iniqua n direx in cspectu oclor meor. In
matutino interficiebā oś peccatores terre:
ut dispderē de ciuitate dni oś opantes
iniqtatē.

IOHES ME FECIT ROGERIO

DNE exaudi oracio
nē meā: & clamor
meus ad te ueniat.
Non auertas faciē
tuā a me: i qua
cūq; die tribulor
iclina ad me aurē tuā. In quacūque

life into religious standards, which everywhere in England had been declining, so that now you may see in every village, town and city, churches and monasteries rising in a new style of architecture.'

A monastery needed books as part of its essential furniture. It is not necessary to ask whether the monks used all the books often (though some monks sometimes certainly did) any more than we need explain liturgy, prayer, or architecture in exclusively utilitarian terms. A monastery was not properly equipped without a library. A famous (though later) quotation from a Swiss Carthusian observes that 'a monastery without books is like a state without resources, a camp without troops, a kitchen without crockery, a table without food, a garden without grass, a field without flowers, a tree without leaves.' Where did monasteries get books from? Reading Abbey, founded in 1121, had nearly three hundred books by the time the catalogue was drawn up in the late twelfth century. With another five hundred or so monasteries in England, all needing books at that time, the efforts put into book production were considerable. They were so successful that English twelfth-century books are the oldest which still survive in comparatively large numbers.

The simple answer to the question of where the books came from, is to say that the monks made them. They sat in the cloisters and wrote them out. Basically, this is true, especially in the twelfth century. But a scribe could not simply write a book. Before anything else, he needed an exemplar, that is, another copy of the same text, carefully corrected and made intelligible, which then acted as the model for the new manuscript. Any manuscript text, unless it is autograph or the scribe knows it by heart, needs a second copy at the time of writing. This is so fundamental that it tends to be overlooked. The mechanics of how this worked in practice, however, are difficult to discover. Let us imagine that the monks of a newly founded northern English Cistercian house had heard that the legal *Decretum* of Gratian was now all the fashion in Italy, that Peter Lombard's *Sentences* were immensely popular in the French schools, or even that William of Malmesbury, away down in the south of England, had written a history which would be of great value for the novice monks. It is tantalizing to know so little about how and where scribes obtained a text, especially if they were monks whose rule did not encourage them to travel freely.

No doubt one monastery often lent books to another. One can easily imagine this happening among the Cistercian houses, for instance, as the order was efficiently centralized. The geographical proximity and the close relationship between Rochester Cathedral and Christ Church, Canterbury, furthermore, probably explains some remarkable parallels between collections of books there. Scribes at Bury St. Edmunds apparently also made use of texts from Christ Church, Canterbury. A ninth-century Cassiodorus from Hereford was the exemplar for a late eleventh-century copy made at Salisbury. The late Dr. N.R. Ker followed up a ninth-century volume of St. Augustine (which was at Burton-on-Trent by the twelfth century) which was the ultimate ancestor of copies made at Salisbury, Hereford, Rochester, and elsewhere.

Sometimes an abbey wanting a book must have found it easier to send a scribe to copy a new text on location than to send a messenger to borrow the precious exemplar and carry it back to the first house for transcription and then to send the messenger all the way back again to return it. There survives part of an interchange of letters, datable to between 1167 and 1173, from the prior and abbot of St. Albans who wrote to Richard, prior of the abbey of St-Victor in Paris, to try to obtain a list of Richard's own writings and to ask whether a copyist might be sent to St-Victor to copy out on location any texts of Hugh of St-Victor still missing from the St. Albans library. Once St. Albans had them, then perhaps other English houses could send scribes there, and so the process could be repeated. There were four of Hugh of St-Victor's works in the Reading library catalogue (one still survives – Bodleian MS. Digby 148) and the scribe perhaps borrowed or used the exemplars from somewhere such as St. Albans.

Having obtained an exemplar, the next stage in making a manuscript was to prepare the blank leaves of vellum. Animal skins for making vellum were no doubt often a by-product left over by the abbey butcher. Since a massive book like the Winchester Bible would probably have needed skins from some two hundred and fifty sheep, it is difficult to imagine so many animals being killed for the sole purpose of supplying vellum. A brief insight into this supply occurs in the contemporary life of St. Hugh of Lincoln. From 1180 to 1186 Hugh was prior of the Carthusian house of Witham in Somerset. He was personally acquainted with King Henry II, and one day in conversation with Henry he mentioned how few books they had at Witham and explained that the problem was the lack of vellum. According to the chronicle, the king then generously gave him ten marks of silver to buy some. Two important points emerge here. One is that vellum was available commercially but it was expensive: ten marks was a large sum (though we do not, of course, know how much vellum it bought). The second is that the monks at Witham had none. It is significant, therefore, that they were Carthusians. According to the austere Carthusian customs of 1130, they never ate meat. Therefore they had no butcher and (we now learn) no vellum. The Cistercians, by contrast, were the largest-scale sheep farmers in Britain. In 1193 they paid their contribution to the ransom of Richard the Lion Heart in wool, not in money. The Cistercians can seldom have been short of vellum.

There is a twelfth-century monastic account of how to make vellum in the *De Diversis Artibus* of Theophilus, probably written at Helmarshausen Abbey in north Germany. Skins are soaked in running water for several days. They are then immersed in a solution of lime and water for up to a fortnight. Then all the hair is scraped off and the skins are put back into the lime solution for as long again. Next they are rinsed, stretched over a frame and dried in the sun, and cleaned over and over again with pumice and water. Plenty of fresh running water was crucial for vellum making. One notices that the manuscripts written at Salisbury in the late eleventh century are on some of the worst possible vellum, thick, yellow and rough, and it is curious that the Norman site of Salisbury, the bleak hill now called Old Sarum, was eventually

79 Eton College MS. 226, f. 94; St. Gregory, Moralia on Job, Reading Abbey, mid-twelfth century.
This manuscript was listed at Reading Abbey in the fourteenth century among the books which the monks used to read to themselves in the chapel in the evenings or had read to them in the refectory during meals.

80 (LEFT) Cambridge, Corpus Christi College MS. 2, detail of f. 281v; Bible, Bury St. Edmunds Abbey, *c.* 1135.
The Bury Bible is described in the abbey's chronicle as having been commissioned by Hervey the Sacrist, brother of prior Talbot, and illuminated by Master Hugo, an artist and metalworker employed at Bury St. Edmunds in the 1130s.

81 (ABOVE) Oxford, Bodleian Library MS. Bodley 717, detail of f. 64r; St. Jerome on Isaiah, Normandy (perhaps Jumièges Abbey), late eleventh century.
This manuscript belonged to Exeter Cathedral in the Middle Ages. It is signed at the end by the illuminator who calls himself 'Hugo pictor' ('Hugh the painter'), who probably also worked on other manuscripts in Normandy.

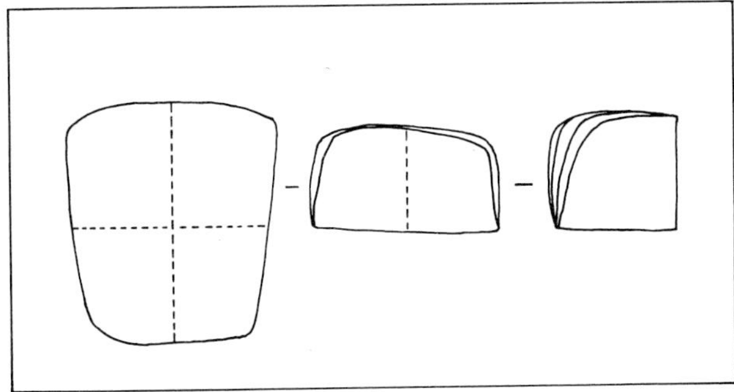

abandoned for the principal reason that it had no access to running water. Perhaps that is why Salisbury vellum was so bad. Again, things must have been easier for the Cistercians whose houses were almost always built by rivers.

There is one curious reference to vellum in the abbey chronicle of Bury St. Edmunds. In describing the huge Bible (Pl. 80) made for the monastery about 1135 and painted by the artist Master Hugo, the chronicle says that as the illuminator could not find suitable material locally, he obtained vellum in Scotland and Ireland ('in Scotiae partibus'). This is rather puzzling. In fact, one of the two volumes of this Bible still survives (Corpus Christi College, Cambridge, MS. 2) and, sure enough, all its miniatures and some of the illuminated initials are painted on separate pieces of vellum pasted into the Bible. It is difficult to think why Master Hugo insisted on importing pieces of vellum for his illuminations, unless for some reason he found the surface of the locally made leaves unsatisfactory.

The way that a sheet of newly made vellum was folded depended on the dimensions of the book that the scribe was planning to make. A really big manuscript, such as a lectern Bible, would be made up of bifolia (pairs of leaves) almost as large as a single skin of vellum, with one fold across the middle. Four of the bifolia would then be placed one inside the other to form a gathering of 8 leaves (or sixteen pages). For a big folio manuscript of a patristic text such as Augustine or Cassiodorus or Josephus, the skin might be folded in half and then in half again, and when the edges were trimmed off there would be a package of four leaves (or eight pages) up to about 14 inches in height. If the sheet was folded yet again before it was cut, it would make eight leaves (sixteen pages), something like 10 by 7 inches (255 by 180mm.). This is a fairly standard size for many twelfth-century texts. If the sheet could be folded in half yet another time, it would end up small and narrow, like many little grammatical and other short treatises of the time. It is worth mentioning too that medieval manuscripts, like modern printed books, are usually taller than they are wide. This is inevitable if one begins by folding an animal skin which is naturally oblong. When paper was first introduced for making pages of books, the makers tended to follow the same custom, though it was no longer essential. Books are still taller than wide: this is because, more than six hundred years ago, their ancestors were made by folding natural vellum.

If you rub your fingers on a sheet of vellum, you can feel the difference between the smooth side (where the hair has been rubbed off) and the rough side which was the flesh side of the skin. There is a slight difference in colour too. If the scribes made their gatherings by folding the vellum in half several times, as explained above, it will always work out exactly that the hair-side faces the hair-side and the flesh-side faces the flesh-side throughout a gathering. This makes for neatness. The first page of a gathering would be the hair-side, and the neatness then applied right throughout the manuscript. Medieval scribes always arranged their leaves like this if it was at all possible. Most twelfth-century manuscripts are made up of gatherings of eight leaves. These gatherings were eventually assembled in order and stitched to form a book.

It always used to be supposed that scribes worked with just a bifolium or pair of leaves open on the writing desk, and perhaps they often did. One would imagine that this would have been simplest. It is odd, however, that almost all medieval pictures of scribes (and there are many of them in Evangelist portraits) show them writing into what seems to be a whole book lying open (Pls. 1 and 72). This may be just an artistic convention, but it is a disconcertingly consistent one. There is some tentative evidence that it was not unknown for twelfth-century scribes to write into the pages of a loosely stitched gathering rather than just on a detached pair of leaves. It has even been argued by some students of manuscripts that small books could have been written on completely uncut vellum with all sixteen pages of one quire still on one huge sheet, some side-by-side and others upside down, so that when the big piece of vellum was finally folded over and over and trimmed, it would form a continuous text.

Before a scribe began to write, he had to measure out the page carefully and rule a grid of faint lines to keep the text straight and within a regular pattern. He would have to decide whether the text would be in one column or two: at the beginning of the twelfth century many books were still in a single column format, but by about 1170 manuscripts were generally larger and often in two columns. By 1200 some small books were in double column. Actually ruling each

82 Durham Cathedral MS. A. I. 10, f. 227; Berengaudus on the Apocalypse, Durham, early twelfth century.
The marginal prickings and the tiny guidewords for the rubricator are just visible down the extreme right-hand edge of the page.

dicunt non posse quenquā bene uera loqui.
qui non possit bene mentiri. Obstulte. quā uana
ē assertio tua. Ecce xp̄c multa bene & ueracit̄
locut̄ ē. qui nunquā potuit mentiri. cui uestigia
te sequi magis oportuisset in quantū uiretus
suppeteret. Simılit̄ ap̄li & ceti predicatores
multa docuer̄t & scripser̄t. sine p̄mistione
mendacii. Et scriptura dic̄. quia om̄e mendaciū
a malo ē. Si mendaciū malū ē. quomō malū bene
potest p̄ferri? Omfelix. quā uana t̄ ē. ira dei
omnipot̄s. quē assidue sine causa offendere
n̄ trepidas. Nam cet̄a uicia quamuis dn̄o
contraria sint. uident̄ tam̄ aliq̄d corpori con
ferre. Auaricia quippe quamuis sit p̄ oīa deo
odibilis. uidet̄ tam̄ aliq̄d conferre corpori.
quia diuitias congregat, ex quib; desideria ei;
expleat. Similit̄ & libido uidet̄ aliq̄d corpori
conferre. quia in p̄fectione ei; uoluntas carnis
extinguit̄. Et ebrietas quamuis dn̄m offendat.
gulę tam̄ desideria p̄ficit. Similit̄ & cet̄a uicia.
ad carnis desideria assumunt̄. Sunt etiam
quędā mendacia quę corpori aliq̄d uident̄ adice
re. sic̄ s̄t auaritię de quib; sup̄ dixim;. Tu aūt
nichil corpori adquiris. & dn̄m sine intermissio
ne offendere n̄ metuis. Ecce mendaciū tuū leue
esset. si tarde accidisset. Verū ex iugi continua
tione grauissimū atq; inportabile efficit̄. Nam
sic̄ luciū leue ē. quā plubū. s; ex multiplicatio
ne sua graui; & p̄iculosi sit. ita ut meo sepe pe
cora demergant̄. sic & quędā leuia peccata ex
congerie sua grauiora quibsdā quę grauia ex
istimant̄ efficiunt̄. Et scito q̄a sic ipse dix̄ ds̄
ueritas ē. nichil plus contrariū potest ēē. ueri
tati quā mendaciū. Hoꝝ g̊ pars erit in stagnum
ignis ardentis sulphure. qd̄ ē. mors s̄cdā. Q̊d sit
mors s̄cdā. in hoc libro manifeste demonstrat.
A sup̄dictis g̊ uiciis ne in morte s̄cdā decidamus.
misedia redeptoris n̄ri nos liberare dignet̄. q̊
cū patre & sp̄u s̄co uiuit & regnat in s̄cłā s̄cłoꝝ
A M E N

EXPLICIT SEX
TE VISIONIS EX
POSITIO.
INCIPIT EXPO
SITIO SEPTIME
VISIONIS.

SEPTIMA
VISIO AD QUAM
DN̄O DONANTE
p̄uenimus: tota
ad illud tempus qd̄
p̊ resurrectionē futu
rum ē. p̄tinet. Et ordo poscebat. ut generali re
surrectione descripta. gl̄am s̄coꝝ quā p̊ resur
rectionē sine fine possidebunt describeret.
Quę sub figura ciuitatis ierlm̄. in hac uisione
describit̄. ET VENIT un; de. vij. angłis qui
habebant fialas. & locut; ē. mecū dicens.
Veni. ostendā t̄ sponsā uxorē agni. Sup̄; in q̊nta
uisione dicit ioh̄s. vij. anglos habentes. vij. fia
las fuisse sibi monstratos. & in sequentib; unū
ex his sibi ciuitatē diaboli dāpnationeq; eius
sub specie mulieris meretricis ostendisse. Simi
lit̄ & hic unū ex eisdē. vij. angłis dic̄ sibi ciui
tatē dī sub figura ierlm̄ demonstrasse. Eandē
g̊ significationē habent singuli isti. quam
illi septē. Significant nanq; predicatores. q̊ fue
runt & er̄t usq; in finē. Ioh̄s ů typū tenet cet̄oꝝ
fideliū. Angłs g̊ iohi se demonstraturū dī ci
uitatē repromittit. quia p̄dicatores s̄ci cet̄is fi
delib; quanta sit beatitudo iustoꝝ in quantū
possunt studeut demonstrare. ut eos ad uitam
et̄nā p̄cipiendā accendant. Quā sponsā &
uxorem agni uocat. Quod sponsa agni ecclā
iure uocet̄: ioh̄s baptista demonstrat dicens.
Qui habet sponsā. sponsus ē. Qd̄ aūt & uxor dicat̄.
scriptura demonstrat dicens. Ppt̄ hoc relinq̄t
homo patrē & matrē suā. & adherebit uxo
ri suę. & er̄t duo in carne una. Quasi g̊ pa

an non offendit in principium [in] seriei, sed manserit ideo cui reposita manebant omnia: et ipse erat spes gentium. hinc quoque summam exordium. Explicit prologus. Incipit liber I.

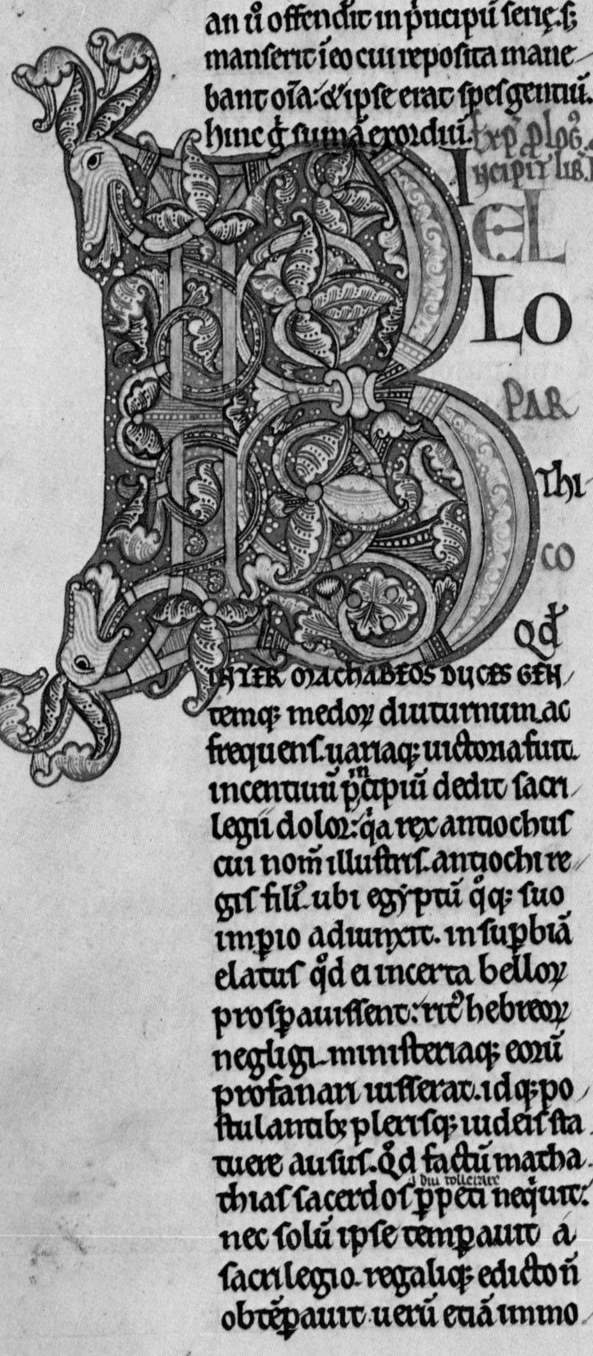

BELLO PARTHICO QUOD INTER MACHABEOS DUCES GENtemque medorum diuturnum ac frequens, uariaque uictoria fuit. incentiuum principium dedit sacrilegium dolor: quia rex antiochus cui nomen illustris, antiochi regis filius, ubi egyptum quoque suo imperio adiunxit, in superbiam elatus quod ei incerta bellorum prosperauissent: ritus hebreorum negligi, ministeriaque eorum profanari iusserat. idque postulantibus plerisque iudeis statuere ausus. Quod factum mathathias sacerdos perpeti [i. diu tollerare] nequiuit. nec solum ipse temperauit a sacrilegio, regalique edicto non obtemperauit, uerum etiam immolantem simulacris hostias de popularibus suis nactus, gladio transuerberauit: et congregata manu atque assideis in societatem ascitis [i. adiunctus]. ipse cum filiis suis temerantes [i. uiolantes] usum patrium et iustitias legis, alios necauit, plerosque expulit. bellique sabbato adoriendi [i. aggrediendi] auctor fuit, ne simili arte ipsi quoque deciperentur: sicut iam plerique eorum dum sabbato bellum suscipere detrectant [i. recusat], irruentibus in se hostibus multi occubuere. Potentiam prosperi [i. sede uictorie] actus dederunt. et perseuerauit in uiro [i. mathathia] usque ad exitum uite studium defensionis et pietatis uigor. Sed cum sibi supremum diem adesse intelligeret, uocatis ciuibus atque assistentibus liberis [i. filiis]: hortatus est ut tuerentur patriam templique religionem. ducemque eis iudam machabeum cure ac sollicitudinis sue successorem reliquit. qui bello strenuus, consilio bonus, ac preceteris fide promptus. quam frequenter innumeras hostium copias parua manu fuderit [i. fugarunt]: prosequi non est presentis negotii [i. operis]. Quod tam breui [i. sermone] colligere datur. quia sepe prosperis usus successibus, excitauit in se magnam hostium multitudinem: qui circumfusi sum

84 Oxford, Jesus College MS.67, f. 3r; Bede on St. Mark's Gospel, Cirencester Abbey, mid-twelfth century.
This manuscript was written by Odo de Wica, a canon of Cirencester.

leaf was tiresomely slow. The scribe would therefore measure up only the first page of a stack of unwritten leaves and with a sharp instrument he would prick the measurements in the extreme margins of a pile of leaves. When he came to each page, therefore, he simply had to join up the prickings in order to multiply the ruling pattern exactly throughout a quire. It is worth looking out for these pricked holes in a twelfth-century book: if nothing else, they may indicate whether the three outer margins have been cropped much by the binder. In the earlier twelfth century the holes are in outer margins only and so had been ruled with the bifolium spread open. By about 1150 one notices the prickings in the extreme inner margins as well, and therefore the scribes must have folded their blank leaves before ruling them. There is a difference too in the instrument used for ruling. Before the twelfth century the lines are almost always scored with an awl or possibly the back of a knife. By the mid-twelfth century, most English scribes ruled their guide-lines with an instrument which draws a line like a modern pencil. Perhaps the graphite mines at Borrowdale in Cumberland supplied this new substance, but sharpened silver and lead also produce very similar marks on a rough surface like vellum. It is worth noting details like ruling and pricking when one examines a romanesque book as, taken together, these can provide interesting clues for dating a manuscript.

One of the ways that we can assign a date to a manuscript is to examine its script. Sometimes this is the only way of guessing a book's age. Of course there is no degree of precision here and it would be foolhardy to date a twelfth-century manuscript within a lesser span than about thirty years on a basis of its script alone. But handwriting evolved, and of course still does: probably all of us could look at an old

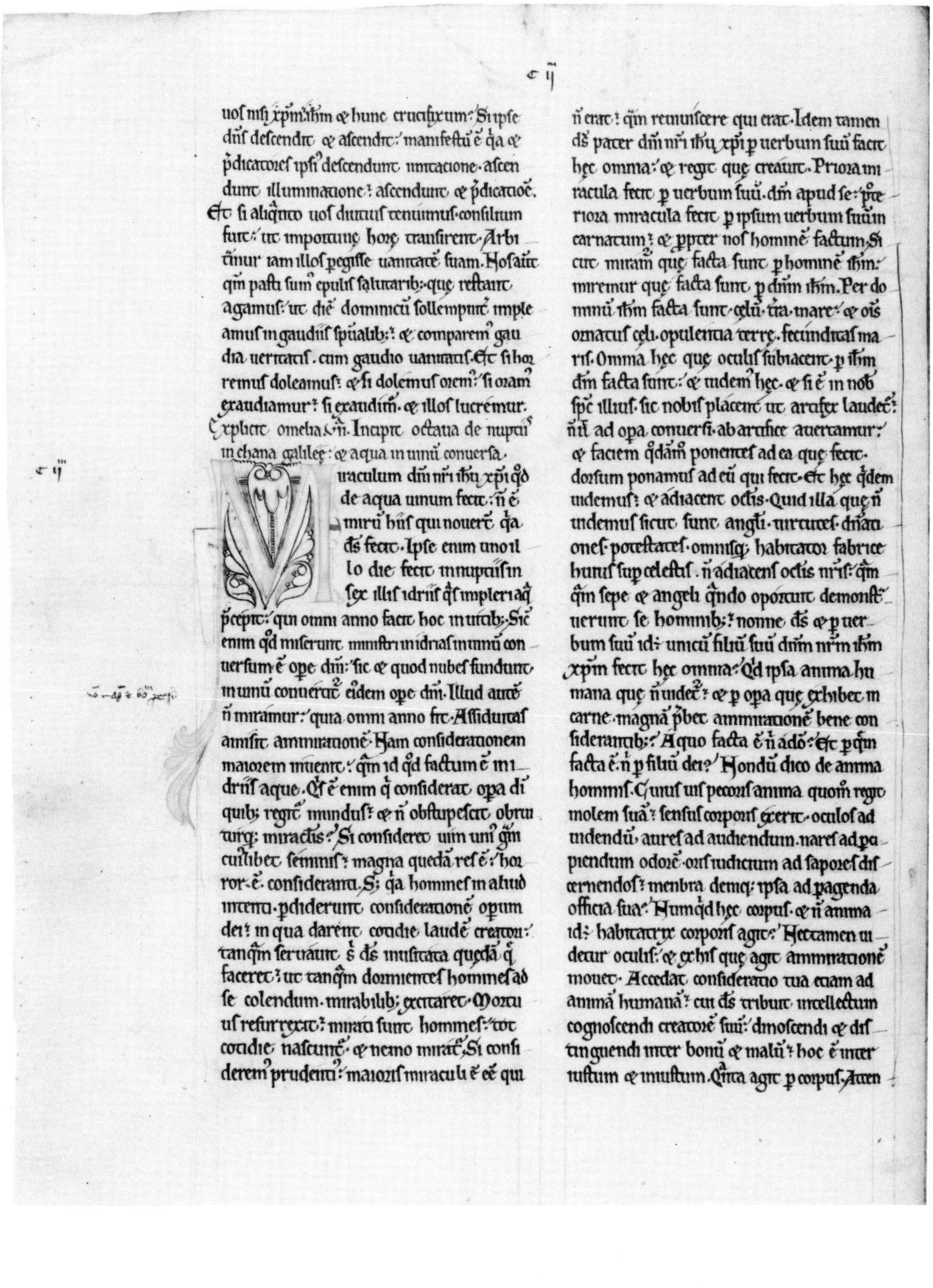

85 Oxford, Christ Church MS. lat. 88, f. 19v; St. Augustine, Homilies, Buildwas Abbey, 1167.
This is the earliest exactly dated English book. It was written at the Cistercian Abbey of Buildwas in Shropshire (founded in 1135) and is a typical Cistercian production using the punctus flexus *punctuation, a mark like a '2' over a dot (after the second word at the top of the second column, for example).*

86 (RIGHT) Lincoln Cathedral MS. A. 1. 18, f. 45v; St. Augustine on the Psalms, Lincoln, second quarter of the twelfth century.
The initial is formed of a mermaid. Lincoln Cathedral probably had its own scriptorium in the twelfth century, and many of its books are handsomely illustrated.

transit. Verbum dei semper dicitur: nunquam transit. Verbum
hominis mox ut dictum fuerit transit. Tenet
in antea: dimittit solida. Si autem deo mutatur
placaturus est sententiam contra inimicum considerante
deo sub quo iudice illam profert. Ille autem contra
quem placata fuerit. et si iam effringi non potest.
quia tenetur iure forte non ecclesiastico sed principum secu-
qui tantum detulerunt ecclesie. ut quicquid in ea iu
dicatum fuerit. dissolui non possit. si ergo effringi
non potest: iam non uult intueri se et caecos oculos
dirigit in iudicem. detrahit quantum potest. Pla
cere illi uoluit inquit. diuiti fauit. aut aliquid
ab illo accepit: aut timuit illum offendere. Ac
cusat. quasi accepta sint munera. Si autem
pauper habuerit contra diuitem. et pro paupere fuerit
iudicatum: dicit item diues. Accepit munera. Que
munera a paupere? Vidit inquit pauperem. et
ne reprehenderetur quod contra pauperem faceret.
oppressit iustitiam. et protulit contra ueritatem
sententiam. Cum ergo necesse sit ut hoc dicatur:
uidete non posse dici ab his qui munera non accipi
unt nisi coram oculis dei. qui solus uidet quis acci
piat. et quis non accipiat: Ego autem in inno
centia mea ambulaui. Redime me domine et
miserere mei: pes meus stetit in rectitudine.
Concussus sum quidem undique scandalis et
temptationibus reprehendentium iudicium huma
ne temeritatis: sed pes meus stetit in rectitu
dine. Quare autem in rectitudine? Quia superius
dixerat et in domino sperans non mouebor. Quid ergo
concludit? In ecclesiis benedicam te domine. Id
est in ecclesiis non me benedicam. quasi certus
de hominibus: sed te benedicam in operibus meis.
Hoc est enim benedicere dominum in ecclesiis fratres:
sic uiuere ut per mores cuiusque benedicatur
dominus. Nam qui benedicit dominum lingua et fac
tis maledicit: non in ecclesiis benedicit domino.
Lingua prope omnes benedicunt: sed non omnes fac
tis. Quidam uoce benedicunt: quidam moribus.
In quorum autem moribus non inuenitur quod dicitur:
faciunt blasphemari dominum. ut illi qui non
dum intrant in ecclesiam quamuis ament
peccata sua et ideo nolunt esse christiani: tamen ex
cusent se per malos. et blandiantur sibi se ducen
tes se ipsos. et dicant. Quid mihi persuades ut christi
anus sim? Ego fraudem a christiano passus sum:
et nunquam feci. Falsum mihi iurauit christianus:
et ego nunquam. Et cum ista dicit: impediunt
saluti ut nichil eis prosit. non quidem quod iam boni
sunt: sed quod mediocriter mali. Quomodo enim nichil pro
dest apertos oculos. si sit quisque in tenebris: ita nichil
prodest esse in luce. si clausi sunt oculi. Ita et pagani
quidem ut de illis potius loquamur uelut bene
uiuens patentibus oculis est in tenebris. qui non
agnoscit lucem suam dominum. Christianus autem male
uiuens in luce quidem est. non nisi dicitur: sed clausit clau
sit oculos. Male uiuendo enim uidere non uult
eum. Inimicus nomine tanquam cecus est in lumine
constitutus.

Explicit tractatus de psalmo xxv. Incipit de psalmo uicesimo sexto.

IPSI DAVID. Priusquam liniretur. Tyro christi
loquitur. cum accedit ad fidem. Dominus illumi
natio mea et salutare meum. quem timebo? Dominus
mihi et notitiam sui. et salutem dabit. quis me au
feret ei? Dominus protector uite mee. a quo trepidabo?
Dominus repellet omnes impetus et insidias hostis
mei. a nullo trepidabo. Dum appropiant super
me nocentes: ut edant carnes meas. Dum accedunt
nocentes ad cognoscendum me et insultandum
ut se mihi preferant mutanti me in melius. ut
maledico dente non me consumant sed potius car
nalia desideria mea. Qui tribulant me in
imici mei. Non solum qui me tribulant amico
animo reprehendentes. et a proposito reuocare
uolentes: sed etiam inimici mei. ipsi infirmati
sunt et ceciderunt. Dum ergo id agunt studio defen
dendi sententiam suam. infirmi facti sunt ad creden
da meliora: et uerbum salutis per quod facio quod eis
displicet odisse ceperunt. Si consistant aduer
sum me castra. non timebit cor meum. Aduersus
me autem si contra dicentium conspirans multitu
do consistat: non timebit cor meum ut in eorum
partes transfugiam. Si exurgat in me bellum.
in hanc ego sperabo. Si exurgat in me persecutio

postcard (for example) and try to guess whether it was written before the First World War, in the 1920s–30s, or in the 1950s, and very often we would be right. Taken with other evidence (the choice of picture on the postcard, the way it is coloured, costumes shown, the way the address is laid out, and so forth) most people, without really knowing why, can date a postcard correctly within a decade or so. This kind of subjective judgement, based on experience, can be applied to manuscripts. Anyone can sometimes be spectacularly wrong, and we have all known the follies of over-confidence. Certain developments in twelfth-century English script can be isolated. A backwards sloping script is not likely to be earlier than the mid-twelfth century. A wavy contraction line (written over a word to indicate that 'n' or 'm' has been omitted) is an early feature: a straight line usually belongs to the second half of the twelfth century or later. The mark like a cedilla under 'e' to represent the 'ae' of classical Latin (e.g. 'caelum' becomes 'cęlum') suggests a date before about 1170, or after about 1450. If the two lower-case letters 'pp' occur together and are actually fused to form a single double form, then the manuscript is not earlier than about 1140 and if they are clearly separate it is not later than about 1180. This is really quite a useful test. If there are combinations of other round letters like 'de', 'be', and 'ho', the manuscript falls within the last third of the twelfth century or later. If the manuscript uses an ampersand (&) for 'et' rather than a mark like a 'z', it is likely to be twelfth century rather than thirteenth.

Localizing a twelfth-century English manuscript on the basis of its script is disappointingly difficult: indeed even whether it was written in England or in France is sometimes very uncertain. Romanesque art was remarkably cosmopolitan and so was monastic discipline, and in any case after 1066 many English monasteries were staffed by Norman personnel. What always used to be thought of as one of the earliest signed English manuscripts, a late eleventh-century copy of Jerome on Isaiah (Bodleian MS. Bodley 717; Pl. 81), has a coloured drawing of the illuminator 'Hugo Pictor', Hugh the Painter; the book comes from Exeter Cathedral but other surviving manuscripts almost certainly by Hugh himself belonged to Jumièges Abbey not far from Rouen in Normandy, and the evidence now suggests that monks of both Exeter and Durham Cathedrals (which had new and energetic Norman bishops) brought in manuscripts ready-made from their home country. To some extent this happened at Canterbury too. Lanfranc, who was archbishop from 1070 to 1089, imported at least one manuscript from his old abbey of Bec in Normandy. It is a volume of *Decretals*, now Trinity College, Cambridge MS. B. 16. 44. It has a contemporary inscription recording that Lanfranc actually purchased it ('dato precio emptum') from Bec, and that he brought it to England and gave it to Christ Church, Canterbury, from which (the note says) no one should remove it on pain of damnation. The Canterbury monks evidently admired its novel rather spiky, prickly Norman script, and for a generation or so the handwriting was imitated and developed by them, a rare local script probably exclusive to Kent.

Who actually were the scribes in a twelfth-century English monastery? Most were probably the monks themselves. Hugh the Painter, whom we have just mentioned, sketches himself holding a pen and an inkpot, and there is every reason to suppose he was a scribe as well as an artist: he is tonsured and wears a Benedictine habit. Diversity of labour was encouraged in monasteries. Making books for the abbey was one of many tasks with which a monk might find himself involved, like gardening, or mending furniture, or teaching in the school. St. Osmund, the Norman bishop of Salisbury (1078–99), is recorded as having encouraged the transcription of books for his cathedral and, it is said, even wrote and bound some himself. Probably monks worked quite slowly, as they had other duties to attend to. One late twelfth-century English glossed Exodus (Lambeth Palace MS. 110) has notes by the scribe on how much work he did each day. He began on 'lundi' and by 'samadi' had written only twelve leaves. When an exemplar was not easily available within a monastery and (as suggested above) the scribe had to travel elsewhere, or when the amount of work to be done exceeded the labour available, the monks could call in professional help. One of the earliest references to professional scribes in England occurs in the chronicle of Abingdon Abbey. It records that Faricius (abbot 1100–17) employed six professional scribes to copy out patristic texts, but he left to the monks (the 'claustrales')

87 Oxford, Jesus College MS. 53, detail of f. 159v.
Ownership inscription in a manuscript of Bede from Cirencester Abbey recording that it was made in the time of abbot Andrew (1147–76) and of the cantor Alexander de Weleu (himself a scribe – he wrote Jesus College MS. 52) and that it was written by the canon Fulco, afterwards prior of the abbey.

88 (RIGHT) New York, Pierpont Morgan Library M. 619, single leaf, recto; Bible, Winchester Cathedral, *c.* 1160–80.
This vast single leaf from a Bible shows scenes from the childhood of Samuel. The size, text, script and artist are all so close to those of the Winchester Bible still in the Cathedral Library there that one would suppose that this was a missing leaf from that manuscript – except that a leaf with identical text is still present in the Winchester Bible (f. 88). Is this the only surviving leaf from a twin copy? Did the monks intend to remove f. 88 from the Winchester and substitute this leaf instead? It is one of the mysteries, as well as one of the masterpieces, of English romanesque art.

89 Camarillo, California, Doheny Library MS.7, detail of f.5r; Zacharias Chrysopolitanus, in Unum ex Quatuor, southern England, late twelfth century.
The initial shows a scribe writing. The manuscript belonged in the late Middle Ages to the monks of Abbotsbury in Dorset.

the task of writing Missals, Graduals, Antiphoners, and other liturgical books. We have seen from the Reading Abbey catalogue that there were a great many of these liturgical manuscripts in a monastery. The point is that they were not books which required difficult journeys in search of accurate exemplars. Monks in the cloister could duplicate them fairly simply. Abbot Simon of St. Albans (1167–83), who corresponded with the abbey of St-Victor in Paris about copying books from there, is also specifically recorded as employing two or three choice scribes at his own expense, and he left an endowment to pay for a scribe for the personal use of abbots in the future. The names of several scribes are preserved in manuscripts from Cirencester Abbey, an Augustinian house in Gloucestershire (Pl.87). Two energetic abbots of Cirencester, Serlo (1131–47) and Andrew (1147–76), supervised the writing out of patristic manuscripts for the house, and about twenty of the books still survive, mostly now in Hereford Cathedral and Jesus College, Oxford, and (remarkably) many still have contemporary notes of the scribes' names. Most were inmates of the abbey. They included Adam (who later became prior), Deodatus, Jocelin, Simon of Cornwall, Odo de Wica (Pl.84), Serlo, Walter, Alexander the Cantor, and especially Fulco (who also later became prior) with six and a half manuscripts to his credit. But among the names is Ralph de Pulleham, described in Jesus College MS.52 as a 'scriptor', a professional scribe, who wrote Jesus College MSS.62, 63 and ff.42–131 of MS.52 in collaboration with Alexander, cantor of Cirencester (Pl.83). Perhaps many monasteries used men like Ralph de Pulleham. The monks did most of the work, but a professional scribe may have been called in to help and advise on the stocking up of a monastic library. It would have been an interesting job to have had in the twelfth century.

Good quality script and elegant layout are features of twelfth-century monastic books, but appearance alone, however agreeable, is no use to a monk if the text is not reliable. Of course all copyists sometimes made mistakes in transcribing. Today even the most professional typist has a self-correcting machine or a little bottle of white paint. Pictures of twelfth-century scribes (like Prior Laurence in Durham U.L., Cosin MS.V.III.1, or Eadwine in Trinity College, Cambridge MS.R.17.1 (Pl.72)) show them scratching away at the page with a little scimitar-shaped knife which they hold in their left hands. This knife was partly to sharpen the pen (a penknife, that is) but also to scratch out mistakes. Vellum is a tough enough material to withstand quite a few erasures. If you peer closely at almost any page of a twelfth-century manuscript you can see little rough patches in the text where the scribe has scraped off a wrong letter or two and rewritten them. This must have happened as the scribe was working: constant vigilance was necessary. The easiest mistake to make is when the scribe has just copied the last word of a phrase and he looks back at his exemplar and his eye alights accidentally on another word which ends like the one he has just written. He then starts to copy out the second half of the wrong sentence in error. The technical term for this is homoeoteleuton. It is especially likely to happen if one is copying Latin because many words end similarly. Another fault a scribe can easily commit is to expand a contraction wrongly. The abbreviation 'mr', for instance, could represent either 'mater' or 'martyr' in the exemplar, and the old schoolboy horrors of 'hic, haec, hoc' and 'qui, quae, quod', which might occur as an abbreviated 'h'' or 'q'' in an exemplar, could easily confuse a scribe to whom Latin was (at best) only a second language.

It would seem as though there was a second scribe who checked through a text after it had been written, comparing it as carefully as possible with the original. If there was the odd word which had slipped in by mistake, he could simply cross it out or (in a way which was less upsetting to the appearance of the page) underline it with a row of dots. A reader would know that he had to omit this word. Longer phrases or whole paragraphs which had to be cancelled could be marked 'va' at the beginning and 'cat' at the end: 'vacat' meaning that the words in between these syllables should not be there. Additions which had to be made were often scribbled in by the corrector in the extreme outer margins and were subsequently transferred into the body of the text, generally by erasing several lines and rewriting them in a more compressed way to include the missing phrase. The words jotted in the margins ought then to have been erased, though they sometimes still remain. One imagines that the corrector was the head or supervisor of the scribes. In manuscripts from

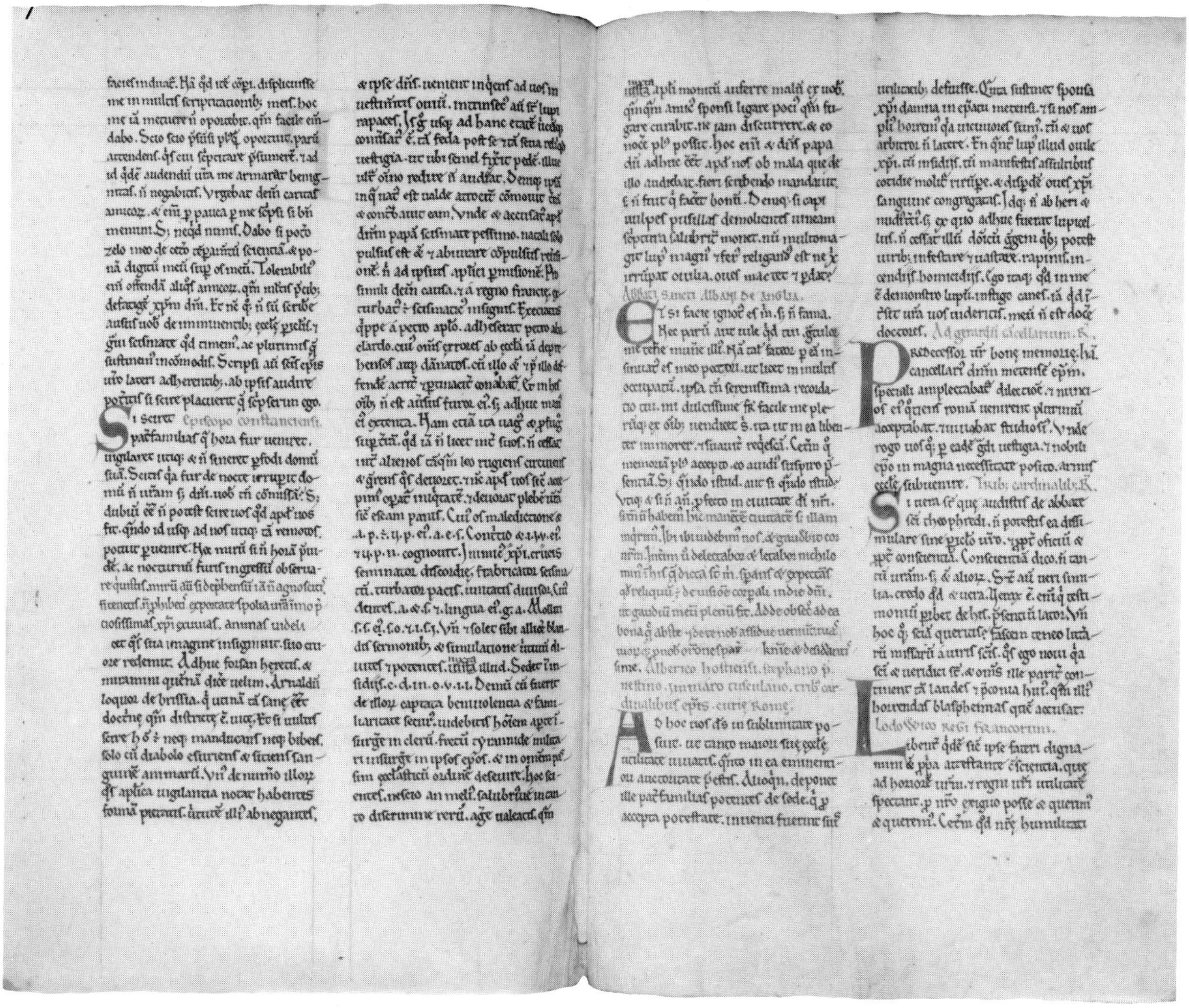

90 London, British Library, Royal MS. 8. F. XV, ff. 58v–59r; St. Bernard of Clairvaux, Epistles, Byland Abbey, late twelfth century.

This is a Cistercian manuscript with plain initials in red and green. In the first column of the second page a long section has been erased and re-written by another scribe.

Salisbury and Winchcombe corrections in the same hand occur in volumes by a variety of scribes. There, at least, one man proof-read books as they were written. When that had been done, the exemplar could be returned to its owner.

The illustration of twelfth-century manuscripts is very much admired today. The paintings of the Winchester Bible (Pl. 88), for instance, must rank among the greatest works of art ever produced in England. The finest have a quality unmatched anywhere in Europe in the twelfth century. There is great elegance too in twelfth-century English coloured initials in the text. These were almost certainly painted by the scribes while they were writing out the book. The main colours of these are red, pale blue, and (particularly in England) green. Sometimes they used brown, purple (especially at Canterbury), yellow, and other colours. Often the initials would be shaped like little flowers and petals. They add great gaiety to a twelfth-century manuscript.

The decision as to whether a manuscript was to be decorated would of course have to be taken before it was written. Spaces would have to be marked out, and the scribe would leave these blank for the miniatures or initials. It raises a fundamental question of why twelfth-century monks decorated their books at all. It is a very difficult question to answer. It obviously worried the medieval Cistercians too: their fundamental principles were for stark simplicity in life-style and architecture, and St. Bernard specifically condemned unnecessary ornamentation formed of distracting animals and monsters (Pls. 90 and 92). Yet their manuscripts often have painted initials and even miniatures and sometimes gold. In the Cistercian statue of 1131, saying that initials ought to be made of one colour only and not illustrated, one can see that they could not imagine books without any painted initials at all. Decoration as such was not simply a luxury. Contemporary descriptions of manuscripts generally do not mention illumination. The St. Albans Abbey chronicle, praising Abbot Simon (1167–83), exalts the great artistic quality of the chalices, crosses, and other gifts commissioned by Simon but in complimenting his illumi-

91 (LEFT) Cambridge, Corpus Christi College MS.4, detail of f.241v; Bible, south east England, mid-twelfth century.
This Bible was at Dover Priory in the Middle Ages. One initial shows a painter and a sculptor at work, both laymen.

92 (BELOW) London, British Library, Royal MS.7.F.V, detail of f.33v; Hugh of St. Victor, In Hierarchia Dionysii, Kirkstead Abbey (Lincolnshire), late twelfth century.
Kirkstead was a Cistercian house and the initials in its manuscripts have no gold.

nated manuscripts says just that they were wonderfully accurate ('authentica') and hurries on to describe the painted cupboard where they were kept. The life of St. Hugh, discussing what must be either the 'Auct' or the Winchester Bible (in any case, a very richly illuminated book), praises not its initials but the corrected text which gave it such a special attraction. The chronicler William FitzStephen, recounting how Thomas Becket obtained manuscripts for his cathedral between 1164 and 1170, mentions only the accuracy of the texts, with no reference to the remarkable illumination. The Reading Abbey library catalogue makes no hint of beauty or decoration as a distinguishing feature of any book, though it lists titles like a Bestiary and an Apocalypse, almost certainly full of pictures. One almost wonders whether they noticed book illumination at all.

This brings us to the true function of decoration in a twelfth-century book. It was clearly not just because it was pretty. The twelfth century was an age which delighted in the classification and ordering of knowledge. Its most admired writers, men like Peter Lombard and Gratian, arranged and shuffled information into an order that was accessible and easy to use. Twelfth-century readers loved encyclopaedias. They wanted books that could actually be consulted. We have seen that the Reading Abbey catalogue singled out as useful not the necessary many-volumed Church Fathers, but the practical summaries and extracts. The fact that monks began making library catalogues at all reflects this fascination with order and accessibility of universal knowledge. Let us then consider book illumination in these terms. It suddenly becomes easy to understand. Initials mark the beginnings of

93 London, British Library, Royal MS. I. B. XI, f. 72r; Gospels, St. Augustine's Abbey, Canterbury, mid-twelfth century.
This page shows the opening of St. Luke's Gospel in an unfinished manuscript. The design has been drawn in pencil and then inked over in preparation for painting. The rubricator has filled in the opening words of the text in alternately red and blue letters following the guidewords faintly written in the top right-hand corner. A note for the scribe is at the top, 'scribatur lucas', ('Luke is to be written').

94 New York, Pierpont Morgan Library MS. 81, f.69r; Bestiary, perhaps Lincoln, *c.* 1185.
The miniature shows a flying fish, which the text calls a sardine. The manuscript was given to Worksop Priory, Nottinghamshire, by Philip, canon of Lincoln, in 1187.

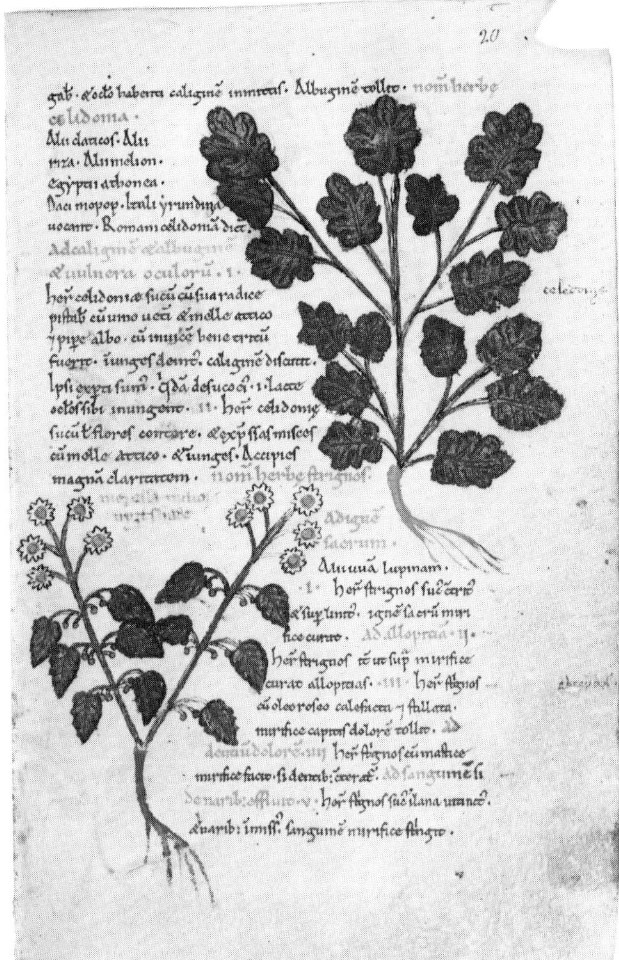

95 Oxford, Bodleian Library MS. Ashmole 1431, f.20r; Herbal, St. Augustine's Abbey, Canterbury, late eleventh century.

books or chapters. They make a manuscript easy to use. A bigger initial is a visual lead into a more important part of the text. It helps classify the priorities of the text. Like the use of bright red ink for headings (something one notices in twelfth-century books after working on earlier manuscripts), coloured initials make a massive text accessible to the reader. A newspaper does this today with headlines of different sizes. In fact, a modern popular newspaper is a good example of a thoroughly accessible text and uses very many of the devices of a twelfth-century illuminated manuscript: narrow columns (less eye strain), big and small letters, running-titles along the top of the page, catchwords (leading a text from page 1 through to page 2, for instance), and, above all, pictures. These help explain a written text visually, they provide a reminder of a familiar image, they help the user to choose which sections to read next, they make for a satisfying page layout, and they can be amusing. Yet any reader of a modern newspaper will fiercely defend his choice of paper by praising the text, not the layout or illustrations. It is not surprising that the twelfth-century chroniclers from St. Albans, Lincoln, and Canterbury complimented the accuracy of manuscripts when what they meant was that they liked using them.

Now we can look at the great illuminated manuscripts of twelfth-century England. Some have miniatures which are really part of the text: diagrams which make texts more comprehensible, like the classified schemes of the universe and charts of the bodily humours in a late eleventh-century handbook of science from Thorney Abbey (St. John's College, Oxford, MS. 17) or the great emblematic illustrations in a copy of Richard of St-Victor's commentary on Ezechiel from Exeter Cathedral (Bodleian, MS. Bodley 494). Others come near to this. A Bestiary, or book of animals (Pl. 94), is really only usable with pictures: B.L. Add. MS. 11283 of about 1170 has ninety-nine of them. The information in herbals too is difficult to extract without illustrations: Bodleian MS. Ashmole 1431, from St. Augustine's, Canterbury (Pl. 95), and MS. Bodley 130, from Bury St. Edmunds, both have about a hundred and fifty miniatures each. But even manuscripts of the Church Fathers must be able to be used. The nine historiated initials and seventy-one decorated initials in Lincoln Cathedral MS. A. 3. 17 must have made St. Augustine's sermons a pleasure to open instead of a burden. The reader would not lose his place either: initials are a visual aid to remembering. The great illustration cycles of the lives of saints must have helped readers understand rather thinly written texts, like the fifty-five miniatures in a copy of the life of St. Cuthbert made at Durham (University College, Oxford, MS. 165) or the thirty-two full-page miniatures and thirteen historiated initials in the Bury St. Edmunds copy of the life of St. Edmund (Morgan Library M. 736). A journalist with not much story today fills out his article with photographs. The famous Bibles of the twelfth century had wonderful historiated initials at the beginning of each book, and for the prologues. A giant Bible is difficult to use without a guide to lead one through the vast text: pictures provide exactly that. They identify and grade the importance of texts. The more ingenious the miniature, the greater its practical function. Decoration is a device to help a reader use a manuscript.

Unfinished manuscripts give an idea of the sequence of

96 London, British Library, Cotton MS. Claudian B. II, f. 341r; John of Salisbury, Letters of St. Thomas Becket, perhaps western England, late twelfth century.
The miniature illustrates John of Salisbury's letter describing Thomas Becket's martyrdom in 1170. It is believed to be the earliest surviving illustration of the event.

97–98 Oxford, Bodleian Library MS. Auct. D. I. 13, f. 1r and detail; Epistles of St. Paul glossed, England (possibly Winchester), mid-twelfth century.
This unusual initial shows three scenes, St. Paul preaching, being lowered in a basket over the walls of Damascus, and being beheaded. In the centre of several areas of painted colour can be seen tiny letters of the alphabet: there is an 'r', for example, on the red tower on the top left of the window from which St. Paul's companions are lowering him, and an 'a' on the hatched blue area just to the right of this. The green cloak of the man in the foreground on the top right is marked with a 'v' and St. Paul's grey-brown tunic seems to be lettered 'g' across his abdomen. One artist must have designed the initial and noted the colours for a second painter to supply.

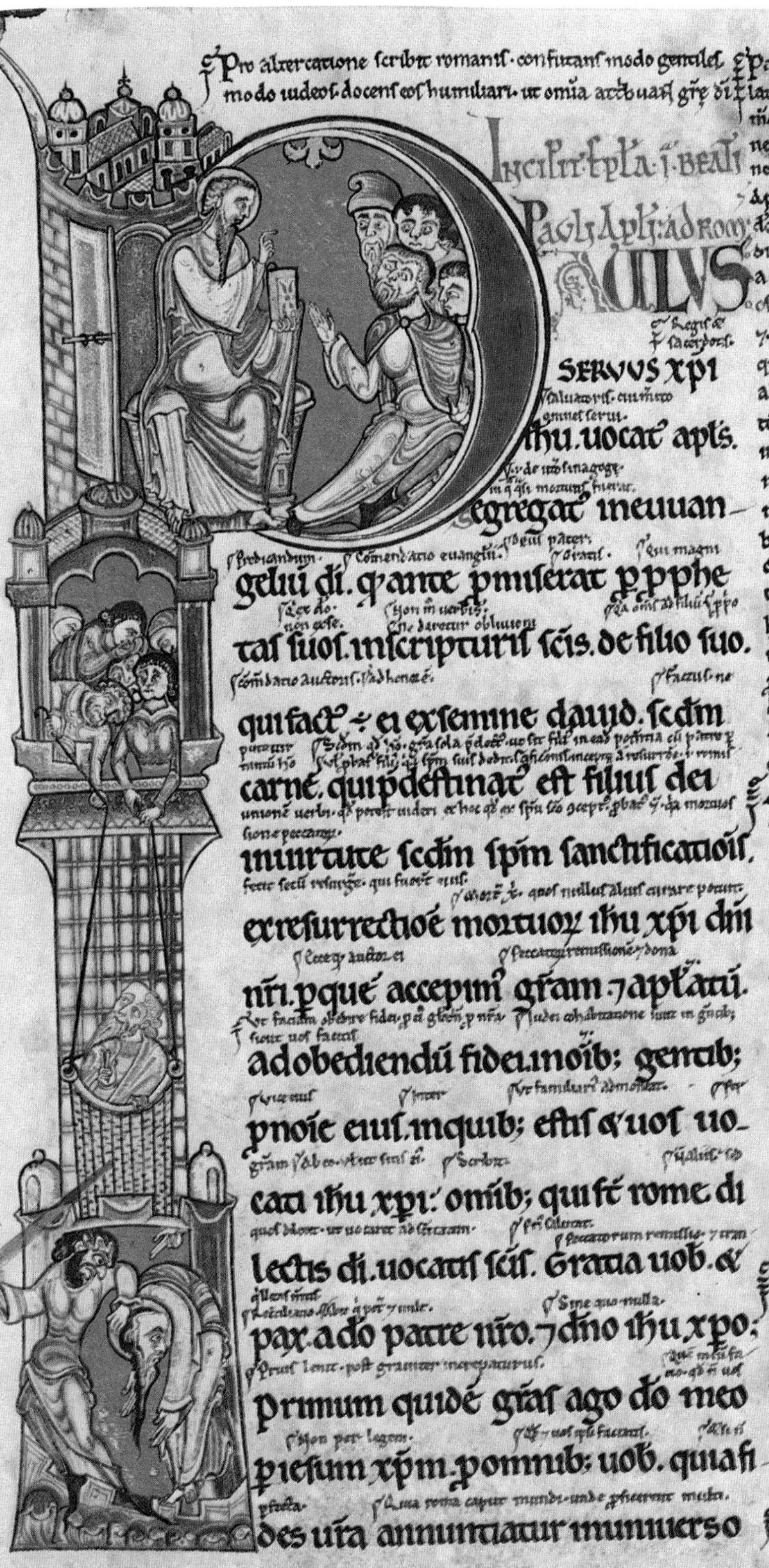

Incipit ep'la .i. beati Pauli ap'li ad Rom[anos]

Paulus servus xpi ihu. uocat' ap'ls.
segregat' in euuan-
geliu di. q'd ante pmiserat p pphe-
tas suos. in scripturis scis. de filio suo.
qui fact' e ei ex semine dauid. scdm
carne. qui pdestinat' est filius dei
in uirtute scdm spm sanctificatio'is.
ex resurrectio'e mortuor ihu xpi dni
nri. p que accepim' gram 7 ap'latu.
ad obediendu fidei. in oib; gentib;
p noie eius. in quib; estis & uos uo-
cati ihu xpi: omib; qui st rome dilectis di. uocatis scis. Gratia uob. &
pax a do patre nro. 7 dno ihu xpo.
Primum quide gras ago do meo
p iesum xpm. p omnib; uob. quia fides ura annuntiatur in uniuerso

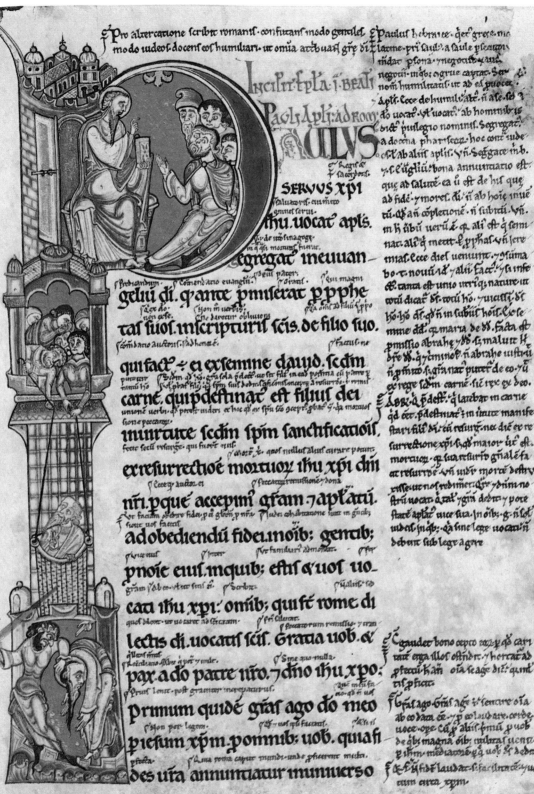

illuminating an initial (Pls. 93 and 100). First of all, the artist lightly sketched in with plummet (or pencil) the design of the letter. Circles and curves were sometimes done by using a pair of compasses and one can see a tiny hole pricked in the middle. The design would then be picked out carefully in pen and ink. Gold is rare in monastic manuscripts before the mid-twelfth century, possibly because until that time most artists worked outside in the cloister and gold leaf is so fragile and thin that it is almost impossible to manipulate in a breeze. But if there was gold, it would be applied at this stage before the colour. That is because it was laid on over glue and then rubbed or burnished until it shone, and the action of burnishing might damage other painted areas. Then the colours were applied with a brush, the basic pigments first and then gradually worked up, no doubt with a finer brush, to a high degree of finish. The colourist was not necessarily the same man as the designer of an initial, particularly if a whole team of artists was working together. The Winchester Bible,

99 (LEFT) Cambridge, Trinity College MS. O. 4. 7, detail of f. 75r; St. Jerome, Commentaries on the Old Testament, Rochester Cathedral Priory, *c.* 1120.
This initial, drawn in outline, shows a man trying to teach a bear to recite the alphabet.

100–101 Winchester Cathedral Library, the Winchester Bible, details of initials on ff. 88r and 342r.
The first initial, showing King Solomon, has been partly sketched in ink and the burnished gold has been added before work was abandoned. The second initial, depicting King Cyrus, has been fully coloured and a tiny guide letter 'a' (indicating blue paint) can be seen to the right of the king's cloak.

for example, was a project which certainly kept a fair number of illuminators employed over a period of some years. Sir Walter Oakeshott, who has spent much of his long life studying this celebrated manuscript, has frequently found evidence of an initial having been sketched by one artist and subsequently painted and subtly altered by another. Another manuscript which shows curious evidence of collaboration is Bodleian MS. Auct. D. I. 13, perhaps from Winchester though later at Exeter (Pls. 97–8). The book is a mid twelfth-century Epistles of St. Paul glossed and has a fine full-length initial on f. 1r showing incidents in the life of St. Paul. If you look closely at the initial, you can make out tiny letters of the alphabet in the middle of each area of colour, and those that are intelligible include 'r' on the red areas, 'v' on the green, and 'a' on the blue. This was, quite simply, what is now called 'painting by numbers'. A good artist drew the initial and indicated the colours for a lesser craftsman to colour in. One thing that emerges is that they were speaking Latin or (more likely) French: 'rouge', 'vert', and 'azure'.

Possibly the artist of this initial was a professional, called in to help the monks decorate their book. What seems to be the work of the same artist occurs in Avranches MS. 159, a chronicle written at Mont-St-Michel in Normandy and completed in 1158. If it was actually the same man, he must have travelled to or from France. The phenomenon of wandering illuminators is the simplest way of explaining what seems to be the work of the same artist cropping up in several quite different places. Examples include the miniatures by the mid-twelfth-century illuminator of the huge Lambeth Bible (Pl. 74), perhaps from Canterbury, which are uncannily similar to the paintings on fragments of a Gospel Book documented as having been made at Liessies Abbey in Hainault in 1146. Another case is the so-called Simon Master who worked at St. Albans around the 1170s: the same artist (so it seems) occurs in manuscripts from Worcester Cathedral, Bonport Abbey in Normandy, and perhaps Troyes in eastern France. But the most weird link of all is the amazing relationship between the style of at least two of the artists of the Winchester Bible and the murals in the chapter house of a monastery at Sigena in northern Spain, more than six hundred miles from Winchester. If any of these are really the same actual artists (as is generally believed), then they must have been travelling professionals. Too little is known about these people. One wonders if they called on monasteries asking for work, or whether the monks sought them out for special projects. What is clear, however, is that monks were anxious to possess decorated books, and monasteries could no longer always do the illumination themselves.

When the script was finished and the decoration complete, the final stage of book production was to bind the volume (Pl. 102). Almost all twelfth-century bindings are of wooden boards covered with leather. The quires or gatherings of a manuscript would be arranged in order (numerical signatures and, later, catchwords helped this) and then sewn onto several horizontal thongs of leather. The thongs were then threaded into tunnel grooves in wooden boards, pulled tight, and pegged into place. Twelfth-century boards had square-cut edges and were made flush with the edges of the pages, not like the covers of a modern hardbound book which overlap slightly. The boards were then covered with leather. Almost always this was white tawed skin, though surviving examples have often mellowed to an agreeable yellow-brown. The spines were flat. Occasionally the leather was coloured red and (in England very rarely) stamped with little impressed pictures. We can assume that all the books in the Reading Abbey catalogue, for instance, were bound in white skin over wooden boards except for eight whose bindings were specified: two Missals in silver, two books in red leather, and four books in stamped leather. A good example of a plain white twelfth-century Reading Abbey binding is B.L. Egerton MS. 2204.

102 Oxford, Jesus College MSS. 70, 68, 53 and 63.
All these are Cirencester manuscripts of the mid-twelfth century in contemporary bindings with remains of tabs at the head and foot of the spines for pulling the books out of the chests where they were kept.

A distinctive feature of a bookbinding in the twelfth century is that it had little tabs shaped like half-moons sewn at the top and bottom of the spine, The titles of the books are sometimes written along the spines too. The Reading Abbey example just mentioned has 'Beda super lucam' written from the bottom to the top of the spine, exactly as listed in the catalogue. These features tell us how the books were stored. They were probably kept in chests with the fore-edge downwards. The edges of the boards were flush with the pages so that it was a neat fit. The title was visible on the spine. The tabs were for lifting the book out of the chest. That is how we would find the manuscripts if we could be miraculously transported back to the twelfth century to rummage through the cloisters in a monastic library.

·4·

Books for Students

Among the most obvious owners of books are students, whether schoolboys learning basic Latin, or postgraduates refining and expanding their researches. The universities of Europe blossomed into international prominence from the late twelfth century onwards, and their need for textbooks brought about a revolution in the medieval book trade. A Bolognese lawyer Odofredo (d. 1265) tells an anecdote about a father who offered his son an allowance of five hundred pounds a year to study at the universities of Paris or Bologna: to the father's distress, the boy went to Paris and squandered his money on manuscripts frivolously decorated with gold initials. The Latin says that he had his books 'babuinare de literis aureis' which literally means the initials were filled with baboons, monkeyed-up, as the father might have said when the student came home penitently at the end of term. It was beyond the father's experience. It would have been almost impossible a century earlier for a private individual to commission textbooks and have them expensively illuminated, and even now the father did not understand the need for them. This chapter will try to take the son's point of view.

Tracing the date of foundation of a medieval university is notoriously difficult. This is partly because the patriotic pride of an antiquarian for his own *alma mater* may beguile his imagination into ascribing the founding of the University of Paris to Charlemagne or of Oxford to King Alfred, and partly because universities did not start issuing their own corporate statutes until some time into the thirteenth century, and there is almost no way of documenting when students began gathering around a master to listen to his teaching. In northern Europe the story must begin in Paris in the first half of the twelfth century. Masters like William of Champeaux (*c.* 1070–1121) and the still almost legendary Peter Abelard (1079–1142) attracted crowds of students to their lectures in the precincts of the cathedral of Notre-Dame in Paris and across the Seine at the church of Ste-Geneviève and at the abbey of St-Victor. These schools certainly existed in the twelfth century. There is nothing especially unusual in the fact of lectures taking place in these surroundings. Really any cathedral chapter had a chancellor whose responsibilities included the education of the cathedral personnel and of various clerical scholars, and he was able to give permission to masters to teach grammar, rhetoric, theology, and other subjects. This was already happening at Laon, Auxerre, Rheims, probably Chartres, Poitiers, and elsewhere in France. These cathedral schools rose and disappeared according to the reputation of the masters, men like Anselm of Laon, Gilbert the Universal, and Gilbert de la Porrée. We have seen in the last chapter that in the mid-twelfth century the abbey of St-Victor in Paris enjoyed a reputation for scholarship which brought monks from St. Albans in England asking for copies of new books written by the masters who taught there. Undoubtedly some students who attended lectures in Paris returned home with books they had somehow acquired or made during their studies. Master Guido of Castello (who died as Pope Celestine II in 1144) had attended Abelard's lectures and he bequeathed to his old monastery of Città-di-Castello in Umbria a set of books which included Abelard's *Theologia* and his *Sic et Non*. It is a very early instance of a student bringing home textbooks. A few decades later there is reasonable evidence of monks studying in the Parisian monastery schools and acquiring their own manuscripts. One of these is Master Robert of Adington, who is documented in Durham in the 1190s and who left to the cathedral there a set of books (Pl. 104), of which one (now Durham Cathedral MS. A. III. 16) includes a list of glossed books of the Bible, with recent works by Peter Lombard, Peter Comestor, Peter of Poitiers, Helduinus, and other Parisian masters, and these books (the list tells us) had been kept by their owner at the abbey of St-Victor in Paris. A very similar list of late twelfth-century textbooks survives in Dijon MS. 34. These belonged to a certain Theobald and were kept by him at the Parisian abbey of Ste-Geneviève. Almost certainly Robert of Adington attended lectures at St-Victor and Theobald at Ste-Geneviève.

However, it is really to the masters around the school of Notre-Dame that we should be looking for the origins of the University of Paris. One of the outstanding teachers there was Peter Lombard, author of the *Sentences* (the greatest twelfth-century theological encyclopaedia, Pl. 106) and of the *Great*

103 Oxford, Bodleian Library MS. Laud Misc. 409, f. 3v; Hugh of St. Victor, De Archa Noe and other texts, England (possibly St. Albans), late twelfth century.
The miniature shows Hugh of St. Victor (c. 1078–1141), one of the first great teachers in Paris, lecturing to three students.

104 Durham Cathedral MS. A. III. 17, f. 4v; Isaiah glossed, Paris, *c.* 1180–90. *This was one of the glossed books owned by Master Robert of Adington who deposited them at the Abbey of St.-Victor in Paris.*

Gloss on the Psalms and Pauline Epistles. Peter Lombard taught in the cathedral schools of Notre-Dame and in 1158 became bishop of Paris. He died in 1160, bequeathing to Notre-Dame his own library including the autograph manuscript of the *Sentences*. Peter Lombard established a tradition of scholarship in Paris which is still unbroken. Peter Comestor, who was probably the Lombard's pupil and died about 1169, wrote the *Historia Scholastica,* a kind of summary of biblical history which was to become a textbook for generations to come. With authors like Peter the Chanter, Peter of Poitiers, and Stephen Langton, all working in and around the cathedral schools within the twelfth century, we are faced with a formidable senior common room.

It is difficult to know whether there was already anything we would now call a university before about 1200. From the third quarter of the century, the masters who taught in the schools at Notre-Dame were still of course licensed formally by the chancellor of the cathedral but they seem to have had an independent admission procedure for newly qualified graduates. In fact, the production of manuscripts is one of the best forms of evidence that the Paris schools were taking on a life of their own in the late twelfth century. The most

105 Paris, Bibliothèque Nationale MS. lat. 16200, f. 4r; Ptolemy, Almagest, Paris, 1213.
The manuscript contains Ptolemy's treatise on astronomy in the Latin translation of Gerard of Cremona. It has a colophon (f. 3v) saying that it was written and perfected from the exemplar at the Abbey of St.-Victor in Paris in December 1213.

fundamental textbook was the Bible, and the form in which the Bible was studied in the cathedral schools was in the twenty or so separate volumes which made up the Gloss on the Bible. We met references to these volumes in the Reading Abbey catalogue (above, pp.78–9) and they were sometimes described there as 'like the copies read in the Schools'. The two biblical Glosses by Peter Lombard were (according to his pupil Herbert of Bosham) left scarcely finished on their author's death and they were edited for publication in the 1160s and issued as part of those huge sets of the Gloss on the Bible. These were published from Paris. A fair number of them survive: large, well-written books with splendid decoration including illuminated initials formed of spirals of vinestems full of tiny yellow lions which clamber through the decoration. A particularly fine example of this kind of book is B.N. MS.lat.11565, a copy of Peter Lombard on the Psalms, which belonged to a cleric who died at St-Victor during the abbacy of Guérin (1172–93). There are examples of this style of decoration in manuscripts of the biblical Gloss (Pl.104), the *Sentences* (Pl.106), the *Historia Scholastica*, the *Decretum* of Gratian, and a few other Parisian textbooks, and we find that the first owners of the manuscripts were often former students of the schools. In a way, the argument is circular: the flourishing of the schools allows us to attribute surviving manuscripts to Paris, and the number of attributable manuscripts enhances our impression of the Paris schools within the twelfth century.

What is almost certainly the earliest medieval reference to a bookshop comes from Paris well within the last quarter of the century. It occurs in the letters of Peter of Blois, archdeacon of Bath, who says that when he was in Paris on business for the king of England he saw some law books laid out for sale by B. the public bookseller. He thought that his nephew would find them useful, he says, and so he agreed a price and left. Subsequently, Peter continues, the provost of Sexeburgh came and offered the vendor more money for the same books and carried them off by force. Peter of Blois says he was extremely annoyed. It is difficult to know how much to read into this anecdote. There is far too little evidence of any real book trade in Paris at this date. The seller is here described as 'B. publico mangone librorum', which is not a flattering term – a public monger of books. Very possibly he owned no more than a market stall. There is little doubt that the law books were second-hand. Manuscripts were always very expensive, and no stallkeeper would tie up capital in new books on the chance of a sale. None the less, here were secular books commercially available with a stallkeeper who was able to haggle over the price and was not averse to breaking his word for a greater profit. The atmosphere had certainly changed from that of the cloistered monk working only for the glory of God. One very early thirteenth-century Parisian manuscript of SS. Luke and John glossed has a contemporary note recording that it was bought for 100 Parisian shillings from 'Blavius bedellus' (Paris, Mazarine, MS.142, f.191v): Blavius the beadle could possibly have been B. the bookseller who cheated Peter of Blois. It may be that we have chanced on the name of the earliest bookseller in Europe.

The manuscript which includes the note of the purchase from Blavius is one of fourteen surviving glossed books of the Bible (now MSS.131–144 in the Mazarine Library in Paris) which were eventually bequeathed to the abbey of St-Victor by brother Peter of Châteauroux, who is recorded as a canon there in 1246. If each volume cost anything like the 100 shillings which Blavius charged, the set came to about 70 pounds. Three volumes from the same set (MSS.131–2 and 136) are decorated by an artist whose hand has been recognized in other manuscripts. By grouping these together we can gain some impression of luxurious textbooks made for wealthy scholars in Paris around 1210. The books by the same illuminator include a copy of Gratian's *Decretum* (Liège University Library MS.499), the *Isagoge* of Joannitius (Bethesda, Maryland, National Library of Medicine), a Latin didactic poem by Gilles de Paris (B.L. Add. MS.22399), and a splendid manuscript of Ptolemy's *Almagest* (B.N. MS.lat.16200), which ends with a colophon by the scribe saying that he wrote and perfected the book from an exemplar at the abbey of St-Victor in December 1213 (Pl.105). These four books are respectively legal, medical, literary, and astronomical. With the glossed biblical books, therefore, the artist produced volumes from each of the four faculties (as they later became) of canon law, medicine, the arts, and theology. The exemplar being kept at St-Victor reminds us to be cautious about ascribing the production to a professional bookshop as early as 1213. These manuscripts belong to that twilight world between the monastic book production of the abbeys and the entirely secular workshops of the stationers who kept their own exemplars. The market, however, was certainly the emerging university.

Another of these very early thirteenth-century Parisian illuminators is actually known by name. A Bible in the Bibliothèque Nationale (MS.lat.11930-1) is signed in gold letters 'Magister Alexander me fecit' (Master Alexander made me). His title may hint at an association with the schools but this does not necessarily mean that he was literally a *magister*. Perhaps he was just a master-craftsman. In any case, he was not a monk. Curiously – unlike books by the painter of the Ptolemy of 1213 – manuscripts illuminated by Alexander are almost all biblical. One of them, a copy of Peter Lombard on the Pauline Epistles, now Troyes MS.175, belonged to Roland, abbot of Montiéramey from 1207 to 1225, which gives some kind of date for the group. The workshop illuminated at least nine surviving one-volume Bibles.

The arrangement and publishing of the Bible was the most enduring monument of the scribes and illuminators of Paris in the early thirteenth century. This deserves some attention. It has a major place in the history of manuscripts. The way that the Latin Bible was redesigned and promoted from the Paris schools was one of the most phenomenal successes in the history of book production. The Bible is not an easy book to

106 Baltimore, Walters Art Gallery, MS.W.809, f.70r; Peter Lombard, Sentences, Paris, late twelfth century.
Peter Lombard (c.1100–1160) taught at the schools of Notre-Dame in Paris and the textbooks that he wrote are among the first to be illuminated in a recognizably Parisian style.

De differentia uoluntatis et intentionis et finis.
Quare uoluntas dicitur peccatum cum sit de naturalibus quorum nullum dicitur peccatum esse.
Quare actus uoluntatis sit peccatum si actus aliarum potentiarum non sunt peccata.
Ex quo sensu dicatur naturaliter omnis homo uelle bonum.
An ex fine omnis actus pensari debeant.
Qui ex affectu et fine omnes sunt boni uel mali. An omnis intentio uel actio infidelium sit mala.
Quibus modis dicatur bonum.
Quomodo intelligendum illud peccatum adeo esse uoluntarium.
Et illud nusquam nisi in uoluntate peccatum est. et item si nisi uoluntate peccatur.
Quod mala uoluntas est. uoluntarium peccatum.
An uoluntas et actio mala meo dem et eadem idem sunt unum peccatum. uel plura.
Si peccatum ab aliquo omissum in eo sit. quo usque peniteat. Quibus accipitur modis reatus.
De modis peccatorum quo differant delictum. et peccatum.
De septem principalibus uitiis.
De superbia.
Quomodo dicatur superbia radix omnium malorum. et cupiditas. cum superbia non sit cupiditas.
De peccato in spiritum sanctum.
De potentia peccandi. an sit homini. uel diabolo a deo.
An aliquando resistendum sit potestati.

T E R T I A

Vnum et non principium esse ostendit non plura ut quidam putauerunt.

CREATIONEM rerum insinuans scriptura diuina. deum esse creatorem. initiumque temporis. atque omnium uisibilium uel inuisibilium creaturarum. in primordio sui ostendit dicens. In principio creauit deus celum et terram. His etenim uerbis moyses spiritu dei afflatus. in uno principio a deo creatore mundum factum refert. Eludens errorem quorumdam. plura sine principio fuisse principia opinantium. Plato namque tria initia extimauit. deum scilicet et exemplar et materiam. et ipsa increata sine principio. et deum quasi artificem non creatorem. Creator enim est. qui de nichilo aliqua facit. Et creare proprie est. de nichilo aliquid facere. Facere uero non tantum de nichilo aliquid operari. sed etiam de materia. Vnde et homo. uel angelus dicitur aliqua facere. sed non creare. Vocaturque factor siue artifex. sed non creator. Hoc enim nomen soli deo proprie conuenit. qui et de nichilo quedam. et de aliquo aliqua facit. Ipse est ergo creator et opifex. et factor. Sed creationis nomen sibi proprie retinuit. Alia uero et cetera communicauit. In scriptura tamen sepe creator accipitur tanquam factor. et creare sicut facere sine distinctione significationis. Quod hec uerba. scilicet facere agere et huiusmodi non dicuntur de deo eam rationem qua dicuntur.
Verumtamen sciendum est. de creaturis. hec uerba. scilicet facere. creare. agere. et alia

I. Beda.

creatione

Vnum esse rerum principium ostendit non plura ut quidam putauerunt.

Strabus

Strabus. plato tria esse dixit principia.

Ex qua ratione dicitur proprie creator. et quid sit creare quid facere.

publish: a very diverse collection of ancient historical and literary texts sanctioned by divine authority and forming a vast and complex record of the Word of God. Of course, the Bible has been central to Christianity from the beginning. We have mentioned manuscript written at Wearmouth or Jarrow for Ceolfrith around AD.700 and those from the Carolingian court. But (with a very few distinguished exceptions) Bible manuscripts had been made up of several separate volumes, usually enormous in size, which were intended as vast monuments to be displayed on a lectern or altar in a church or in the refectory of a monastery. The monks of Reading Abbey had kept a two-volume Bible in the cloister, and a three-volume copy for use at meals. These volumes were not portable in the usual sense, and they were not designed for private study. Twelfth-century students of the Bible text (and naturally there were many) would make use of those twenty or so distinct volumes which made up a glossed Bible. Fundamentally, however, they regarded the Scriptures as a collection of separate texts, which could be read in any order. One studied the Psalms, or the Gospels, or the Minor Prophets, for example. Biblical scholars were known as 'Masters of the Sacred Page', a term which echoes this concept of the biblical corpus as the sum of a great many pages of Holy Writ rather than as a single book within two covers.

107 Paris, Bibliothèque Nationale MS.lat.11560, f.93v; Moralized Bible, Paris, c.1220.
The three volumes of this vast illustrated Bible (now divided between Paris, Oxford and London) include a total of over 13,000 miniatures.

108 (OPPOSITE, TOP) London, British Library, Add.MS.54235, f.577r; Bible, Paris c.1250–70.
This page shows the opening of the Interpretation of Hebrew Names in the version beginning 'Aaz apprehendens'.

109 (OPPOSITE, BOTTOM) London, Sotheby's, 11 December 1984, lot 37, ff.178v–179r; Bible, Paris, mid-thirteenth century.

Sometime in Paris in the late twelfth or early thirteenth century all this began to change. This is really very significant. The Bible was now put into a single volume. The order and names of the biblical books were standardized, the prologues ascribed to St. Jerome were inserted systematically, and the text was checked for accuracy as far as possible. For the first time the text was meticulously divided up into numbered chapters which are still in use today. The so-called *Interpretation of Hebrew Names*, an alphabetical dictionary of the Latin meanings of Hebrew proper names, was added at the end (Pl. 108). More important in the history of publishing are the changes to the physical appearance of the book. Scribes used the thinnest silky vellum. The pages became extremely small. They employed headings at the top of each page, little red and blue initials throughout the text to mark the beginning of each chapter, and the text was now written in black ink in a microscopic script in two columns. The effect was dramatic. The new type of Bible was an absolute best-seller (Pls. 109 and 112). These tiny manuscripts were evidently sold in vast numbers in the thirteenth century. They were produced in such huge quantities that copies served the needs of all the rest of the Middle Ages: fourteenth- and fifteenth-century Bibles are remarkably rare because the ubiquitous thirteenth-century copies must still have been easily available. Even now, these are by far the most common surviving books from the thirteenth century. More than that, the Bible design masterminded in the early thirteenth century has so fundamentally entered the subconsciousness of all of us that, even now, seven hundred years later, Bibles still look the same. Choose a traditional printed Bible from a good bookshop today. Look at its physical layout. It is on tissue-thin paper, very like the

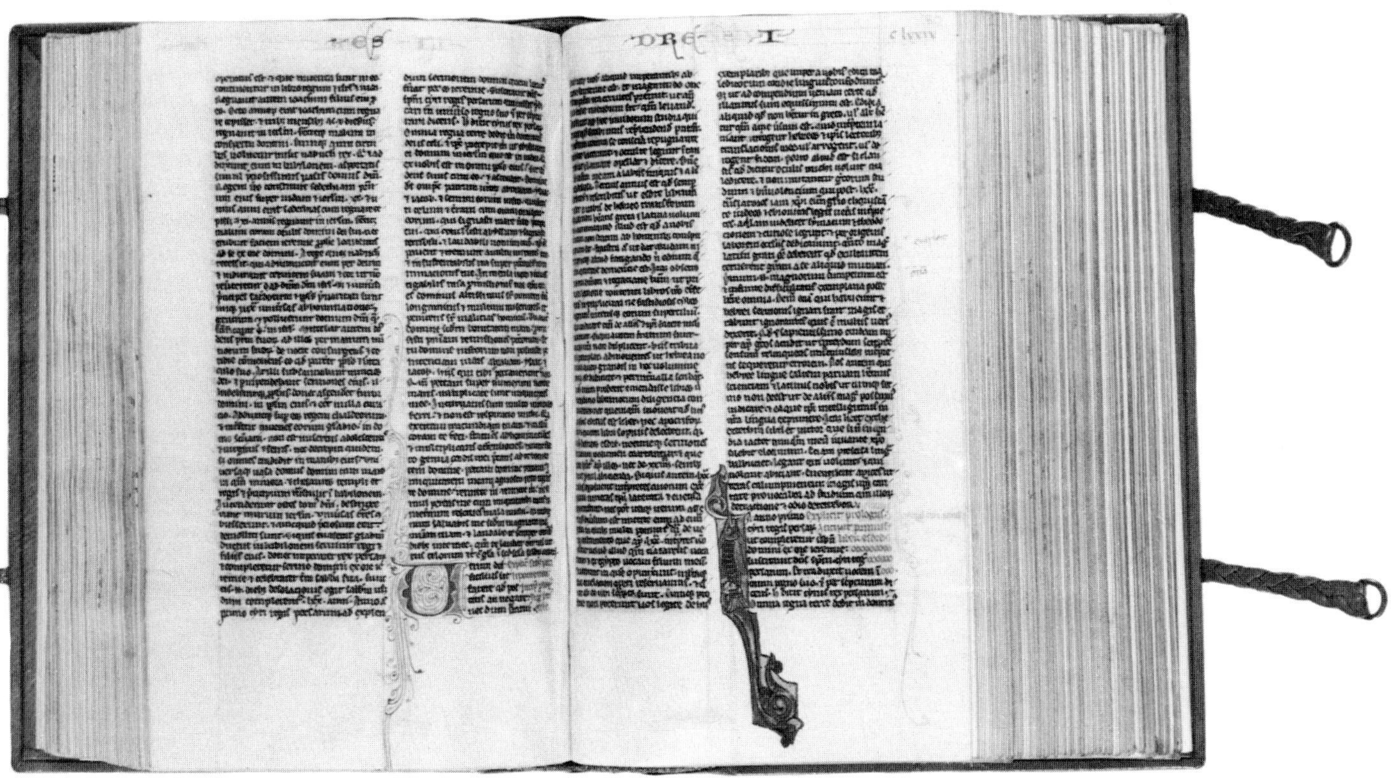

110 New York, Pierpont Morgan Library M.240, f.8r;
Moralized Bible, Paris, *c.*1220.
The Moralized Bible now divided between Toledo and New York may have been commissioned by Louis VIII (d.1226) and his wife Blanche of Castile, parents of Saint Louis. This miniature shows a king and queen enthroned and a cleric instructing a secular artist in the writing and painting of the manuscript.

111 (RIGHT) London, British Library, Harley MS.1527, f.27;
Moralized Bible, Paris, *c.*1220.
This copy of the Moralized Bible is from the same set as volumes now in Oxford and Paris (Pl.108).

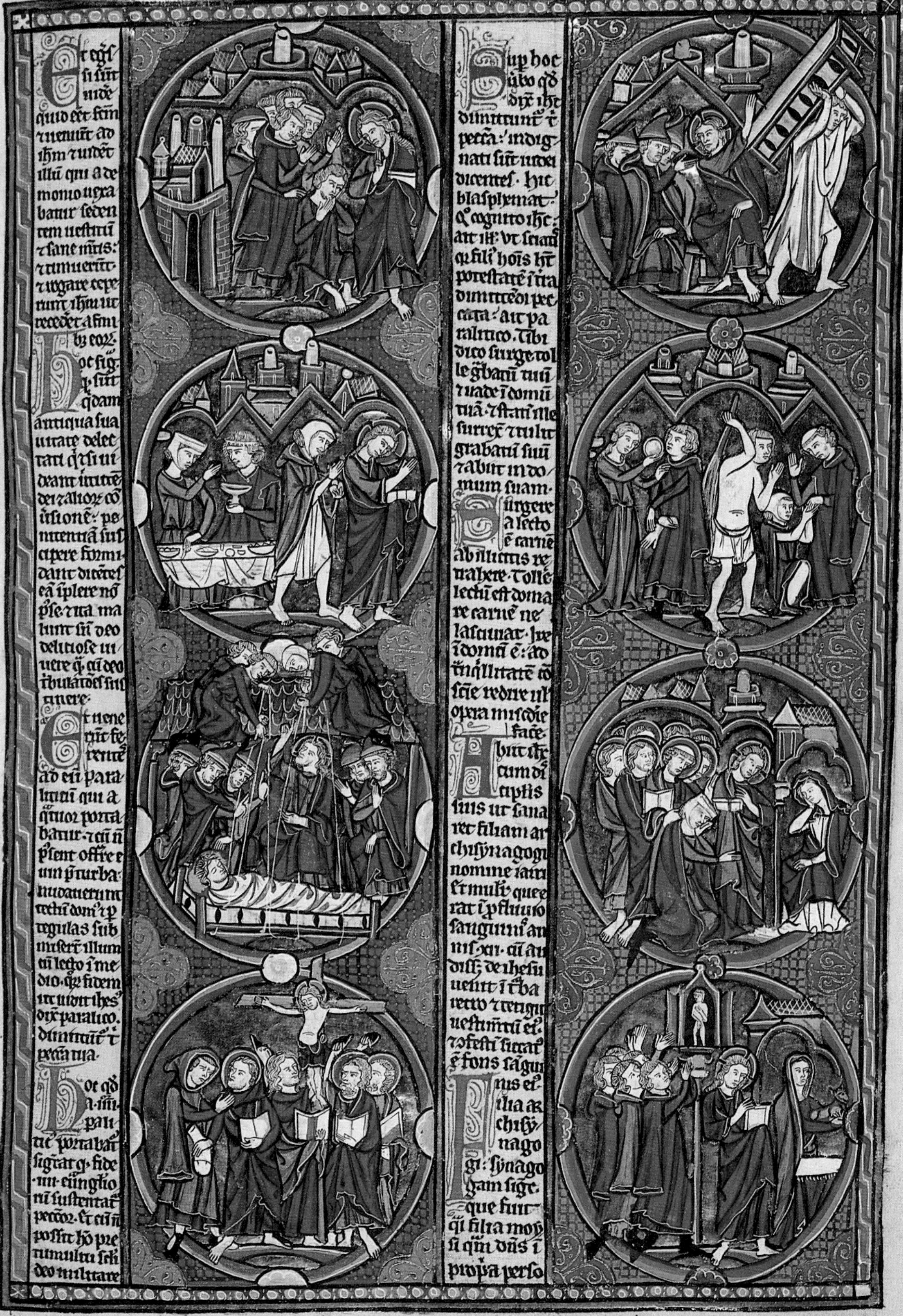

ascendat ad claustrũ · 7 sic sup̃ carnales uoluptates·

na saluare ueniat· mulier sanguinaria ypsum gentile ·e· que longo tempore ydolatrie fetore 7 carnis oblatione fedabatur·

112 Oxford, Wadham College MS. 1, f. 397v; Bible, Paris, 1244.
This Bible is dated 1244 and signed by the scribe Guillelmus, 'known as the knight of Paris' (f. 434v).

'uterine' vellum of the thirteenth century. It is probably octavo in size, like almost every thirteenth-century copy. It has the same order of biblical books, headings, the same division into chapters (with verses, not introduced until the sixteenth century) and – many centuries after this layout has been dropped from most other texts – it is in minute writing in two narrow columns. Look at the binding and the coloured edges. The chances are that the cover will look like leather and be black or red or blue: these are the three colours of thirteenth-century Parisian painting. It is hardly possible to find another object which was so new in 1200 and which is still made with so little modification today.

It is difficult to know exactly when this new form of Bible was devised. Thomas Becket owned a Bible in one volume which was shelved at Canterbury among glossed books and copies of Peter Lombard which Becket almost certainly brought from Paris in 1169–70. It may have been an extremely early example. Generally one-volume Bibles are very rare before about 1200, and unusual before about 1220. Probably the Paris masters contributed to the new format, and the name of Stephen Langton comes to mind. He was lecturing on the whole Bible in Paris from the early 1180s until 1206. The division of the Bible into chapters is usually ascribed to him. The earliest dated use of chapter numbers is in a manuscript of Stephen's commentary on the Minor Prophets made in 1203 (Troyes MS.1046). Probably he was one of those who helped transform the concept of the sacred page into that of the Bible as an entity, and Stephen Langton deserves even greater fame than is already accorded to him for drafting Magna Carta.

Some time in the second quarter of the thirteenth century the text of the Latin Bible was thoroughly revised in Paris and attempts were made to standardize the manuscripts. Roger Bacon, writing in about 1267, says this was done by the masters and stationers of Paris some forty years before. This takes us back to about 1227. Perhaps there were already some stationers in Paris by then but Roger Bacon was probably just trying to belittle the accuracy of the so-called modern text by implying commercial rather than exclusively academic motives. The suggested date, however, is very close to 1229, when the Dominicans opened their general theological school at St-Jacques in Paris. By 1236 they had their own list of corrections to the Bible text. The Dominicans are to be taken very seriously indeed when we are considering biblical scholarship and publishing in the thirteenth century. St. Dominic (1170–1221) had founded the Order of Preachers with the primary aim of teaching and confirming fundamental truths in order to resist heresy and to educate intellectuals in orthodox religion. The new universities had an important place in their campaign. The Dominicans set up their French headquarters in Paris in 1217, and in Italy at Bologna and in England at Oxford. Soon every major university town had a Dominican convent. The Dominicans had two reasons to welcome the publication of the new one-volume Bibles. First of all, Bible scholarship was at the heart of their teaching at St-Jacques in Paris, and men like Hugh of St. Cher and Thomas Aquinas himself, who both lectured there, were among the greatest biblical scholars of any age. All Dominican convents had a *lector*, whose duties included teaching the Bible. Secondly, the friars were preachers. They literally went out across Europe with the Word of God. The Bible was as useful as a Breviary (and the size of thirteenth-century Bibles may have been inspired by Breviaries). It was the ideal book for the preacher's satchel. Many-volumed folio Bibles were no use during a sermon: a preacher needed a copy he could carry. Many of the greatest publishing successes in history have been with very small books: Aldines, Elzevirs, and Penguins; the friars used the Paris Bibles because they fitted into a medieval pocket.

Not long after the Dominicans established themselves in Paris, the Franciscan friars came into prominence too and set up their own schools there in 1231. They too travelled widely, preaching as they went. The rivalry between the two orders can be exaggerated, and no doubt both groups used similar kinds of manuscript. As a generalization, however, the Dominicans zealously promoted traditional scholarship while the Franciscans tended to be concerned with more humble social problems and popular piety. St. Bonaventura, the great Franciscan theologian teaching in Paris between 1248 and 1257, remarked that the Dominicans put learning before holiness, but that the Franciscans put holiness before learning. Both orders of friars were important in the history of the university (Pl. 114). The Dominicans certainly wrote out some manuscripts themselves, and their constitutions of 1220–21, 1240, and 1243 stated that the prior might assign manuscript copying to any Dominican friar whose script was good enough. Often these must have been just sample sermons or other books for their own use. Perhaps they sometimes wrote out manuscripts for outside customers. The Franciscan General Council of 1260, however, specifically prohibited their friars from making books for sale. Franciscans were bound by a vow of poverty, and book production was dangerously profitable. A prohibition usually implies that the opposite is sometimes taking place. Some Dominicans and a few Franciscans were probably among those involved in making books in Paris in the thirteenth century.

By the mid-century the secular book trade was evidently taking over much of the business of producing manuscripts. A bookseller called Nicolaus Lombardus, for instance, appears in the tax lists for the district of Ste-Geneviève between 1239 and 1260. His surname makes one wonder if he was originally an Italian. He occurs again in a university document of August 1254 in which he stands as surety for Odelina, widow of Nicholas the Parchmenter (another colleague from the trade), who was selling her house between the law schools and the Mathurin Convent; the house was bought for £32 on behalf of the chancellor of Paris. We find his name too in a note in a manuscript (B.N. MS.lat.9085) which records that Gui de la Tour, bishop of Clermont (1250–86), had bought from Nicolaus Lombardus, 'venditor librorum', a whole set of glossed books of the Bible written out by a single scribe ('de una manu'), and that the bookseller undertook to supply one of the three remaining volumes by the feast of St. Remigius (19 January) and the other two by Easter or Pentecost, and that on the delivery date Gui would then trade in two other volumes in part exchange and pay over 40 Parisian pounds in money. There is a lot of information here. It tells us that the bookseller was the agent for commissioning new manuscripts. We learn that a single scribe was employed on one expensive commission for very many months, and that the customer paid the bookseller and not the scribe. The figure of £40 is now only about half the £70 which we calculated earlier as the theoretical price for the partial set of glossed books sold by Blavius in the first years of the century. It is, however, more than the price of the house where the late Nicholas the Parchmenter had lived. It is important that the price of Gui's manuscripts was propped up by two other manuscripts which the customer traded in to the bookseller. Clearly, therefore, Nicolaus Lombardus dealt in second-hand books too.

The fact that Gui de la Tour ordered a set to be written in a single hand suggests that the scribe was somehow in the bookseller's employment. A few thirteenth-century Parisian Bibles preserve the names of their scribes. One is dated 1244 and signed by William, 'known as the knight of Paris' ('dictus miles Parisiensis'; Wadham College, Oxford, MS.1;

Frater
filius filia
Nepos Neptis
GAUTIER·LEBAUBE·FIT·LABRE

113 (LEFT) New York, Pierpont Morgan Library G.37, f.11; table of consanguinity, Paris, mid-thirteenth century.
The two figures at the foot of the page hold a scroll with the name of the artist 'Gautier Lebaube fit labre' ('Gautier Lebaube made [the] tree'.)

114 (ABOVE) London, Estate of the late Major J. R. Abbey, JA.7345, detail of f. 1; Bible, Italy, perhaps Bologna, *c.*1262.
The miniatures at the foot of the first page of this Bible show SS. Dominic (1170–1221) and Francis (1181–1226) teaching their respective rules to order of friars.

Pl. 112). Another is dated on the *feast* of St. Leonard (6 November) 1267 and signed by frater Johannes Grusch (Sarnen, Collegium MS. 16). Was he a friar perhaps? A third is signed by Adam (B.N. MS.lat. 16748-9), who could be the Adam of St-Michel who is recorded in a scribbled note in B.N. MS.lat. 12950, f. 125v, as having written out a volume of Peter Lombard's *Sentences* in 1284. St-Michel is on the left bank opposite Notre-Dame, in the heart of the university. Sometimes specific illuminators can also be identified by name. Two mid-thirteenth century Parisian miniatures from a canon law manuscript, probably the *Decretum* of Gratian, are signed on a scroll with the name of Gautier Lebaube (Morgan Library G. 37; Pl. 113). The late Robert Branner ingeniously proposed that this artist was the 'Gualterus illuminator' who appears on the tax roll for the parish of Ste-Geneviève in 1243. Features of the artistic style include twisting vinestems, and one can note in passing that Gualterus paid 9 pence tax for owning a vineyard.

We began this chapter with the tale of the student squandering his allowance on illuminated manuscripts. By the mid-thirteenth century one can see how this happened. There were many professional illuminators in Paris. The surviving manuscripts are often beautifully ornamented and the gold really sparkles in the light. Whereas gold in monastic manuscripts had generally been applied flat onto the page, these thirteenth-century illuminators built up their initials underneath with gesso ('plaster of Paris', in fact) to achieve a highly burnished raised finish which sometimes looks like great droplets of golden mercury. The effect must have been very seductive to bibliophiles. Miniatures were in bright colours, predominantly red and blue, with clear black outlines. They look very like tiny stained-glass windows, both in colour and design.

Robert Branner's *Manuscript Painting in Paris during the Reign of St. Louis* (University of California, 1977) is the first serious attempt to classify the illuminators of thirteenth-century Paris acording to their styles of painting. The author shuffled a great many illuminated manuscripts into clusters which he cautiously termed 'workshops'. However this worked in practice (artists working from home, one imagines, perhaps with an apprentice or two in the attic), there was considerable business in manuscript decorating for the student market. One 'workshop' illuminated Bibles and liturgical books as well as three glossed books of the Bible, a Peter Lombard, two textbooks of civil law, and the *Decretals* of Gregory IX. Another workshop illuminated seven glossed books of the Bible, two copies of Peter Lombard, a Bible dated 1260, and a copy of Hugh of St. Cher. These were all the sort of books a student would need. Students with a hundred pounds to spend could acquire marvellous copies.

It is quite clear that by the mid-thirteenth century the University of Paris was drawing scholars and masters from all over Europe. Books go hand in hand with scholarship, in terms of both buying and writing. There were four principal areas of teaching. They all needed manuscripts. The first of these was the faculty of arts. This incorporated such subjects as grammar, logic, arithmetic, geometry (Pl. 115), music, and astronomy, and was formally recognized as a faculty in the area of Ste-Geneviève on the left bank in 1227. The district is still known as the Quartier Latin after the principal study. A statute of 1255 listed the books on which a master in the faculty of arts was required to lecture: they included Priscian for Latin grammar and a very substantial run of the Latin translations of Aristotle, including all the logical works, the *Physics, Metaphysics, On the Soul, On Animals,* and *On the Heaven and Earth*. The second faculty was law. This may have been one of the oldest disciplines in the Paris schools, to judge from surviving twelfth-century manuscripts of Gratian and from the story of Peter of Blois finding law books for sale. However, Paris never achieved in legal studies the reputation of Bologna or even Orléans, Angers, or Toulouse. The fact that many Paris students owned glossed law manuscripts which seem certainly to have been written in Italy (presumably Bologna) suggests that these books were imported into France ready made and that they did not form the stock-in-trade of the Paris scribes. Even the richly illuminated Sorbonne copy of Gratian (now Sorbonne MS. 30) is Italian work. The third faculty was medicine. Here we have a specific list of reading for students in the statutes of *c.* 1270–74. Medical students needed the compendious *Ars medicinae* collected by Constantinus Africanus (*c.* 1015–87) together with the *Viaticum* and the works of Isaac usually associated with it. They required the *Antidotarium* (a twelfth-century pharmaceutical textbook ascribed to Nicholas of Salerno) and they needed two unspecified volumes of *Theoretica* and *Practica.* A particularly finely illuminated Parisian manuscript of Constantinus Africanus' translation of Hippocrates (now Vienna Cod. 2315) is signed by the scribe Hugo Cappellarius, which literally means Hugh the Hatter. Perhaps he had two trades to tempt wealthy medical students. Finally there was in Paris the faculty of theology. This was the most prestigious course of study. The student spent six years as an undergraduate, four of them attending lectures on the Bible and two years studying the *Sentences* of Peter Lombard. He then became a bachelor of theology and proceeded to further biblical studies. It is hardly surprising that manuscripts of the Bible and of Peter Lombard are the most common surviving books from thirteenth-century Paris. They were actually used in the lecture room.

It is worth stressing too the influence of Aristotle's works in the literary life of the University of Paris. The enormous awakening of interest in Aristotelianism swept through the universities late in the first half of the thirteenth century. In fact, much of Aristotle was not unknown in the romanesque period (there had been a copy of the *Elenchi* and *Topica* in the twelfth-century Reading Abbey catalogue, for instance), but in the Latin translations of Gerard of Cremona, James of Venice, Michael Scot, and others, Aristotle's immense

115 Oxford, Corpus Christi College MS. 283, f. 165r; Euclid and other texts, Paris, *c.* 1266–77.
This mathematical manuscript was brought back from Paris by William de Clara who, in October 1277 at the age of 35, became a monk at St. Augustine's Abbey, Canterbury. It later belonged to the Elizabethan mathematician and astrologer John Dee (1527–1608).

equales magnitudines et perpendiculares equaliter se iacenti epipedo aliquotiens inequales aliquotiens inequales apparent.

epipedo. Ducantur linee recte ab a. ad b. et ab c. et sit oculus in medio c. ducantur due linee ad c. una veniat a termino a. ad e. alia a b. et ab d. ad e. ... [illegible] ... Iterum sit oculus in k. ducantur due linee una a termino h. alia a termino a. ... [illegible] ... maior an. h. ... [illegible] ... angulus est maior ... [illegible] ... et sic habes propositum.

84 Sunt loci quidam in quibus oculo posito inequales magnitudines in eodem spatio equales utrimque mensium apparent.

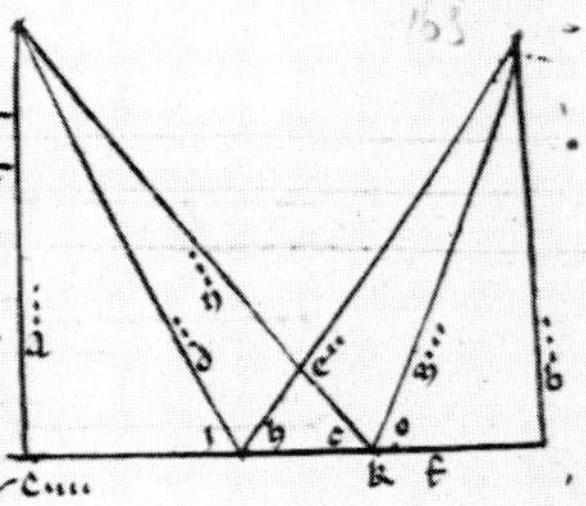

Sint a. et b. due magnitudines inequales constituantur due semicirculi ... [illegible] ... et ibi perveniant due linee ... [illegible]

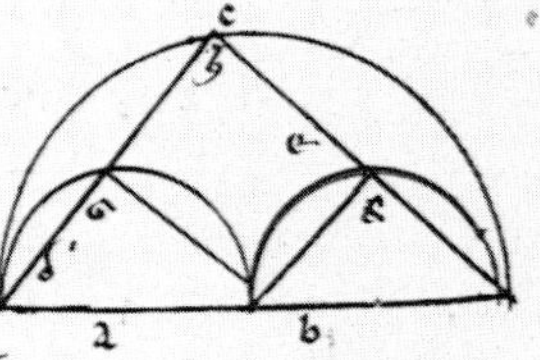

14 Invenire locos a quibus equalis magnitudo medietas apparet ut circa partes ut universaliter in fine in qua et angulus dividitur.

Esto a. magnitudo a. b. ... ducantur due linee ... [illegible] ... et sic de aliis ... angulus semper maior.

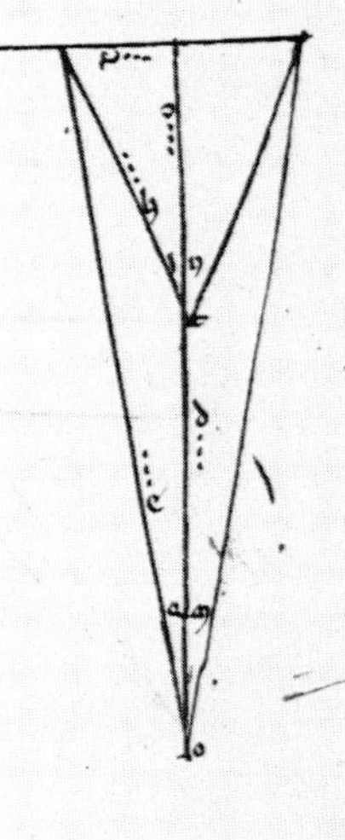

74 Equali celeritate latorum et super unam ad rectos ipsis existentium in easdem partes extremos habentium antecedentibus quod adiacet perceptionem equidistantem ducere quod remotius est videtur precedere id quod propius est. Non tamen mutantibus precedens eadem videtur subsequi quod non sic videtur precedere.

Esto a. ... et b. sint ... linee recte ... perpendiculares et una ... [illegible] ... moveantur eque velociter ... [illegible] ... et solida figura de facili patebit.

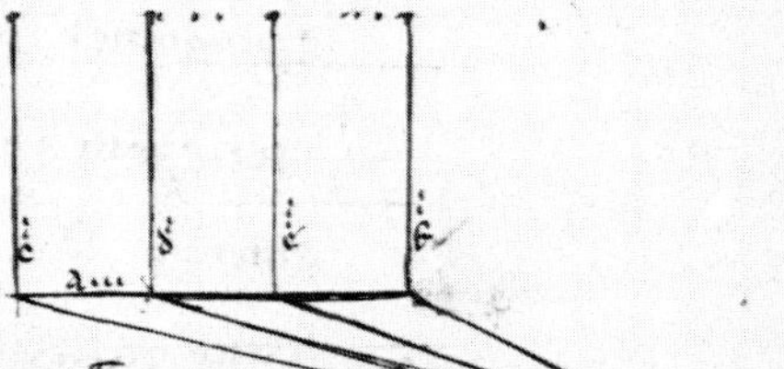

34 Si aliquibus latis et pluribus inequali celeritate transferentur in easdem partes et oculus quoque cum oculo equali celeritate

Sint a. et b. et c. tres quantitates ut plures. Et oculus d. et moveantur a. et b. et c. et d. in eandem partem ... d. movetur duplo velocius ... [illegible] ... dico quod illa que est equali celeritate moveri videtur stare ... [illegible] ... stare.

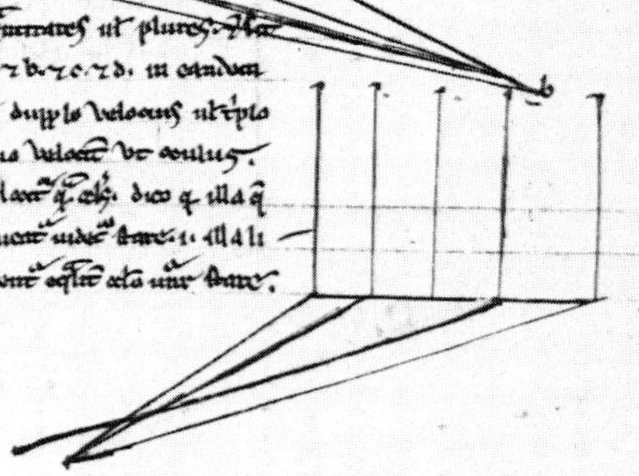

116 (LEFT) Oxford, Bodleian Library MS. Holkham misc. 47, f. 254r; Azzo, Summa, Bologna, late thirteenth century.
This is a richly illuminated Bolognese legal textbook with several miniatures signed by 'Maister gulielmo'. In the inner margin here, just above the miniature, is a pecia *note 'fi.xxv.pec': this means that the scribe had just finished copying the twenty-fifth piece of his hired exemplar.*

117 (RIGHT) Paris, Bibliothèque Nationale MS. lat. 14563, f. 1; Richard of Mediavilla, Commentary on the Sentences, Paris, early fourteenth century.
The initial shows the author, a Franciscan, lecturing to a group of friars. This manuscript belonged to the Abbey of St.-Victor in Paris and has their ownership inscription along the foot of the page.

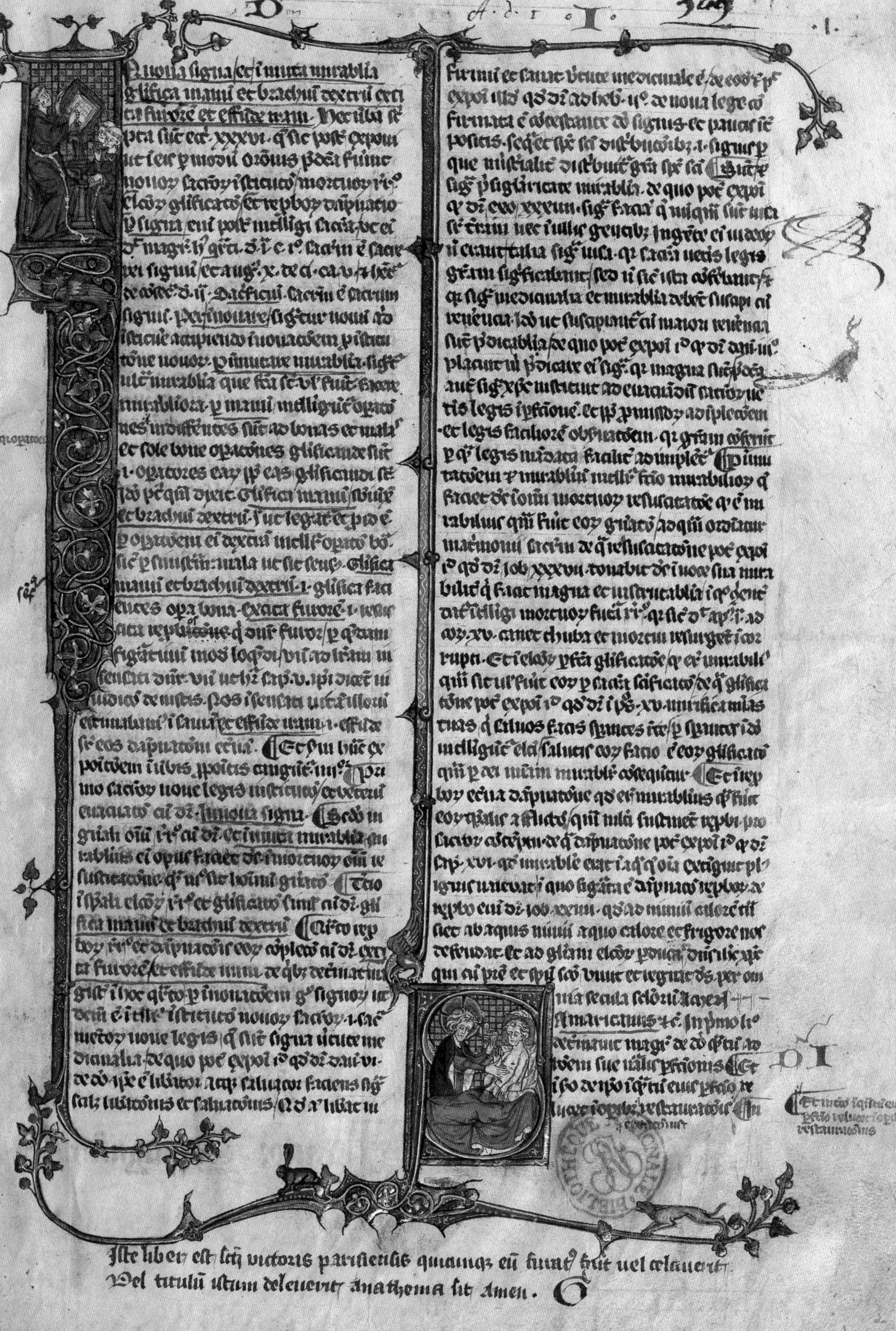

Iste liber est sci victoris parisiensis quicunqz eu furat fuit uel celauerit
Vel titulu istum deleuerit anathema sit Amen.

Et ille magnus textus est ypocratis qui eum scripsit in greca littera et post hoc quidam transtulit in latinum in hec verba

[Q]UI DE EGROTANTIUM accidentibus in singulis egritudinibus tractantes pocius consensisse ferunt eos quod in his qui tradiderunt invenisse quidem dubium non est. Potest etiam quivis non medicus quis id idem facere ut egrotantium accidentia percipiens denotaverit. Secundum eciam que cum his medico scire necesse est. ab se egri indicio nota fiunt: plurima intacta omiserunt.

Alia translatio verbi ypocratis

ILLI QUI SENTEN[TIAS]

[Qu]as illius de assidiis relatas scripserunt in eo quod scripserunt de accidentibus que in egris in unaquaque earum egritudinum accidunt non invenerunt. potuit autem fieri et sic invenire in eo et qui medicus non est. quod volo intelligere in unaquaque egritudinum illud quod ipse invenitur de infirmitatibus et cetera. aut quas medico necesse est scire cum iste preter quod infirmus ipse dicat ei: plurima dicere omiserunt. Sed intendit quod illa accidentia divisa sunt in egritudinibus divisis et quorundam eorum sollicitudo magnificatur in significatione.

Non solum cum scripserunt rememorati sunt sententias relatas illis de assidiis omiserunt aliquid dicere ex accidentibus que infirmis accidunt. immo invenimus eos dixisse de accidentibus plus quam oporteat: sed omnium fuit unum posse autem actio in non est opus prudentium in arte. Sed ut non dimittunt dicere aliquid de rebus quas vulgus scire potest. cum intentio prudentium in arte sua non est hec. sed ut sciliant totum quod est inveniendum in medicatione egritudinum donec ipsius in eius sit necessarium addere ad illud res quas omnes sciunt vulgi. et dimittunt rememorari res multarum ex illis quas ipsi sciunt cum videat quod in ipsis non est iuvamentum in fine artis.

Hoc quod in divisis egritudinibus diversi ex parte obscuris et intelligi difficiles habent significationem.

Quoniam illa accidentia divisa sunt in divisis egritudinibus et quorundam eorum magnificatur studium in significatione. Significatio est scientia sumpta ex significationibus. consueta autem utuntur hoc nomine scilicet significatio. sed per signa coniunctiva sicut omnia in quod exposui de accidentibus et significationibus. Dicit ergo ypocras de quibus ad quarum cognitionem et scientiam fit in hac scientia cognitio vel curatio in quibus iuvantur medici quod non omne invenitur scriptum in sententiis relatis illius de assidiis. sed diminuuntur in multis locis.

Secundum scientiam inoportuna in investigatione collecta discutiuntur in unitate morbi typo: non nulla ab eorum sententiis discrepantia poterunt inveniri. inveniri.

Et quando suscipiuntur res iste ad significationem. sicut in significatione unicuiusque egritudinis: tunc sciuntur ex eis res alie quam narraverunt illi.

Postquam dixit quod media qui fuit de illis de assidiis dimiserunt dicere res multas quibus fit iuvamentum in significatione: sequitur est illud et narravit illud per intentionem sermonis sui in significatione et dicit. sicut in sanatione cuiusque egritudinis. Quod quod omne quo fit iuvamentum in inventione sanationis egritudinis est exacte medici.

corpus of writings on logic, natural science, and philosophy became the starting point for new research not only in the arts but also in Christian theology. In essence what Aristotle provided was a method of academic argument. It was a way of systematically speculating on both sides of a proposition in order to reach a solution. A master would cite a whole series of authorities and linked arguments in favour of a hypothesis. He would then bring together another series of similar arguments in support of the opposite view. The conclusion then ingeniously redefines the original question and presents a logical solution. This may seem to us rather trite, but in the thirteenth century it was remarkably new (and, in the opinion of many, dangerously so) to argue out the case against Christianity, for instance, in order to reaffirm (and perhaps even to define more exactly) a fundamental truth. This became the scholastic method of argument. It can be applied to almost any proposition. The famous satirical example of the schoolmen debating how many angels could stand on the head of a pin may seem ridiculous (that was why it was invented) but it conceals an academic discipline which was enormously influential in a medieval university.

One fact that very clearly emerges from even a brief look at

118 (LEFT) Vienna, Österreichische Nationalbibliothek MS.2315, f.100v; Hippocrates, Liber Regimenti Acutorum, Paris, second half of the thirteenth century.
This is a medical text; the miniature shows two doctors discussing a patient.

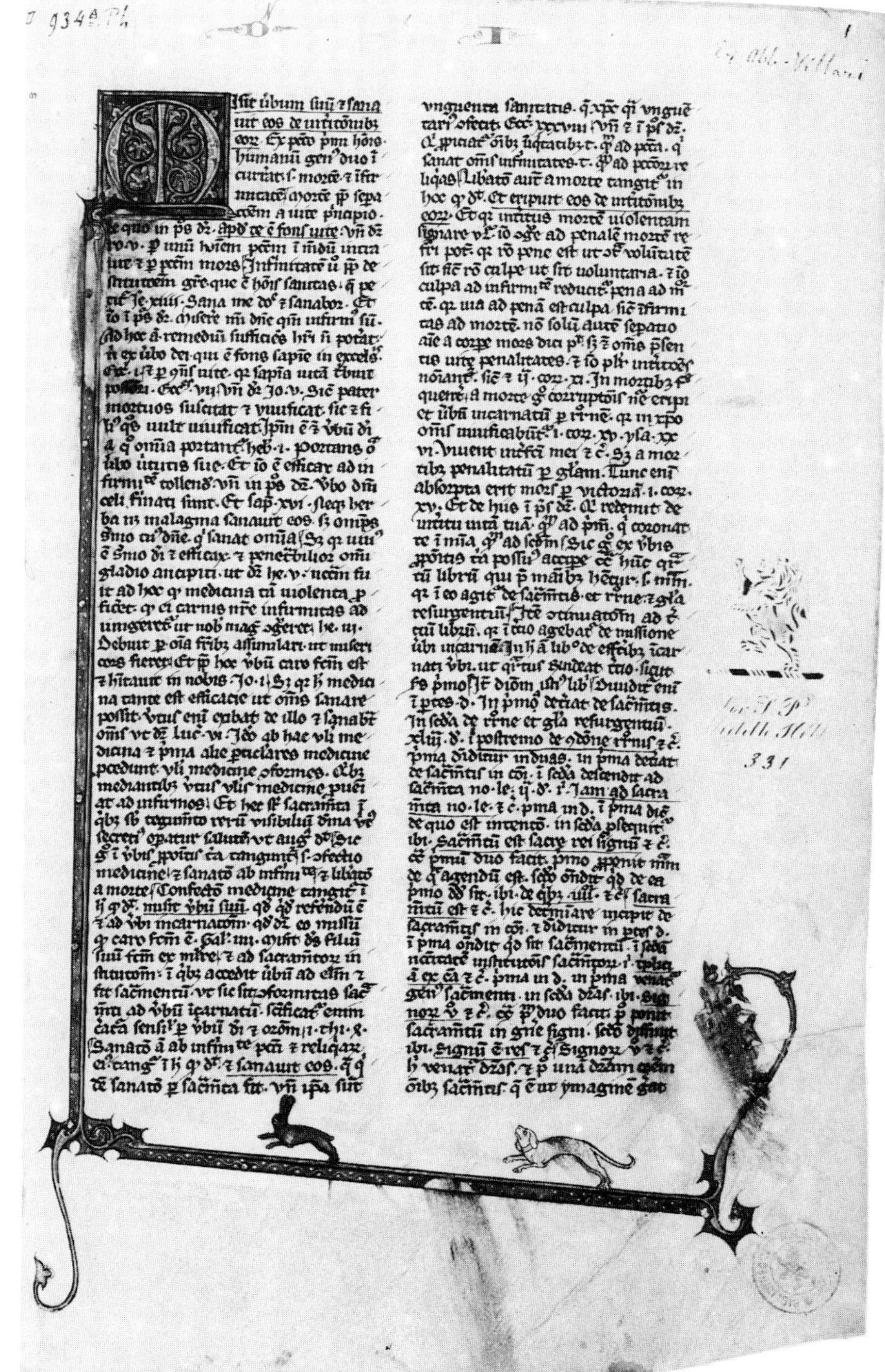

119 (RIGHT) Brussels, Bibliothèque Royale MS.II.934, f.1r; Thomas Aquinas, Commentary on the Sentences, Paris, 1286.
This manuscript is signed by the scribe Bernier de Nivelles and dated in Paris in 1286. It belonged to Sir Thomas Phillipps (1792–1872) and has his crest in the outer margin.

the book business in thirteenth-century Paris is the immense number of texts being published by members of the university. It seems as though everybody wanted to write a book. The wealth of scholastic commentaries on the *Sentences* of Peter Lombard, for example, is really daunting. The greatest author among them all was St. Thomas Aquinas (*c.* 1225–74), who taught at the Dominican convent of St-Jacques from 1252 to 1259 and from 1269 to 1272, and it was at Paris that much of his finest writing was done and from Paris that it was disseminated. His best-known work is the monumental *Summa Theologiae*, the vast corpus of theological knowledge, but his scholastic output included a commentary on the *Sentences* (composed at St-Jacques, 1252–57; Pl. 119), commentaries on Aristotle (Pl. 121), and the *Catena Aurea*, a Gospel commentary composed of a 'chain' of quotations from the Church Fathers. The fact that over 1900 manuscripts of works by Aquinas were listed by the Leonine Commission in 1973 attests to the author's immense popularity. It is only just exceeded by the 2200 manuscripts of Latin texts of Aristotle recorded in the census published in 1937 and 1961. The ultimate point of dissemination was the book trade in the schools of Paris.

But Thomas Aquinas was not alone in writing books for students. The Dominicans at St-Jacques included Hugh of St. Cher (*c.* 1190–1263), the great biblical commentator and philosopher Albertus Magnus (*c.* 1206–80), who was regent master in Paris from 1242 to 1248, Peter of Tarentaise, who taught from 1259 to 1264 and probably 1267 to 1269 and who died as Pope Innocent V in 1276, William of Moerbeke (*c.* 1215–86), the great Aristotle translator who was probably trained in Paris, Eckhart (*c.* 1260–1327), regent master 1311–13, and Durand of St. Pourçain (d. 1334). The Franciscans in Paris included the celebrated Alexander of Hales (d. 1245), Alexander's even greater pupil St. Bonaventura himself (1217–74), Richard of Mediavilla (d. 1300; Pl. 117), and later Duns Scotus and Nicholas of Lyra. Among the secular masters in the schools of Paris were prolific writers such as Peter of Poitiers, regent master 1167–1205, Simon of Tournai (d. *c.* 1203), Robert of Courçon (d. *c.* 1218), Stephen Langton, Philip the Chancellor (d. 1236), Odo of Châteauroux (d. 1273), William of Auvergne (d. 1249), William of St. Amour (d. 1272), Gerard of Abbeville (d. 1272), Henry of Ghent (d. 1293), and Arnold of Villeneuve (d. *c.* 1311). These are just a few selected from the faculty of theology only. Paris masters produced a tide of new texts, often long ones, and the problems of publishing them must have been stupendous for the newly founded book trade. 'Here ends the second part of the *Summa* of the Dominican brother Thomas Aquinas', wrote one scribe after 750 pages of closely written script, 'the longest, most verbose and most tedious to write; thank God, thank God and again thank God' (New College, Oxford, MS. 121, f. 376v).

How did they do it? How could so many massive texts be multiplied at comparative speed and without enormous expense? The answer is really very important, and it will take some detail to explain. They used what is known as the *pecia* system. It was very ingenious, and it was completely new. Briefly it worked as follows. From the second half of the thirteenth century, certain booksellers in Paris had a special title. They were known as university stationers. A stationer owned a great many specially made exemplars of university textbooks and these were kept unbound in loose gatherings. Each of the gatherings was numbered and known as a piece, or *pecia*. The stationer would hire out the *peciae* to scribes or students who wanted to copy the text. Because the pieces were separate, he could rent out a text to many customers at once and each could transcribe a different part of one exemplar. The scribe then had to bring back the *pecia* he had just copied and collect the next number in the sequence. In the meantime the one he had just returned could be hired out to another client. Thus a text of 312 leaves (for example) instead of being lent to one scribe for six months while he copied it out at the rate of twelve leaves a week (for instance), could be used to reproduce up to twenty-six identical copies during the same time and each one would be only one remove from the original exemplar.

This direct link with the exemplar is crucial too. Normally a manuscript book was copied one from another in a long chain of relationships which delight and dismay textual critics who record how a text gets more and more corrupt as scribes made little mistakes and unknowingly passed them on. Under the *pecia* system, however, there was only one occasion for error as every scribe had the master-copy before him.

A further essential aspect of the *pecia* method of publishing is that it was closely controlled by the university. Each year during the vacation a commission of masters would examine the stationers' exemplars for accuracy. If the majority (or at least six) of the *peciae* were found to contain errors, they had to be corrected at the stationer's expense. The commission would then issue an official list of texts available, with the titles of the approved *peciae*, the number of pieces in each, and the price for hiring them. Thus in the 1275 list, the earliest known, there is a copy of Aquinas's commentary on St. Matthew comprising fifty-seven pieces at a fixed rental of 3 *sous d'or* for the set. The same set was still available in the second surviving list dated 1304 but the price for hiring them had gone up to 4 *sous* for the set. This official list would be displayed publicly in the stationer's shop. The 1275 list offers 138 different texts and that of 1304 has 156 texts, many of them in the same *peciae* as the list of almost thirty years before. There was thus a considerable choice for the student visiting a bookshop.

The fundamental university regulations controlling the hire of *peciae* were published in the nineteenth century. The understanding of how the method worked in practice will forever be associated with the name of the indefatigable Jean Destrez (d. 1950), who spent his life systematically peering at

120 Oxford, New College MS. 288, second frontispiece; the Chaundler Manuscript, Oxford, *c.* 1461–65.
This is a late medieval view of New College in Oxford, founded in 1379, with the Fellows and members of the College in the foreground. The buildings in the main quadrangle shown here survive almost unchanged today.

121 Paris, Bibliothèque Nationale MS.lat.14706, f.122v; Thomas Aquinas, Commentary on the Metaphysics of Aristotle, Paris, late thirteenth century. *In the left-hand margin is a* pecia *note, 'xxxv.pe'.*

university textbooks of the thirteenth and fourteenth centuries. What he found was very remarkable. He noticed that at regular intervals in the margins of scholastic books were consecutive series of numbers sometimes with the letter 'p' or even 'pecia' in full (Pls.116 and 121), and that the totals of these often corresponded with the number of pieces in the university lists. What must have happened is that the scribe noted down the number of the *pecia* he was beginning to copy (or at Bologna, which we shall consider in a moment, which he had just finished copying). This would not only remind him which piece to ask for next when he returned to the stationer but might also serve as a way of assessing his payment, if he was a professional scribe. The marks are very valuable for us in localizing surviving manuscripts in the schools and particularly crucial for a modern editor anxious to get as close as he can to a correct version of an authentic text. By 1935 Destrez had inspected more than seven thousand university manuscripts and said that he found about a thousand with *pecia* markings of some sort; by the time of his death he had seen very many more. It is still a hope that one day Destrez's lists of these manuscripts will be published.

Very occasionally the sets of actual *peciae* still survive. These are the original numbered gatherings which the stationer hired out. At some time the stationer would have decided that a set was obsolete and so would bind it up like a book and sell it off cheaply. They are usually rather unattractive volumes on thick over-thumbed vellum. One example is B.N. MS.lat.3107, the actual set of fifty-seven *peciae* for Thomas Aquinas's *Summa contra Gentiles* dating from about 1300. Apparently some pieces in the set had got lost when it was in circulation and have been replaced by a different scribe. Perhaps this happened during one of the annual inspections as the volume is full of corrections too, some signed 'R' or 'Rad', presumably Radulphus. Another surviving manuscript, B.N. MS.lat.15816, is one of the contemporary copies taken by a client from this set of fifty-seven *peciae* when they were in circulation. It includes the *peciae* numbers which correspond with those on the separate sections of the original exemplar.

There are still many controversies about exactly how the *pecia* system operated. Mention of the subject is the quickest possible way of starting an argument among a party of palaeographers. One area of contention is the relationship between the author's final draft of a text and the pieces which the stationer lent out. This matters a great deal to a modern editor of a medieval text. Did an author take his newly written textbook round to a stationer (or did the stationer ask for it first, or did it have to be on some textbook list, or did a stationer just buy a copy in the trade?) and then what happened? Presumably the stationer would not want to hire out his only set and so one imagines that he prepared and retained an office copy. Was it this version or only the loose lending copies which were checked by the university? Despairing scholars have found that *pecia* manuscripts are often less accurate than one might have hoped. Something of the mechanics of thirteenth-century publishing emerges from Father P-M. J. Gils's work on Thomas Aquinas's commentary on the third book of the *Sentences*. This text was in circulation in Paris by 1272 but it was later revised by Aquinas himself. By remarkable good fortune the original set of *peciae* still survives in Spain, now bound up as a book (Pamplona Cathedral MS.51). It has actually been updated from the original text into the revised edition, presumably by the Dominicans at St-Jacques where Aquinas was living. It seems as though the stationer called in his old set of pieces for this text and literally sent them back to the author's convent for revision. The Pamplona Cathedral volume has the name of the stationer at the top of each of the numbered pieces, and he was called William of Sens.

Here the recent researches of Richard and Mary Rouse have been remarkable. They have traced a whole family of Parisian booksellers 'of Sens': Margaret, Andrew, Thomas, and William, who successively lived in the rue St-Jacques in the university quarter of Paris from before 1275 until at least 1342. It is important that their business was on the same side of the same street as the convent of St-Jacques itself. This must have been an ideal location for a shop which seems to have had an exceptionally good stock of Dominican texts and which was perhaps somehow involved in the publication of Thomas Aquinas. The friars only had to walk a few paces from their convent to the bookshop. It is not surprising, therefore, to find William of Sens updating his *peciae* of Thomas Aquinas as soon as the new version was available.

The question of when the *pecia* system began is complicated by Italian documents which hint at some kind of hiring out of exemplars in the universities there as far back as 1228. In fact, however, the earliest datable surviving manuscript with *pecia* numbers seems to be the copy of Hugh of St. Cher on the Pauline Epistles, which was bequeathed to Durham Cathedral by Bertram of Middleton who died in 1258 (Durham MS.A.I.16). Therefore the *pecia* method was in operation by that year at the very latest. The author was another Paris Dominican and the book is certainly a Parisian copy. It is extraordinarily difficult to follow the *pecia* method back any earlier than the circle of the masters from St-Jacques in the mid-thirteenth century.

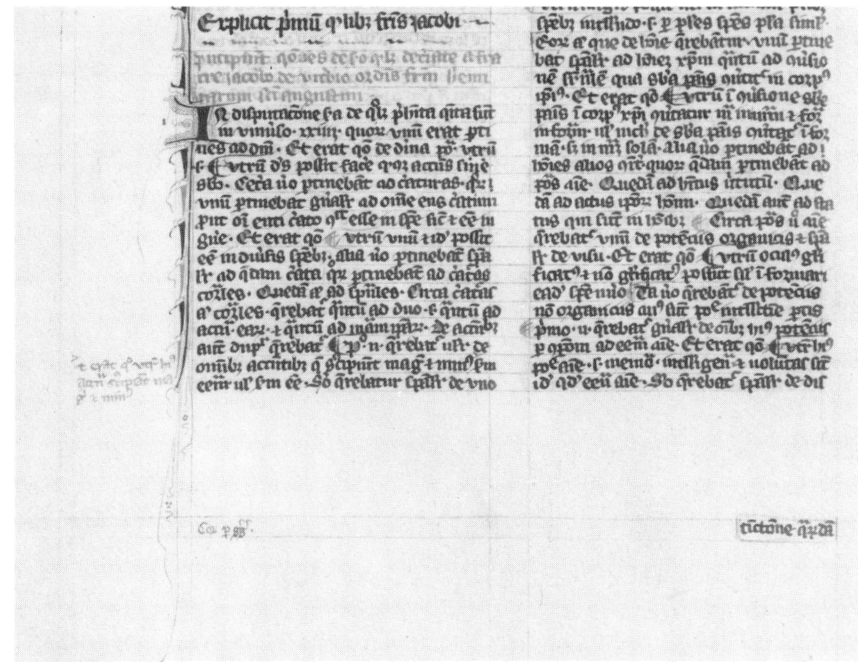

122 Paris, Bibliothèque Nationale MS.lat.15362, detail of f.36v; Jacques de Viterbe, Quodlibeta, Paris, *c.*1293–4. *This manuscript has been checked for accuracy: at the bottom of the last page of each quire is a note 'Cor per gg. (corrected by Gg', perhaps Gregorius). It was bequeathed to the library of the Sorbonne by Pierre de Limoges (d.1306).*

By 1300 the Parisian book trade was thoroughly organized, efficient, and under full control of the university. Even the sale of vellum was under the strict supervision of four official university assessors. There were regulations in 1316 requiring booksellers to take an oath of allegiance to the university and laying down guide-lines on the hiring out of *peciae* and restricting the profit on the sale of second-hand books. There were blacklists of those who refused to subscribe. Booksellers benefited from coming under university control not only because of the business advantage in official recognition but also, quite simply, because after 1307 membership of the university provided exemption from taxation. This was no doubt a huge bonus to members of the book trade. It is a disadvantage for us in trying to identify who made books, because their names and addresses disappear from the surviving tax rolls.

As it happens, one way and another we know a fair amount about the personnel of the book trade in Paris around 1300. Thus there is a record, for example, of Geoffroi de St-Ligier both in the stationers' oath list of 1316 (when his shop was in the rue Neuve in front of Notre-Dame Cathedral) and in a manuscript he must have sold, Ste-Geneviève MS.22, a richly illustrated *Bible historiale* with Geoffroi's name on ff. 37v and 56r. The names of very few scribes have come down to us. Probably they were very often students making books for their own use or supplementing their allowances with extra pocket money. Pierre Giraut is one on the tax lists of 1297–1300. The names of illuminators are not at all rare in the tax rolls. About forty-five are known by name in the decade or so around 1300, including several women. Sometimes they had other trades too, such as Estienne le Roy and Enart de St-Martin, who were both illuminators and bookbinders (*c.*1297–1300), Gilbert l'Englais, who was an illuminator and lawyer (1292–1300), and Thomasse, a woman illuminator and innkeeper in 1313. Jehan d'Orli, who had been an illuminator and innkeeper in 1297, devoted himself entirely to his second profession in 1298–1300. Probably it was more profitable. The image of a man selling pints of beer while decorating manuscripts is very appealing, and perhaps not ridiculous. An inn was a good place for students to congregate too.

So far in this chapter we have been looking exclusively at the University of Paris. This is deliberate. Not only was Paris the most international of the medieval universities but probably too it was the innovator in the great advances of the book trade: the devising and marketing of pocket Bibles, the establishment of organized bookshops, and the publishing of textbooks by the *pecia* method. But Paris was certainly not the only place where students needed books. Bologna must undoubtedly have been the second most important city in Europe for the production of books in the thirteenth century. It too had bookshops and a trade controlled by the university. It too made one-volume Bibles, and textbooks with *pecia* marks. The university there was probably older than Paris, and it was second to none in the Middle Ages for the study of law. There were law schools in Bologna from at least 1100, traditionally associated with Irnerius who was perhaps teaching as early as 1088. By the late twelfth century Bologna had an international reputation for legal studies (Pl.123). As Paris published theology, so Bologna published law.

There were two fundamental categories of legal studies in the Middle Ages. Both were taught at Bologna. Both

123 West Berlin, Staatliche Museen Preussischer Kulturbesitz, Kupferstichkabinett, min.1233; cutting from a manuscript, Bologna, fourteenth century.
This miniature, signed by the artist Laurentius de Volterra, shows Henricus de Allemania lecturing to his students in Bologna.

124 (RIGHT) Oxford, Bodleian Library MS.Lat.th.b.4, f.168r; the Decretals of Gregory IX with the gloss of Bernard of Parma, Bologna, 1241.
The scribe Leonardus de Gropis of Modena records that he finished this manuscript on Wednesday, 12 July 1241. The gloss itself has been glossed by a contemporary reader, possibly during lectures.

125 (LEFT) New York, Pierpont Morgan Library M.821; cutting from a manuscript of Decretals, Bologna, *c.*1330.
This miniature shows the laity studying manuscripts of the Decretals of Boniface VIII *and listening, like the doctors in the Temple of Jerusalem, to the wisdom of Christ.*

126 (RIGHT) London, British Library, Harley MS.531, ff.11v–12r; Johannes de Sacrobosco, Algorismus, etc., England (possibly Cambridge), 1272.
The reputation of Cambridge for science can be traced back to the Middle Ages. This manuscript was certainly in Cambridge by the fifteenth century and may have been written there.

provided manuscripts. The first was civil (or secular) law, and the second was canon (or ecclesiastical) law. Written civil law went back to the great code assembled for the Emperor Justinian in the sixth century. It is made up of extracts from ancient Roman law and legal textbooks and was supplemented in Justinian's lifetime by additions known as the *Novellae*, the *Digest*, and the *Institutes*. All these together formed the corpus of civil law. Manuscripts are enormous in size, often include commentaries by Bolognese masters (Pl.116), and mostly date from the thirteenth and fourteenth centuries.

By contrast, canon law was entirely medieval in origin. Its basic encyclopaedia was the *Decretum*, or *Concordantia Discordantium Canonum*, of Gratian, an otherwise almost unknown Camaldolese monk working about 1140 in Bologna. It is a textbook which became a best-seller. It was like Peter Lombard's *Sentences* in that it organized information under subject headings, and for centuries it was the most popular student guide to canon law. It is not a book of laws as such. This was the role of the *Decretals*. These were official collections of papal and episcopal letters which actually laid down Church law on specific subjects. *Decretals* could be enforced in the Church courts. They are all associated with names of popes. The first are known as the *Decretals* of Gregory IX (Pl.124), and were compiled in 1234, probably by the Dominican Raymond of Peñafort (1185–1275). They were supplemented by two further sets of *Decretals*, those of Boniface VIII in 1928 (Pl.125) and of Clement V in 1317.

The three comprised the corpus of canon law. *Decretals* were dispatched by the papacy to the universities of Bologna and Paris with the command that the text should be taught in the schools. There could be no greater compliment to manuscript production in Bologna and Paris than this papal confidence in the publishing skills of those two universities.

In fact, Bologna largely cornered the market in legal manuscripts and there were 119 civil and canon law texts on the Bolognese *pecia* list of the first half of the fourteenth century. Manuscripts were published with marginal commentaries by masters of the law faculty there such as Bernard of Parma (d. 1263) and Giovanni d'Andrea (d. 1348). With the commentaries, these were huge manuscripts. It is said that students would walk into the lecture hall followed by servants carrying these heavy volumes. Perhaps the Bolognese scribes liked large books (unlike those of Paris) since the only other substantial category of manuscripts ascribed to that city before about 1300 are choirbooks, also huge. In the thirteenth century at least, the business of illuminating textbooks was not as well organized in Bologna as in Paris. The student who in the story wasted his money on books was given by his father a choice of going to Paris or to Bologna; he chose Paris. Dante mentions one Bolognese illuminator, Oderisi da Gubbio (recorded 1268–71, in fact), who excelled (wrote Dante, *Purgatorio* XI:80–81) in that art which in Paris is called illumination. Paris had the reputation, quite clearly. It seems to have been not uncommon to make and export Bolognese legal manuscripts with the illumination left blank. When the volumes were remarketed through the book trade of the northern universities the miniatures would be added. It would be fascinating to know exactly how this happened. Bodleian MS. Laud Misc. 307 is an early fourteenth-century *Decretals* collection in Italian script with *pecia* marks, but its miniatures are French, perhaps Parisian. B. L. Royal MS. 10. E. IV is a copy of the *Decretals* of Gregory IX with the prologue addressed to the University of Paris, but the script is Italian and the miniatures are English: one could imagine that it might have been written at Bologna, sold in Paris, and illuminated in Oxford.

In England before the fifteenth century, Oxford was the only university of importance. Of course Cambridge had existed from the thirteenth century but it is incredibly difficult to point to any manuscripts certainly made there. B. L. Harley MS. 531 is a volume of scientific texts by Sacrobosco dated

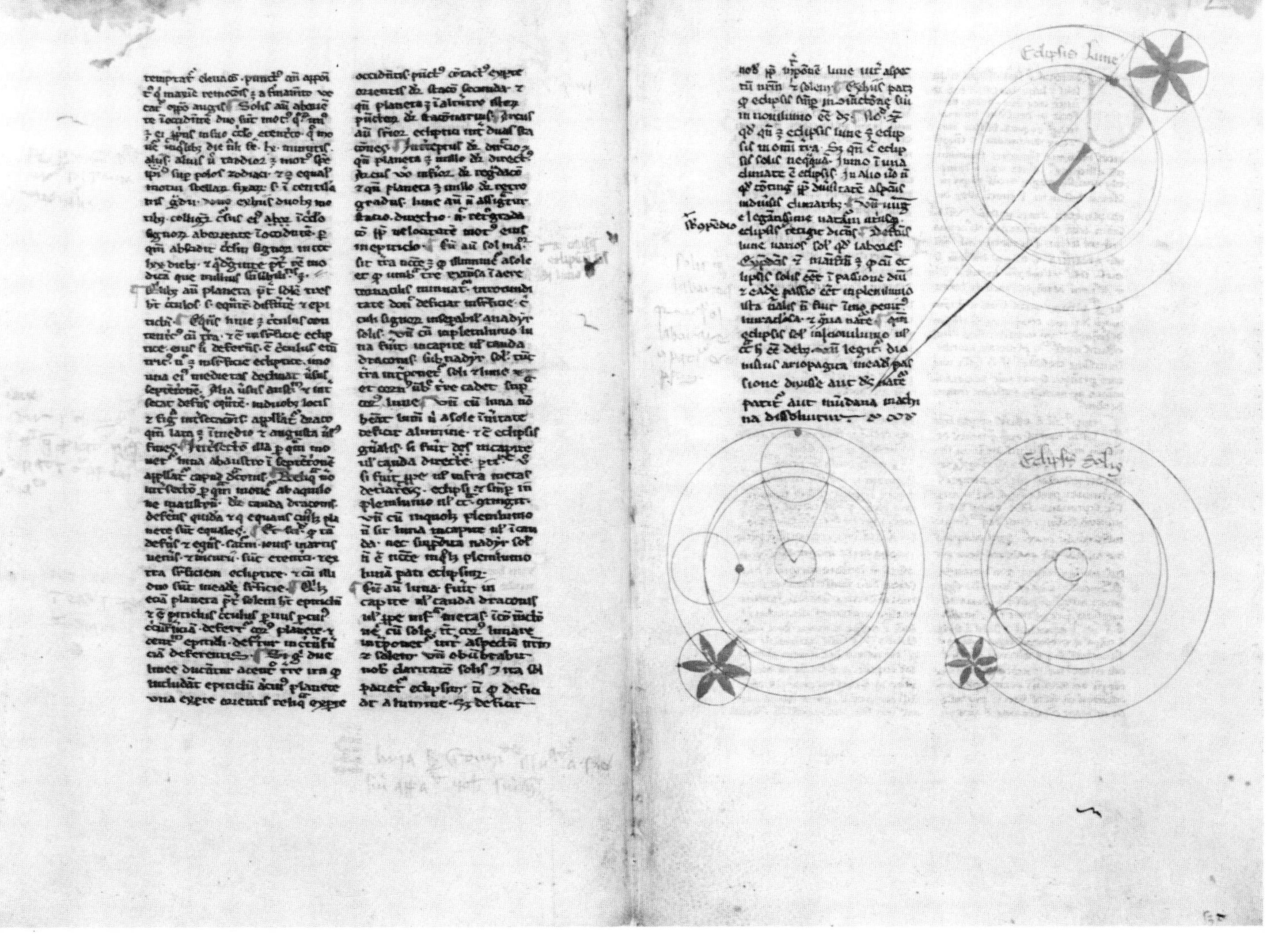

1272 (Pl. 126): it was certainly in Cambridge by the fifteenth century but whether it had been written there is a different question. Oxford, however, had many of the attributes of a university book trade: one-volume Bibles, stationers of some sort, and possibly (not certainly) the *pecia* system. Even now Oxford is known for publishing books. One of the first pieces of evidence for the existence of Oxford, in fact, is a late twelfth-century charter witnessed by a bookbinder, a scribe, two vellum-makers, and three illuminators. One Oxford manuscript is dated 1212, which is remarkably early (B.N. MS.fr.24766; Pl. 128). It may be that Walters Art Gallery MS.W.15 is as old: it is a glossed Gospel Book with added legal formularies which have been plausibly ascribed to Oxford in 1202–09. By the middle third of the century we have a good clutch of surviving manuscripts illuminated (and two of them signed) by William de Brailes (Pl. 127), who is documented in Catte Street in Oxford between about 1230 and 1260, including a Bible possibly as old as 1234 (Bodleian MS. Lat. bibl. e. 7). There are other illuminators recorded in Oxford at this time too, including Robert, Job, Walter of Eynsham, Robert de Derbi, and Reginald. A set of glossed books of the Bible may be the work of Reginald, who (Mr. Graham Pollard discovered) lived at no. 94 High Street with his wife Agnes between about 1246 and 1270. The manuscripts are B.L. Royal MSS. 3. E. I–V and the last volume includes a note (f. 102v) that a defective gathering was given to Reginald at Oxford to continue. Furthermore, someone (presumably the illuminator) has added up exactly how much decoration has been supplied for the book. He counts a total of 12,406 little initials and paragraph-marks and 1453 large initials. Clearly he expected payment by the initial. Here is really a student manuscript frivolously decorated.

We can conclude this survey of books for students with a glance at one Oxford manuscript of the end of the Middle Ages. It must stand as the most extreme example of a basic textbook produced in haste (no doubt) and inexpensively in the very midst of a university, bypassing the stationers and the book trade. It is Eton College MS. 44, a copy of the commentary of Albertus Magnus on SS. Luke and Mark,

127 London, British Library, Add. MS. 49999, f. 1; Book of Hours, Oxford, mid-thirteenth century.
William de Brailes, the illuminator of this manuscript, is documented as living in Catte Street in Oxford, the street where the Bodleian Library now stands, between about 1230 and 1260.

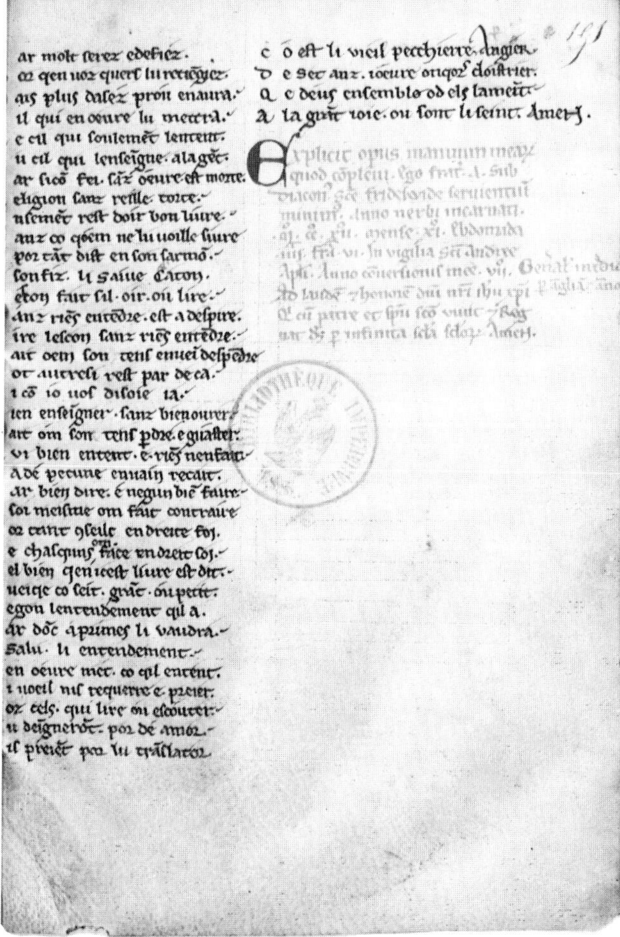

128 Paris, Bibliothèque Nationale MS. fr. 24766, f. 151v; St. Gregory in French verse, Oxford, 1212.
This manuscript was completed by the subdeacon of St. Frideswide's Priory in Oxford on 29 November 1212, the earliest surviving dated Oxford manuscript.

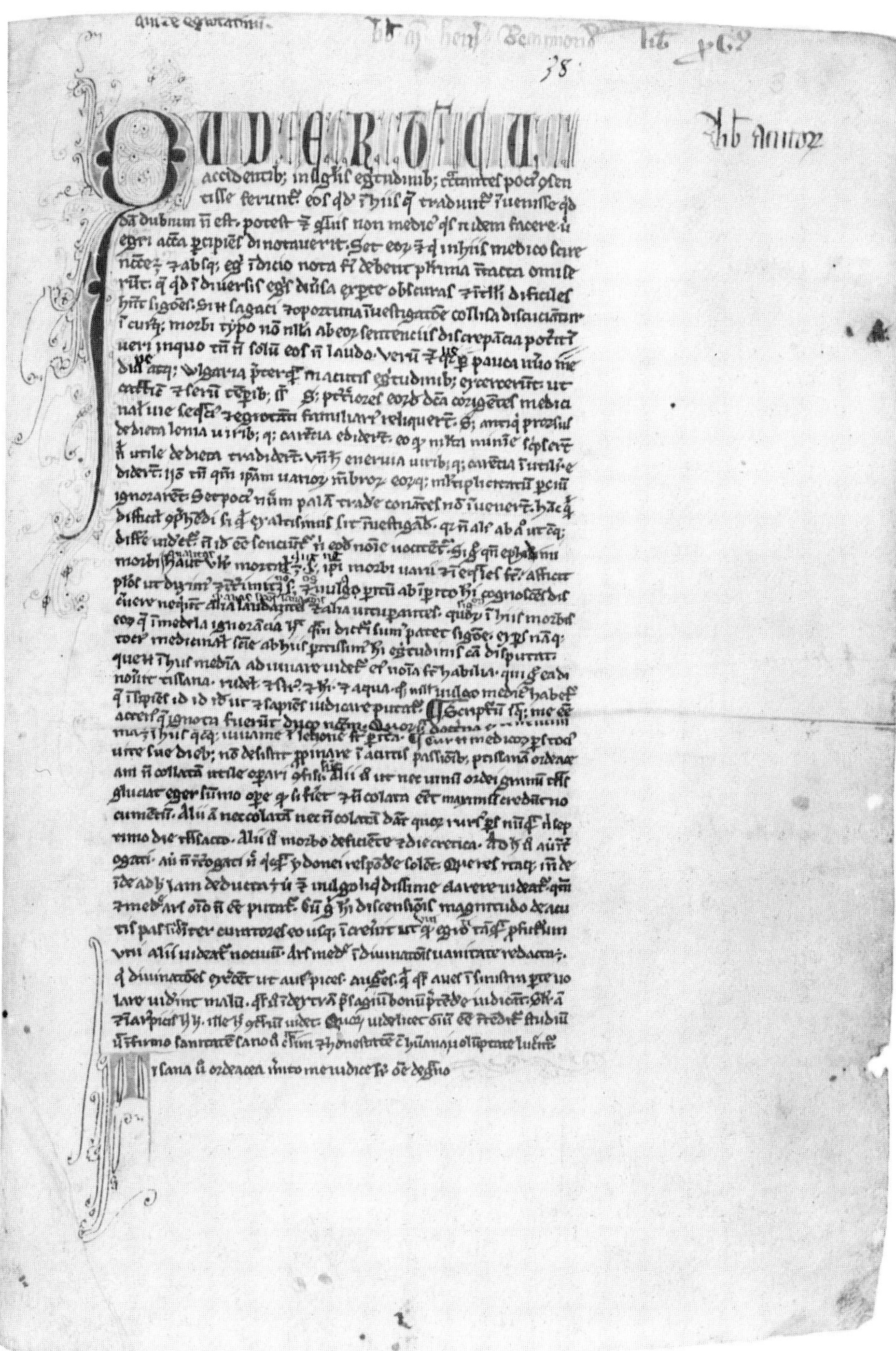

129 Oxford, New College MS. 166, f. 3r; Hippocrates, Liber Regimenti Acutorum, England (presumably Oxford), late thirteenth century.
This is one of two anthologies of medical textbooks which belonged to Henry Beaumont (d. 1415), a Fellow of Exeter College in Oxford in 1372. A Parisian manuscript of the same text is illustrated in Pl. 118.

written about 1480. In fact we even know the manuscript it was copied from, Balliol MS. 187. The extraordinary feature of the Eton volume is that it was a collaborative effort by approximately fifty-three different scribes. They all seem to have come from New College, Oxford. Of the thirteen scribes who signed their names, ten were Fellows of the college and all had been at school together in Winchester. They mostly came up to Oxford in the late 1470s. One had been the school chaplain. They were all of course amateur scribes, students contributing to copying out a book, and no doubt they worked in New College itself. The manuscript is a reminder to us that books are made in universities and (despite all the professionalism of the book trade) students are first and last the reason for university manuscripts.

·5·

Books for Aristocrats

Emperors and kings, dukes and marquises, counts, knights, townsfolk . . . take this book and have it read to you.' With these words Marco Polo addresses his audience and begins his account of a journey across the world in the second half of the thirteenth century, a tale which introduces Genghis Khan, Prester John, the One-Eyed Cobbler, and the Wrestling Princess, as well as his historically accurate description of the almost unknown world he had seen between Venice and China. The emperors and kings, to whom the book was supposed to be read, must have felt that the whole story sounded like a romance. One of the finest Marco Polo manuscripts, made about 1400, was bound up with Bodleian MS. Bodley 264, an Alexander romance dated 1338. It has a famous miniature of Marco Polo about to sail from Venice, which is shown like the backdrop of a pageant on a sunny day with bridges, flags, boats, swans, islands, and little groups of richly dressed citizens hurrying along cobbled streets or standing, talking, or waving. The reminiscences of the shrewd Venetian merchant were transformed by scribes and illuminators into a text to be enjoyed by the rich with stories of Alexander the Great, Charlemagne, and King Arthur. Many listeners must have enjoyed Marco Polo as fiction. King Charles V of France owned five copies, one of them bound in a cloth of gold.

Marco Polo's book describes his adventures on an incredible voyage. A journey or a pilgrimage is the setting of much medieval fictional narrative. Travelling was slow in the Middle Ages and often adventurous. It also provided occasion for travellers to pass the time by singing and telling stories, and this in itself contributed something to the rise of literature. This chapter, which concerns fiction and romance, will take us along the pilgrim road through France to the shrine of St. James of Compostella, to the Crusades and back, up the waterways of the Rhine and into northern Europe and unsteadily out into the north Atlantic in wooden boats, and safely in April from London along the pilgrims' way to Canterbury.

Elements of vernacular literature go back to campfires and taverns, centuries before anything was written down. The word *Edda* in Icelandic means 'great-grandmother', a name evocative of a distant past. The *jongleurs* of France were certainly singing and dancing from time immemorial. Their name has the same derivation as 'juggler' in English, and entertainers and acrobats belong to a profession far older than that of manuscript illumination. The *troubadours* of Provence were chanting their songs of love and heroism long before these were first recorded in the twelfth century. As wayfarers passed through southern France, they must have picked up

130 (LEFT) Oxford, Bodleian Library MS. Holkham misc. 49, detail of f. 5r; Boccaccio, Decameron, Ferrara, 1467.
The miniature at the foot of the first page of text shows youths entering the church to Santa Maria Novella in Florence where a group of girls are sheltering from the plague. The stories they tell to pass the time make up the Decameron. This manuscript was made in 1467 for Teofilo Calcagnini in the Este court in Ferrara.

131 (RIGHT) London, British Library, Add. MS. 24189, f. 8r; Sir John Mandeville, Travels, Bohemia, early fifteenth century.
This scene from Mandeville's fictional journey to the Far East shows the travellers sailing into Syria and paying a landing tax to the local customs officers.

132 Paris, Bibliothèque Nationale MS.fr.782, detail of f.2v; Benoit de Ste-Maure, Roman de Troie, Italy, early fourteenth century. *A whole cupboard of Trojan romances is illustrated in this miniature of Cornelius, nephew of Sallust, who is said to have discovered the books while looking for a grammar.*

wandering minstrels or listened to their songs on the journey. Pilgrims from northern Europe travelling to Compostella in Spain came past the tomb of the Carolingian hero, Roland, who was buried at the foot of the Pyrenees, and they crossed the pass at Roncevaux where Roland and his troops were said to have been killed by the Saracens in the eighth century. Of course travellers were shown these sites and they heard the *chansons de geste*, the songs of deeds, recited by professional entertainers. When someone wrote it down, then the *Chanson de Roland* became literature. There are fewer than ten surviving manuscripts and fragments of the *Chanson de Roland* (despite its enormous fame now as the greatest *chanson de geste*) and they are all unillustrated, except for one copy in Venice with a small initial showing Charlemagne. The oldest manuscript (Bodleian MS.Digby 23) was made in England in the twelfth century – perhaps even within the first half of the century though this is highly controversial – and it is an unassuming little manuscript, suitable for a minstrel's wallet. Even the fact that it is English shows how far the story had travelled.

Some Charlemagne romances probably crossed Europe with the crusaders who no doubt enjoyed singing of legendary heroes conquering the infidel. The *Chanson d'Aspremont* was apparently composed in Sicily or the far south of Italy, and it was known to the knights of Philip Augustus and Richard the Lion Heart spending the long winter of 1190–91 camping in Sicily before setting sail on the final leg of the ill-fated Third Crusade against Saladin. The *Chanson* concerns Charlemagne and his allies in Italy crossing the mountainous 'Aspremont' in the Apennines to march against the Saracen king Agolant. Crusaders must have found it easy to identify themselves with the heroes of the story. One of the earliest manuscripts of the *Chanson d'Aspremont* is English in origin (B.L. Lansdowne MS.782) and dates from about 1240–50. It has forty-five coloured drawings of rather home-made quality. The same workshop probably illustrated another romance on the life and travels of Alexander the Great, Thomas of Kent's *Roman de Toute Chevalerie* (Trinity College, Cambridge, MS.O.9.34), which has 152 coloured drawings of knights and battles. It is easy to imagine returned soldiers ordering illustrations for these old songs in order to demonstrate to admiring relatives at home the valour of holy warfare.

The movement of legends went the other way too. Modena Cathedral in northern Italy has carvings of the very early twelfth century showing King Arthur of Britain and his knights rescuing Winlogee (a variant of Guinevere) from the wicked knight Mardoc. The twelfth-century mosaics in Otranto Cathedral in the extreme south-eastern tip of Italy depict 'rex Arturus' among the famous men of the past, such as Noah and Alexander the Great. Some British traveller had brought songs and tales to Italy. In France the twelfth-century poet Chrétien de Troyes began to collect the Arthurian stories told (as he says) at the royal court and to write some of the earliest French poems on the Holy Grail and on Lancelot. Something over thirty manuscripts (at least half of them in the Bibliothèque Nationale) contain poems ascribed to Chrétien de Troyes.

These heroic tales also passed over into Germany. The warrior duke Henry the Lion (whose Gospel Book, described in chapter 2, proclaims his descent from Charlemagne) commissioned from Konrad the priest a German version of the song of Roland, the *Rolandslied*, written about 1170. There are twelfth-century German poems on Alexander the Great and King Arthur too. The great writers of epic poetry in Germany all belong to the decade or so on either side of 1200. They are Hartmann von Aue (fl.1170–1215), who translated Chrétien de Troyes; Wolfram von Eschenbach (d. after 1217; Pl.134), author of *Parzival*, the tale of a young knight errant who is eventually admitted to the Round Table of King Arthur and to the company of the guardians of the Holy Grail at Munsalväsche; and Gottfried von Strassburg (*c.*1210), who wrote *Tristan*, the romance of a nephew of King Mark (of 'Tintajoel' Castle in Cornwall) who accidentally drinks a love potion with Isolde, the king's betrothed. Only slightly later is Rudolf von

133 (RIGHT) Paris, Bibliothèque Nationale MS.fr.12577, detail of f.74v; Chrétien de Troyes and others, Romances of the Holy Grail, Paris, *c.*1330. *The miniature shows a courtly procession bearing the Holy Grail, the Lance and the Sword.*

134 (BELOW, RIGHT) Munich, Bayerische Staatsbibliothek, CGM.193/III; fragments from Wolfram von Eschenbach, Willehalm, Germany, *c.*1250–75.

Ems (fl.1220–54), whose huge poems include a massive *Weltchronik*, a history of the world as far as King Solomon and which in some manuscripts has bold illustrations throughout. John Ruskin owned a very fine copy, now in Berlin, painted with 102 miniatures and completed in 1411 for Count Frederick of Toggenburg, not far from Zurich. The greatest German medieval poem of them all is the *Nibelungenlied*. The most important manuscript of the text is still owned by a German princely family (Donaueschingen MS.63), an unilluminated but handsome thirteenth-century volume of 114 leaves. The epic is long and immensely complicated. Briefly, it concerns Siegfried who helps King Gunther marry the terrible Brunhild because Siegfried wants to marry Kriemhild, Gunther's sister, but Brunhild (misunderstanding Siegfried's rank) has him killed; so Kriemhild, who has in the meantime married Etzel, king of the Huns, cunningly invites the enemies of Siegfried to a feast with the intention of avenging his death and obtaining the Nibelung treasure (which has been thrown in the Rhine), but in the massacre which ensues everybody dies horribly.

Not all German secular writing was quite so bloodthirsty. The *Minnesingers* are still romantic figures in history (Pl.142). The word *Minne* is often translated as 'love' (for these were knightly minstrels who sang of fair damsels) but these were not mere songs of passion but of a courtly aristocratic wistful secret love for an unattainable woman. There is an almost fairytale atmosphere about the wandering *Minnesingers* like Reinmar von Hagenau (fl.1160–1210) and Heinrich von Morungen (*c.*1200).

The minstrels brought vernacular entertainment into the courts of southern Europe also. Troubadours like Rambertino Buvarelli (d.1221) sang in Bologna in the Provençal language. Dante ascribes the origin of Italian poetry to the court of the Emperor Frederick II (1194–1250), king of Sicily and Jerusalem, who gathered around him a group of writers known (not strictly correctly) as the 'Sicilian poets' and there exist poems by Frederick himself and by his chancellor Pier della Vigna. It must be stressed that the rise of

celle foi que vos me devez

Ha dame fait il. bien vos
di quil me covient dire. Da
me ce estes vos. je fait elle. Par moi
ne por autre vos mie les .ij. lan
ces. que ma pucelle vous porta
de cui je mestoie nule hors dou
mandement. Dame je sui par elles
ce que je dui. Et par vous sui ge ce
que je poi. Or me dites les choses
et les proesces que vos avez faites
par qui les feistes vos. Dame fait
il por vos. Coment fait elle amez
me vos dont tant. Et dont me vint
celle amor. Dame fait il des que
je fui primes apellez chevalier et je
ne lestoie mie. A ces paroles tos
sist la dame de malohaut a es
ciant. Et leva la teste quelle a
voit embrunchiee. Et cil lentendi
tantost. Car maintes fois lavoit
oie. Et il la regarde si la conut
si en out tel dolor et tel anguisse

Et il sesforce plus quil puet de par
ler. Dame je voi que je vos ai dit
coment fu ce dont fait elle. Da
me fait il vos feistes de moi vostre
ami. se vostre bouche ne me ment
mon ami fait elle et coment

Dame quant je oi pris congie
de mon signor le roi Artu
je ving devant vous. et je estoie
touz armez fors dou chief et des
mains. Si vous comandai a dieu
et dis que je estoie vostre chevalier. en
quel que lieu que je fusse. Et vos
deistes que vostre ami et vostre chevalier
volez vos bien que je fusse. Et
je dis dame granz merciz et puis apres
dame adieu vos comant. Et vos
deistes. Adieu biaus douz amis. Et
onques puis li mos dou cuer ne
ne me pout issir. Cest li mos qui
preudome me fera se je sui mes
longuement. Ne onques puis
ne fui a si grant meschief que de

fors le duc. Et vostre pensers ne
fu mie vilains. Ainz fu douz et de
bonaires. Et vos en est bien avenu
quant preudome vous a fait. Et
nonporquant la costume nest mie
tele a amant chevalier. qui tient en
tendant maintes choses a main
tes dames dont nule lor est petit
pres au cuer. Et vos semblanz me m
ostre que vos avez une de ces
dames la. plus que vos ne faites
moi. Car vos avez plore ne de
paour tornez vos regarz vers
eles a droit. Si voi bien que li vostre
pensers nest mie si a moi com
vos faites le semblant. Et par
la foi que vos me devez laquele
est ce que vos amez tant. Ha da
me fait il dieu merci ainsi mait diex
nulle delles na mon cuer. Ce na
mestier fait la roine. Vos ne me
poez riens embler. Car jai veut
maintes choses aveler. Et je quois

tessiez cuer que il ne pooit respon
dre a ce que la roine disoit. Si quen
ca a souspirer molt durement
et les lermes li coulent contreval
les vis. Si que li samis quil avo
it vestu en fu touz moilliez. Et quant
plus resgardoit la dame de malo
haut et plus estoit a malaise.

De ceste chose se prent gar
de la roine. Et voit quil res
garde molt piteusement les dames
Dites moi fait elle dont celle a
amor vient que je vous demant

cest mot ne me sovenist. Cist mi
mos ma conforte en toutes mes a
nuis. Cist moz ma tout mes maus
garis. Cist moz ma touz anuiz
fait oublier. Cist moz ma fait
en toutes mes fains. Cist moz ma
fait riche en toutes mes povre
tez. Par foi fait la roine cist moz
fu dit de bone eure. Et diex en soit
aourez quant il dire le me fist.
Mais je nel pris pas si a certes com
me vos feistes. Et a maint chevalier
lai ge dit. ou je ne pensai onques

bien vostre cuer. qui est la plus al
nest ci. Et de ce fist elle por vour
quelle le puet metre a malaise
Car elle cuidoit bien savoir quil
ne pensoit dame se li non.
Jamar eust il fait por la roine
dir vocres armes. Ha ma elle se
delitoit en sa malice veoir. Et cil
fu si anguisseus que par .j. pau
quil ne se pasme. Et la roine le
prent par la chevece quil ne
cheut. et apella Gal. et il saut et
vient devant li. Si voit que cis

secular poetry throughout Europe from about 1200 onwards does not mean that poetical manuscripts are common. They are, in fact, exceedingly rare. Many troubadours were probably hardly literate and the audiences listened to literature rather than reading it. The significance of secular verse, however, is that (within a couple of generations at most) the fashion for vernacular literature spread through the courts of Europe, and the minstrel lad of the Dark Ages gave way to the writer of medieval romances. An early *jongleur* composed his songs as he went along, but a thirteenth-century poet prepared a specific text and when that happened, he needed manuscripts.

Among the most remarkable literary manuscripts of the thirteenth century are the songbooks of Alfonso X, 'el Sabio' (the Wise), king of Spain from 1252 to 1284. Like Frederick II, Alfonso encouraged the arts of astronomy, law, and history. From his youth he had begun to collect and write in Galician a series of songs or *Cántigas* in honour of the Virgin Mary, and he commissioned spectacular Castilian manuscripts of these and had them richly decorated (Pl. 136). Four of the volumes survive, one in Madrid (from the Cathedral of Toledo and probably the oldest copy), one in Florence (unfinished), and two marvellous volumes which Philip II obtained at great expense from Seville Cathedral for the royal Monastery he was building at the Escorial. They are still in the sixteenth-century library there. The second of these manuscripts (Escorial MS.T.j.I) has the astonishing total of 1255 miniatures, usually arranged six to a page with captions in Spanish and ornamental borders (Pl. 143). They illustrate miracles described in the songs. The first page opens with a miniature of King Alfonso himself holding up one of his songs on a long scroll which he points out to his admiring courtiers. The second miniature shows three musicians playing as the king listens to them and dictates words to two clerics who write first on scrolls and then transfer the text and music into a big volume, from which four cantors are singing. The following thousand or so miniatures form an amazing documentary on medieval secular life: singing, fighting, feasting, church building, riding, being shipwrecked, going to church, attending a hanging, stealing money, sleeping, travelling, dying, praying, wrestling, hunting, besieging a city, sailing, painting frescoes (the scaffold collapses but the artist is saved because he was painting the Virgin Mary), giving birth, playing dice, serving in a shop, keeping bees, hawking, bull-fighting, shearing sheep, writing books, frying eggs, ploughing, fishing, and so forth. The manuscript deserves to be better known. It must have delighted the court of Alfonso the Wise.

In France the tradition of illustrating literary manuscripts probably began with versions of the tales of King Arthur. The *Lancelot* romance exists in many forms, including that ascribed to Walter Map, and it brings together the legends of Camelot, the Lady of the Lake, the Holy Grail, and the death of Arthur, which all still form part of our folk culture (Pls. 133 and 135). One of the earliest illustrated manuscripts of the prose text of *Lancelot du Lac* (as Alison Stones has recently suggested) must be Rennes MS.255, which can be ascribed to the circle of the royal court in Paris perhaps as early as the 1220s. It comes from that moment in Parisian book production which was discussed in the last chapter when professional artists moved in to supply the needs of the court on the one hand and the students on the other. In a rhymed preface to a chronicle of Philip Augustus written in the second half of the 1220s (B.L. Add.MS.21212) the author says he will use French prose 'si com li livres Lancelot', as if such books were well known to his readers. Certainly *Lancelot* manuscripts are not rare in that about fifty copies are known, including twenty in the Bibliothèque Nationale, and some are profusely illustrated like the manuscript in Bonn University Library (MS.526) which has over 230 miniatures and was written in 1286 at Amiens by a scribe called Arnulphus de Kayo (Pl. 137). This must have been an expensive book to make and it supposes a wealthy patron. One *Lancelot* manuscript whose first owner can be identified from its heraldry is in the Beinecke Library at Yale University (MS.229), a splendid copy in three volumes illuminated for Guillaume de Termonde (d. 1312), son of the count of

135 (OPPOSITE) New York, Pierpont Library M.805, f.67; Roman de Lancelot du Lac, north eastern France, *c.* 1300. *The miniature illustrates the first kiss of Lancelot and Guinevere.*

136 (BELOW) El Escorial, Real Biblioteca, MS.J.b.2, f.125r; Canticles of Alfonso the Wise, Castile, second half of the thirteenth century.

Flanders. The inventory of the possessions of Jean d'Avesnes, count of Hainaut (d. 1304), includes a Lancelot manuscript described as bound in red, and the will of the count's brother, Guillaume d'Avesnes who was bishop of Cambrai (d. 1296), mentions a 'livre de gestes' which was to be given to the abbey of St-Sépulchre in Cambrai because (the will says) one of the monks had made it. These minor nobles therefore are the kind of people who must have owned and enjoyed the romances of King Arthur's knights.

The best-known French romance of the thirteenth century is the *Roman de la Rose*, a huge poem of over 20,000 lines, which was written by two authors who never met each other (Pl. 138). The story begins with a lover going to bed one night and dreaming that he has found himself by a stream on a lovely May morning with the sun shining and the birds singing. He is admitted into a garden where he sees and falls in love with the Rose in bud. He is rebuffed in all his advances and only after elaborate adventures and debates with

137 Bonn, Universitätsbibliothek MS. S. 526, f. 1; Roman de Lancelot du Lac, Amiens, 1286.
This manuscript, though worn and well used, contains the earliest entirely complete dated cycle of the Lancelot stories. The six miniatures on the first page show scenes in the life of Joseph of Arimathea.

allegorical gods is he finally able to achieve his heart's desire by winning the Rose. It sounds rather trite in this brief summary but in fact is entertaining to read and is crammed with fascinating incident and observation. The first 4058 lines of the poem were composed about 1230–35 by Guillaume de Lorris, who probably came from Lorris near Orléans and who abandoned his text unfinished. It was then continued and completed after 1268 and perhaps before 1274 by Jean de Meun who writes a reference to himself into the text. The God of Love is made to appear in the story and to bemoan the death of all the love poets of the past, including his faithful servant Guillaume de Lorris. Then (the God of Love predicts) Jean Chopinel from Meung-sur-Loire will come more than forty years later and will be so fond of the poem that he will try to finish it in order that the knowledge of love may be carried 'through crossroads and through schools, in the language of France, before audiences throughout the kingdom'. Thus another 17,000 lines were added and the poem completed. Jean de Meun (d. 1305) was well known as a poet and translator and lived in Paris in the rue St-Jacques, the same street as the Dominican convent and the Sens family of stationers whom we met in chapter 4. He was an experienced author fully aware of the value of books 'in the language of France'.

The *Roman de la Rose* was a great success throughout the rest of the Middle Ages. Over two hundred manuscripts are known. Its reputation of being mildly erotic helped its circulation. There is a thirteenth-century glossed Acts, Canonical Epistles, and Apocalypse in the Bibliothèque de Ste-Geneviève in Paris (MS.75) with a medieval note that its owner, a priest in Senlis, exchanged it for a *Roman de la Rose*. No doubt he hurried away delightedly from the deal. Many copies are beautifully illuminated and at least five have over a hundred miniatures each. Two surviving copies belonged to the Duc de Berry (B.N. MSS.fr.380 and 12595). One manuscript (B.N. MS.fr.2195) is dated at the end 31 May 1361 and includes an acrostic which spells out the name of its scribe as 'Johan Mulot'; this copy was still being enjoyed a century later as it has an ownership inscription of Massiot Austin of Rouen who says he bought it in June 1470 from a book dealer in Rouen called Gautier Neron, and that if he loses it the finder who returns it to him shall be rewarded with a good pot of wine (f. 146v). Another *Roman de la Rose* was written at Sully-sur-Loire in 1390 (Arsenal MS.3337), and the scribe records that he began it on 26 August and worked without a break until 8 November. This is seventy-five days, which works out at about 290 lines a day.

The great Italian medieval poem, which far eclipses the *Roman de la Rose* in quality and imagination is, of course, the *Divina Commedia*, or *Divine Comedy*, of Dante Alighieri (1265–1321). In fact, Dante knew Jean de Meun personally and their poems are sometimes compared, but the tremendous power and artifice of Dante's writing is quite unique in all the Middle Ages. It may not be necessary to remind ourselves that the *Divine Comedy* is an account of an astonishing voyage through the underworlds and into heaven itself. The scene opens on Easter Thursday in the year 1300 when the poet has lost his way in a dark wood. He is rescued by the poet Virgil who has been sent by three women, the Virgin Mary, St. Lucy, and Beatrice, the girl Dante loved. Virgil escorts Dante right down into the centre of hell, and up through purgatory, and Beatrice herself leads him on into paradise. It is a poem of enormous intelligence and majesty, and it was extremely widely read. Over six hundred fourteenth-century manuscripts survive and probably even more from the fifteenth century (Frontispiece and Pl. 140). It attracted no fewer than fifteen medieval commentaries, beginning with one written before 1333 by Dante's son Jacopo (Pl. 139). From the distribution of manuscripts one can guess that the text was especially popular in Florence in the mid-fourteenth century and again around 1400. Some manuscripts are very grand productions (like those owned by the Visconti family in Milan and the Aragonese royal library in Naples or the amazing late fifteenth-century unfinished copy with full-page drawings by Botticelli) but others are quite humble in execution and are quite often written on paper. The first dated illustrated copy was written out in 1337 by Ser Francesco di Ser Nardo da Barberini (Milan, Biblioteca Trivulziana, MS.1080) and was illuminated in Florence by the artist known as the Master of the Dominican Effigies. The legend is

138 Oxford, Bodleian Library MS.e.Mus.65, detail of f. 12v; Guillaume de Lorris and Jean de Meun, Roman de la Rose, Paris, late fourteenth century.
Narcissus admires himself in a fountain.

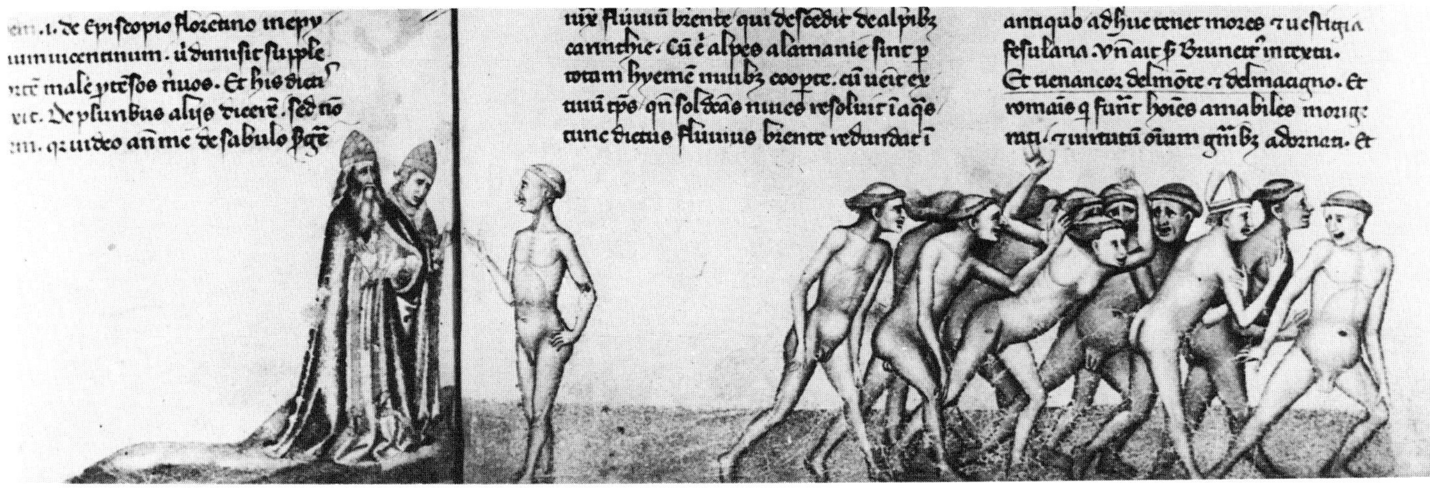

139 Chantilly, Musée Condé MS.1424, detail of lower margin of f.114r; Dante, Inferno, with the commentary of Guido da Pisa, probably Pisa, *c.*1345.

140 (RIGHT) London, Sotheby's, 25 June 1985, lot 82, lower cover of binding; Dante, Divina Commedia, Florence, *c.*1400, bound in the late fifteenth century.

that Ser Francesco provided dowries for his daughters by writing out a hundred manuscripts of the *Divine Comedy*, and it is curious that there are at least three other copies so closely related to the signed manuscript in their script and decoration that they must all have been produced together: Florence, Bibl. Laur. Strozz. MS.152, Bibl. Naz. Palat. MS.313, and Pierpont Morgan Library M.289. The proceeds of even a few such books would make any daughter worth chasing.

The third of the great triumvirate of medieval poems with the *Roman de la Rose* and the *Divine Comedy* is Geoffrey Chaucer's *Canterbury Tales.* It too describes a journey and the stories told by pilgrims as they travel the fifty miles or so from Southwark in London to the shrine of St. Thomas Becket in Canterbury Cathedral. There exist about eighty-five manuscripts of all or part of the *Canterbury Tales*, but they are not lavishly illustrated like the French romances. Only one, the famous Ellesmere Chaucer (Huntington Library MS.26.C9) has marginal illustrations of the twenty-three pilgrims who recounted stories in the text, and two others (Cambridge University Library MS.Gg.4.27, and the fragments now in Manchester and Philadelphia, Pl.146) perhaps once had similar pictures which have now mostly disappeared. B. L. Harley MS.1758 has blank spaces for miniatures which were never added. All the other manuscripts are without illustrations, and a third of them are written on paper. It is difficult to know how to interpret the fact that there was no developed tradition of illumination for secular texts in England as there was in France and Italy. Perhaps the tales were meant for reading out loud and pictures would have been superfluous if the poems were ever recited in public as shown in the famous frontispiece to Chaucer's *Troilus and Criseyde* in Cambridge, Corpus Christi College MS.61, where the author declaims from a lectern in the midst of an aristocratic picnic. This miniature, however, is completely French in style and must represent a courtly ideal rather than a common practice. It seems likely that literary patronage was different in England. There were no great English aristocratic art collectors in the lifetime of Chaucer (*c.*1340–1400) except perhaps Richard II himself whose little library in 1384–85 comprised Arthurian romances in French and a *Roman de la Rose* (valued at one pound), all inherited from his grandfather. The two earliest references to copies of the *Canterbury Tales* in English wills date from 1417 and 1420. The first belonged to Richard Sotheworth, a priest and chancery clerk, and the second to John Brinchele, a London tailor. It is interesting that Sotheworth came from Canterbury and was Master of Eastbridge Hospital there, and Brinchele is recorded as living in Southwark: thus these two owners of manuscripts lived at either end of Chaucer's fictional journey. They may have had very local reasons for buying the text.

The *Roman de la Rose* is in French, the *Divine Comedy* in Italian, and the *Canterbury Tales* are in English. With all the great medieval aristocratic literary texts, however, there is the implication that the most appropriate language for romance was French; and the word *romance* originally meant simply the vernacular speech of France. Marco Polo's memoirs were almost certainly first written down in French, though the author was a Venetian. Sir John Mandeville's fictional *Travels* (Pl.131) were composed in French in order to reach a wider public than in English or in Latin 'pour ce que pluseurs entendent mieulx rommant qe latin' (says the writer). Brunetto Latini, the first great literary figure of thirteenth-century Italy, wrote one of his books, the *Trésors,* in French because he thought this was 'plus delitable et plus commune a tous langages'. The fact that nearly thirty illuminated copies of the text survive shows that he was at least partly right. Obviously many English aristocrats spoke French as their mother tongue, as their Norman ancestors had done. But in Italy too literature in French was quite intelligible. A surprising number of Arthurian romances in French seem to have been written out by Italian scribes in Italy. A really beautifully illuminated example is B.N. MS.nouv.acq.fr.5243, the *Romance of Guiron le Courtois*, one

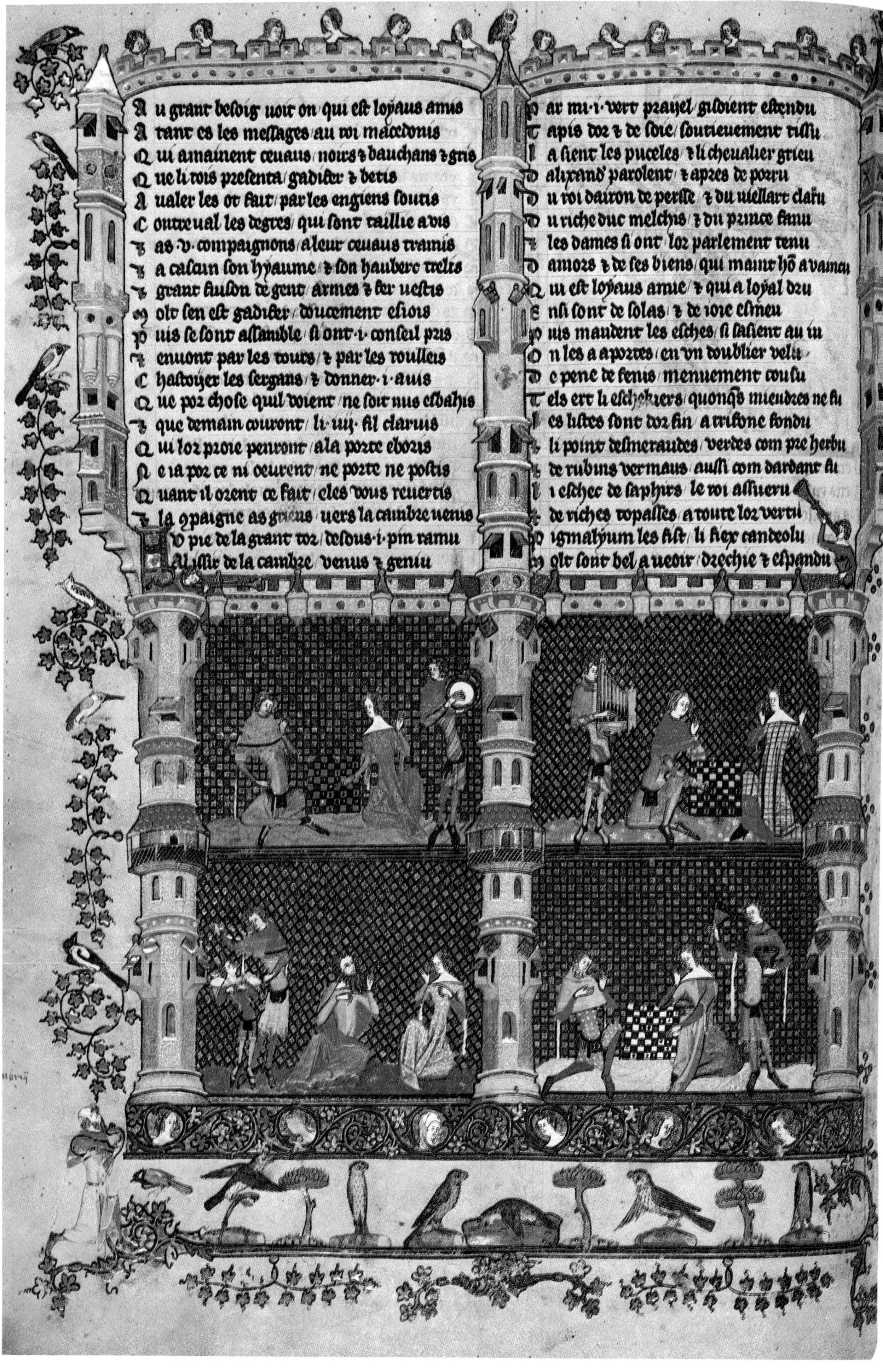

A u grant besoig uoit on qui est loyaus amis
A tant es les messages au roi macedonis
Q ui amainent ceuaus noirs ⁊ bauchans ⁊ gris
Q ue li rois presenta gadifer ⁊ betis
A ualer les ot fait par les engiens soutis
C ontreual les degres qui sont taillie a vis
⁊ as ·v· compaignons a leur ceuaus tramis
⁊ a casain son hyaume ⁊ son hauberc trelis
⁊ grant foison de gent armes ⁊ fer uestis
M olt sen est gadifer doucement esiois
P uis se sont assamble si ont ·i· conseil pris
⁊ enuoint par les tours ⁊ par les roulleis
C hastoyer les sergans ⁊ donner ·i· auis
Q ue por chose quil voient ne soit nus esbahis
⁊ que demain courront li ·iiij· fil clarus
Q ui lor proie penront a la porte eboris
S e ia por ce ni oeurent ne porte ne postis
Q uant il orent ce fait e les vous reuertis
⁊ la compaigne as grieus uers la cambre uenus
Au pie de la grant tor desous ·i· pin ramu
Al issir de la cambre venus ⁊ geniu

P ar mi ·i· vert prayel gisoient estendu
T apis dor ⁊ de soie soutieuement tissu
L a sient les puceles ⁊ li cheualier grieu
D alixand' parolent ⁊ apres de porru
D u roi dauron de persse ⁊ du uiellart claru
D u riche duc melchis ⁊ du prince fanu
⁊ les dames si ont lor parlement tenu
D amors ⁊ de ses biens qui maint hō a vaincu
Q ui est loyaus amie ⁊ qui a loyal dru
E nsi sont de solas ⁊ de ioie esmeu
P uis maudent les esches si sasient au iu
O n les a aportes en vn doublier velu
D e pene de fenis menuement cousu
T els ert li eschekiers quonques mieudres ne fu
L es listes sont dor fin a trifone fondu
L i point desmeraudes verdes com pre herbu
⁊ de rubins vermaus aussi com dardant fu
L i eschec de saphirs le roi assueru
⁊ de riches topasses a toute lor vertu
P ignalyum les fist li fiex candeolu
M olt sont bel a uedoir drechie ⁊ espandu

141 (LEFT) Oxford, Bodleian Library, MS. Bodley 264, f. 127v; Roman d'Alexandre, perhaps Tournai, written in 1338 and illuminated in 1344.
The colophon of this huge illustrated Alexander romance records that the writing was completed on 18 December 1338 and that the illumination was finished by Jehan de Grise on 18 April 1344, five and a half years later. The manuscript was in England in the Middle Ages, and was purchased in London on 15 January 1466 by Richard Woodville, first Earl Rivers (d. 1469), whose daughter Elizabeth married King Edward IV.

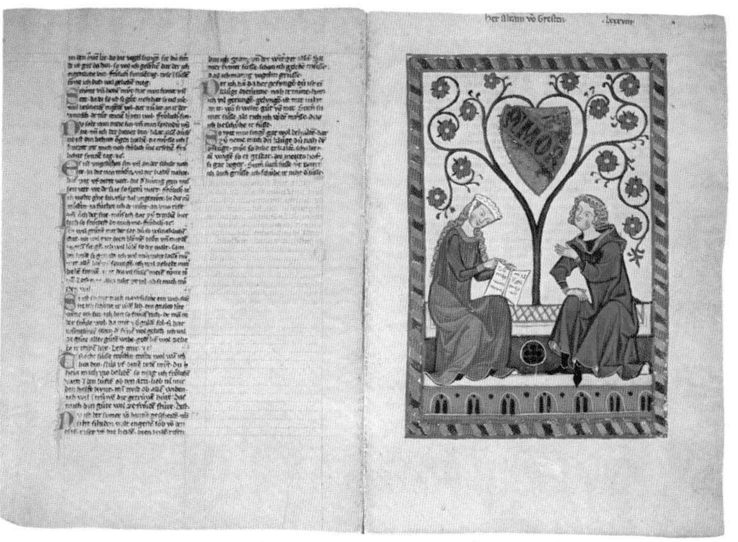

142 (ABOVE) Heidelberg, Universitätsbibliothek MS. Pal. germ. 848, ff. 310v–311r, the Manasse Codex, Switzerland (probably Zurich), early fourteenth century.
This is the best-known collection of poems of the Minnesingers*; it belonged to the Manasse family of Zurich. The miniature here shows the lover presenting his songs to his lady.*

143 (LEFT) El Escorial, Real Biblioteca, MS. T. I. 1, f. 200r; Canticles of Alfonso the Wise.
The miracle story here concerns a bull fight. A man prays to the Virgin Mary and then goes off to buy his ticket to the fight. Unfortunately he falls into the arena and is about to be gored to death when the Virgin sends the bull to sleep and the man escapes. When the bull wakes up everyone congratulates it.

of Arthur's knights, painted in Lombardy or perhaps even Venice in the late fourteenth century. In the mid-fifteenth century Borso d'Este, duke of Ferrara, wrote asking a friend to dispatch 'as many French books as possible, especially of the story of the Round Table, for I shall receive from them more pleasure and contentment than from the capture of a city.'

The old unanswered question which has haunted linguists for generations is to decide at what time national languages came into common use and when (and why) they were first written down, since all education came from the Church and all churchmen knew Latin. It is frequently said that women had an important role in promoting vernacular writing because girls were not customarily taught Latin as thoroughly as boys. It is quite true that vernacular prayerbooks can often be traced to nuns rather than to monks, for example. One cannot tell who gathered round the poet who recited epics by the fire after dinner in the medieval hall, but women may well have been there. In 1252 the queen's chamber at Nottingham Castle was painted with scenes of Alexander the Great. The audience listening to Chaucer in the *Troilus and Criseyde* manuscript mentioned above includes nine women, and it is doubtful whether they would have been so attentive if the lecture had been in Latin. In fact, the earliest dated Lancelot manuscript must have been written by a female scribe (B.N. MS.fr.342). It was made in 1274 and ends with the request that the reader will pray for the scribe, 'pries pour ce li ki lescrist'; 'ce li' is a feminine pronoun.

The aristocratic patronage of manuscript illuminators in the court of France in the first half of the fourteenth century was often associated with women. Famous manuscripts were commissioned for noblewomen such as the Countess Mahaut d'Artois, Jeanne d'Evreux, Blanche de France (daughter of Philip V), Jeanne de Belleville, Jeanne de Navarre, Bonne of Luxembourg, and Yolande of Flanders. By no means all their manuscripts were secular romances (many were prayer-books) but their support strengthened the tradition of expensive manuscript illumination which merged with a passion for vernacular literature during the reigns of John II (1350–64) and Charles V (1364–80).

By the mid-fourteenth century a great many massive folio texts were being translated into French and richly illuminated for aristocratic libraries. They included weighty texts such as Boethius, Vegetius, Livy, Aristotle, and St. Augustine, all translated into French. A rather surprising success was an adaptation of Peter Comestor's *Historia Scholastica,* a twelfth-century university textbook which enjoyed a remarkable revival among the newly literate nobility of the fourteenth century (Pl.152). It consists of a summary of the historical sections of the Bible which, like the legends of Troy or Alexander, include some first-rate stories. The *Historia Scholastica,* or *Bible Historiale* in French, was translated by Guyart des Moulins, canon and later dean of St-Pierre d'Aire (about thirty miles south east of Calais), in the four years leading up to February 1295 and it was revised by him before about 1312. Over seventy manuscripts of the text are known, mostly richly decorated. The earliest is a single volume in the British Library (Royal MS.I.A.XX) which is dated in Paris in 1312 by a scribe Robert de Marchia who says in the colophon that he is in prison. It is not a beautiful manuscript (perhaps his cell was uncomfortable) but it nevertheless has forty-eight miniatures. Five years later Arsenal MS.5059 was written and signed by the scribe Jean de Papeleu in the rue des Ecrivains in Paris. This is no rough production: it has 176 fine miniatures and is of excellent quality. Another copy with ninety-three miniatures belonged to John II of France and has an extraordinarily dramatic provenance. According to an early fifteenth-century inscription on its flyleaf (B.L. Royal MS.19.D.II, f.i), it was captured from King John at the battle of Poitiers on 19 September 1356 and was bought for 100 marks (just over £66) by William de Montacute, earl of Salisbury, as a present for his wife Elizabeth, and when she died in 1415 her executors resold it for £40. It is a massive book, 16½ by 11¼ inches (420 by 285 mm.), with 527 leaves which were probably originally bound in three volumes, and it is interesting to visualize the king of France struggling onto the battlefield with such a manuscript under his arm.

The loss of this *Bible Historiale* was soon made up in the French royal court, however. In 1371 Charles V was given another glorious copy, which is now in the Museum

144 London, Sotheby's, 26 November 1985, lot 107, detail of f.117v; Histoire Ancienne jusqu'à César, Bourges or the Loire valley, *c.* 1470.
The miniature shows a party of Amazons, proto-feminists of ancient Greece, approaching a fortified city.

Meermanno-Westreenianum in The Hague (MS.10.B.23). Its full-page frontispiece by Jean Bondol shows Charles V himself sitting in an armchair and gazing admiringly at an illuminated manuscript which a kneeling courtier holds open for him to read the beginning of Genesis in French (Pl. 151). At the end of the text is a long French poem explaining to the king that the manuscript was presented to him by his servant Jehan Vaudetar, who is shown in the miniature, and that (says the poet) never in his life has he seen a *Bible Historiale* decked out like this with portraits and events by one hand, for which (the verse continues) he went backwards and forwards, night and morning, through the streets and often with rain falling on his head, before it was finished. Perhaps he should not have bothered to go to all this effort. The copy of the *Bible Historiale* which the royal family really liked must have been B.N. MS.fr.5707, dated 1363, which has autograph ownership inscriptions on one amazing page (f.367v) signed by Charles V, the Duc de Berry, Henri III (1574–89), Louis XIII (1610–43), and Louis XIV (1643–1715).

The great fascination of the *Bible Historiale* was not only that it was scriptural but also that it was historical. It might be fairer to call it a chronicle of biblical history. Medieval aristocrats loved history, and history (like Bible stories, saints' lives, and oriental travel) mingled with romance, especially when rendered 'de latin en romans', as Pierre Bersuire put it in the heading of Livy's history which he translated for John II in the 1350s. Romantic history took several forms. The first was ancient history. Here fact became entangled with legends of the fall of Troy and of Alexander the Great. The *Histoire Ancienne jusqu'à César*, a romantic account of ancient heroes and battles, was composed between 1206 and 1230 and survives in nearly forty manuscripts (Pls. 144 and 147). Three of these were actually made in Acre in the Holy Land during its occupation by the crusading forces: Brussels B.R. MS.10175, Dijon MS.562, and B.L. Add.MS.15268. It is pleasant to think of crusaders reading up their ancient legends while they were out in the Middle East. Even Troy cannot have seemed far away as they gazed out on the eastern Mediterranean over the ramparts of Acre. Trojan history had an extraordinary fascination for the medieval aristocracy (Pl. 132), and Guido delle Colonne's *Historia Destructionis Troiae* (completed in 1287) was adapted and translated into almost every vernacular language, including Icelandic. The English claimed that their country had been founded by refugees from the sack of Troy, and they derived the name 'Britain' from Brutus, a Trojan prince whose story begins the *Brut Chronicle*, the best-known Middle English history book. The first book ever printed in the English language was a Trojan history, *The Recuyell of the Histories of Troy*, published in Bruges by William Caxton probably in 1473–4 and issued under the patronage of Margaret, duchess of Burgundy (Pl. 145). The Burgundian ducal family were passionate admirers of Troy, and Philip the Good owned at least seventeen manuscripts tracing his own descent from the Trojans.

The great patriotic chronicle in the French court was the *Grandes Chroniques de France* (Pl. 148). It too opens with the siege of Troy but quickly moves to the history of the Franks and the chivalric descent of the French kings. The text was compiled in the royal abbey of St-Denis in the mid-thirteenth century and was translated into French in 1274. It is extravagantly partisan, and obviously caught the imagination of the kings of France who made sure it was updated from time to time to include themselves. They presented luxurious copies to visiting kings and dignitaries. It was the favourite reading of Charles V. The Duc de Berry owned several copies including one he had originally borrowed from St-Denis to show to the Emperor Sigismund. More than a hundred manuscripts have survived and it became the first dated French book to be printed (Paris, 1476).

Only slightly more serious history was represented by the *Speculum Historiale*, or 'Historical Mirror', by Vincent of Beauvais (*c.*1190–*c.*1264). Vincent was an immensely hard-working Dominican encyclopaedist and protégé of King Louis IX. His huge compilation on the history of the world comprises thirty-one books divided into 3,793 chapters and begins with the creation of the world and ends with the Crusade of Louis IX in 1250. The early manuscripts are in Latin and not illustrated. Curiously, the first translation was

145 London, British Library, C.11.C.1; The Recuyell of the Histories of Troy, translated into English by William Caxton and printed by him in Bruges probably in late 1473 or early 1474. *This is the first printed book in the English language, a Trojan romance.*

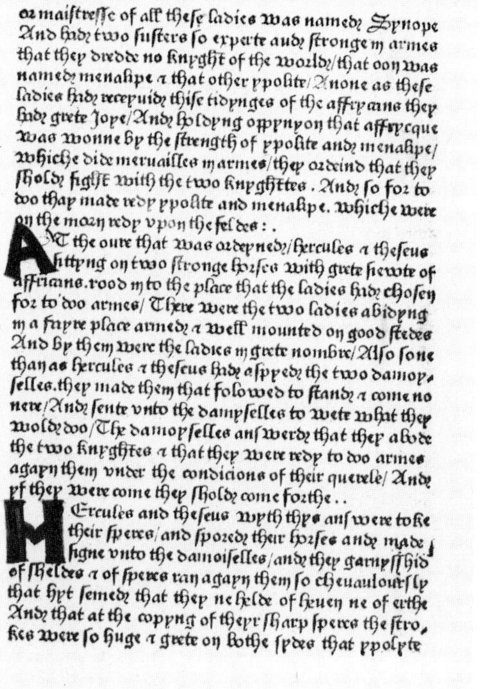

146 Manchester, John Rylands Library, Eng. MS. 63, fragment, f. 1v; Chaucer, Canterbury Tales, England, *c.* 1440.
Only thirteen leaves of this manuscript survive, two in Manchester (including this drawing of the Miller) and eleven in the Philip H. and A. S. W. Rosenbach Foundation Museum in Philadelphia.

147 (RIGHT) Paris, Bibliothèque Nationale MS. fr. 301, f. 147; Histoire Ancienne jusqu'à César, Paris, *c.* 1400.
The Duc de Berry purchased this manuscript in Paris in April 1402. The full-page miniature here shows the Greeks bringing the wooden horse into Troy and their subsequent sack of the city.

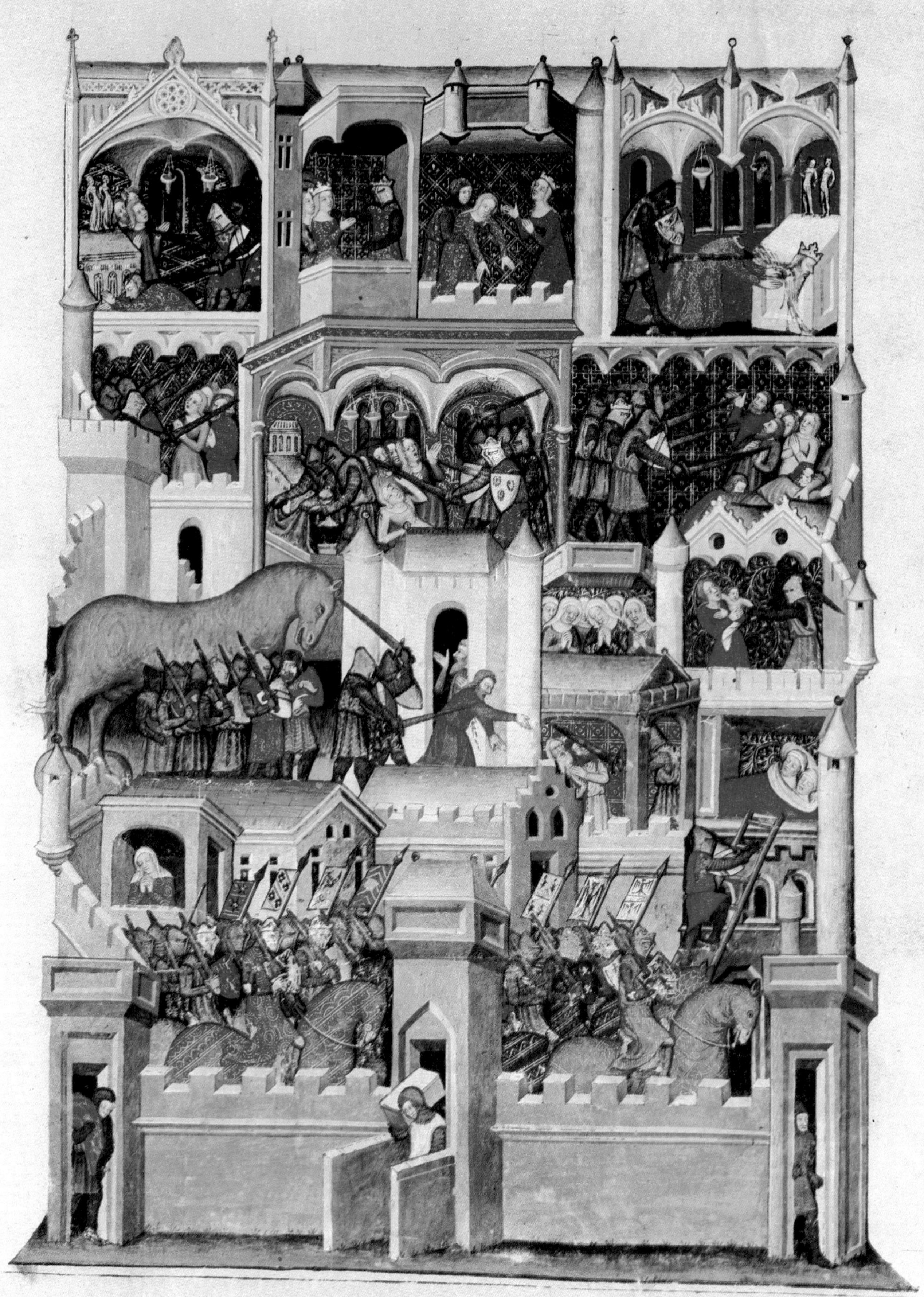

not into French, the usual channel by which academic texts passed into romance, but into Middle Dutch, the *Spieghel Historiael*, a verse adaptation prepared in the 1280s by Jacob van Maerlant at the request of Florent, count of Holland. The only surviving manuscript was made about 1330 (The Hague MS. Ak. XX) and has forty-nine miniatures (Pl. 149). A French edition, translated by Jean de Vignay and finished in 1333, was extremely popular. Manuscripts are often magnificently decorated, like the former Chester Beatty manuscript (now B.N. MSS. nouv. acq. fr. 15939–15944) which has no fewer than 708 miniatures. There are five sets of the *Miroir Historial*, as they called it, in the inventory of the library of Charles V, mostly described as 'très bien hystoriez', which means well illustrated. A version by William Caxton, *The Mirror of the World* (Westminster, 1481), is in fact the first English book printed with illustrations.

It is difficult to know exactly why vernacular manuscripts came to be illustrated so grandly. It is in marked contrast to the humble little troubadour texts of the twelfth century. Aristocratic owners loved gothic miniatures, and a French *Bible Moralisée* made for John II of France in the mid-fourteenth century has the scarcely credible total of 5,122 miniatures. There is certainly enormous charm in the delicate little figures with swaying hips, like gothic carvings, and the abstract tessellated backgrounds. French secular texts usually have almost square miniatures set into one column of a

148 (ABOVE) London, Sotheby's, 3 July 1984, lot 47, detail of f. 218v; Grandes Chroniques de France, Paris, *c.* 1320–30.
This miniature shows Louis VII and his court on horseback.

149 (BELOW) The Hague, Koninklijke Bibliotheek MS. Ak. XX, detail of f. 213v; Spieghel Historiael, Netherlands, *c.* 1330.
The battle of Charlemagne and Roland is illustrated in the earliest Dutch translation of the Speculum Historiale by Vincent of Beauvais.

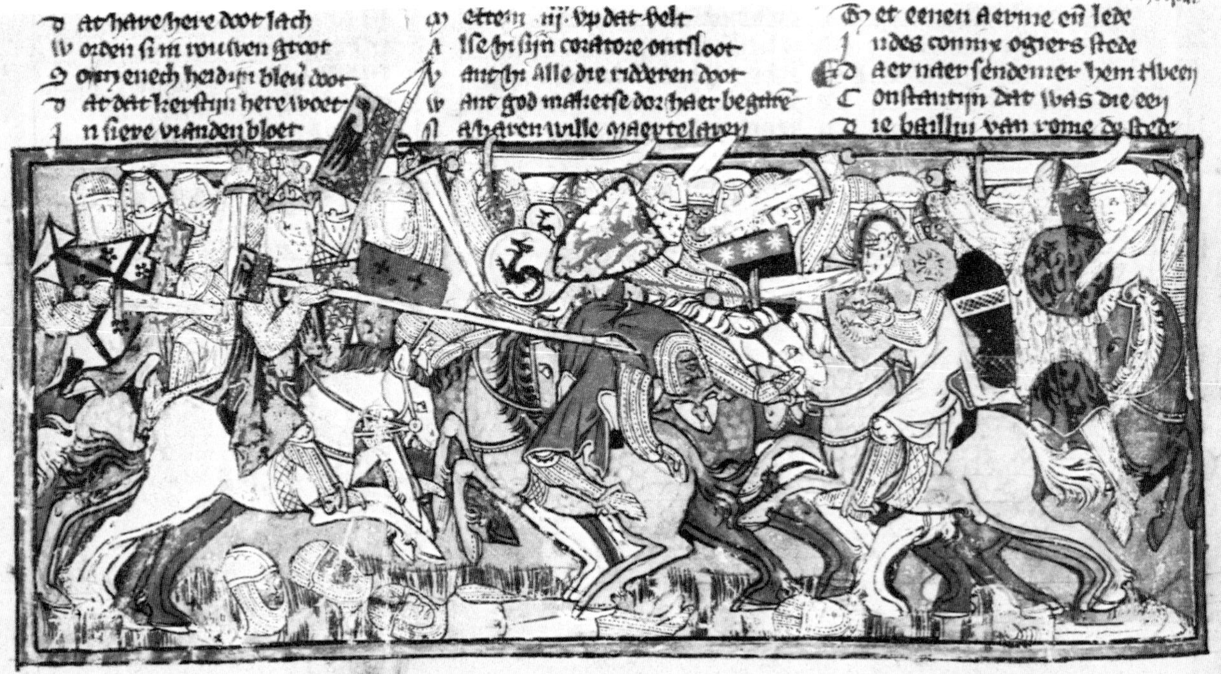

150 New York, Pierpont Morgan Library M. 1044, detail of f. 11r; Gaston de Foix, Livre de Chasse, Paris, early fifteenth century.

The Livre de Chasse is the great illustrated guide to hunting, with chapters on the animals of the chase and the aristocratic art of pursuing them. The miniature here begins the chapter on fallow deer.

double-column text. They are sometimes within cusped architectural frames in red, white, and blue, the colours of the French royal family (Pl. 152). Often formal ivyleaf borders run up and down the margins, sometimes terminating with tiny butterflies or imaginary animals. The first page of a French romance often has a half-page composition formed of four smaller miniatures placed together, and sparkling ivyleaf borders surround the page. In Germany, Italy, and England miniatures are no less frequent, but tend to be more informally placed on the pages. They are often without frames and spill over across the columns or even along the lower margins (Pl. 139).

There is something quintessentially medieval about an illustrated romance. 'I can't conceive anybody being ever tried with a heavier temptation than I am,' wrote John Ruskin in the nineteenth century, 'to save every farthing I can to collect a rich shelf of thirteenth century manuscripts.' These books were probably originally intended to be carried in by the librarian, bound in beautifully coloured silks, and placed on a lectern so that the owner might listen to readings from his favourite authors. The miniatures are probably not much more than decoration to be admired as the reading was going on. A statute of the Sienese painters' guild of 1356 describes the purpose of painting as being for 'those who do not know how to read'. It is too harsh to say that aristocratic owners were illiterate, but there are gradations of literacy, and for any inexperienced reader illustrations convey scenes and atmosphere which someone reading fluently and fast can gain from

151 The Hague, Rijksmuseum Meermanno-Westreenianum MS. 10. B. 23, f. 2r; Bible Historiale, Paris, 1371.
The frontispiece by the artist Jean Bondol shows Jehan Vaudetar presenting his manuscript to Charles V, who is dressed as a Master of Arts of the University of Paris.

152 (RIGHT) London, British Library, Royal MS. 17. E. VII, f. 1; Bible Historiale, Paris, 1357.
This is the opening page of a manuscript of the Bible Historiale which concludes with an acrostic whose initial letters spelled backwards reveal the date 1357.

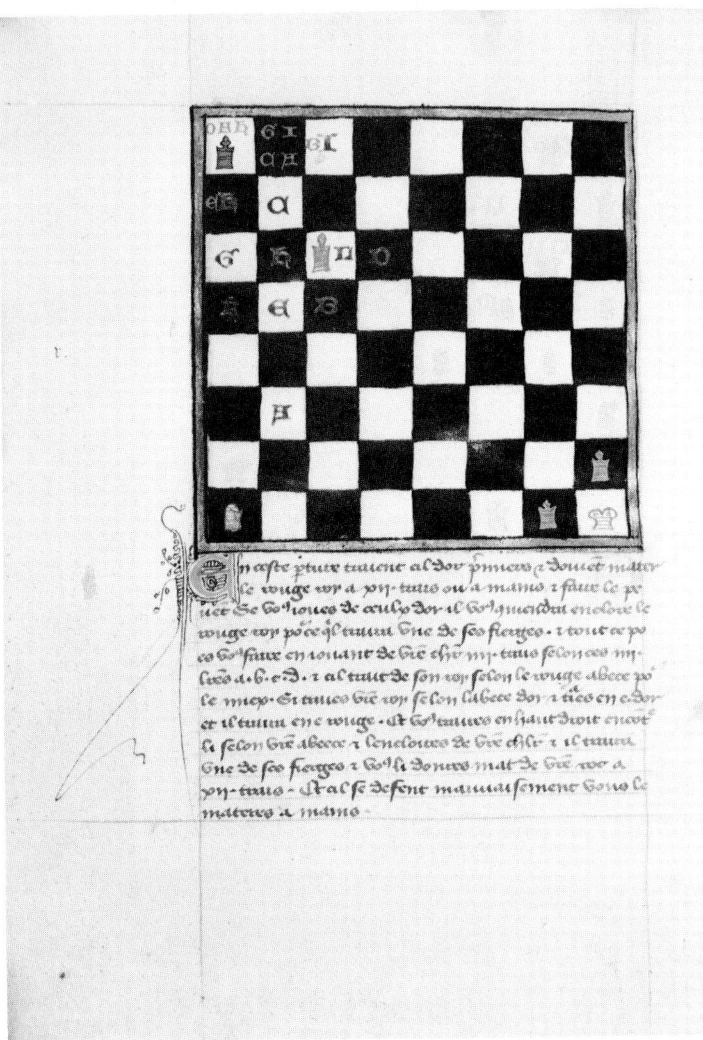

153 Malibu, The J. Paul Getty Museum MS. Ludwig XV. 15, f. 88v; Bonus Socius, northern France, late fourteenth century.
The manuscript illustrates chess problems.

the text. Pictures of battles and ships and kings and lovers convey pleasure to those who see them, and really the main purpose of a romance is to provide enjoyment.

The rise of literacy is one of the old themes of historians of the Middle Ages. At one time few except the monks and priests could read, but by the fifteenth century education was broad enough for middle-class families to write letters to each other with some fluency and to conduct their business with written documents. Merchants began to see the advantage of books. Marco Polo's travels are on one level a wonderful holiday tale, but to the medieval businessman they provide much practical information. Geographical treatises were useful too, such as Gregorio Dati's *La Sfera*, a poem in Italian composed about 1400, which was often illustrated and which furnished valuable information about navigation in the Mediterranean and northern Atlantic. It went through thirteen printed editions between 1472 and 1490, and was eventually rendered obsolete by Columbus's discoveries in 1492. Manuscript maps were evidently popular as well in the fourteenth and fifteenth centuries. We know the names of about forty makers of portolan charts (nautical maps which mark ports and headlands) between the early fourteenth century and 1500. Merchants must have gazed at them with fascination. Law was also a subject of great practical value for the middle classes. Legal manuscripts were especially produced in England, where volumes of the *Statutes of the Realm* were issued (probably often from London) from the early fourteenth century, and also in Germany, where the *Sachsenspiegel*, or 'Saxon Mirror', a legal anthology by Eike von Repgow (fl. 1209–33), was popular for three centuries. It survives in more than two hundred manuscripts, and one of them (Dresden M. 32, written *c.* 1375) has nearly a thousand illustrations. With books on horses, chess, plants, popular medicine, astrology, love, the craft of warfare, the art of dying, agriculture, alchemy, polyphonic music, fables, heraldry, cooking, politics, painting, hunting, and many other secular subjects, not only the nobleman, but even the moderately prosperous and fairly literate layman could enjoy books. The manuscripts were no longer exclusively aristocratic.

154 (OPPOSITE) Chantilly, Musée Condé MS. 1389, f. 130r; the fables of Bidpai in German translation, Württemberg, *c.* 1480.
This full-page drawing shows a cat chasing a mouse, in a manuscript of fables decorated for Eberhard, duke of Württemberg.

14v

•6•

Books for Everybody

No one has ever counted up how many Books of Hours still exist. It would be possible to do (and very useful) but would require patience, as Books of Hours are now more widely scattered around the world than any other object made in the Middle Ages. Though fair numbers of them have ended up in major national libraries (something like four hundred in the British Library and well over three hundred in the Bibliothèque Nationale in Paris), these manuscripts have always been rather despised by serious librarians and have been enormously admired by private collectors. That is exactly why Books of Hours were made. They were not for monks or for university libraries but for ordinary people. They are small and usually prettily decorated books. They were intended to be held in the hand and admired for the delicate illumination rather than put on a library shelf and used for their text. They still appeal enormously to bibliophiles. A Book of Hours is almost the only medieval work of art which a moderately wealthy collector today can still hope to own. At least at the moment, a single leaf from a manuscript Book of Hours need be no more expensive than the book you are now reading. It is an extraordinary tribute to the energy and industry of those who produced Books of Hours that even now, five hundred years later, their manuscripts have still not quite disappeared from circulation in the bookshops. The enchanting miniatures in Books of Hours are successfully reproduced now for Christmas cards and postcards: we all take an innocent delight in the scenes of shepherds singing under the starry sky, the Flight into Egypt past fairytale castles and Tolkien-like landscapes, and in the borders of flowers and animals sparkling with gold and colour. It is a very direct appeal, and a very old one. The poet Eustache Deschamps (1346–1406) describes the bourgeois wife who feels she is not properly fitted out unless she owns a Book of Hours, beautifully made, illuminated in gold and blue (says the poem), neatly arranged and well painted and bound in a pretty binding with gold clasps. It was the first time that any kind of book became really popular, even among people who had never owned books before. The very great appeal of Books of Hours was understood by the medieval booksellers who manufactured and sold these volumes in immense numbers.

Books of Hours today are probably most famous for their association with the names of great medieval aristocrats, like the Duc de Berry (1340–1416) and his brother Charles V (1338–80, king of France from 1364), Mary of Burgundy (1457–82), and Anne of Brittany (1477–1514), and it is certainly true that the patronage of the immensely rich nobility must have given a great boost to the fashion for owning illuminated manuscripts. It must have made a few artists very rich too. But the Duc de Berry, for example, would not have seen himself primarily as a collector of Books of Hours: he owned about three hundred manuscripts, of which only fifteen were Books of Hours, sixteen were Psalters, and eighteen were Breviaries. He also possessed at least ten castles, fifty swans, fifteen hundred dogs, a monkey, an ostrich, and a camel. It is fair to suggest that it was hardly a typical household. His greatest manuscript, the *Très Riches Heures* (now in the Musée Condé at Chantilly) is famous precisely because it is such a freak (Pls. 157–8). It is far bigger and far richer than any normal Book of Hours, and it was left unfinished when the duke died.

For the present chapter it will be more useful to leave aside the very opulent royal Books of Hours and to consider the more typical manuscripts which any well-to-do medieval family might have purchased. A Book of Hours is a compendium of different devotional texts which the owner could read in private. One learns to recognize each of the separate sections of a Book of Hours. This is quite easy to do. The core of the manuscript (usually about a third of the way through the volume) comprises the Hours of the Virgin: a standard series of prayers and psalms intended to be used in honour of the Virgin Mary at each of the canonical hours of the day. These are Matins, Lauds, Prime, Terce, Sext, None, Vespers, and Compline. It is because of these that the text is called a 'Book of Hours'. Each one begins at least with a big illuminated initial and generally with a painted illustration too. They are almost always in Latin. Matins starts 'Domine labia mea aperies' ('Lord, open thou my lips') and goes on

155 Vienna, Österreichisches Nationalbibliothek MS. 1857, f. 14v; the Hours of Mary of Burgundy, Flanders, *c.* 1480.
This miniature shows Mary of Burgundy (1457–82), daughter of Charles the Bold and wife of the Emperor Maximilian, using her Book of Hours as she sits by an open window through which one can see a chapel where Mary and her family are kneeling before the Virgin and Child.

'Et os meum annunciabit laudem tuam' ('And my mouth shall show forth thy praise' – to use the translation which is still used in Matins in the English prayerbook). All the other hours, except Compline, begin 'Deus in adiutorium meum intende' ('God make speed to save me'). Sometimes the words are abbreviated but they should always be recognizable. They occur below the miniatures on all those Christmas cards reproduced from manuscripts. Compline, which is the last hour of the day, begins 'Converte nos deus salutaris noster' ('Direct us, God of our salvation'). Each of the hours, then, consists of a very short hymn, psalms (usually three of them – such as Psalms 119 to 121 at Terce, or 122 to 124 at Sext), a brief reading or *capitulum* (chapter) and a prayer. All these are interspersed with sentences headed with 'Ant.', 'V', and 'R'. These are the antiphons, versicles, and responses and they can differ greatly from one manuscript to another.

The owner of a Book of Hours was meant to stop eight times a day and read the appropriate text, probably speaking it quietly under the breath. There are certainly some contemporary descriptions of people doing exactly this. Monks and nuns, of course, were obliged to read their Breviary the same number of times a day, and the central text of a Book of Hours is basically only a shorter and lay version of the same round of monastic prayers. Cynics will ask whether Books of Hours were really used much. We do not know the answer. Some existing manuscripts are in such fresh condition that it is difficult to imagine that they were read often, but perhaps the examples that survive are just the exceptions; possibly the ordinary copies were simply read to pieces. It sounds a great nuisance to have to go through a whole service so often in the day, but in fact you can experiment with reading a Book of Hours aloud and it takes only about three and a half minutes to mumble through one of the shorter offices.

Other fundamental texts in a Book of Hours are as follows. Manuscripts almost always open with a calendar of the Church year, listing saints' days for each month and headed with an illuminated 'KL' at the top of the page. Ordinary saints' days are usually written in black ink and special feasts are in red ink (this is the origin of the term 'red-letter day'). A pretty variation (typical of Paris and later of Rouen too) is for the saints' names to be written alternately in red and blue throughout with the important festivals written in burnished gold. Then there are sometimes short texts between the end of the calendar and the Hours of the Virgin. Often these comprise four short readings from the Gospels and two prayers to the Virgin which are known from their opening words as the 'Obsecro te' and 'O intemerata'. Following the Office of the Virgin in a Book of Hours we can expect more texts. Again these vary, according to date and region and (very probably) just how much a customer was prepared to pay. The most easily recognizable are the Penitential Psalms with a Litany, and the Office of the Dead. The Penitential Psalms are seven in number (Psalms 6, 31, 37, 50, 101, 129, and 142) and are all on the theme of the sinner seeking forgiveness. The Litany is an exceedingly ancient incantation. It lists a whole series of saints' names followed by 'OR', which is 'ora pro nobis', pray for us:

Holy Mother of God – pray for us,
Holy Virgin of Virgins – pray for us,
St. Michael – pray for us,
St. Gabriel – pray for us,

and so on, including angels and archangels, apostles and evangelists, martyrs, confessors and virgins, and then pleas such as

from hardness of heart – Good Lord deliver us,
from lightning and tempest – Good Lord deliver us,
from sudden and unexpected death – Good Lord deliver us.

It is a very emotive text, going right back to the earliest Christian liturgy and associated with the Penitential Psalms from at least the tenth century. The fear of sudden death was a real one in the Middle Ages, plague and warfare being always imminent. One can see during the fifteenth century the development of the obsessive fascination with death, the skeletal spectre attacking indiscriminately, and with the symbols of death which remind us all of our mortality. This brings us to the Office of the Dead in a Book of Hours. It is a long section usually towards the end. It is a comparatively late element in medieval piety in that, though its origins go back to the ninth century, it hardly came into general use until the thirteenth century. The Office of the Dead comprises further psalms and readings primarily intended to be said around the bier of a dead person, but also recited daily as a reminder of one's mortality and (as some thought) as a protection against dying suddenly and unprepared.

These are some of the essential elements in a Book of Hours. The selection varies enormously, however. Many manuscripts include short rounds of Hours of the Cross and

156 (RIGHT) Chantilly, Musée Condé MS.71, f.8; the Hours of Etienne Chevalier, Paris, *c.*1452–60.
The Book of Hours made by Jean Fouquet for Etienne Chevalier (c.1410–74), Treasurer of France, must have been one of the finest fifteenth-century French manuscripts before it was cut up and its miniatures framed separately in the late eighteenth century. The illustration of the Nativity of Christ marked the opening of Prime in the Hours of the Virgin and shows the first line of text at the foot of the page.

157 (OVERLEAF, LEFT) Chantilly, Musée Condé MS.1284, f.86v; the Très Riches Heures of the Duc de Berry, Paris, *c.*1413–16 and Bourges, *c.*1485.
The Très Riches Heures was one of the most ambitious of all illuminated manuscripts and is the most famous surviving Book of Hours. The patron, Jean, Duc de Berry (1340–1416), and the three artists, Paul de Limbourg and his brothers, all died before the project was completed. The miniature illustrated here was designed by the Limbourgs but was executed seventy years later by the Bourges illuminator Jean Colombe who was employed by Charles, Duc de Savoie (d.1489), a later owner of the manuscript. It shows the opening of the Office of the Dead.

158 (OVERLEAF, RIGHT) Chantilly, Musée Condé MS.1284, detail of f.2v; the Très Riches Heures of the Duc de Berry, Paris, *c.*1413–16.
This extraordinary evocation of a winter's scene illustrates the page for February in the Calendar of the Très Riches Heures. It is certainly one of the finest paintings by the Limbourgs and among the greatest images in medieval art.

DEVS IN ADIVTORIVM MEVM INTENDE DNE AD ADIV

ribus percipe domine:
intellige clamorem
meum
tionis mee: rex meus et
deus meus.

Hours of the Holy Ghost. Frequently they include prayers to particular saints, known as the Memorials (or sometimes Suffrages) of the Saints. These generally come right at the end. Other prayers may include two in French, the Quinze Joyes and the Sept Requêtes. One also finds eccentric little texts like the verses of St. Bernard, sometimes preceded by an anecdote explaining their origin. One day (the rubrics in the Book of Hours tell us) the Devil appeared to St. Bernard and boasted that he knew of seven special verses in the Psalms so efficacious that whoever recited them daily could not die in sin. St. Bernard cried, 'What are they? Tell me at once!' 'I shan't', said the Devil, 'You shall not know them.' St. Bernard then replied that he would have to recite the entire Psalter every day in order to be sure of including the seven magic verses, and the Devil, fearing that this excessive devotion would do too much good, quickly revealed the verses.

Because a Book of Hours was not an official Church service-book of any kind but a compendium largely made by secular booksellers for use at home by the laity, variations (and mistakes) abound. The makers of Books of Hours added what was required by the customer rather than by some Church authority. To the modern social historian there can be great interest in these peculiar prayers grafted on to the end of the essential Book of Hours text. St. Margaret was invoked during childbirth, St. Apollonia was called upon by sufferers from toothache (a historically minded dentist could do a fascinating survey plotting in which parts of Europe these prayers occur most), and credulous incantations and extravagant offers of thousands of years' indulgence for the use of some little prayer all have their place in coming to an understanding of lay piety in the fifteenth century. The fact is that Books of Hours were extremely popular. Families who had never owned another manuscript went out to purchase a Book of Hours. Manuscripts are sometimes crammed with added dates of domestic births and deaths and christenings, like the Victorian family Bibles. We can gauge something of the vast market for Books of Hours from the fact that when printing was invented there were at least 760 separate printed editions of Books of Hours published between 1485 and 1530. When we think that surviving manuscript copies are even more numerous than printed versions, we realize that even more must have been produced by hand than were ever printed. It was the basic book for medieval households. Some of its texts (almost forgotten today) must have been known by heart by half Europe. We should remember too that it was from the Book of Hours that children were taught to read. Isabelle of Bavaria is known to have ordered a Book of Hours for her daughter Jeanne in 1398 and an 'A, b, c, d, des Psaumes' for her younger daughter Michelle in 1403: both girls were then about six or seven. The word 'primer', meaning a first reading book, is said to derive from the office of Prime. To the great majority of the medieval population of Europe, the first book they knew, and often the only one, must have been the Book of Hours.

It sometimes seems surprising, therefore, that there is no up-to-date edition of the text for use by students of the Middle Ages. Its cultural impact (if that is not too pompous a term for an illuminated prayerbook) was wider and deeper than that of many rare literary texts worked over and over again by modern editors. It reached people too with no other knowledge of literacy. Anyone who could be encouraged to edit the first printed edition of the Book of Hours since the sixteenth century would win the gratitude of all historians of manuscripts. The task, however, will be made immensely complicated by the number of surviving manuscripts and their endless subtle differences.

These variations should be a delight, however, to historians of books. They can help us localize and sometimes date manuscript Books of Hours. This makes the Book of Hours a particularly valuable text for the study of fifteenth-century art. Whereas a panel painting or a pottery jug or a piece of furniture, for example, could often have been made almost anywhere in Europe, a Book of Hours can sometimes be localized to the very town where it was to be used. The first thing to check is the 'Use' of the Hours of the Virgin. This is

159 London, British Library, Add. MS. 35216, ff. 62v–63r; Book of Hours, Paris, *c.* 1475. *These pages show part of the text for None in the Hours of the Virgin. On the left are the antiphon* 'Sicut lilium' *and the capitulum* 'Per te dei', *characteristics of the Use of Paris.*

a test principally of value for manuscripts made in France. We have mentioned that the psalms and readings within the Hours of the Virgin are interspersed with verses and responses. These often varied greatly according to the local custom ('Use') of a particular diocese. Exactly why they varied is difficult to understand: some really quite small towns like Thérouanne, Bayeux, and Le Mans patriotically had their own Use. There are other more general Uses such as that of Utrecht (which was normal for all the Netherlands), Sarum or Salisbury (which was used throughout England and in continental manuscripts intended for English customers), and the ubiquitous Use of Rome which occurs in all Italian Books of Hours, in most Flemish Books of Hours (this is particularly frustrating), and increasingly often in France by the end of the fifteenth century. None the less it must be the first priority of the student of a Book of Hours to identify its Use.

The simplest method is to look for the offices of Prime and None in the Hours of the Virgin. If the book has miniatures, these are the ones illustrated with the Nativity and the Presentation in the Temple. Then turn to the end of the office and locate the *capitulum*, which is a short reading of several lines and ought to be marked 'c' or 'cap'. Just before this, perhaps in smaller script, will be an antiphon indicated with 'a' or 'ant' (Pl. 159). Note down the antiphon and *capitulum* both for Prime and for None. The most common variations are shown in the table.

Be fairly careful. There can be deceptive exceptions. B.L. Add. MS. 35218 is of the Use of Besançon but the manuscript is signed and dated in Barcelona in Spain. B.N. MS. lat. 1425 is of the Use of Limoges but the scribe explicitly claims that he made it in Paris in 1449. Sometimes scribes must have copied their exemplars without really noticing the antiphons. One can imagine too a merchant from Besançon (for example) visiting a bookshop in Paris to order a Book of Hours to take back to his home town. The big workshops in Rouen were evidently able to supply manuscripts of the Use of Coutances, Lisieux, Evreux, and elsewhere in Normandy as well as of the Use of Rouen itself. Flemish workshops had a long-standing tradition of making books to sell to the English merchants in Bruges: they made Books of Hours of the Use of Sarum and marked them 'secundum usum Anglie' (according to English use). None the less, it is useful (and quite fun) to delve into antiphons and to come up, like a conjurer, with a really obscure local use.

Now turn to the calendar at the beginning. This indicates the saints commemorated on particular days of the year and was useful both for Church observance and for writing the date on documents (which are likely to be dated on the Eve of Michaelmas, for instance, or the Feast of St. Martin, rather than 28 September or 11 November). Look for local saints singled out in red (Pl. 161). If your Book of Hours is of the Use of Paris and the patron saint of Paris, St. Geneviève, is in red or gold on 3 January, then almost certainly the manuscript is Parisian. If you think it may be from Rouen, check for St. Romanus singled out in red on 23 October; the calendar may also include other Rouen feasts such as the Translation of St. Romanus on 17 June, and SS. Ouen, Austrebert, and Wandrille. For Ghent and Bruges, try SS. Bavo (1 October) and Donatian (14 October); for Tours, try St. Gatian (18 December) as well as St. Martin (11 November); for Florence, try St. Zenobius (25 May); and for Venice, try the Dedication of St. Mark (8 October). The Litany and Memorials are also worth looking at. There may be invocations of local saints there too. Both the calendar and the Litany may provide clues for dating a manuscript, especially if they include saints who were not canonized until the fifteenth century. St. Nicholas of Tolentino (10 September) became a saint in 1446, St. Vincent Ferrer (5 April) in 1455, St. Osmund (4 December) in 1457, and St. Bonaventura (14 July) in 1482. An especially useful name is St. Bernardinus of Siena, who died in 1444 and was canonized in 1450. His cult spread very quickly, and when a determined owner assures you that his Book of Hours is fourteenth century, look at 20 May in the calendar; if Bernardinus is there, the book cannot be older than the mid-fifteenth century.

PRIME		NONE		
antiphon	*capitulum*	*antiphon*	*capitulum*	
Assumpta es . . .	Quae est . . .	Pulchra es . . .	In plateis . . .	USE OF ROME
Benedicta tu . . .	Felix namque . . .	Sicut lilium . . .	Per te dei . . .	USE OF PARIS
Maria virgo . . .	Per te dei . . .	Pulchra es . . .	Et radicavi . . .	USE OF ROUEN
O admirabile . . .	In omnibus . . .	Germinavit . . .	Et radicavi . . .	USE OF SARUM
Ecce tu pulchra . . .	Ego quasi . . .	Fons hortorum . . .	Et radicavi . . .	USE OF BESANÇON
O admirabile . . .	Virgo verbo . . .	Ecce Maria . . .	Et radicavi . . .	USE OF POITIERS
Doe du ontsprekeliken . . .	Van aen beghin . . .	Siet Maria . . .	Ic bin verhoget . . .	USE OF UTRECHT

160 (LEFT) London, Sotheby's, 3 July, 1984, lot 89, f.7v; Book of Hours, Flanders, *c.*1430–50. *This miniature from the opening of Matins is in the style of the Master of Guillebert de Mets, a southern Netherlandish artist who is possibly to be identified with Jean de Pestivien. It shows the Annunciation. The Virgin herself has been reading a Book of Hours and has other manuscripts on a high shelf by the ceiling.*

161 (RIGHT, ABOVE) London, Sotheby's, 10 December 1980, lot 102, ff.3v–4r; the Hours of Nicolas von Firmian, probably Flanders, *c.*1500. *This manuscript was made for a Tyrolese nobleman Nicolas von Firmian (d.1510) and was probably illuminated in Bruges. The illustrated Calendar shows the nobility riding out in June and the peasants mowing grass in July.*

162 (RIGHT, BELOW) London, Victoria and Albert Museum MS.L.39–1981, ff.21v–22r; Book of Hours, Bruges, *c.*1520. *This manuscript is in the style of Simon Bening, the best-known Bruges illuminator of the early sixteenth century (pl.164), and shows here the opening of the Office of the Dead.*

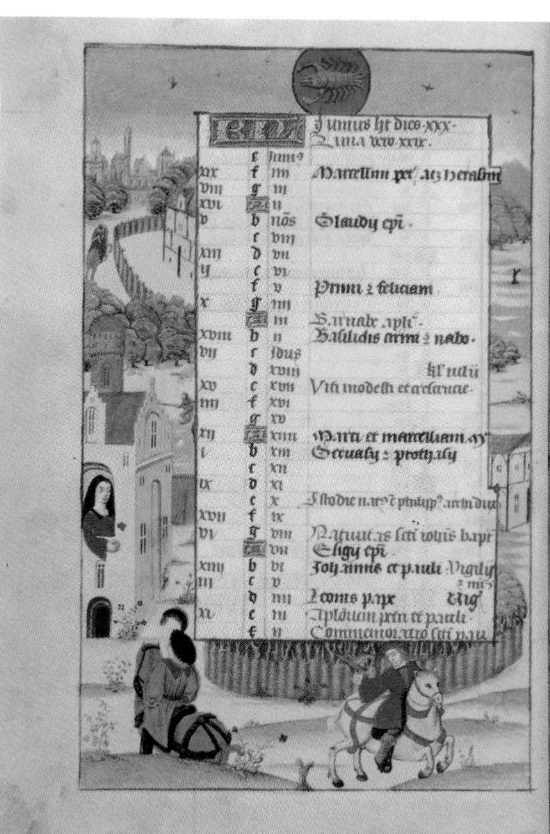

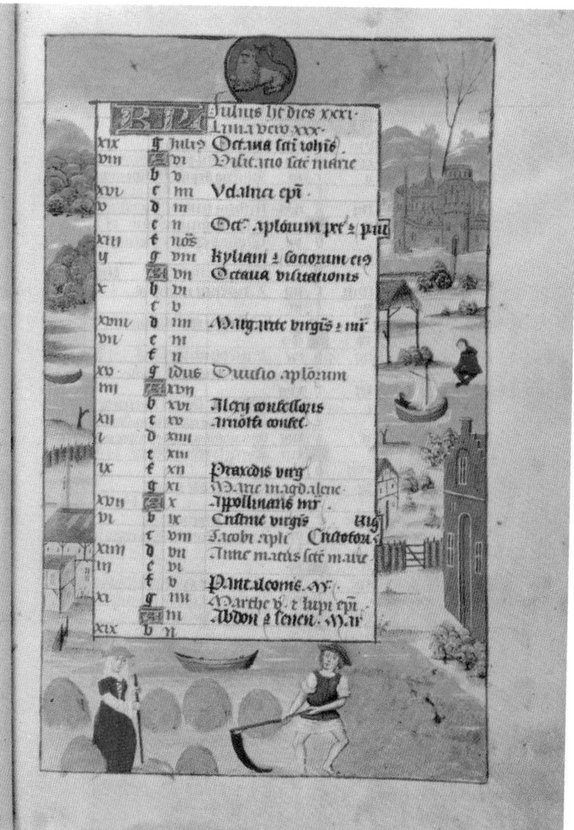

Using these tests for dating and localizing Books of Hours and aided by the more usual techniques of script and decoration, the history of Books of Hours can be plotted from surviving manuscripts. There are a few thirteenth-century copies from England, France, and Flanders. They are generally very small manuscripts, rather like the little Psalters of the period which were intended to be slipped in the pocket or carried at the waist. Fourteenth-century Books of Hours exist in reasonable numbers for France and England, and some are expensively illuminated manuscripts like the charming Hours of Jeanne d'Evreux, queen of France, painted in Paris about 1325 and now in the Cloisters Museum in New York. We have already seen how Paris had an organized book trade around its university from the thirteenth century and we must certainly ascribe to Paris many of the best-known Books of Hours of the period of Jean, Duc de Berry. The *Très Belles Heures* of the Duc de Berry was begun about 1382, and his *Petites Heures* dates from about 1388. Both are Parisian manuscripts. By about 1400 a great many Books of Hours were being written and illuminated in Paris. Probably for the first time books were being produced in quantity for sale. The generation of about 1400 to 1420 was the greatest for the manufacture of Books of Hours of the Use of Paris. They are often of lovely quality (Pl. 166). In the meantime we start to find some of the earliest Italian Books of Hours. There is in Adelaide, Australia, a delightful little Perugian Book of Hours of about 1375. The first Books of Hours that can be attributed to London date from the late fourteenth century. Flanders too began to make Books of Hours commercially, followed in the early fifteenth century by the Netherlands. These are usually rather uninspired and provincial-looking manuscripts: the greatest Netherlandish illuminators still moved to Paris to practise their trade. Artists like the Limbourg brothers and the Boucicaut Master came to Paris from the north to the centre of the book trade. The principal business for most of them must have been Books of Hours.

Sadly (from the point of view of art, anyway), politics intervened. The English invaded and defeated the French at the battle of Agincourt in 1415. Their prisoners included Jean de Boucicaut, marshal of France, and owner of one of the finest of all Books of Hours. Paris was already torn by the civil war between the Armagnacs and the Burgundians, which lasted until the assassination of John the Fearless, duke of Burgundy, in 1419. A year later the English armies of Henry V entered Paris. This seems to have marked the end of the first great period of the production of Parisian Books of Hours. It is extraordinary how difficult it becomes to localize manuscripts in Paris between about 1420 and the mid-century. The social disturbance caused by civil war and foreign occupation must have been terrible. Hungry people

163 (LEFT) Germany, private collection, Book of Hours, ff. 85v–86r; Flanders (probably Bruges), 1466.
This Book of Hours, written in the round italianate script suited to the taste of southern European clients, is dated 1466. The pages here mark the opening of None in the Hours of the Virgin.

164 (ABOVE) New York, Metropolitan Museum of Art, Robert Lehman Collection, RLC. 191; self-portrait of Simon Bening (1483–1561)
This tiny portrait of Bening at the age of 75 shows the great artist working by the window of his house in Bruges.

do not buy books. Only one outstanding illuminator stayed on in Paris, the so-called Bedford Master who takes his name from a Breviary and a Book of Hours associated with the English regent of France, the Duke of Bedford, brother of Henry V (Pl. 172). It really seems as though all the scribes and illuminators fled to the provinces. Certainly the fashion for owning Books of Hours spread right over France in the middle third of the fifteenth century. We can ascribe Books of Hours to Amiens, Rouen, Rennes, Nantes, Angers, Tours, Bourges, Dijon, Besançon, Troyes, Rheims, and elsewhere in a huge circle around Paris. An enormous number of manuscripts were made – not necessarily expensive ones, but capitalizing on a vast market for books. In certain provincial cities, such as Rouen and Tours, the trade in Books of Hours was so successful that it continued to flourish even after the middle of the fifteenth century when other illuminators drifted back to the capital.

An independent tradition of manuscript production in Flanders was in the meantime moving rapidly into the making of Books of Hours. They were not just for local customers, but (with typical Belgian business acumen) for export as well. After the Treaty of Arras in 1435, the dukes of Burgundy were able to move the seat of their vast dominions to Flanders, and some great illuminators worked for the Burgundian court in Lille, Tournai, Valenciennes, and elsewhere. Ducal patronage attracted the personnel of the book trade, as it had in Paris in the late fourteenth century. The market towns of Ghent and Bruges were ready when the last duke of Burgundy died in 1477. These essentially bourgeois towns, unburdened by warring local princes, became world centres for Books of Hours. Many were made for sale to England; in fact, probably just about the majority of surviving fifteenth-century Books of Hours of the Use of Sarum give away their true origin by featuring saints such as St. Donatian of Bruges in the calendar. Books of Hours were being made in Bruges for the Italian market as early as 1466 if one can judge from a hitherto unpublished example of the Use of Rome dated in that year and written in a rounded Italian script (Pl. 163). Another, in the Newberry Library in Chicago (MS. 39) is probably not much later; it is in a Spanish script and several rubrics are in Catalan. The style of illumination is so typical of Bruges that it seems certain to have been made there, perhaps by a Catalan scribe, for sale to Spanish visitors. By 1500 the art of manuscript illustration in Ghent and Bruges was second to none in Europe (Pls. 161 and 162). The Flemish Books of Hours were especially famous for their realistic borders looking as though flowers had actually fallen onto the pages (Pls. 182 and 183), and for their delicate miniatures with marvellous landscapes. Simon Bening, the best-known Bruges painter of Books of Hours (Pl. 162), was praised in his own time as the greatest Flemish artist for painting trees and far distances. The customers evidently adored these jewel-like manuscripts.

Books of Hours were made elsewhere in Europe too. German examples are curiously rare (Austrians like Nicolas von Firmian and Franz Thurn und Taxis, postmaster in the Tyrol, ordered theirs from Flanders), but Spanish and Portuguese Books of Hours exist. Italian examples are numerous, usually small books without elaborate decoration. English Books of Hours might have been even more common if they had not been discarded at the Reformation. Dutch Books of Hours are very numerous especially from the later fifteenth century. They can be particularly fascinating because the text was usually translated into the Dutch language, and the miniatures have biblical scenes set in a homely atmosphere with tiled floors and crowded domestic interiors filled with the paraphernalia of the sitting rooms of the bourgeois families who first owned the manuscripts.

Very few Books of Hours are signed by their makers. Most of these are either very early or very late. A Book of Hours in Leningrad was written by Gilles Mauleon, monk of St-Denis, for Jeanne of Burgundy in 1317. Another in Châlons-sur-Marne was made for a local musician there by J.

165 (LEFT) London, Estate of the late Major J. R. Abbey, JA.7398, f.43v; the Hours of Margaret, Duchess of Clarence, London, *c.*1430.
The first owner of this little-known English royal Book of Hours was Margaret (d.1439), widow of Thomas, Duke of Clarence (1388–1421), brother of King Henry V and of John, Duke of Bedford, and Humfrey, Duke of Gloucester.

166 (ABOVE) Oxford, Bodleian Library MS.Douce 144, f.131r; Book of Hours, Paris, 1408 (1407, old style).
The colophon of this manuscript is dated in the year that the bridges of Paris fell (pl.170). The miniature here, which is in the style of the Boucicaut Master, is from the Memorials to the Saints and shows St. Paul on the road to Damascus.

167 London, British Library, Add. MS. 58280, ff. 10v–11; Book of Hours, England, 1474.
This tiny English Book of Hours, illustrated here life size, is signed by the scribe Roger Pynchebek and is dated 1474. It was given to the British Library in 1974.

168 Paris, Bibliothèque Nationale MS. lat. 1169, f. 42r; Book of Hours, probably Besançon, early fifteenth century.
This home-made little manuscript is signed on several pages by the scribe Alan with the information that his wife illuminated it.

Bruni in 1537. A copy of about 1410 is signed by the scribe Alan with the information that his wife illuminated the book (B.N. MS. lat. 1169; Pl. 168). It is a rather roughly made manuscript of the Use of Besançon, and it is possible that this was not a commercial partnership but simply that Alan and his wife could not afford to buy a manuscript and so made one themselves. Arsenal MS. 286 is a beautifully illuminated Book of Hours made in 1444 by a monk Jean Mouret for his own use. There is an English book of 1464 written and signed by William Fairfax, who says that the manuscript is to be passed to his son and heir and to his descendants forever. Jehan de Luc made a Book of Hours for his wife in 1524 (The Hague, Mus. Meerman. W. 10. F. 33). All these are rather peculiar manuscripts. Most people wanting a Book of Hours probably went to a bookshop.

We know something about the bookshops in Paris from the documents of the university book trade there. Many are recorded in the rue Neuve-Notre-Dame opposite the Cathedral of Notre-Dame and it was probably from there that many people would have ordered a Book of Hours around 1400. A very rich collector, like the Duc de Berry, doubtless put his commissions in the hands of a big agent like Jacques Rapondi, a member of a great family of international brokers and merchants originally from Lucca in Tuscany. The Duc de Berry probably never entered a bookshop, and his scribes and illuminators were paid members of his household. Most people went to shops, however. One of these was owned by Pierre Portier, recorded as one of the university stationers in 1376 and still in business in 1409. In November 1397 he received 64 shillings from Isabelle of Bavaria for writing eight vellum quires for a Book of Hours (this works out, in fact, at a shilling a leaf) and a further 54 shillings 'pour avoir nettoyé, blanchy, corrigé, reffourni, doré, relié et mis à point lesdictes heures'. Thus there were two separate accounts, one for writing out the book, and the other for cleaning and whitening the vellum before writing, correcting the text afterwards, filling it in, applying the gold, binding, and finishing off the new book. Pierre Portier no doubt subcontracted out the writing of the text and had to supply the vellum and to bind it up afterwards. If there had been miniatures too he might have had to take the leaves to yet another craftsman. Some professional scribes and illuminators are recorded as living on the left bank in the rue des Enlumineurs (now rue Boutebrie).

It is very rare for Parisian Books of Hours to contain exact information about when they were made, and it is only by historical deduction that we can date major manuscripts like the Hours of Charles the Noble to around 1405 or the *Belles Heures* of the Duc de Berry to around 1409. Two Books of Hours, however, contain very interesting dated colophons. The first is Bodleian MS. Douce 144 (Pl. 166) which has the inscription on f. 271 that it was made and completed in the year 1407 when the bridges of Paris fell (Pl. 170). The second manuscript was formerly in the Chester Beatty collection (W. MS. 103) and its miniatures are now dispersed among several libraries including Princeton University, the University of North Carolina (Pl. 169), and the Barber Institute in Birmingham. It is written by the same scribe as the Douce manuscript and had an inscription on f. 158v that it was made in the year 1408 when the bridges of Paris fell. The three bridges of Paris were swept away by floods between 29 and 31 January 1408 (they called this 1407 in the Bodleian volume as the year was still reckoned as beginning on 25 March). Obviously the event was of great importance to the makers of these two Books of Hours. One wonders if the bookseller's stall was on the bridge, perhaps the Petit Pont which joined the Ile de la Cité to the left bank and the student quarter. We know that the bridges included the covered shops of merchants, money changers, drapers, smiths, and other craftsmen, and one can see the Petit Pont built up with houses in miniatures of Paris such as that on a Book of Hours in the Rylands Library in Manchester (MS. lat. 164, f. 254r; Pl. 174) or on the leaf from the Hours of Etienne Chevalier in the Metropolitan Museum in New York.

Both the Books of Hours of 1408 have miniatures by more than one illuminator. The two distinct styles in the Bodleian volume have led art historians to ascribe it to the Boucicaut Master or a close follower and to an artist whose style is very like the early work of the Bedford Master. These are the two big names in Parisian manuscript painting in the early fifteenth century (Pls. 171–2). There is circumstantial evidence for identifying these two artists with Jacques Coene (who is documented in Paris from 1398 to 1404) and perhaps Jean Haincelin (who seems to be documented in Paris from 1403

169 (RIGHT) Chapel Hill, University of North Carolina, The Ackland Art Museum, Ackland Fund, 69.7.2; single miniature from a Book of Hours, Paris, 1408.
This miniature of King David, marking the opening of the Penitential Psalms, was formerly f. 64r in Chester Beatty W. MS. 103. *Like Bodleian* MS. *Douce 144 (Pls. 166 and 170), it is dated in the year that the bridges of Paris fell.*

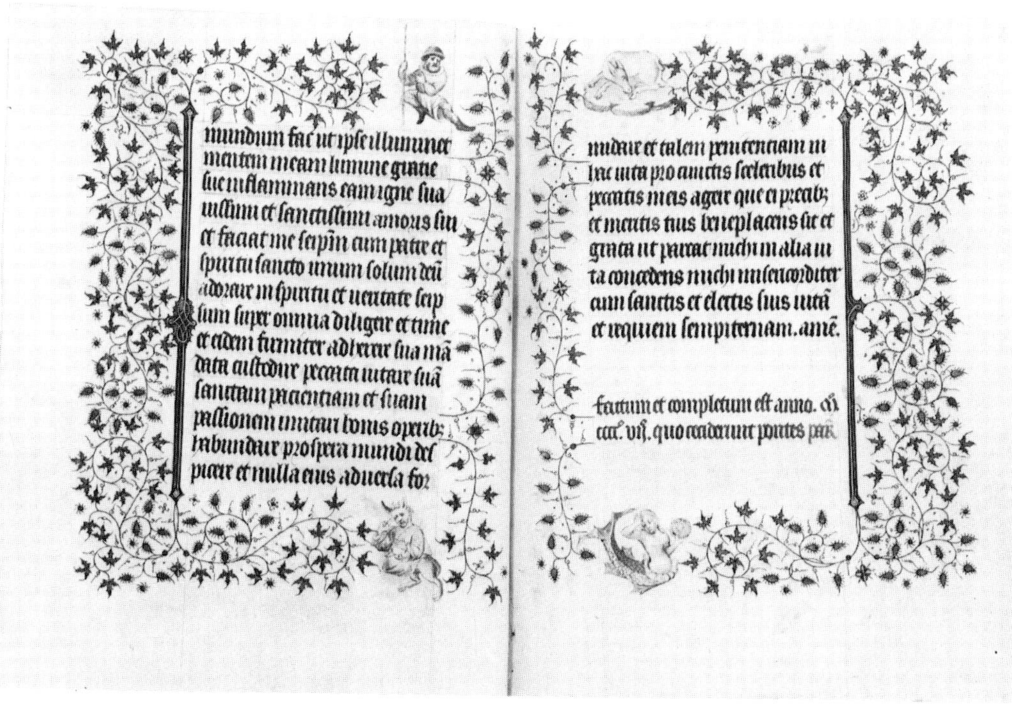

170 (LEFT) Oxford, Bodleian Library MS. Douce 144, ff. 26v–27r; Book of Hours, Paris, 1408 (1407, old style).
The colophon from the manuscript illustrated in Pl. 166 says that it was made and completed in 1407 when the bridges of Paris fell. The bridges over the Seine were swept away by floods on 29–31 January 1408. The scribe is using the archaic dating whereby the year was thought of as ending on 31 March, and so the Book of Hours must have been made in February or March that year. The same scribe wrote Chester Beatty W. MS. 103 *(Pl. 169) after 1 April since he dates that colophon 1408.*

to 1448). Their styles of illumination are quite distinct: the Boucicaut Master paints tall, haughty, aristocratic figures in beautiful clear colours: the Bedford Master depicts shorter, more human figures with snub noses. They are the most famous artists among many anonymous painters who worked on Books of Hours and who have been given such names as the Egerton Master, the Troyes Master, the Master of the Brussels Initials, and the Master of the Harvard Hannibal. Because Parisian miniatures are so outstanding, it is too easy to suppose that each painter had a studio there (like a Renaissance artist in Italy) and Books of Hours are often given attributions such as 'workshop of the Egerton Master'. Perhaps one tends to think of the Boucicaut and Bedford styles as representing two rival operations. Their collaboration in a single Book of Hours in 1408, for example, is very puzzling to art historians. Probably the truth was very different. The client probably went to the bookshop on the Petit Pont or perhaps in the rue Neuve-Notre-Dame and explained what he wanted. It is possible (but not probable) that the keeper of the shop had some unbound gatherings in stock. The customer would discuss which texts he wanted added to the basic core of the Book of Hours. He would perhaps choose a script from a sheet of sample handwritings like the fascinating one dated 1447, now in The Hague

171 (PREVIOUS PAGE, LEFT) Paris, Musée Jacquemart-André MS.2, f.90v; the Hours of the Maréchal de Boucicaut, Paris, *c.*1405–8.
The Boucicaut Master, perhaps to be identified with the artist Jacques Coene, takes his name from the huge Book of Hours made for Jean de Boucicaut (d.1421), Marshal of France, who was taken prisoner by the English at the Battle of Agincourt in 1415.

172 (PREVIOUS PAGE, RIGHT) London, British Library, Add.MS.18850, f.15v; the Bedford Hours, Paris, *c.*1423.
The Bedford Master, the second great Parisian illuminator (possibly identifiable with Jean Haincelin), is named from his work in this Book of Hours and a later Breviary (BN, MS.lat.17294) associated with John of Lancaster, Duke of Bedford (1389–1435), brother of Henry V and Regent of France during its occupation by the English.

173 (BELOW) The Hague, Koninklijke Bibliotheek 76.D.45, 4a; scribe's specimen sheet written by Hermannus Strepel, of Münster, in 1447.
From a pattern such as this, exhibited in a bookshop, a customer could select a script when commissioning a manuscript.

174 (RIGHT) Manchester, John Rylands Library, Lat.MS.164, f.254r; Book of Hours, Paris, *c.*1430.
The bridges and houses of Paris appear in this miniature of St. Geneviève, patron saint of Paris, painted in the style of the Bedford Master.

de sainte geneuiefue
felix ancilla dei nos
pondere pressos exonera ⁊ fes
sos mordacibus exue culpis

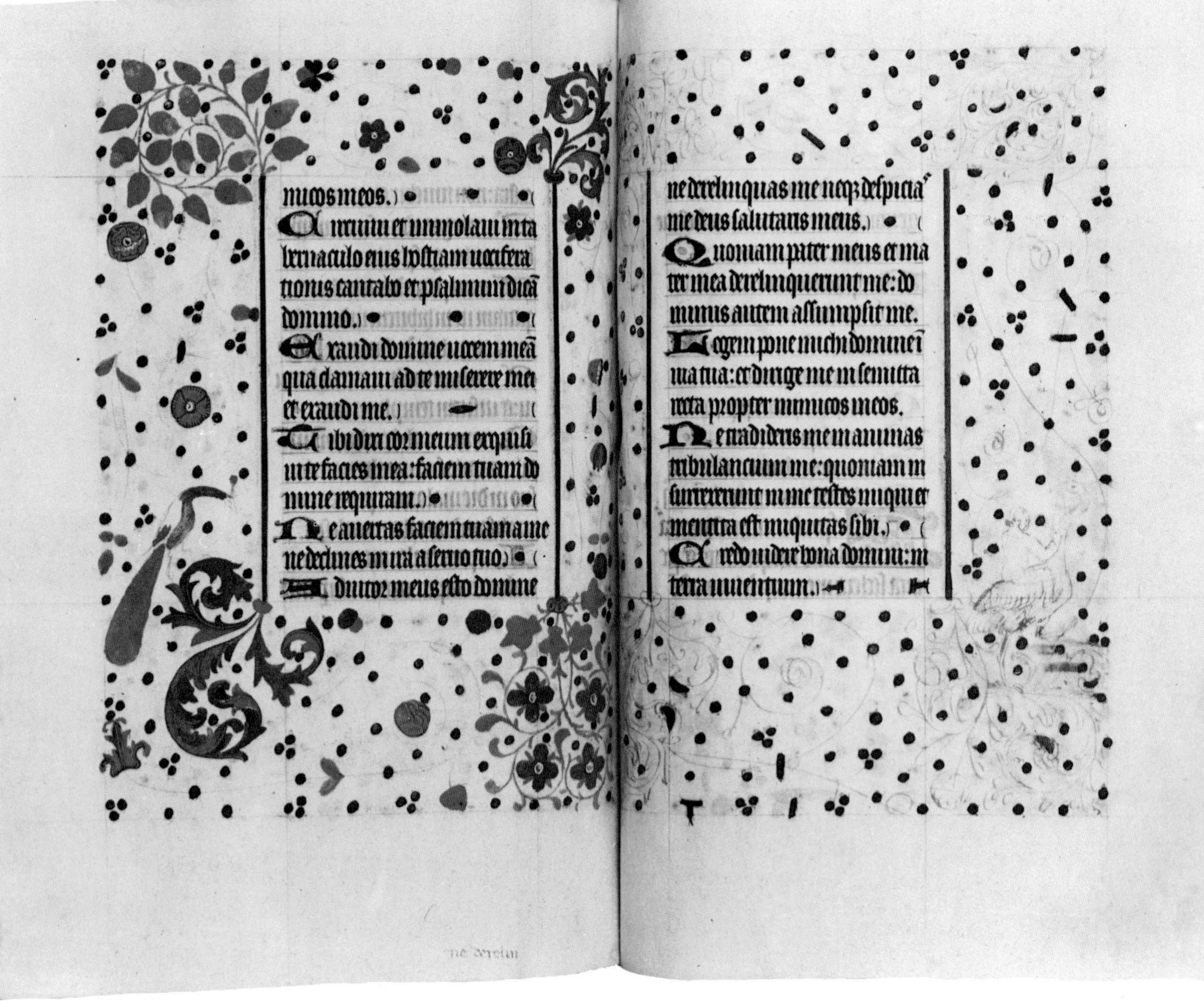

175 New York, Pierpont Morgan Library, M.358, ff.169v–170r; Book of Hours, France (perhaps Provence), *c.*1440–50.
This manuscript was abandoned unfinished. The illuminators have sketched in the designs for borders and have supplied the gold first so that the process of burnishing it would not smudge the painting. On the right-hand page they have begun to paint in the colours. Since f.169v is the last page of a gathering (note the catchword 'ne derelin'), the illuminators were no doubt working on each quite separately.

(MS.76.D.45; Pl.173). Sometimes the bookshop owner may also have been a scribe (as stationers like Raoulet d'Orléans and Jean l'Avenant certainly were) but he was not the artist. It was only after the client had left that they set about making the Book of Hours. Some quires were sent out to one illuminator and some to another (Pl.175). With a little imagination one can visualize the bookseller's apprentice hurrying across the street with several gatherings for the Boucicaut Master to paint, and dropping off a few further up the road at the house of the Bedford Master, and leaving the less important leaves with the assistant who worked for the Master of the Coronation of the Virgin. Some weeks later, when these were done, the bookshop collected up the separate sections, paid the artists, tidied up and bound the leaves (we have seen Pierre Portier doing this in 1397), and then presented the book to the customer, with an invoice. The image is fanciful, but there is no other way to explain the apparently enormous output of some artists and the bizarre collaboration of different painters in an otherwise unified Book of Hours.

Understanding what was going on in the artist's house is even more difficult. The Boucicaut Master, whose style is in the main miniatures of both the Books of Hours dated 1408, takes his name from a vast and lovely Book of Hours with forty-four miniatures made about 1405–08 for the Maréchal de Boucicaut (Musée Jacquemart-André, MS.2; Pl.171). The artist himself was no doubt called upon to paint such a grand manuscript with his own hand. Altogether, however, more than thirty other Books of Hours have been ascribed to the same workshop, all between about 1405 and 1420 (Pls.176 and 177). If one adds together the number of miniatures in each, the total is not far off seven hundred. To add in too the richly illustrated secular texts in the style of the Boucicaut Master (texts like the *Bible Historiale* with over a hundred miniatures each) the grand total of surviving miniatures ascribed to the circle of the Boucicaut Master in a space of only about fifteen years is just over eighteen hundred. That is more than a hundred paintings a year, judged merely from those that happen to survive.

The only way they can have achieved this kind of output must have been with pattern sheets which were designed by the master and which could be copied out at great speed. One sees remarkably similar miniatures from one manuscript to the next. Sometimes pictures are the same but exactly in reverse, suggesting that designs were copied on tracing paper (which was called *carta lustra*) and applied back to front. There must have been model sheets for all the standard scenes required in a Book of Hours: the Annunciation at Matins, the Visitation at Lauds, the Nativity of Christ at Prime, the Annunciation to the Shepherds at Terce, the Adoration of the Magi at Sext, the Presentation in the Temple at None, the Flight into Egypt at Vespers, and the Coronation of the Virgin at Compline. Sometimes figures from one composition were used for another: the calendar miniature of courting couples in April could provide a pretty girl with a garland to accompany the shepherds in their vigil at Terce, and the sower in October could be transferred to the background of the Flight into Egypt at Vespers. The source of some of these compositions can occasionally be traced back to known paintings. The Limbourg brothers adapted a Florentine fresco by Taddeo Gaddi for one of their miniatures in the *Très Riches Heures,* for example. Another less well-known instance occurs in Books of Hours produced according to patterns of the Bedford Master. One of the most splendid portraits by Jan van Eyck, now in the Louvre, shows the French chancellor Nicolas Rolin (1376–1462) kneeling before the Virgin and Child (Pl.178). In the background, seen over the rampart and battlements of a castle, is a marvellous distant view of a winding river and a bridge with people hurrying across and (if one peers closely) a castle on an island and little rowing boats and a landing-stage. It was painted about 1435–37. The view is now famous as one of the earliest examples of landscape painting. The Bedford Master must have admired it too, perhaps in Rolin's house where the original was probably kept until it was bequeathed to the church at Autun. The same landscape was copied almost exactly, even to the little boats and the

176–177 London, Sotheby's, 26 October 1948, lot 436, single leaf, and Brussels, Bibliothèque Royale MS.11051, f.138r; Books of Hours, Paris, *c.*1410–15.

These miniatures from the Office of the Dead are derived from the same model. They are both from Books of Hours in the style of the Boucicaut Master.

178 Paris, Musée du Louvre, Jan van Eyck, portrait of Nicholas Rolin kneeling by his Book of Hours and adoring the Virgin and Child, *c.*1435–7.

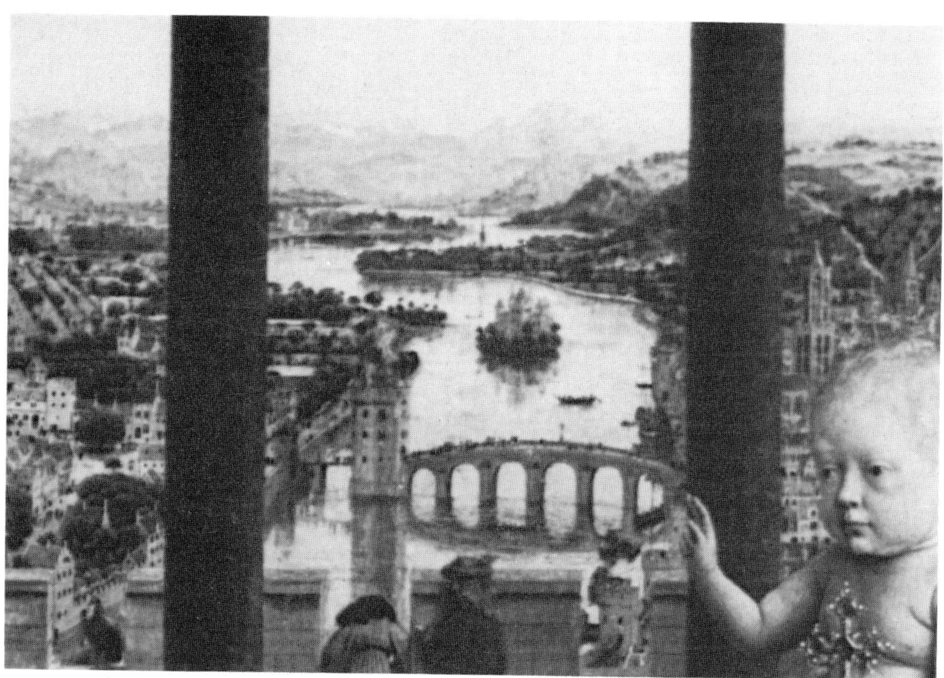

179 (RIGHT) Detail of pl. 178.

180–181 (BELOW) Malibu, The J. Paul Getty Museum MS. Ludwig XI.6, f. 100r, and London, Sotheby's, 13 June 1983, lot 11, f. 105r; Book of Hours, Paris, *c.* 1440–50. *The backgrounds of these miniatures in Books of Hours in the late style of the Bedford Master are derived from the Rolin portrait. The kneeling figure of Rolin himself has been replaced by that of King David and the subject now illustrates the Penitential Psalms.*

bends in the river, into the backgrounds of several Bedford Master miniatures such as the former Marquess of Bute MS.93, f.105r (Pl.181) and the mid-fifteenth-century Hours of Jean Dunois in the British Library (Yates Thompson MS.3, f.162r). It was adapted slightly for Bedford miniatures such as Getty Museum, MS. Ludwig IX.6, f.100r, where the fortified bridge has contracted into part of a castle (Pl.180). The scene gets gradually transformed in other manuscripts into the usual view from the palace of King David in the miniature to illustrate the Penitential Psalms in northern France and then in Flanders. The battlements stay on but the river becomes a lake and then a courtyard (still with little people hurrying to and fro) in the Ghent/Bruges Books of Hours of the sixteenth century (Pl.185). The Bedford Master's sketch of a detail in a portrait that had interested him was transformed remarkably over a hundred years as one illuminator after another duplicated and adapted the original pattern.

Too little information survives on exactly how illuminators kept and copied these patterns. It is important to break away from the modern notion that an artist should strive for originality and that a creator has a kind of monopoly on his own designs. A medieval artist was expected to work according to a specific formula, and this must often have meant using designs and compositions with a familiar precedent. In fact, the genius of a medieval illuminator is reflected in the skill with which he could execute an established subject. Careful adherence to an artistic tradition was required of an artist, as a violinist today is praised for following his score with consummate skill, or as a medieval author often begins a great work of literature by explaining or claiming that he is retelling an old story. A customer would expect a particular subject, especially in a book as naturally conservative as a prayerbook. Illuminators must have borrowed patterns from each other. There was probably a lot of knocking on doors in the rue des Enlumineurs. This

182–183 London, Sir John Soane's Museum MS.4, f.23v; and London, British Library, Add. MS.35313, f.31r; Books of Hours. Ghent or Bruges, *c.*1500.
These miniatures, illustrating the opening of Compline, are in the style of the Master of James IV of Scotland, a Flemish artist whose miniatures are often duplicated almost exactly from one manuscript to the next. The script, however, is quite different, the rounded writing on the left following the fashion of southern Europe (as in pl.163) and that on the right being in accordance with northern taste.

184 Paris, École des Beaux Arts, M.2235; pattern sheet showing scenes from the story of David and Goliath, early sixteenth century.

185 (RIGHT) Malibu, The J. Paul Getty Museum MS. Ludwig IX.18, f.166r; the Spinola Hours, Ghent or Bruges, early sixteenth century.

The marginal scenes are derived from a pattern sheet such as that shown in pl.184. The scene of David in the centre derives ultimately, and through many stages of transmogrification, from the Bedford design illustrated in pls.180–181, and there are faint echoes from the Rolin portrait itself in the distant double tower in the far left, the tiny hurrying horsemen, and the low wall behind the kneeling figure of David.

practice of reusing old designs extended far beyond Paris. Artists took their experience with them, like the Fastolf Master who left the capital about 1420 and apparently moved to Rouen and by about 1440 seems to have been in London. If he did not travel himself, his models certainly did. Thus general Bedford designs occur in Books of Hours made far from their place of origin. Three compositions from the Boucicaut Hours are repeated in Morgan M.161, a Book of Hours probably made in Tours around 1465. One architectural border in a Lyons Book of Hours of about 1480–90 (Sotheby's, 13 July 1977, lot 76, f.19r) is copied from a pattern used in the Hours of Isabella Stuart of about 1417–18 and repeated in the Rohan Hours of about 1420 (Fitzwilliam Museum MS.62, f.141v, and B.N. MS.lat.9471, f.94v). The calendar of the *Très Riches Heures* entered the pattern-books of the Ghent/Bruges illuminators of the early sixteenth century and recurs in the Grimani Breviary and in the December miniature by Simon Bening in B. L. Add.MS.18855, f.108v. Many Rouen Books of Hours of the 1460s to 1480s mirror each other so exactly that one must visualize some kind of production line to multiply almost identical illuminations at great speed (Pls.186–9). We find the same in Paris in the last quarter of the century. The most extreme instances of duplicating miniatures are in the Ghent/Bruges Books of Hours of around 1500. Manuscripts like the Hours of James IV, the Spitzer Hours, the Spinola Hours, the Hours of Eleanor of Portugal, a fine Book of Hours in the Sir John Soane's Museum, and a whole shelf of lesser Flemish manuscripts all have miniatures and borders which must have been reproduced from almost identical patterns (Pls.182–3). What may be one of these actual model sheets is now in the Ecole des Beaux-Arts in Paris (Pl.184): it shows a typical high-quality Flemish border with scenes from the life of David (this is to illustrate the Penitential Psalms) and versions of it reappear in the Spinola Hours (Pl.185) and elsewhere. Clearly, the public appetite for Books of Hours was so huge that the mass multiplication of miniatures was regarded as quite ethical, being the only way to meet the demand.

If the evidence of the bulk production of miniatures tends to undermine our image of the artists as the original geniuses

Ad primam.
Eus in adiuto
rium meum
intende .

49
Eus in adiutori
um meum in
tende
omine ad

Eus in adiutorium
meum intende
omine ad adiu

Eus in adiutoriu
meum intende.
omine ad ad

186–189 (LEFT) Paris, Bibliothèque de l'Arsenal MS.562, f.41v; Paris, Bibliothèque Nationale MS.lat.13277, f.49r; Oxford, Bodleian Library MS.Douce 253, f.50r; and Waddesdon Manor, National Trust, MS.12, f.49r; all miniatures for Prime in Books of Hours, Rouen, *c*.1470.

190 (RIGHT) Paris, Bibliothèque Nationale, MS.nouv.acq.lat.3117, f.41v; Book of Hours, central France (probably Lyons), *c*.1485.
The jagged landscape background and the square-cut faceted architectural border are distinctive features of the Lyons manuscripts in the style of Guillaume Lambert.

that we once thought, we must remember that it was not the artist who designed the book. He was merely a subcontractor in the business. It was the keeper of the bookshop who dealt with the public and who invested money (and therefore responsibility) in the manufacture of Books of Hours. The sending out of written leaves to be illuminated was only part of the business of assembling and selling manuscripts. In Flanders the two operations were so clearly distinct that very many miniatures for Books of Hours were actually painted on separate single leaves, blank on the back, that could be made miles away and only afterwards purchased by the bookseller and bound into Books of Hours. If you peer into the sewing of a Ghent/Bruges Book of Hours you can easily see how the miniatures have been pasted in by wrapping the stub around the back of the quire.

Occasionally we can pick up isolated details about these bookshops. One in Lyons was perhaps owned by Guillaume Lambert as there is a Book of Hours (Quaritch catalogue, 1931, no.47) with an inscription saying it was written in Lambert's house by the gate in 1484, and there is a Missal still in Lyons (MS.516) which Guillaume Lambert wrote in 1466. The illumination of the Book of Hours belongs to a well-defined group of central French manuscripts with characteristic prismatic architectural borders, and no doubt Lambert or his agents sent the manuscript out to be painted by the Lyons artists. His house was near the gate (*'près le portal'*) which may be a city gate, a good place for trade, or the great triple door of Lyons Cathedral. In Rouen the bookshops were certainly around the cathedral, as they had been in Paris, and the courtyard by the north door of Rouen Cathedral is still called the Portail des Libraires, a name already in use by 1479. We know the names of some booksellers who rented their shops from the cathedral in Rouen: different members of the Coquet and Boyvin families, for instance, were in the bookselling business there throughout much of the fifteenth century. We should be looking to these kind of people to understand the manufacture and marketing of such vast numbers of Books of Hours. The customer paid a lot of money and a Book of Hours was specially made for him. The customer paid less money and bought a little one ready-made or a second-hand copy. So appealing were these manuscripts that every moderately well-to-do person in Europe in the fifteenth century seems to have walked out of some bookshop with a Book of Hours under his or her arm. One owner of an English Book of Hours, now privately owned in Denmark, was so proud of his new manuscript that he wrote on the flyleaf: 'He that stelles thes boke he shal be hanked upon on hoke behend the kechen dor.' In the little domestic world of the owner, to hang a thief on the hook behind the kitchen door was the most awful threat imaginable. The Book of Hours was a very precious possession in that household. It was probably their only book.

·7·

Books for Priests

More manuscripts have come down to us from the Middle Ages than anything else, but the most visible survivals of the period are the parish churches. The rural landscape of Europe is still dotted with towers, steeples and onion-shaped domes, and it is easy to picture the old arrangement of village houses clustered around a parish church. Anyone entering one of these churches today will see many books: a shelf of hymnbooks by the door, prayerbooks and perhaps a rack of general Christian literature. There may be guidebooks to the building and parish newspapers. By the chancel steps there will probably be a lectern with a large Bible opened for the daily reading. Modern church pews have a ledge where members of the congregation place their books to participate in the service. Books are very visible in churches. In the Middle Ages it would certainly have been different. There were no pews (people usually stood or sat on the floor), and there would probably have been no books on view. The priest read the Mass in Latin from a manuscript placed on the altar, and the choir chanted their part of the daily office from a volume visible only to them. Members of the congregation were not expected to join in the singing; some might have brought their Books of Hours to help ease themselves into a suitable frame of mind, but the services were conducted by the priests.

The local priest was often a man of some status in the village, usually moderately well educated and reasonably articulate. He supervised the spiritual life of the parishioners: he preached the Christian faith, taught reading and writing, visited the sick, prayed in time of tribulation and led the services of thanksgiving, he heard confessions, conducted baptisms, marriages, funerals and burials, and maintained the constant round of liturgical worship.

Most medieval priests probably had a number of manuscripts. The most important were used regularly in church. It is a paradox that, because of the obsolescence of service-books, many liturgical fragments now survive. A Breviary goes out of date quite quickly: as new festivals are introduced and liturgical practices are modified, the old book is discarded. Pages can work loose and tend to fall out of manuscripts handled frequently, and the whole volume becomes unusable and is laid aside. The Reformation caused the disposal of vast numbers of obsolete Romish service-books. Because of the wear and tear to which liturgical books are subject, they had usually been written on vellum rather than on paper, and discarded sheets of second-hand vellum were always useful. Leaves from medieval service-books were reused as flyleaves and to strengthen the sewing in sixteenth-century bookbindings, and as folders for documents, for patching windows, lining walls, covering jam jars and other domestic uses, and single leaves from medieval Missals, Breviaries and liturgical music manuscripts are really quite common. This chapter will examine these manuscripts, and consider how the priest used them.

First of all, it should be remembered that the church year is based on two simultaneous cycles of services. The first is the Temporal, or Proper of the Time, which observes Sundays and festivals commemorating the life of Christ. It opens with the first Sunday in Advent (the Sunday closest to 30 November) and continues with Christmas (including Epiphany, the Twelfth Day of Christmas), Lent, Paschal Time (from Easter to Ascension eve), and the season of the Ascension (which includes Pentecost, Trinity Sunday, Corpus Christi, and the Sundays after Pentecost). Christmas, of course, is a fixed feast and is always celebrated on 25 December, whether it is a Sunday or not. Easter, however, falls on the Sunday after the first full moon following the spring equinox and it varies considerably, thus changing the dates of other feasts calculated from Easter, such as Ascension Day, which is forty days later, and Pentecost, which is seven weeks after Easter. These are movable feasts. The second quite distinct cycle of the church year is the Sanctoral, or Proper of the Saints. This celebrates the feast days of saints, including those of the Virgin Mary, and it opens with St. Andrew's day (30 November). Some saint's name could be assigned to every day of the calendar year. Local observances varied from place to place, and the calendars in liturgical manuscripts classified or 'graded' saints' days according to the importance to be given to them: ordinary days, important or *semi-duplex*, and of

191 Utrecht, Bibliotheek der Rijksuniversiteit MS. 402, f. 180r; Missal, northern Netherlands, mid-fifteenth century.
The opening leaf of the Canon of the Mass in this Dutch Missal shows a priest reading from a manuscript on the altar as an acolyte stands behind with a candle.

Te igitur clemen
tissime pater per
ihesum xpm̄ fili
um tuū dominū
nostrū supplices
rogamus ac pe
timus. uti accep
ta habeas et be
nedicas hec ✠
dona. hec ✠ mu
nera. hec sc̄a ✠
sacrificia illibata.

In primis que ti
bi offerimus pro
ecclesia tua sc̄a
catholica quam
pacificare custodi
re. adunare et re
gere digneris to
to orbe terrarum
una cū famulo
tuo papa nostro.
N. et antistite nr̄o.
N. et rege nostro.
N. et omnibus
orthodoxis. atque
catholice et apos
tolice fidei cultori
bus.
Memento

192 (ABOVE LEFT) Oxford, Bodleian Library MS. Lat. liturg. d. 11, upper cover of binding; Missal, Bohemia, mid-fourteenth century.
The manuscript has an inscription of Johannes, subdean and rector of the church of Maršovice, near Prague, in 1348.

193 (ABOVE) New York, Pierpont Morgan Library M. 629, lower cover of binding; Pseudo-Bonaventura, Speculum Beate Marie Virginis, etc., Schwäbisch-Gmünd, *c.* 1470.
This manuscript of theological texts and sermons was written out by Bartholomeus Scherenbach, parish priest at Schwäbisch-Gmünd, for his own use. It was bound by another parish priest, Johannes Richenbach, of Geislingen (about 20 miles north-west of Ulm), who has stamped his name around the binding.

exceptional importance or *totum duplex*. The greatest feasts of the Sanctoral, like the Annunciation on 25 March and Michaelmas on 29 September, are ranked with Christmas Day and Trinity Sunday in the Temporal among the most honoured days of the religious year.

The Sanctoral and the Temporal were kept quite distinct in medieval service-books and sometimes even formed separate volumes. A medieval priest would not confuse them. It should be quite straightforward, in examining a page from a liturgical manuscript, to assign it to one or the other. The Temporal will have the services with headings such as *Dom.ii in* xl^{a}. (second Sunday in Lent – or *Quadragesima* in Latin) and *Dom.xiii post Pent.* (thirteenth Sunday after Pentecost), but the Sanctoral will refer to saints' names, *Sci. Hilarii epi. et conf.*, St. Hilary (14 January), *Decoll.sci.Joh.bapt.*, the Beheading of St. John the Baptist (29 August), and so on.

An even more fundamental distinction in the services of the late medieval church is between the Mass and the daily offices. These were completely different in function and in form. The Mass is the communion service or Eucharist, one of the most solemn and important Sacraments of the Church, instituted by Christ at the Last Supper and consisting of consecrating and partaking of the bread and wine which represent the Body and Blood of Christ. It was celebrated at the altar, and its service-book was the Missal. The Mass is not to be confused with the daily services performed in the choir: Matins, Lauds, Prime, Terce, Sext, None, Vespers and Compline. We discussed the shortened versions of these offices in the chapter on Books of Hours. They are not sacramental services, but are basically prayers and anthems in honour and praise of Christ and the saints. Their service-book was the Breviary. In the eighteenth and nineteenth centuries, antiquarians used to call any medieval liturgical manuscript a 'Missal' (be cautious therefore of titles added on the spines of manuscripts), and even now cataloguers sometimes confuse Breviaries and Missals. To the medieval mind, this would be unthinkable. The Mass is on an altogether different level from the eight offices, and the words of the service were in quite distinct manuscripts.

Having distinguished the Temporal from the Sanctoral and the Missal from the Breviary, one can see how these would slot in together throughout the church year. On an important feast day in the Temporal or Sanctoral, the priest would celebrate Mass at the altar. Further down in his church he

195 London, British Library, Add.MS.30337, detail; Exultet Roll, southern Italy, tewlfth century.
Exultet rolls are one of the rarest and most remarkable classes of liturgical manuscript, typical of south-western Italy. They were illuminated scrolls for the chants used on Easter Eve for the service of consecrating the Paschal candle. As the deacon recited the text, unfurling the scroll as he went, so the part that he had read would hang upside-down unrolled in view of the congregation. The text and pictures, therefore, faced opposite ways, the script for use by the clergy and the illustrations for the admiration of their audience.

194 (OPPOSITE) London, Sotheby's, 26 November 1985, lot 2, detail; leaf from a large noted Breviary, England, early fifteenth century.
The leaf shows part of Matins on the feast of Corpus Christi. The manuscript was no doubt discarded at the Reformation and this fragment survived as a wrapper around the outside of a bookbinding.

would usually also recite two or more of the offices, at least Matins and Vespers. The basic shape of these services would remain the same throughout the year but could be adapted according to the progress of the Temporal and the coincidence with the feasts in the Sanctoral. Special prayers could be inserted for the day appropriate within each cycle. Thus, for example, St. Mark's day (25 April) might one year happen to be on the second Sunday after Easter, but in the next year on the Tuesday after the third Sunday after Easter. The liturgy would therefore be different. In this way, the round of services, though fundamentally the same year after year, was capable of considerable variation.

Let us now suppose we are examining a manuscript Missal. A few moments glancing at the rubrics will confirm that it is indeed a Missal, not a Breviary, as it includes headings like *Introitus*, *Offertorium*, *Secreta*, *Communio* and *Postcommunio*, which would not be found in a Breviary. (A Breviary, by contrast, would have headings such as *Invitatorium*, *Hymnus*, *In primo nocturno*, *Lectio i*, *Lectio ii*, *Lectio iii*, *In secundo nocturno*.) The Missal will probably open with a Calendar. It is then likely to contain the Temporal (starting with the Introit, or opening words, 'Ad te levavi animam meam' for the First Sunday in Advent), consisting of the words in each Mass, which vary from day to day: the Introit (sung), the collect or prayer for the day, the appropriate readings from the New Testament Epistles and from the Gospels (with a sung Gradual verse between them), the Offertory or scriptural quotation read or sung before the collection, and the Secret, which is read quietly after the offerings have been received, with the communion verse from the Bible and a short prayer used after the communion. These are all quite short. The Masses itemized in the Temporal repeat these sub-headings over and over again as the section runs through the whole church year from the beginning of Advent to the last of the many Sundays after Pentecost.

The Missal will then have the central core of the Mass itself, more or less in the middle of the volume. This will be the most thumbed section in a manuscript. It is the unchanging part which the priest read at every Mass, inserting the daily variations where appropriate. There will be some short prayers and the Common Preface ('Vere dignum et justum est') and the Canon of the Mass ('Te igitur clementissime pater'; Pls. 191 and 197) and the solemn words of consecration followed by the communion itself. It was sometimes written out in a larger script, perhaps because the priest used both hands for the acts of consecration and would at this point leave the manuscript open on the altar or hand it to an acolyte with the result that he now needed to read it from a greater distance than if he held the book himself (Pl. 201).

The script will then return to the smaller size for the beginning of the Sanctoral which, in the manner of the Temporal just described, gives the variable sections of the Mass for saints' days of the whole year. This takes up most of the rest of the volume. It will be followed by the Common, comprising Masses which can be used in honour of saints not included by name: for an apostle, a confessor bishop, a virgin martyr, several virgins, and so on. If an officiating priest wanted to celebrate a Mass for a local saint not named in the Sanctoral, he would select the appropriate category from the Common. Finally, a manuscript Missal usually concludes with special sections of votive Masses (against the temptations of the flesh, for travellers, for rain, for good weather, and others for similar special occasions) and probably the Mass for the Dead.

This is a very brief summary, and of course manuscripts differed from each other in their exact contents. The Temporal, like a Book of Hours, might vary according to the liturgical 'use' of a diocese or region. Feasts for different saints followed local venerations. Are Masses for rain rarer in Missals from England than from Italy? Almost certainly. The most solemn part, it must be stressed again, is the Canon of the Mass. It never varied. This is the page where a typical late medieval Missal will now usually fall open of its own accord, partly because the priest needed to read this page every time he used the book and partly because it has the most elaborate illumination in the manuscript and generations of admiring bibliophiles will have sought out this opening first of all. Do not be ashamed to be among them. There will generally be one or even two full-page miniatures. We see the Crucifixion often preceded by a painting of Christ in majesty enthroned in glory between symbols of the Evangelists or presiding over the court of heaven. Often these are splendid pictures, and in the fifteenth century the Crucifixion is sometimes shown with all the crowds and pageantry of a state occasion.

As a generalization (with notable exceptions, like all generalizations), manuscript Missals are not elaborately illustrated. The Canon miniatures are normally the only large pictures in the book. Their subjects symbolize the text: the Crucifixion, the actual sacrifice of Body and Blood, and God the omnipotent Father who (according to the Common Preface) should now be glorified. 'Holy, holy, holy', the priest recites at this point, 'Lord God of hosts – heaven and earth are full of your glory'. The Missal paintings are devotional images representing just this: the glory of God in heaven and the glory of the Son on earth at the most glorious moment of the Crucifixion. Sometimes God is represented holding the orb made of heaven and earth together.

It is very difficult, without getting entangled in theology, to explain the full-page miniatures in a Missal in the traditional terms of art history. Elsewhere we have tried to understand the purpose of illumination in different kinds of manuscript: educative, explanatory, decorative, entertaining, and so forth – all recognizable functions of art and presupposing a medieval reader who uses illustrations as part of the business of reading. But a Missal is a unique kind of book. It is the vehicle for a Sacrament. Pictures cannot be strictly illustrative in a text which, taken on its own terms, is not for the use of a reader as such, but rather to re-create the most holy moment of religious worship. Already this explanation is beyond the framework of secular science and, to those to whom the Eucharist is unfamiliar, it must seem complicated. Perhaps a comparison is possible between Missal paintings and icons. An icon is itself regarded as the holy object it represents. The subject and the medium become indistinguishable in the eyes of the believer. The bread and wine in the Eucharist *are*, at that moment, the Body and Blood of Christ. On an infinitely

196 London, Sotheby's, 26 November 1985, lot 120, detail of f. 9, Missal, Rouen, *c.* 1430–50.
These miniatures illustrate the opening of the Mass for Easter Day. A blank space has been carefully left by the illuminator for a coat-of-arms to be inserted in the large initial. At the time of painting either the identity of the patron or the blazon of his arms must have been unknown to the artist.

lower level, the images of Christ on the Cross and of the Father in majesty become part of the presence of God in the Sacrament. At any other time they would just be paintings; but as the priest was reciting the Canon, these miniatures were the subjects of literal veneration. The picture of Christ on the Cross was kissed devoutly by the priest. With the late medieval mingling of spirituality and common sense, artists realized that frequent kissing smudged a fine painting, and so they sometimes illustrated a second much smaller Crucifix or a Cross in the lower margin of a Canon miniature so that it could be physically venerated without damage to the main composition (Pl. 197).

Because the Canon had the richest decoration in a Missal manuscript, it is on these pages that we most often find representations or coats-of-arms of the original owners. One sees medieval priests or laity depicted beside the Crucifixion or in the illuminated margins. Patrons were no more bashful about having their names and portraits inserted in the most holy part of a Missal than they were about being commemorated on a monumental brass before the altar in the chancel of a church, and the same kind of images appear with kneeling figures holding scrolls commending posterity to pray for them. Volume III of Leroquais's *Sacramentaires et Missels*, 1924, describes about 350 late medieval manuscript Missals in public collections in France: of these, just over 100 contain original coats-of-arms or other explicit indications of the original patrons. It is a high proportion. Though this may not be a statistically random survey, it shows between a quarter and a third of fifteenth- or early sixteenth-century French Missals having been commissioned by individuals who wished to be remembered as donors.

These patrons varied considerably. Many were bishops, and some of the grandest surviving Missals were illuminated for the use of prelates of the Church, the high priests (Pl. 200). However, since episcopal visitations of parish churches included an inquiry as to whether a church had an accurate and usable Missal, a bishop's coat-of-arms in a Missal might simply indicate that he had made up a deficiency himself. It would be a very worthy thing to do. Often the donors were the local priests or the parishioners themselves. One Missal was written by brother Yvo in 1441, according to a note at the start of the Canon (B.N. MS. nouv. acq. lat. 1690, f. 228r), on the commission of Hugues de St.-Genèse, then vicar of the parish church of Bassan (in the diocese of Béziers, in the far south of France), '*cuius anima requiescat in pace, Amen*'. Another Missal was made in 1451 for presentation by the priest Guillaume Jeudi, rector of the parish church of Notre-Dame d'Olonne (in the diocese of Poitiers), for the commemoration and salvation of his own soul: this is all recorded in a scroll at the foot of the Canon miniature which includes a picture of the donor asking the Virgin and Child to remember him (B.N. MS. lat. 872, f. 156v). There is a long and complicated inscription at the end of a Missal of 1419, now in Avallon (MS. 1, f. 257r), recording that it was made by Bernard Lorard in the town of Villaines-les-Prévostés (Côte d'Or) while Jean Odini de Reomo was curate of the church there, and that the parishioners paid Bernard forty crowns for his labours and that, when Bernard himself made a personal contribution to the cost, they awarded him a supply of red wine. The manuscript sparkles with little miniatures of grotesque animals and faces, and (unusually for a Missal) it has twelve Calendar scenes. It cannot have been simple to make. Probably very local Missals like these were hardly professional products in the normal sense. In a provincial village the priest himself must often have been almost the only person who could write. A Missal made in 1423 for the church of St.-Sauveur, diocese of Aix, is signed by the scribe Jacques Murri, 'clericum beneficiatum' (Aix MS. 11, p. 829), and another Missal, paid for by the vice-chancellor of Brittany in 1457, was written out by Yves Even, parish priest of the village of Troguéry in the north Breton diocese of Tréguier (B.N. MS. nouv. acq. lat. 172, f. 266r). Writing books may have helped supplement a clerical stipend. The first of these two manuscripts has many small miniatures but they are not well executed and may have been made at home. A century earlier there is a colophon in a Flemish Missal completed in Ghent in 1366 by Laurence the illuminator, priest of Antwerp (The Hague, Mus. Meerm.-Westr. MS. 10. A. 14), and probably the priest both wrote and decorated it.

Next to the Missal, the book which a priest would need most regularly in his church was the Breviary. This too must sometimes have been made by the priest himself. A hastily written Breviary in Brussels (B.R. MS. 3452) is signed by the scribe Hugues Dubois ('de Bosco'), priest in the diocese of Amiens, who records on f. 156v that he finished copying it from the exemplar owned by Pierre Alou, priest of the church of St-Éloi in Abbeville, in 1464 on 6 November, 'hora secunda post prandium' – at two o'clock, after lunch. A Breviary, as we have seen, was not a book for use at the altar. Its dimensions are often smaller than those of a Missal, and it is usually a squat thick volume or is divided among several small volumes. In medieval England a Breviary was generally called a 'portiforium', a book which a priest carried outdoors ('portat foras'), a term which reflects its convenience of size. The handwriting was often very small. A Breviary comprises hymns, readings, Psalms, anthems and other prayers for the

197 London, Sotheby's, 3 July 1984, lot 52, ff. 153v–154r; Missal, Ghent, mid-fifteenth century.
A full-page miniature of the Crucifixion faces the opening of the Canon of the Mass in this small Missal made for the Abbey of St. Bavo in Ghent.

198 Fribourg, Bibliothèque Cantonale et Universitaire, MS.L.64, Breviary, Switzerland, *c.*1400.
Some little Breviaries are written in very small script. The medieval owner of this manuscript hollowed out the inside of the original front cover to insert a pair of spectacles.

199 London, British Library, Egerton MS.2865, f.165r; Breviary, north-east Italy, 1402.
The scribe concludes this manuscript (f.171r) with a long inscription explaining that he is Antonio de Ubertis, beneficed priest at the church of Santa Maria de Valtorta; that he is getting elderly for he is nearly 47 years old and has been priest for 22 years; and that he finished the book on Friday 17 March 1402 in reasonable time and for a sufficient fee.

offices from Matins to Compline and, in the full version, includes the whole Psalter, marked up with rubrics and responses, as well as the appropriate offices to be used throughout the long sections of the Temporal and the Sanctoral.

There is one major problem in considering Breviaries in a chapter called 'Books for Priests'. Not only priests used them. All monks required Breviaries, and some of the finest surviving examples seem to have been used by the laity. Missals are rather different: only an ordained priest could celebrate Mass, and, though many monks and abbots were ordained as well, it is reasonable to consider a Missal as a priest's book even if the priest was also a monk. Many Breviaries, however, were intended simply for monks and nuns, and they, probably more than parish priests, actually read from the volume eight times a day. A priest often recited

HIESVS NAZARENVS
REX IVDEORVM

200 (LEFT) London, Sotheby's, 11 December 1984, lot 44, f.45v; Missal, Rome, *c.*1520–21.
This vast Missal was illuminated for Cardinal Bernardino de Carvajal (1456–1522), who is shown in prayer in his chapel in the lower margin of the miniature of the Crucifixion, facing the Canon of the Mass.

201 (ABOVE) Malibu, The J. Paul Getty Museum, MS. 3, single miniature of the Mass of St. Gregory, Bruges, *c.*1520–30.
One day when St. Gregory was celebrating Mass, the legend recounts, Christ appeared to him exhibiting his wounds and surrounded by the emblems of the Passion. The miniature, attributable to Simon Bening himself (see pl. 164), shows the scene as it might have taken place in the artist's lifetime. The actual page measures $5\frac{1}{2} \times 4$ inches.

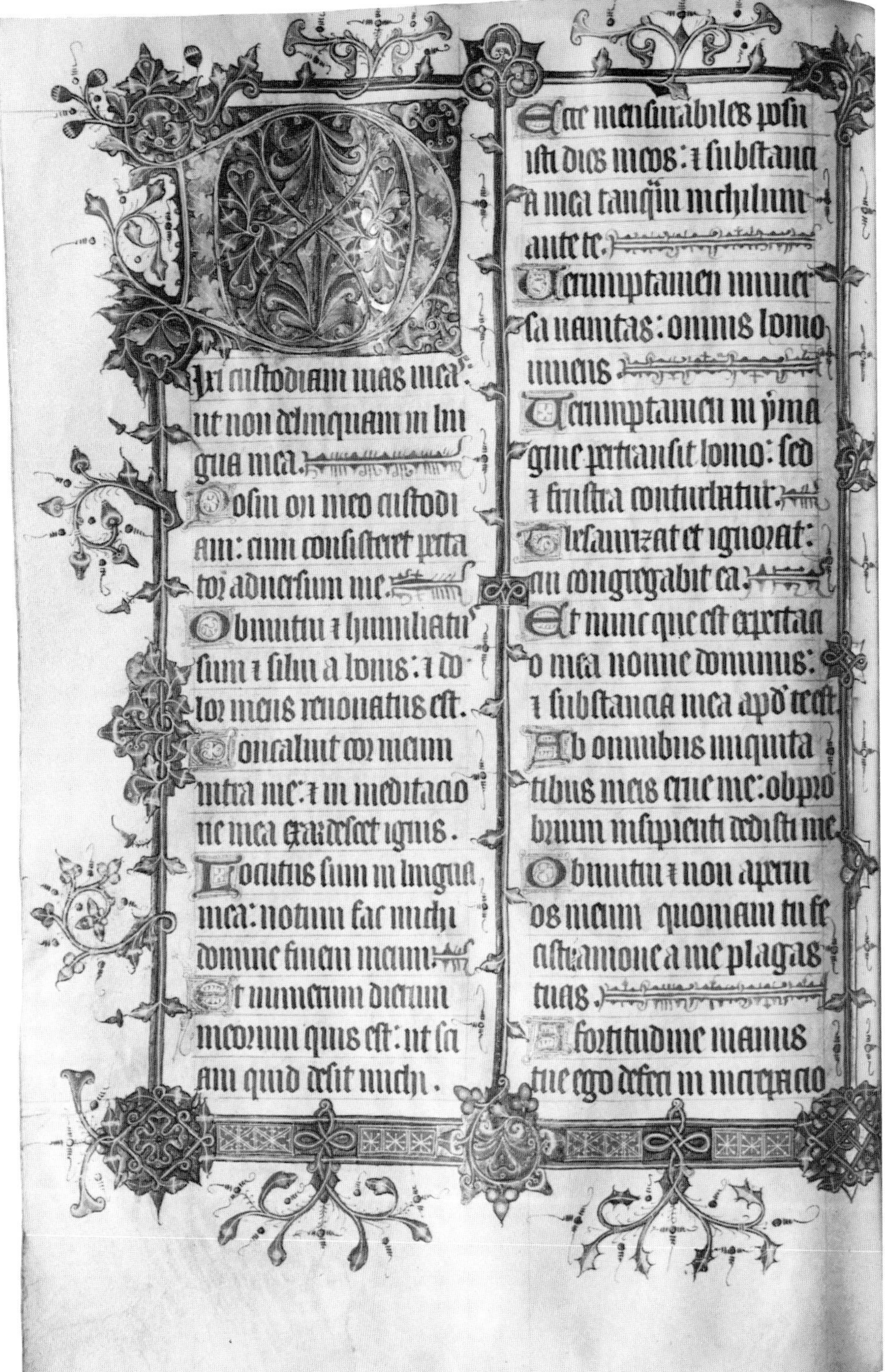

202 (LEFT) Ushaw College, Co. Durham, MS. 8, Psalter, southern England (probably London), *c.* 1400–10.
This manuscript belonged in the Middle Ages to the parish church of High Ongar in Essex.

203 (OPPOSITE) Oxford, Bodleian Library MS. Laud. misc. 419, f. 433r; Breviary, northern France (possibly Noyon), *c.* 1525.
This is the opening of the Common of the Saints in a large Breviary illuminated for Jean de Hangest, who succeeded his uncle as bishop of Noyon in 1525. He died in 1577.

only Matins and Vespers. One distinction between a 'secular' Breviary (that is, one used in a church) and a monastic Breviary is in the number of lessons or readings in the office of Matins. A parish priest or a friar used nine lessons on Sunday and on feast days and three on ordinary weekdays; monks, by contrast, read twelve lessons on Sundays and feast days and three on weekdays in the winter and one in summer. This difference ought to be reflected in the manuscripts themselves, and the readings are usually numbered *Lectio i*, *Lectio ii*, and so forth, and are not difficult to find. A second method of checking whether a Breviary is monastic or secular is to look through the Calendar. Feast days are 'graded', and so if special honour is given to St. Benedict (21 March), for example, and to the translation of his relics (11 July and probably also 4 December), the Breviary was presumably intended for use by a Benedictine monk. If the Calendar singles out feasts such as

St. Bernard (20 August), St. Robert of Molesmes (29 April), St. Peter of Tarantaise (8 May) and Edmund of Abingdon (16 November – he died at Pontigny Abbey), then the Breviary is probably Cistercian. Thus, with the help of a dictionary of saints, it should be possible to say whether a Breviary is Augustinian, Dominican, Franciscan, and so forth. If it was made for a parish church, it is likely to accord special honour to local saints of the diocese, and it may well have an entry in the Calendar for the anniversary of the dedication of the church itself. A nondescript '*Dedicatio huius ecclesie*' will be of little help, but the entry '*Dedicatio ecclesie Sancti Stephani Cathalaunensis, Totum duplex*' under 26 October in B.N. MS. lat. 1269, for instance, localizes that Breviary to the church of St.-Etienne in Châlons-sur-Marne.

Breviaries were sometimes illuminated for the laity, especially in the late Middle Ages, and some of the very grandest surviving copies are associated with secular aristocrats such as Charles V of France (B.N. MS. lat. 1052), the Duke of Bedford (B.N. MS. lat. 17294), Reinald of Guelders (Pierpont Morgan M. 87), and Queen Isabella of Castile (B.L. Add. MS. 18851). The most famous of all, the Grimani Breviary in Venice (Marciana MS. lat. I. 99), was not designed for Cardinal Grimani (1461–1523), but was bought by him second-hand from Antonio Siciliano, who had been Milanese ambassador in Flanders in 1514. But even these grand books were primarily for use by priests or monks. All princely families had their own private chapels. The splendid Breviaries must often have been chanted by the domestic chaplains rather than by the nobility in person. The aristocrats were the patrons, not the daily readers.

Related to Breviaries are Psalters, and the Psalms arranged liturgically form a principal component of any Breviary. Many parish priests must have owned Psalters, especially in the later Middle Ages when the Psalter often included liturgical elements such as a Calendar, Litany, and the Office of the Dead. About a dozen surviving manuscript Psalters can be specifically associated with English parish churches, and they were perhaps more common in England than on the Continent (Pl. 202). There is an interesting contract for the writing of a liturgical Psalter for the use of a priest in York in 1346. In August that year, Robert Brekeling, scribe, appeared before the Chapter at York Minster to confirm his agreement to make for John Forbor a Psalter with Calendar for which he would charge 5s. 6d., and then, for a further 4s. 3d., to write out, in the same script and in the same volume, the Office of the Dead with hymns and collects. Then there are details of exactly how the illuminated initials were to be supplied. Robert Brekeling was to do the work himself. Each verse of the Psalms had to be given a capital letter in good blue and red. The Psalms themselves were to begin with large initials in gold and colours, and each of the seven liturgical divisions had to be indicated with a five-line initial, except for the psalms *Beatus Vir* and *Dixit Dominus* (Psalms 1 and 109 – those used at Matins and Vespers on Sundays), which required initials six and seven lines high. All this is carefully specified in the contract. All large initials in the hymnary and collectar, according to the arrangement, were to be painted in gold and red, except those of double feasts, which should be like the big gold initials in the Psalter. For this extra work of illuminating, Robert was to charge an additional 5s. 6d. plus 1s. 6d. for buying the gold. The total comes to 16s. 9d., which was quite a lot of money in the fourteenth century.

A further expense that one sometimes finds in medieval accounts is for the 'noting' of service-books. This means supplying music. Both the Mass and the daily offices contain substantial sections of musical chant. The origins of liturgical music were traditionally said to go back to St. Gregory the Great (d. 604), who is sometimes shown in medieval art being inspired by the Holy Dove to record the principles of 'Gregorian' chant. As there were two main service-books in the medieval Church, the Missal and the Breviary, so there were two corresponding volumes of music. The Gradual contained the musical parts of the Missal; the Antiphoner contained the musical parts of the Breviary. The difference is

204–205 (OVERLEAF) London, Sotheby's, 13 June 1983, lot 20, ff. 111v–1v r; Missal, Paris, *c.* 1480–90.
These full-page miniatures originally preceded the Canon of the Mass (they are now misbound at the beginning of the manuscript); the slight smudging on the face of Christ may have been caused by pious kissing during the recitation of Mass.

ure filius dei erat iste

as important as that between the Missal and the Breviary, and the same words in the rubrics will distinguish one from the other: headings such as *Introitus*, *Graduale* and *Offertorium* are found in a Gradual, and *Invitatorium*, *Hymnus* and *Responsum* in an Antiphoner. In its original sense, the Gradual comprised the musical response sung between the reading of the Epistle and the Gospel, and the word derives from the steps ('gradus') where the Epistle was read. It came, however, to mean all the sung parts of the Mass. Similarly, an Antiphoner took its name from the short antiphons, verses sung by one choir in response to another at the end of a Psalm, but it was taken to include all musical sections of the offices.

All medieval churches were expected to have a Gradual and an Antiphoner, and all monasteries certainly owned them. There is a fine illustrated manuscript Gradual in Zittau in East Germany (Christian-Weise-Bibliothek MS. A. V) with an inscription recording that it was completed in 1435 for the parish church in Zittau, the Johanneskirche, at the expense of brother Johann Gottfried von Goldberg, the incumbent priest there (1418–39), for whom prayers should be offered and for

206 Cambridge, Massachusetts, Harvard College, The Houghton Library pfMS. Lat. 186, f. 101v; Gradual, Rouen, *c.* 1510–20. *This page marks the opening of the Mass for a bishop confessor in the Common, and the initial shows a priest kneeling with his manuscript before a saintly bishop.*

207 Oxford, Bodleian Library MS. Lat. liturg. a. 7, p. 146; Gradual, Mexico, seventeenth century. *This enormous manuscript Gradual was made for a church in the Spanish colonies in Mexico. It shows the Introit for Mass on the First Sunday after Easter.*

rimum
quidē ser
monem
feci de om
nibus o theophile que
cepit ihesus facere et do
cere usqz in diem qua
precipiens apostolis p

208 (LEFT) London, British Library, Harley MS. 2897, f. 188v; the Breviary of Jean sans Peur (1371–1419), Duke of Burgundy, Paris, *c.* 1415.
The miniature illustrates the office of the Ascension and shows Christ's feet disappearing into the clouds.

209 (ABOVE) West Berlin, Staatliche Museen Preussischer Kulturbesitz, Kupferstichkabinett, min. 14707; cutting from a Missal, Regensburg, *c.* 1480–90.
This Canon miniature is attributable to Berthold Furtmeyr, documented in Regensburg from c. *1470 to 1511.*

all benefactors of Christ. Such books must once have been extremely widespread. Examples from southern Europe, Italy, and more especially Spain and Portugal, are among the most common of all illuminated manuscripts, and there are now vast numbers of framed single leaves from these books, often sixteenth- or seventeenth-century (though dealers may claim them to be earlier). They are usually huge in size because a choir would sing from a single manuscript (Pls. 207 and 214). One could possibly guess the size of the choir (or perhaps the darkness of the church) by propping up one of these giant choirbooks and experimenting how many people could in practice read it clearly at once. Partly because of the size and partly because every page of music was different, these were complicated books to set in printed type, and so plain-chant manuscripts were still being handmade in the traditional way in south-west Europe for centuries after the introduction of printing.

The music was written in black neumes on staves of four or five lines. It is sometimes asserted that the use of a five-line stave indicates a date of later than the fifteenth century: while in practice this is often true, there are far too many exceptions for it to be an indicator of a manuscript's age. There are examples of five-line staves as early as the thirteenth century. The staves could be drawn with what was called a 'rastrum' (the word literally means a rake), consisting of four or five evenly spaced pens joined like a multi-pronged fork to rule the lines simultaneously across a page. One can see where a rastrum has been used when the scribe has accidentally bumped the implement as he was working and all the parallel lines quiver in unison.

The very earliest manuscript Graduals and choirbooks had no staves at all, and from at least the tenth century simple indications of liturgical music were given by whiskery little neumes written in above the line of text (Pl. 210). Several types of Carolingian notation were used, and some of the best known are associated with St. Gall and Lorraine. In their primitive form, these marks look rather as if a spider had trodden in the ink and wandered across the page. In Germany and the Low Countries these zig-zag marks evolved into more angular shapes with linked vertical tails, and, after the stave

210 London, British Library, Add. MS. 62104, fragment from a Missal, Exeter, mid-eleventh century.

This half-leaf of a late Anglo-Saxon Missal, recovered from use as a sewing-guard in a bookbinding, has several lines of musical neumes without a stave

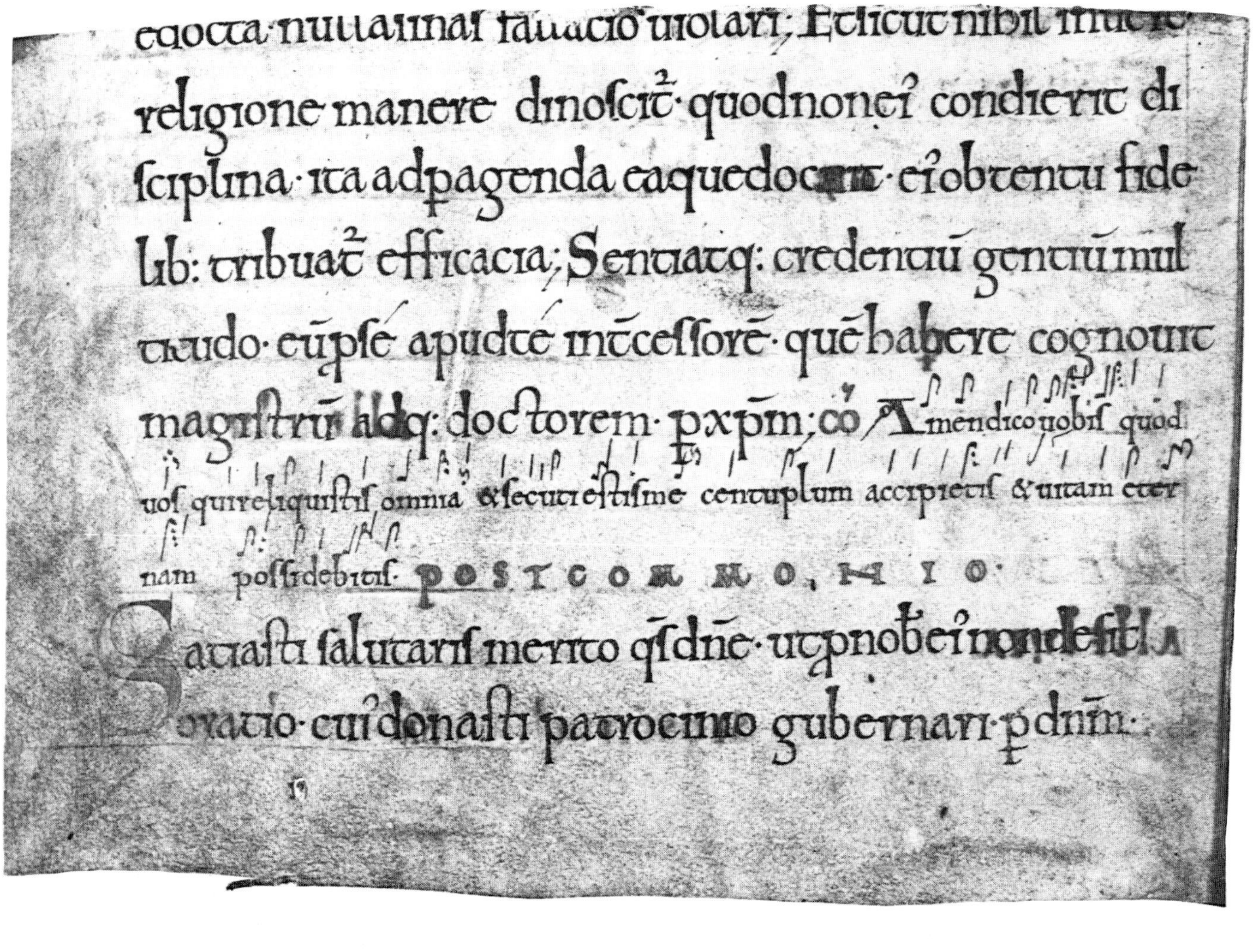

was introduced in the thirteenth century, they resemble clusters of short nails. Because of this resemblance, the distinctive neumes in German choirbooks are known as *Hufnagalschrift*, which means 'horseshoe-nail writing' (Pl. 211). The staves are usually in black ink in German and Netherlandish manuscripts.

In southern Europe, England and France, the stave was usually drawn in red and the neumes are generally without tails. They worked approximately as follows. One of the four or five lines was marked at the beginning of the row with a clef sign to indicate that a particular line was 'c' or 'f'. These clef marks are derived from the form of the alphabetical letters, 'c' being usually written and 'f' something like (or in eastern Europe). Quite simply, then, the notes on or between the lines of the stave are pitched in accordance with this known note: the neume above 'c' is 'd', the neume below it is 'b', and so on. The clefs can shift up and down, even on one page of a manuscript, and the raising and lowering of the clef allows melodies of different range to be written on a stave of only four lines. There are no bar lines. The faint vertical lines in many manuscripts simply indicate the corresponding division of words in the line of text below. A tick at the end of a line is a silent warning to the singer of what is to be the first note on the following line. The spacing of the neumes indicates the length of the note. Neumes spread out across the page are sung slowly. Two neumes close together, or even contiguous, are sung as if quavers. If the neumes are side-by-side , the notes repeat quickly . If a pair of neumes is written vertically , the lower note is sung first . Two neumes joined in their corners thus are sung in descending order . These are the simplest forms in medieval choirbooks. There can be many combinations of neumes, or diagonal lines instead of repeated notes, such as which is . All these can be interpreted in terms of a modern stave, and enthustiastic medievalists, with a good ear and a little practice, can actually sing straight from a page of a medieval choirbook, re-creating for a few moments the sound of a parish church or monastery five hundred or more years ago. It can be enthralling to listen to. Some ancient hymn tunes, such as the *Veni creator spiritus* ('Come Holy Ghost'), emerge from the manuscripts almost unchanged from antiquity.

In addition to a Gradual and an Antiphoner, most medieval parishes would have used other liturgical manuscripts from time to time. The churchwardens' accounts of St. Margaret's church in New Fish Street in London list the books owned there in 1472. Amongst them are six Antiphoners (including 'a gret & a newe Antiphoner covered with Buk skynne . . . of the gyft of sir Henry Mader, preest'), five Graduals, ten Processionals (including two given by the priest, Henry Mader), three Manuals (one from Henry Mader's gift again – they were for occasional services such as baptisms, marriages, and visiting the sick), an Ordinal (directions for conducting the liturgy), four Psalters, and a gratifying number of books for simple instruction in the Christian religion: the Miracles of the Virgin, in English, a *Catholicon* (this is Balbus's practical encyclopaedia of religious knowledge), 'a boke called compendium veritatis theologice'

211 London, Sotheby's, 26 November 1985, detail from lot 62; Missal, Rhineland (probably Warburg), first half of the fourteenth century.
This fragment shows the typically German Hufnagelschrift *neumes.*

(presumably the popular handbook by Hugo Ripelinus which opens 'Veritatis theologice sublimitas . . .'), a tract by St. Bernard and the *Prick of Conscience*, both chained in the church, and so forth. The books were not merely for conducting services.

In considering books which a priest would have used, we must not overlook the pastoral side of the parish duties. A priest's occupation included instructing the laity, hearing confessions, comforting the bereaved, teaching Bible stories to children, and preaching and interpreting the Scriptures, and there existed books to assist with all these. They are usually unspectacular. Humble little booklets on matters of practical theology were not as impressive as richly illuminated service-books, but they were probably nearly as common in the possession of priests. There is a modern index of the opening words of medieval treatises on the virtues and vices, the fundamental guides for administering day-to-day religious advice: M. W. Bloomfield, B.-G. Guyot, D. R. Howard and T. B. Kabeale, *Incipits of Latin Works on the Virtues and Vices, c.1100–1500 AD*, published by the Medieval Academy of America in 1979. It cites well over 10,000 surviving medieval manuscripts and more than 6,500 different texts, and it is by no means comprehensive. 10,000 extant volumes is an extraordinary number. For medieval sermons, historians have J. B. Schneyer's monumental nine-volume *Repertorium der Lateinischen Sermones*, published from 1968 and listing very many thousands of sample sermons in vast numbers of manuscripts dating from the two hundred years after 1150; no one has yet tackled the task of recording all the sermons and preaching guides for the fifteenth century. The sheer bulk of surviving manuscripts of pastoral theology is really daunting. Not all these manuscripts belonged to priests; perhaps the majority were used by friars, and others by monks and literate laity, but they represent a huge body of grass-root theology in an age when a casual visitor to a church might have thought it bare of books. Two of the most popular handbooks were Raymond of Peñafort's treatise on penance, the *Summa de*

AVE REGINA CELOR

212 (LEFT) London, British Library, Add. MS. 17440, f. 13v; Missal, Ghent, 1483.
The dedication miniature of this Missal for St. Bavo's Abbey is dated in the upper border and shows the patron, Willem van Bossunt, being commended to the Virgin and Child.

213 London, British Library, Add. MS. 16578, f. 17v; Speculum Humanae Salvationis, Osterhofen (Bavaria), 1379.
This manuscript was written by a priest Ulric of Osterhofen, son of Conrad the public scribe and imperial notary, and was finished on 15 November 1379. It has fifty-three coloured drawings, probably by Ulric himself, including this scene of the Entry into Jerusalem and of Jeremiah lamenting over the city.

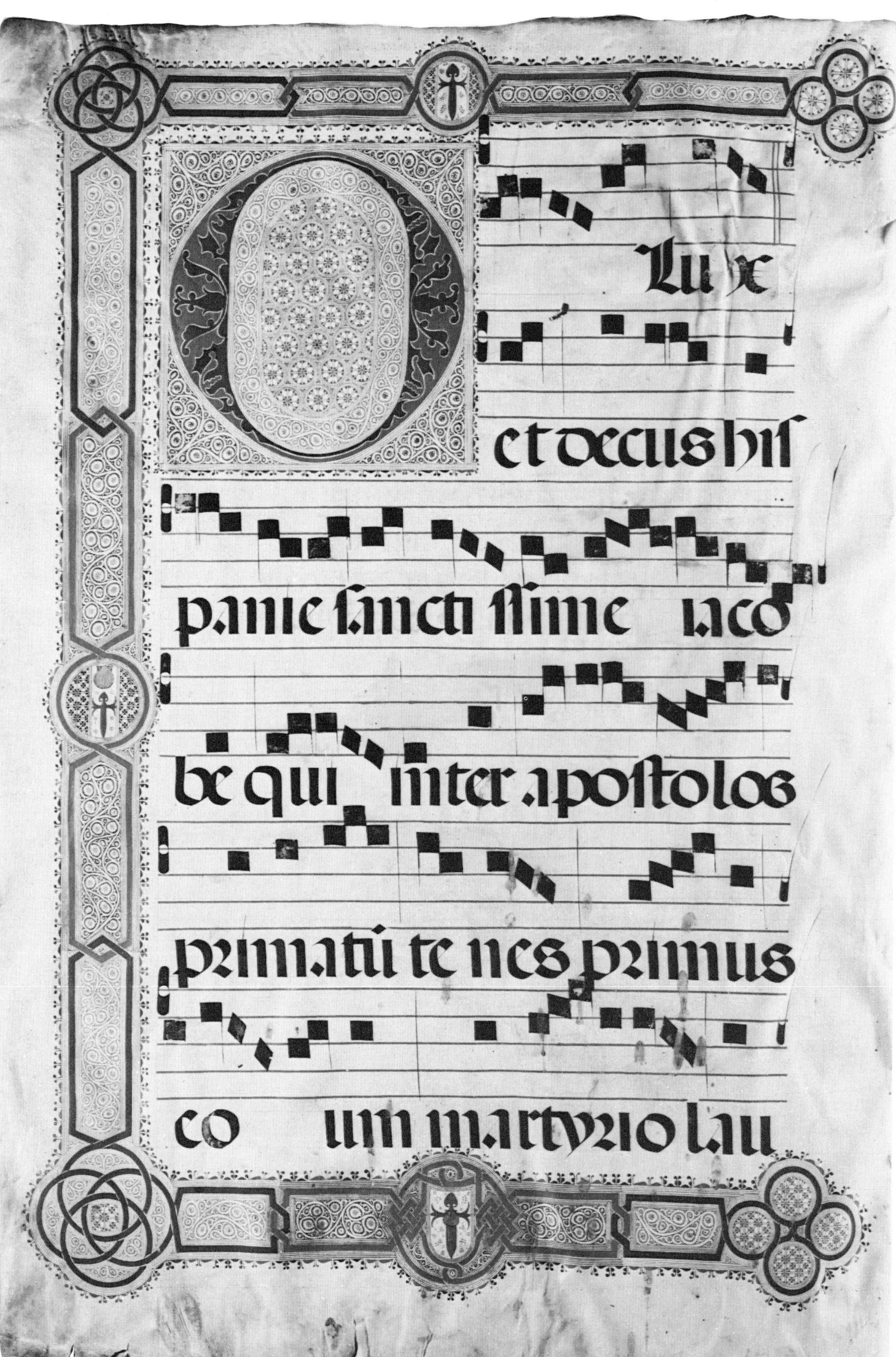
Lux
et decus his
panie sanctissime iaco
be qui inter apostolos
primatū tenes primus
eo um martyrio lau

Casibus Penitentie, and Guillaume Pérault on the vices and virtues, the *Summa de Vitiis et Virtutibus*, both written by thirteenth-century Dominicans. One of the thirteenth-century *exempla* (or moral tales for use by preachers) tells how a common woman used to lend out separate gatherings of her copy of Pérault's *Summa* for priests to copy, and thus did more practical good to the parishes of her region (the story says) than the masters of theology in Paris ever did. Especially useful were texts like Guy de Montrocher's handbook for priests, the *Manipulus Curatorum*, Gerson's guide for confessors, the *De Praeceptis, de Confessione et Scientia Mortis*, and the *Compendium Theologice Veritatis* cited above. At the most basic level, a late medieval priest's teaching of the Scriptures would benefit from using a simple textbook such as the *Biblia Pauperum* (Poor Men's Bible; Pl. 216), an album of Bible stories with pictures and quotations from the prophets, and the slightly later *Speculum Humanae Salvationis* (Mirror of Human Salvation; Pl. 213), which has nearly 5,000 lines of doggerel Latin verse explaining how the life of Christ was prefigured by the Old Testament. It survives in over 200 manuscripts, of which about half are illustrated with vigorous and dramatic pictures. It was used like the Doom paintings in churches to teach the life of Christ and the inevitability of the Last Judgement.

A perceptive reader will have noticed that there has been no mention so far in this chapter of the one book found in every parish church today – the Bible. Readings from the Bible form an essential part of a Christian service. They were always used in medieval services, but lessons followed a fixed programme which laid down which passage was to be read on each day. It was often much more convenient for the priest to have these readings in a Lectionary or within the Missal or Breviary than to try to find the appropriate passage in a complete Bible which was not, at this time, divided into verses. Those little thirteenth-century portable Bibles were still in circulation, but their microscopic script is not suited to declaiming from a lectern.

Sometime in the late fourteenth or early fifteenth century, the lectern Bible began to return into fashion (Pl. 218). It is difficult to know how far this was related to the use of a Bible in church, or for reading during meals in a monastery, or for private study (probably all three, in fact), but it seems to have been a phenomenon of the Low Countries and then later of the Rhineland. From the fourteenth century, the rhyming Bibles in the Dutch language were popular, rather as the *Bible Historiale* was in France, and in the fifteenth century monumental copies of the Dutch vernacular Bible histories were among the finest Netherlandish manuscripts. Nearly forty copies survive, and the two known first owners were both priests: Herman van Lochorst (d. 1438, deacon of Utrecht Cathedral) probably owned B.L. Add. MSS. 10043 and 38122, and Evart van Soudenbalch (canon of Utrecht 1445–1503) owned Vienna ÖNB. MS. 2771–2. Similarly, huge Latin Bibles were being written out in the Low Countries in the first half of the century. A good example is Brussels B.R. MSS. 106–7 and 204–5, a giant four-volume Bible made in Utrecht in 1402–3 by Henricus van Arnhem, presumably a professional scribe since he worked both for the Carthusian Abbey of Nieuwlicht and for Utrecht Cathedral. Another fine copy in two volumes is now in Auckland, New Zealand (Public Library, MS. G. 128–131), written in or soon before 1419. A three-volume copy is in Cambridge (Fitzwilliam Museum MS. 289), illuminated with the arms of Lochorst of Utrecht, *c.* 1420. In Utrecht University Library (MS. 31) there is a splendid lectern Bible in six volumes written at Zwolle between 1464 and 1476 at the expense of the dean of Utrecht Cathedral. These are all very grand manuscripts, and they are not isolated examples. It is probable that the movements known as the *Devotio Moderna* and the Brothers of the Common Life had something to do with the revival of lectern Bibles. Gerard Groote (1340–84), founder of the movement in the Low Countries, taught a return to the basic teaching of the Bible and initiated a spiritual renewal whose

214 (LEFT) London, Sotheby's, 8 December 1981, lot 102, f. 1r; Antiphoner, Spain, mid-sixteenth century.
The large initial here opens the office for the feast of St. James the Greater (25 July), patron saint of Spain.

215 London, British Library, Add. MS. 38021, f. 3r; Jacobus de Voragine, Sunday sermons, Würm, 1421.
The manuscript was copied by a priest, Hermann, vicar of Würm, probably for his own use.

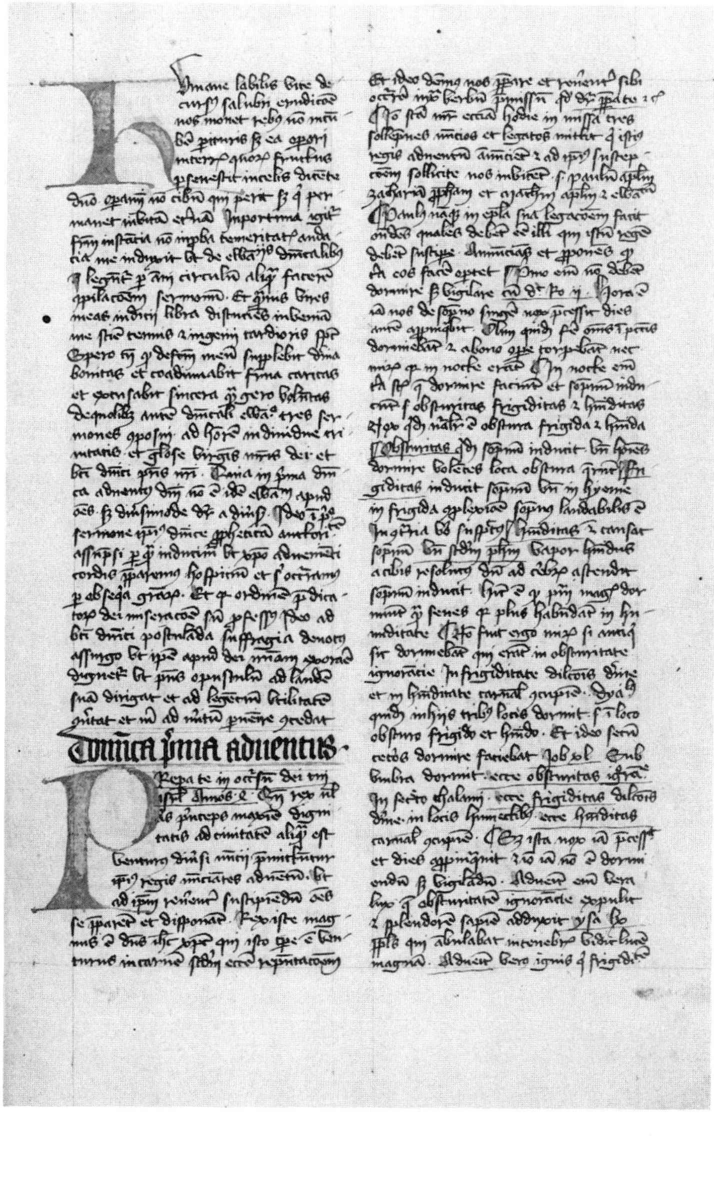

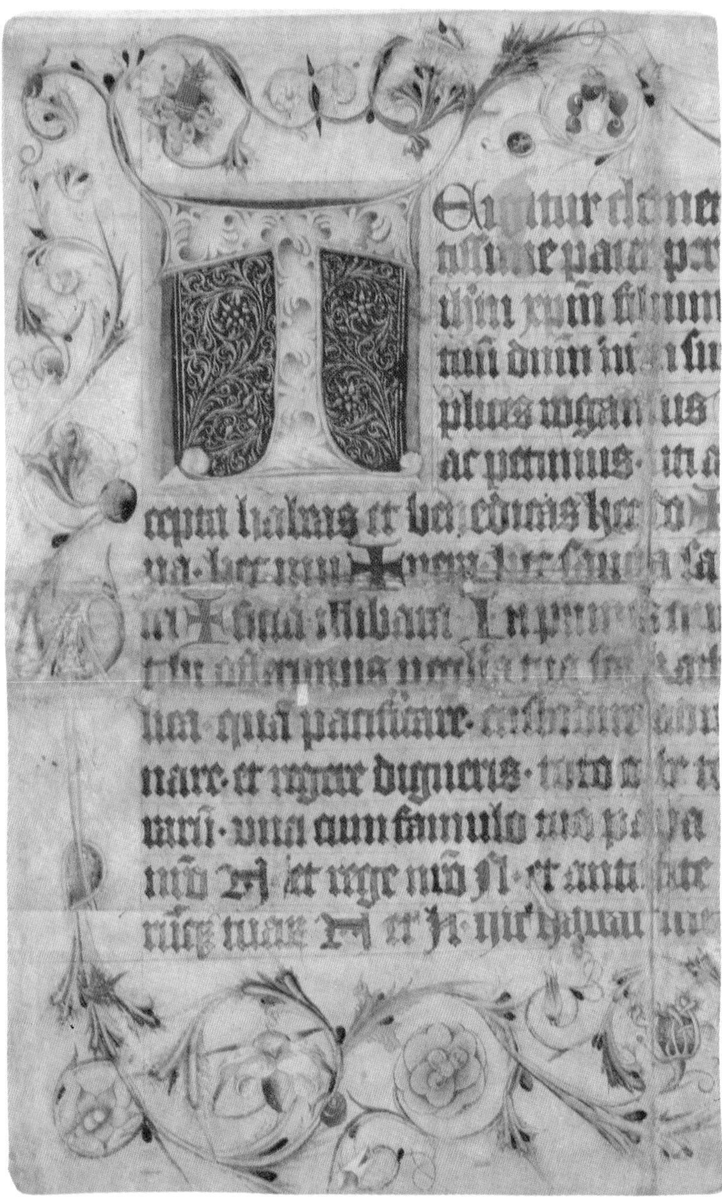

216 (ABOVE) London, British Library, King's MS. 5, f. 20r; Biblia Pauperum, Netherlands, early fifteenth century.
The Poor Men's Bible *was a simple picture book used to explain biblical prophecies and symbolism. Here the image of Christ breaking forth from the Tomb is paralleled by Samson breaking the gates of Gaza and by Jonah coming out of the mouth of the whale.*

217 (LEFT) London, Sotheby's, 11 December 1984, lot 5, single leaf; Missal, Mainz, *c.* 1450–65.
This fragment of the Canon of the Mass in a manuscript Missal, recovered from use as the wrapper around the outside of a bookbinding, was illuminated by an artist who seems to have been employed by Johann Gutenberg and by his successor Johann Fust to decorate some of the earliest printed books including several copies of the Gutenberg Bible.

218 (RIGHT) Oxford, Bodleian Library MS. Rawl. G. 161, f. 426r; Bible, Austria, 1399.
This is a large lectern Bible dated 1399.

credidit et baptizatus fuerit salvus erit. Qui vero non crediderit condempnabitur. Signa autem eos qui crediderint hec sequentur: in nomine meo demonia eicient, linguis loquentur novis, serpentes tollent, et si mortiferum quid biberint non eis nocebit; super egros manus imponent et bene habebunt. Et dominus quidem Ihesus postquam locutus est eis, assumptus est in celum et sedet a dextris dei. Illi autem profecti predicaverunt ubique, domino cooperante et sermonem confirmante sequentibus signis. Explicit Marcus. Incipit prologus beati Ieronimi in Lucam evangelistam.

Lucas Antiocensis natione Syrus arte medicus discipulus apostolorum, postea vero Paulum secutus usque ad confessionem eius, serviens domino sine crimine. Nam neque uxorem habuit unquam neque filios; septuaginta et quattuor annorum obiit in Bithinia plenus spiritu sancto. Igitur cum iam descripta essent evangelia, per Matheum quidem in Iudea, per Marcum autem in Ytalia, sancto instigante spiritu in Achaie partibus hoc scripsit evangelium, significans etiam ipse in principio ante suum alia esse descripta. Cui extra ea que ordo evangelice dispositionis exposcit, ea maxime necessitas laboris fuit, ut primum grecis fidelibus omni perfectione venturi in carnem dei Christi manifestata esset humanitas, ne iudaicis fabulis attenti in solo legis desiderio tenerentur, neve hereticis fabulis et stultis sollicitationibus seducti exciderent a veritate psimpta laborarent. Dehinc ut in principio evangelii Iohannis nativitate presumpta cui evangelium scriberet et in quo electus scriberet indicaret, contestans in se completa esse que essent ab aliis inchoata. Cui ideo post baptismum filii dei a perfectione generationis in Christo implete et repetende a principio nativitatis humane potestas permissa est, ut requirentibus demonstraret in quo apprehendens erat per Nathan filium David introitu recurrentis in deum generationis admisso indisparabilis dei, in se predicans in hominibus Christum suum perfecti opus hominis redire in se per filium faceret, qui per David patri venientibus iter prebebat in Christo. Cui Luce non immerito scribendorum apostolicorum actuum potestas in ministerio datur, ut deo in deum pleno et filio perditionis extincto, oratione ab apostolis facta, sorte domini electionis numerus compleretur. Sicque Paulus consummationem apostolicis actibus daret, quem diu contra stimulum recalcitrantem dominus elegisset. Quod et legentibus ac requirentibus deum, etsi per singula expediri a nobis utile fuerat, sciens tamen quod operantem agricolam oporteat primum de fructibus suis edere, vitavimus publicam curiositatem, ne non tam volentibus deum demonstrare videremur quam fastidientibus prodidisse.

Incipit prohemium beati Luce in evangelium suum

Quoniam quidem multi conati sunt ordinare narrationem que in nobis complete sunt rerum, sicut tradiderunt nobis qui ab initio ipsi viderunt et ministri fuerunt sermonis, visum est et michi assecuto a principio de omnibus diligenter ex ordine tibi scribere, optime Theophile, ut cognoscas eorum verborum de quibus eruditus es veritatem.

Incipit Lucas evangelium

Fuit in diebus Herodis regis Iudee sacerdos quidam nomine Zacharias de vice Abia, et uxor eius de filiabus Aaron, et nomen eius Elyzabeth. Erant autem iusti ambo ante deum, incedentes in omnibus mandatis et iustificationibus domini sine querela. Et non erat illis filius, eo quod esset Elyzabeth sterilis, et ambo processissent in diebus suis. Factum est autem cum sacerdotio fungeretur Zacharias in ordine vicis sue ante deum secundum ordinem sacerdotii, sorte exiit ut incensum poneret ingressus in templum domini; et omnis multitudo populi erat orans foris hora incensi. Apparuit autem illi angelus domini stans a dextris altaris incensi. Et Zacharias videns turbatus est et timor irruit super eum. Ait autem ad illum angelus: Ne timeas Zacharias, exaudita est deprecatio tua, et uxor tua Elizabeth pariet tibi filium, et vocabis nomen eius Iohannem. Et erit gaudium tibi et exultatio, et multi in nativitate eius gaudebunt. Erit enim magnus coram domino et vinum

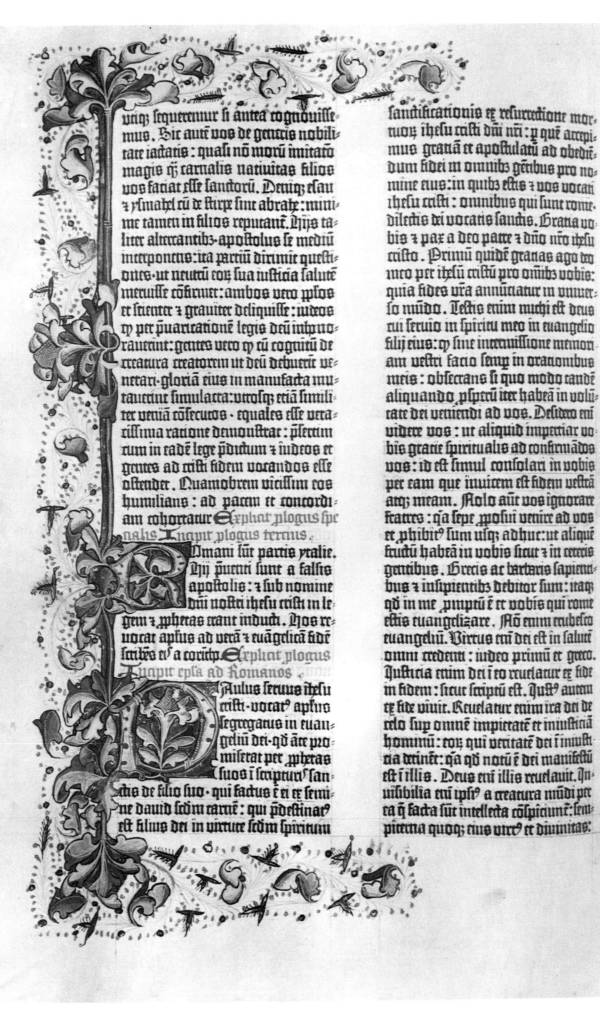

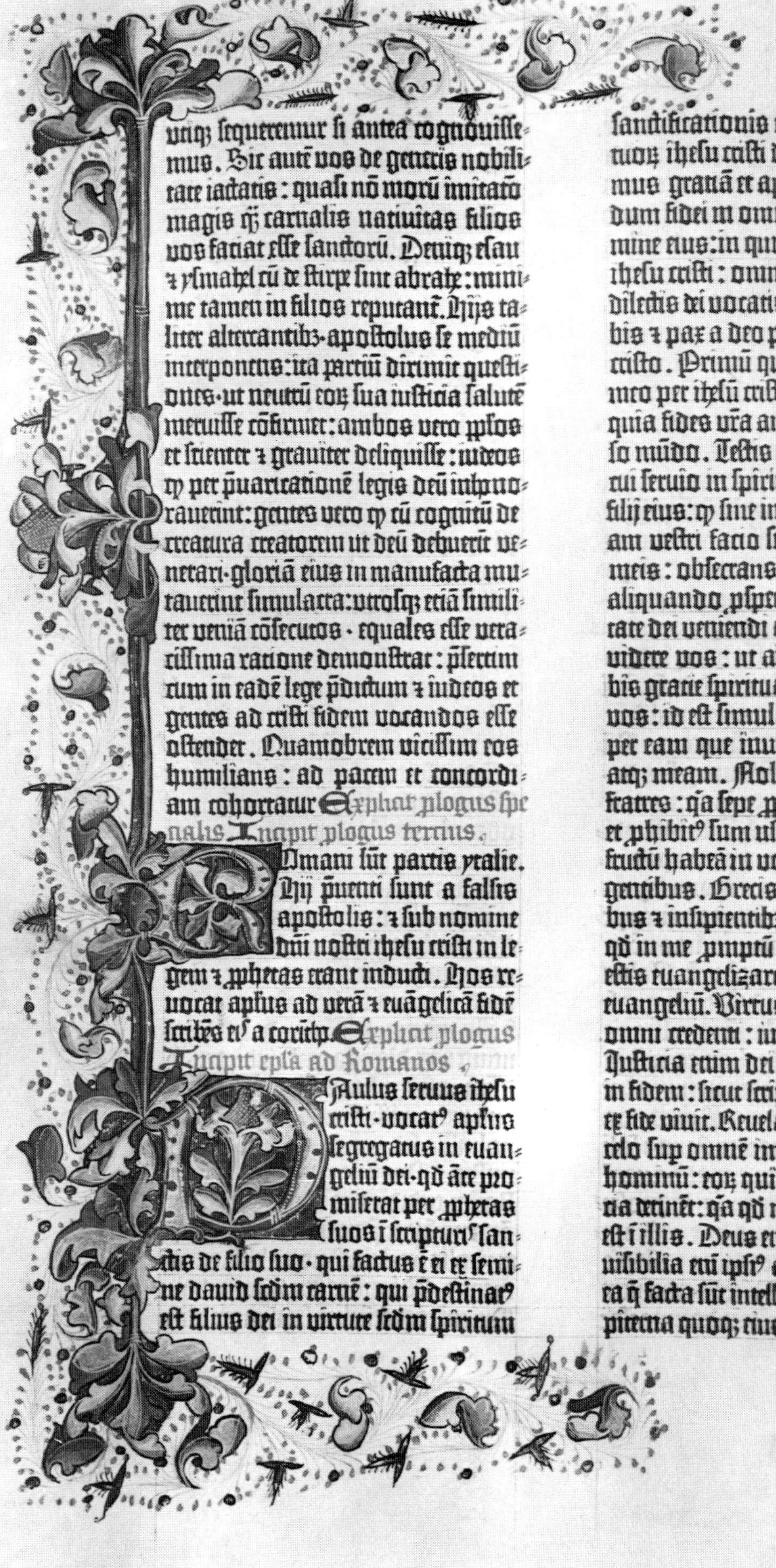

uniq; sequeremur si antea cognouisse-
mus. Sic autē vos de generis nobili-
tate iactatis: quasi nō morū imitato
magis q̄ carnalis natiuitas filios
vos faciat esse sanctorū. Deniq; esau
⁊ ysmahel cū de stirpe sint abrahe: mini-
me tamen in filios reputant̄. Hijs ta-
liter altercantib; apostolus se mediū
interponens: ita partiū dirimit questi-
ones· ut neutrū eorꝫ sua iusticia salutē
meruisse cōfirmet: ambos vero ꝑpulos
et scienter ⁊ grauiter deliquisse: iudeos
qꝫ per ꝑuaricationē legis deū inhono-
rauerint: gentes vero qꝫ cū cognitū de
creatura creatorem ut deū debuerit ve-
nerari· gloriā eius in manufacta mu-
tauerint simulacra: utrosq; etiā simili-
ter veniā cōsecutos· equales esse vera-
cissima ratione demonstrat: ꝑsertim
cum in eadē lege ꝑdictum ⁊ iudeos et
gentes ad cristi fidem vocandos esse
ostendet. Quamobrem vicissim eos
humilians: ad pacem et concordi-
am cohortatur. Explicit ꝓlogus spe-
cialis. Incipit ꝓlogus tercius.

Romani sūt partis ytalie.
Hij ꝑuenti sunt a falsis
apostolis: ⁊ sub nomine
dñi nostri ihesu cristi in le-
gem ⁊ ꝓphetas erant inducti. Hos re-
uocat apl̄us ad verā ⁊ euāgelicā fidē
scribēs eis a corintho. Explicit ꝓlogus.
Incipit ep̄l̄a ad Romanos.

Paulus seruus ihesu
cristi· vocat⁹ apl̄us
segregatus in euan-
geliū dei· qd̄ āte pro-
miserat per ꝓphetas
suos ī scripturis san-
ctis de filio suo· qui factus ē ei ex semine dauid scd̄m carnē: qui ꝑdestinat⁹
est filius dei in virtute scd̄m spiritum
sanctificationis ex resurrectione mor-
tuorꝫ ihesu cristi dñi nr̄i: ꝑ quē accepi-
mus graciā et apostulatū ad obedien-
dum fidei in omnib; gētibus pro nomine eius: in quib; estis ⁊ vos vocati
ihesu cristi: omnibus qui sunt rome·
dilectis dei vocatis sanctis. Gracia vobis ⁊ pax a deo patre ⁊ dño nr̄o ihesu
cristo. Primū quidē gratias ago deo
meo per ihesū cristū pro omīb; vobis:
quia fides vr̄a annūciatur in vniuer-
so mūdo. Testis enim michi est deus
cui seruio in spiritu meo in euangelio
filij eius: qꝫ sine intermissione memoriam vestri facio semꝑ in oracionibus
meis: obsecrans si quo modo tandē
aliquando ꝓsperū iter habeā in volū-
tate dei veniendi ad vos. Desidero enī
videre vos: ut aliquid impertiar vobis gratie spiritualis ad confirmādos
vos: id est simul consolari in vobis
per eam que inuicem est fidem vestrā
atq; meam. Nolo aūt vos ignorare
fratres: q̄a sepe ꝓposui venire ad vos
et ꝓhibit⁹ sum usq; adhuc: ut aliquē
fructū habeā in vobis sicut ⁊ in ceteris
gentibus. Grecis ac barbaris sapienti-
bus ⁊ insipientib; debitor sum: itaq;
qd̄ in me ꝓmptū ē et vobis qui rome
estis euangelizare. Nō enim erubesco
euangeliū. Virtus enī dei est in salutē
omni credenti: iudeo primū et greco.
Iusticia enim dei ī eo reuelatur ex fide
in fidem: sicut scriptū est. Iust⁹ autem
ex fide viuit. Reuelatur enim ira dei de
celo sup omnē impietatē et iniusticiā
hominū: eorꝫ qui veritatē dei ī iniusti-
cia detinēt: q̄a qd̄ notū ē dei manifestū
est ī illis. Deus enī illis reuelauit. In-
uisibilia enī ipsi⁹ a creatura mūdi per
ea q̄ facta sūt intellecta cōspiciunt̄: sem-
piterna quoq; eius virt⁹ et diuinitas:

219 London, Lambeth Palace Library MS. 15, f. 16v; Gutenberg Bible, printed in Mainz, *c.* 1450–55, and illuminated in London.
The Gutenberg or 42-line Bible is the first substantial book ever printed in Europe. This copy, sent from Mainz for sale in England, so closely resembles contemporary illuminated lectern Bibles that until the nineteenth century it was mistaken for a manuscript.

characteristics included lay participation in worship, sincerity, and practical study. Thomas à Kempis, author of the *Imitation of Christ*, wrote out a lectern Bible in five volumes between 1427 and 1438 (Darmstadt, Staatsbibl. MS. 324). The Brothers of the Common Life at Deventer made manuscripts professionally, and their fraternity's regulations included a paragraph on the writing of books, giving instructions to show specimens of scribes' hands to potential clients, to make clear contracts before beginning work, and to obtain payment for work done.

It would be interesting to know if there was a correlation between the dissemination of lectern Bibles in the fifteenth century and the books' most essential equipment – lecterns. These too were dispersed across Europe from the Low Countries and Germany. There are extremely few surviving lecterns in parish churches dating from before the fifteenth century, but late medieval examples are relatively common in the Rhineland and in the southern Netherlands (like one in Tournai dated 1483 and another at Chievres near Ath dated 1484). Renier van Thienen of Brussels (fl. 1464–94) was celebrated for making brass lecterns and other church fittings. Fifteenth- and early sixteenth-century lecterns from Dinant and Brabant were used as far afield as Edinburgh, Venice and Sicily. The style of their manufacture in brass is still known as Dinanderie after its origin in Dinant in what is now eastern Belgium.

In considering the apparent success of lectern Bibles in north-west Europe in the fifteenth century, one can look briefly at the very first products of the printing press, an invention that has long had a legendary association with the Netherlands but which was brought into practical realization with movable type by Johann Gutenberg and his partners in Mainz in the Rhineland in the mid-fifteenth century. A fundamental difference between writing by hand and printing (apart from the obvious difference of technique) is that the publisher of manuscripts accepted a commission first and then wrote out a book to order, whereas a printer, making an edition of several hundred copies simultaneously, was obliged to tie up capital in creating a stock which was subsequently marketed. Therefore a printer selected texts which had a certain sale. It is significant to consider what he chose. It will give us an interesting insight into the most secure market for books in the mid-fifteenth century. After experiments with ephemeral pieces, Gutenberg's first major project was a Latin Bible, the celebrated Gutenberg or 42-line Bible (*c.* 1450–5). It is a typical lectern book in two volumes. Copies were sold across northern Europe, and there are Gutenberg Bibles with original decoration which can be attributed to illuminators in Mainz, Leipzig, Melk, Augsburg, Erfurt, Basle, Bruges (three copies) and London. These books often look exactly like manuscripts, and the Lambeth Palace copy was actually mistakenly described as a manuscript Bible in H. J. Todd's catalogue of 1812 (Pl. 219). Quite clearly, the first printer took sensible advantage of a rich and wide market existing for lectern manuscripts.

Other books from the very earliest years of the first printing press in Mainz include a second lectern Bible, a liturgical Psalter, 1457 (not intended for monastic use but for that of a secular church), Durandus's *Rationale Divinorum Officiorum*, 1459 (the basic parochial guide to church services), the *Catholicon*, 1460 (we have seen that there was a copy at St. Margaret's parish church in London) and, in the early 1460s, St. Augustine on the art of preaching.

It may well be, to return to the opening of this chapter, that if one were to walk into a parish church in the fifteenth century there would have been few books on view, but to the calculating printers who looked about them, priests and churches were the greatest users of books.

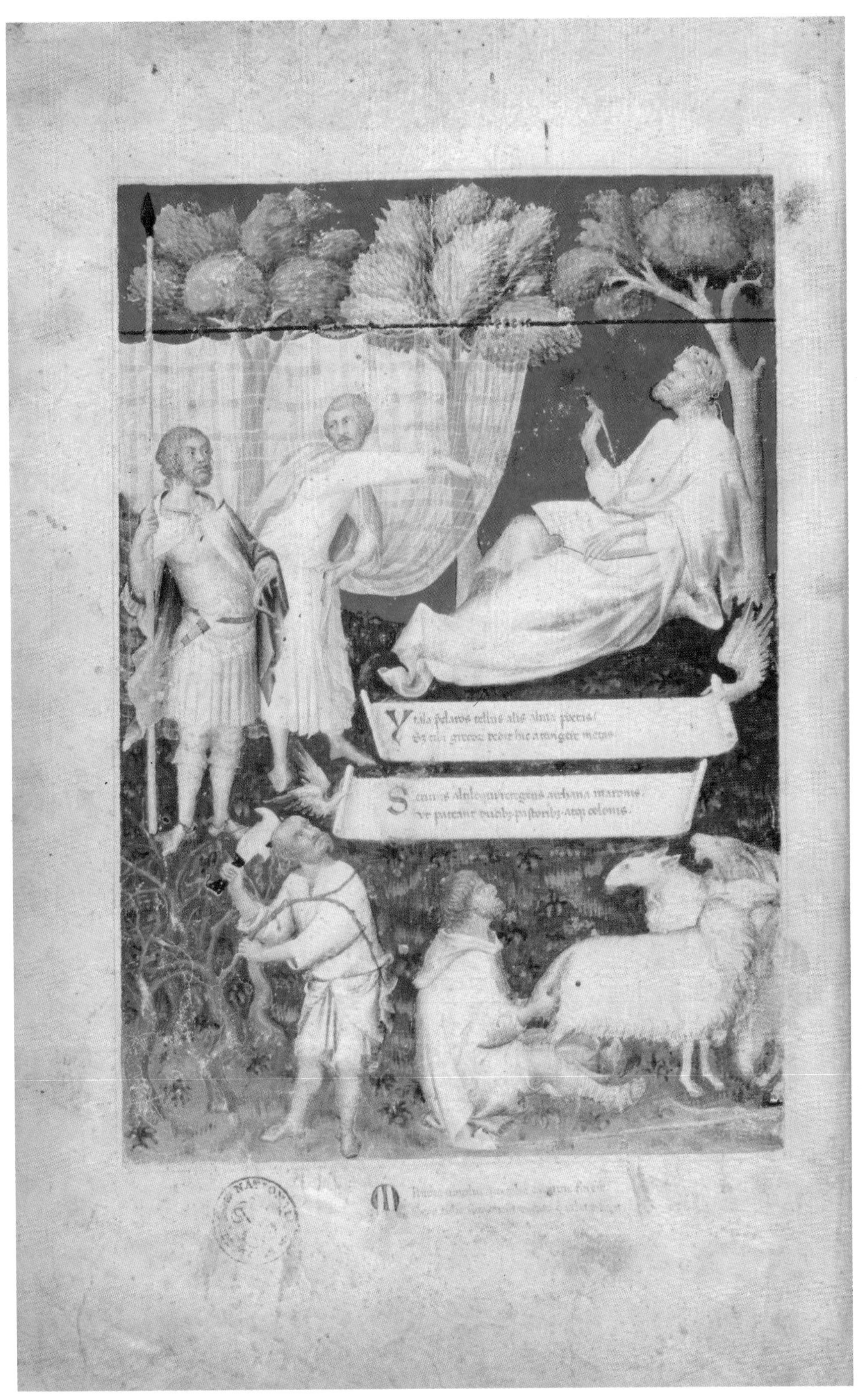

220 Milan, Biblioteca Ambrosiana MS. S. P. Arm. 10. scaf. 27, f. 1v; Virgil, Aeneid with the commentary of Servius, Avignon, *c.* 1325, with frontispiece *c.* 1340. *This is Petrarch's copy of Servius's gloss on Virgil, written perhaps in 1325, stolen from Petrarch in 1326 and recovered in 1338. The frontispiece was illuminated for Petrarch by Simone Martini (1283–1344) who settled in the papal court of Avignon in 1339.*

·8·

Books for Collectors

Book collectors have always taken a delight in owning volumes which belonged to famous bibliophiles of the past, and one can dream about what is the most ideal provenance for any surviving book. A candidate from the gothic period must certainly be the Psalter probably made for Geoffrey Plantagenet (Leiden MS. lat. 76 A): it was afterwards owned by Blanche of Castile, St. Louis of France, Jeanne of Burgundy, Blanche of Navarre, Philip the Bold, and the library of the dukes of Burgundy. From the period of the early humanists there are some copies with irresistible associations. B.N. MS. lat. 1989/1 is an eleventh-century St. Augustine inscribed from Boccaccio to Petrarch in 1355. Exeter College in Oxford has a Suetonius manuscript (MS. 186) which belonged to Petrarch, was bequeathed to Francesco Novello da Carrara, was captured in 1388 by Prince Giangaleazzo Visconti, impounded in 1499 by Louis XII of France, bound for Jean Grolier, and sold in 1827 by Henry Drury (Pl. 223). The most ideal book of all is now in the Vatican (MS. Vat. lat. 3199). It is the copy of Dante's *Divine Comedy* which Boccaccio gave to Petrarch and which was acquired by Bernardo Bembo. One can imagine Bembo (1433–1519) proudly showing this volume to his friends, together with the two books he wrongly believed to be in Petrarch's own handwriting (now MSS. Vat. lat. 3357 and 3354), and they must all have been very impressed.

The figure of Francesco Petrarch (1304–74) stands as a giant among the founders of Italian humanism and book collecting. It is now argued that he was not really the first scholar inspired by the love of the classics and that he was following the Paduan tradition led by men like Lovato Lovati (1241–1309). None the less, Petrarch towers above them all as one of the very greatest of writers, poets, classicists, and collectors (Pl. 221). He was born at Arezzo during his father's exile from Florence and was brought up in Tuscany and Avignon. While he was still a boy his father gave him a twelfth-century manuscript of Isidore which still exists (B.N. MS. lat. 7595), and there is a story that the father thought Petrarch was spending too much time on classical verse and that he flung the boy's manuscripts into the fire and then repented, pulling out Virgil and Cicero already smouldering. By his early twenties, Petrarch had begun assembling as complete a text as possible of the works of Livy. One of his exemplars came from Chartres Cathedral and was itself copied from that fifth-century Livy which we mentioned earlier (p. 68) in the possession of the Emperor Otto III. While still based in Avignon, Petrarch searched the old libraries for classical texts new to him and he found Seneca's *Tragedies*, Propertius, and Cicero's *Pro Archia*. He later acquired books from Pomposa Abbey and Montecassino in Italy, and he was overjoyed to discover Cicero's *Letters to Atticus* in 1345 in the ancient chapter library at Verona. He systematically set out to build up a full set of surviving texts by ancient writers. He wrote poetry, fell in love with Laura, climbed mountains, travelled, talked, wrote, studied, and represented to future generations the ideal of the all-round humanist scholar and antiquarian. His enthusiasm and determination seem to have inspired everyone he met. His library must have been one of the greatest private collections ever put together. In 1362 he offered to bequeath his books to Venice on condition that the city housed both them and himself during his lifetime. The republic agreed to the proposal, and Petrarch moved into the palace supplied for him. Some years later he left Venice again and apparently considered the bargain void. He lived on and died in his little house not far from Padua on 18 July 1374. Some of his books were scattered among his family. Others went to his last patron Francesco Novello da Carrara and passed into the Visconti-Sforza library. Altogether, some forty-four surviving manuscripts from Petrarch's library have been identified. Any one of them would be a relic worthy of veneration by the sect of humanists which flourished after his death.

The direct link between Petrarch and the humanist bibliophiles of the Renaissance is one of shared enthusiasm which was passed on from one person to another. The poet Giovanni Boccaccio (1313–75) in his later life became passionately involved in the circle of poets and collectors who gathered round Petrarch, and from the 1350s they became close friends, frequently staying in each other's houses (Pl. 222). He too had a wonderful collection of books which he bequeathed to the Augustinian convent of Santo Spirito in Florence, including an autograph copy of the *Decameron* now in Berlin (Hamilton MS. 90). Boccaccio knew and encouraged Coluccio Salutati (1331–1406), chancellor of Florence from 1375 until his death, and Salutati's protégés included Leonardo Bruni (1369–1444), Niccolò Niccoli

221 (LEFT) Darmstadt, Hessischen Landes- und Hofschulbibliothek MS. 101, f. 1v; Petrarch, De Viris Illustribus in the Italian translation of Donato degli Albanzani, Padua, late fourteenth century.
This drawing of Petrarch at his desk represents the ideal humanist's study strewn with manuscripts.

222 (BELOW) Paris, Bibliothèque Nationale MS. lat. 1989 (1), detail of inscription on f. 1r; St. Augustine, Enarrationes in Psalmos, eleventh century.
An autograph inscription by Petrarch records that Boccaccio, 'poet of our time', gave him this huge book when he came from Florence to Milan to visit him in April 1355.

223 (RIGHT) Oxford, Exeter College MS. 186, f. 24r; Suetonius, De Vita Caesarum, 1351.
This manuscript was written for Petrarch and belonged subsequently to the Visconti library, Louis XII of France, Jean Grolier (who had it bound) and Henry Drury. The marginal notes are in Petrarch's handwriting.

(*c.* 1364–1437), and Poggio Bracciolini (1380–1459). Their enthusiasm inspired Cosimo de' Medici (1389–1464), and so we are taken into the period of the princely libraries of the Renaissance based on the revival of classical learning and antique art.

It is sometimes difficult, in looking at the careers of these early Florentine enthusiasts, to distinguish the love of pure Latin scholarship from the unashamed delight in collecting texts and, though it has always been possible for cynics to make fun of bibliophiles or collectors of any sort, the gusto

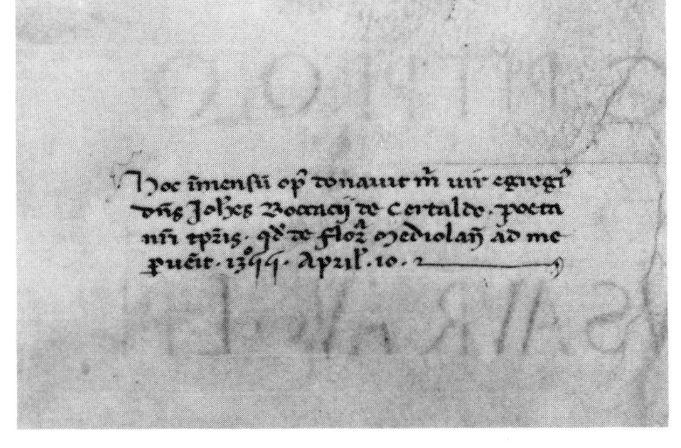

ma est ex textu a Catullo secus abnepos obtin
ma. Adversus Graecos optimatium patronus senat
des filium reliquit. quem in simili dissensione
multa varie molientem diversa factio perstratum
interemit. De patre Tyberii.

Tiberius nero tyberii cesaris pater. — Pater Tiberii quaestor G. Caesaris Alexandrino
bello classi oppositus plurimum ad victoriam
contulit. Quare et pontifex in locum P. Scipio
nis substitutus. et ad deducendas in Galli
Narbo et Arelate. — am colonias in quis Narbo et Arelate erant
missus est. Tamen Caesare occiso cunctis turbarum
metu abolitionem factorum decernentibus etiam de praemiis ty
rannicidarum referendum censuit. Praetura deinde
functus cum exitu anni discordia inter triumvi
ros orta esset retentis ultra iustum tempus insignibus
vel Antonium — L. Antonium consulem triumviri fratrem ad Perusi
am secutus deditione a ceteris facta solus perman
sit in partibus ac primo Praeneste inde Neapolim eva
sit. Servisque ad pilleum frustra vocatis in Si
ciliam profugit. Sed indigne ferens nec statim se in
conspectum Sexti Pompeii admissum et fascium usu
prohibitum ad M. Antonium traiecit in Achaiam.
Cum quo brevi reconciliata inter omnes pace Ro
mam redit. Uxoremque Liviam Drusillam et
tunc gravidam et ante iam apud se filium [tyberium] enixam
petenti Augusto concessit. nec multo post diem
obiit: utroque liberorum superstite Tiberio Drusoque
Neronibus. De loco et tempore nativitatis Tyberii.

Tiberium quidam Fundis natum existimave
runt. secuti levem coniecturam. quod materna ei
avia Fundana fuerit et quod mox simulacrum
Felicitatis ex S. C. publicatum fuerit ibi sit. Sed
ut plures certioresque tradunt. natus est Rome in Pala
tio. xvi. kl. decembris. M. Emilio Lepido iterum
L. Numa. Munatio Planco consulibus post
Sic enim — bellum Philippense. Sic enim in fastis actisque in publicum re
vel tamen — latum est. Nec tamen desunt qui tamen antecedente an
no Hirtii ac Pansae partim insequente Servilii Is
aurici Antoniique consulatu genitum eum scribant.

Infantiam De infantia et pueritia Tyberii.
pueritiamque habuit laboriosam et exercita
tam. comes usque quaque parentum fuge. quos quidem
apud Neapolim sub irruptionem hostis navigi
um clam petentes vagitu suo pene bis prodidit.

Tiberius et Drusus — Nerones

De primo agit hic liber. de secundo [illegible]

semel cum a nutricibus ubere et cum a sinu matris
rapta auferretur ab his qui pro necessitate temporis mu — vel ius
lierculas levare onere temptabant. Per Siciliam
quoque et Achaiam circumductus ac Lacedemoni
is publice qui in tutela Claudiorum erant de
mandatus digrediens inde itinere nocturno dis
crimen vite adivit. flamma repente e silvis undi
que exorta: adeoque omnem comitatum circumple — periculum tyberii infantis.
xa ut Livie pars vestis et capilli amburerentur.
Munera quibus a Pompeia Sexti Pompeii sorore
in Sicilia donatus est clamis et fibula. item bulle
auree durant ostendunturque adhuc Baiis. — vel Bais.

Post reditum in urbem a M. Gallio senato
re testamento adoptatus hereditate adita mox
nomine abstinuit quod Gallius adversarum Augu
sto partium fuerat. Novem natus annos defun
ctum patrem pro rostris laudavit. Dehinc pube
scens Actiaco triumpho currum Augusti comi
tatus est. sinisteriore funali equo cum Marcellus
Octavie filius dexteriore veheretur. Presedit
et Actiacis ludis et Troianis circensibus ductor
turme puerorum maiorum. De adolescentia et

Virili toga sumpta. adolescentiam iuventute eius.
omnemque spatiumque insequentis etatis usque ad
principatus initia. per hec fere transegit. Mu
nus gladiatorum in memoriam patris et alterum
in avi Drusi dedit. diversis temporibus ac locis. pri
mum in foro secundum in amphitheatro. Rudia
riis quoque quibusdam revocatis auctoramen
to centenum milium dedit. dedit et ludos sed ab
sens. cuncta magnifice inpensa matris ac vi
trici. Agrippinam M. Agrippe genitam neptem — ex filia pomponii agrippe uxore.
Cecilii Attici equitis R. ad quem sunt Cice — Cecilii Attici.
ronis epistole duxit uxorem. sublatoque ex eo filio
Druso quamquam bene convenientem rursusque gravidam — Drusus.
dimittere. ac Iuliam Augusti filiam confestim — quam fuerat uxor Agrippe Iuliam.
coactus est ducere non sine magno angore animi
cum et Agrippine consuetudine teneretur et Iulie mo
res improbaret. ut quam sensisset sui quoque sub priore
marito appetentem quod sane vulgo etiam exi
stimabatur. Sed Agrippinam et abegisse post divor
tium doluit. et semel omnino ex occursu visam
adeo contentis et tumentibus oculis prosecutus est.
ut custoditum sit ne umquam in conspectum ei post hac

Agrippinam hanc [sic] dimissam post Iulie et Augusti obitum
reduxit in uxorem et Augustam huius. hoc quidem quod
meminimus nusquam legi in libris. sed patet in numis
mate aureo quod michi nuper advenit, fuit [illegible]
Augustam et meus.

and excitement of book acquisition shines through in antiquarians like Coluccio, Niccoli, and Poggio. This in itself represents a major stride into humanism and the Renaissance, and away from the pragmatic book ownership of the Middle Ages. To be a humanist was not a necessary occupation. They bought books because they liked them and enjoyed being surrounded by books. This is a very modern attitude. Like many great collectors today, Coluccio began when quite young. By his mid-twenties he was certainly buying Latin manuscripts such as his copy of Priscian which is still in Florence (Bibl. Laur. Fies. MS. 176). His famous library came to include the oldest complete manuscript of Tibullus, one of the three primary manuscripts of Catullus, and Cicero's long-lost *Letters to his Friends* which was discovered in the cathedral library at Vercelli. Coluccio must have found himself comparing his own life with that of Cicero: a long-serving politician and man of affairs acknowledged to be the centre of a wide network of urbane and civilized friends. All fellow-enthusiasts were encouraged to visit his library in Florence, and something like 120 of its manuscripts have survived, including (for example) a signed Seneca entirely in Coluccio's hand (B.L. Add. MS. 11987).

Niccolò Niccoli was some thirty years younger than Coluccio and he lived until 1437, well into the true Renaissance. He was not a rich man (his father had a cloth manufacturing business), but was wealthy enough to devote his life to collecting. He once sold several farms in order to buy manuscripts, and he died with a superb library and a substantial debt at the Medici bank. He was an austere and rather frightening man. While his friends scattered themselves across Europe seeking out manuscripts, Niccoli stayed in Florence encouraging their expeditions and receiving the treasures they brought back for his approval. There is an irresistible modern comparison with Old Brown, the owl in Beatrix Potter's *Tale of Squirrel Nutkin*, before whose door the young squirrels in the story have to make presents to gain permission to gather nuts on Old Brown's island. Niccoli was an exacting critic. He lived fastidiously and dressed stylishly, wearing a red gown which reached to the ground. He never married though, as we are told by Vespasiano whom we shall be meeting soon, 'he had a housekeeper to provide for his wants' (we learn elsewhere that her name was Benvenuta). His manuscripts were superb, and his library became a meeting place for scholars and bibliophiles. It is well known that incipient collectors can be greatly inspired by the infectious example of a persistent enthusiast, and (to judge by the results) the long evenings at Niccoli's house were spent discussing and comparing acquisitions with such excitement and sense of fun that a whole generation of collectors became caught up in the search for books. This can be explained in historical terms which define humanism as the love of learning for its own sake (that is certainly true here) and the recovery of classical Latin texts as an academic discipline which required books as working tools, but there is a more fundamental straightforward enjoyment of being a collector.

This *joie de vivre* certainly appears in Poggio Bracciolini, the third of the great Florentine classicists who brought bibliophily to the Renaissance. Poggio arrived in Florence in the late 1390s when he was less than twenty and had just given up law school at Bologna. He had no money and was looking for a job, and he was befriended by Coluccio and Niccoli. Between them they devised a new method of writing out manuscripts (we shall return to this in a moment). Late in 1403 Poggio secured a job as a notary with the papal court in Rome. His real chance for book collecting came in October 1414 when he moved as papal *scriptor* to Germany for the great Council of Constance. The Council sat for four years, and one local chronicler proudly listed the astonishing total of 72,460 people who attended. It was a huge gathering and inevitably there was spare time, which Poggio used to his very best advantage. He made expeditions to libraries all around Lake Constance and further afield and he discovered and extracted (where he could) a wealth of new classical texts that really attracted the admiration of his bibliophile friends back in Florence. Early in 1415 he came upon the Cluny Abbey manuscript of Cicero's speeches and sent it off to Niccoli. In the summer of 1416 he got into the old monastery library at St. Gall where his finds included part of Valerius Flaccus, then unknown, and, for the first time, a complete text of Quintilian. The monks would not let him take their Quintilian (and by good fortune it is still in Switzerland, Zurich MS. C. 74a), but he borrowed it and copied it out in full, a task which is variously reported as taking him thirty-two days or fifty-four days. In any case it was a big book to transcribe and Poggio must have wished that they would release the original. The next year he and a few friends from the Council went to other monasteries in Germany and Switzerland, and in the summer crossed into France. They turned up copies of Lucretius, Silius Italicus, Columella, Vitruvius, and even more hitherto unknown Cicero. Many of the manuscripts had got there in the first place hundreds of years before when the northern emperors had been imitating ancient Romans with imperial libraries. Now the books began to flow back to Italy again. Poggio did not always find it easy to extract volumes from their 'prisons', as he called them: he described their owners as 'barbari et suspiciosi' and one finds it hard not to sympathize with the monastic librarians face to face with this articulate young Italian determined to talk them into giving up manuscripts.

After the council ended, Poggio visited England (where he said the dinner parties were unbelievably boring) and finally returned to Italy. Here his newly found texts passed into the canon of classical literature. There was a growing band of book collectors passionately keen on ancient Roman culture and each was inspired to put together as complete a set as possible of classical Latin texts. If they could not own original Roman manuscripts, which was an impossible hope, they had to make do with copies. The style in which this was

224 West Berlin, Staatsbibliothek, Preussischer Kulturbesitz MS. Hamilton 166, f. 96r; Cicero, Epistolae ad Atticum, Florence, 1408.
This manuscript is in the hand of Poggio Bracciolini and was probably later owned by Cosimo de'Medici. It is one of the earliest examples of the humanistic script and of the new 'white vine' illumination.

eius lucerias horrent. Itaq: quero qui sint isti oppimates qui me exturbent cu
mis si domi maneant. Sed tamen quicunq: sunt ἀιδέομαι τρῶας. & si qua spe
proficiscar uideo: coniungoq: me cum homine magis ad uastandam italiam q̄ ad
uincendū parato dominū quem expecto. & quidem cū hec scribebam uti nonas iam ex
pectabam aliquid a brundusio. quid autē aliquid q̄ inde turpiter fugisset: & ui
ctor hic qua se referret & quomodo dubij audissem. si ille appia ueniret ego arpinū
cogitabam.

M. TULLII. CICERONIS. EPISTOLARUM. AD. ATTICUM. LIBER. OCTAUUS. EXPLICIT. INCIPIT. LIBER. NONUS.

CICERO ATTICO SALUTEM. ETSI CUM has tu
litteras legeres putabam fore ut scirem iam qui brundusij actum esset. nā canu
sio. viii. kl. profectus erat. cn.. hec autē scribebam pridie non. xiiii. die postq̄ ille
canusio mouerat. tamen angebar singularū horaꝝ expectatione: mirabarq: nihil
allatū esse ne rumoris quidem. nā erat mirū silentiū. sed hec fortasse κενόσπουδα
sunt: que tamen iam sciantur necesse est. Illud molestū me adhuc inuestigare nō
posse ubi P. lentulus noster sit. ubi domitius. Quero autē quo facilius scire possim
quid acturi sint. ituri ne ad pompeiū. & si sunt qua quandoue ituri sunt. Urbē
q̄dē iam refertam esse optimatū audio sosium & lupū quos. cn. noster ante putabit
brundusium uenturos esse q̄ se ius dicere. hinū uulgo uadunt etiā. M. lepidus
quo cum diem conterere solebam cras cogitabat. Nos autē in formiano morabamur
quo citius audiremus. deinde arpinū uolebamus. inde iter q̄ maxime ἀπαντητικὸν
esset ad mare superū remotis siue omnino missis lictoribus. Audio enim bonis uiris
qui & nunc & sepe antea magno presidio r. p. fuerunt. hanc cunctationē nr̄am non
probari. multaq: mihi esse uere in conuiuijs tempestiuis quidem disputari. Cedam
igitur: & ut boni ciues simus. bellū italie terra mariq: inferamus. & odia improboꝝ
rursus in nos que iam extincta erant incendamus: & luccei consilia ac theofani per
sequamur. Nam scipio uel in syriā proficiscitur sorte. uel cū genero honeste. uel
cesarem fugit iratū. Marcelli quidem nisi gladiū cesaris timuissent manerent.
Appius in eodem timore & inimicitiaꝝ recentiū. & tamen preter hunc & C. cassiū
reliqui legati faustus proq: ego unus cui utrū uis liceret. frater accesserit. quē sociū

225 (LEFT) London, Victoria and Albert Museum MS.L.1504–1896, detail of f.209r; Pliny the Elder, Historia Naturalis, Rome, *c.* 1460–70.

226 (RIGHT) London, Sotheby's, 25 April 1983, lot 10, initial cut from a twelfth-century central Italian manuscript.
Romanesque initials of this type provided the early fifteenth-century humanists with their models for reviving white vine ornament.

done had been thought out by Salutati, Niccoli, and Poggio in Florence around 1400. In short, they introduced humanist script. Precisely how or when this happened is difficult to discover, but it is accepted that the young Poggio was a key figure in the operation. The old-fashioned fourteenth-century gothic script, full of abbreviations, was not always easy to read. We know of complaints by the elderly Coluccio in 1392 and 1396 that ordinary gothic writing was too small for his eyes. The collectors had been able to acquire many very old manuscripts from the Carolingian period (in fact, about a third of what survives from Coluccio's library dates from before 1200) and they must have admired the elegant pre-gothic minuscule in which they found their earliest classical texts. We do not know how good their palaeographical judgement really was: they appreciated that these manuscripts were extremely old, but surely they did not actually think they were Roman books? However, they began to make manuscripts in a version of this old rounded neat script. One of the earliest specimens is thought to be Bibl. Laur. Strozzi MS. 36, a volume of texts by Coluccio himself with corrections by the author (therefore datable to before his death in 1406) and copied out almost certainly by Poggio in 1402–3 before he left to take up his first job in Rome. Another is a Cicero copied by Poggio in 1408 (Berlin, MS. Hamilton 166; Pl. 224). Already by 1418 they were describing this kind of script as *'lettera antica'*. It was a deliberate attempt to revive an old script and they admired it simply because they knew it was ancient. These men were antiquarians, not inventors. They adopted a new kind of decorated initial too. In both the Coluccio book of 1402–3 and in the Cicero of 1408 there are initials with branching entwined vinestems left white against a coloured ground. These initials became typical of Florence in the fifteenth century, but they were quite new in the time of Coluccio, Niccoli, and Poggio. They are formed of what are known as white vines ('bianchi girari' in Italian). The initials look rather like the acanthus foliage which the humanists knew on ancient Roman marble columns, but their actual models must have been the vinestem initials found in many central Italian manuscripts of the mid-twelfth century. Once again they thought they were reviving an old tradition.

This new style of book appealed enormously to the collectors of classical texts in Florence in the early decades of the fifteenth century. Scholars began to practise it themselves and to ask their friends to do it. It was the style used for reproducing the texts which Poggio and others were finding in ancient monasteries. Giovanni Aretino could write a fine version of this *lettera antica*, for example, and he copied out manuscripts of Cicero (1410), Livy (1412), Cicero (1414 and 1416), Francesco Barbaro (1416), Justinus (1417), and so forth (Pl. 227). It was Aretino who wrote out Bibl. Laur. 46.13, a fine copy of the text of Quintilian which Poggio had recovered from St. Gall a year or so before. When Poggio came back to Italy he actually seems to have taught scribes to write in his humanistic minuscule. In June 1425 he wrote to Niccoli to say he was trying to train a new Neapolitan scribe and, two months later, said the scribe was proving unreliable, fickle, and disdainful, but that a French scribe he had was even worse. There is a marvellous despairing letter from Poggio dated 6 December 1427 recounting that he has spent four months attempting to teach a bumpkin scribe: 'I have been shouting, thundering, scolding and upbraiding', wrote Poggio, now aged nearly fifty, 'but his ears are blocked up – this plank, this log, this donkey . . .'.

The circle of bibliophiles in Florence shared the most common complaint of collectors at all periods: they did not have enough money. They must have been particularly pleased to welcome Cosimo de' Medici into their company. It was like a Getty applying to join a local arts society. Suddenly there was a collector with really unlimited wealth. Cosimo the Elder (1389–1464) was a brilliant banker and a calculating and successful politician. His hobby was book collecting. Niccoli cultivated his enthusiasm. He planned a holiday in Palestine with Cosimo to look for Greek manuscripts, and he got him to buy for the huge price of 100

227 (RIGHT) Oxford, Bodleian Library MS. D'Orville 78, f. 261r; Cicero, Orationes, Florence, soon after 1417.
Giovanni Aretino wrote this manuscript of Cicero after Poggio had discovered an exemplar of the text in 1417. It belonged to Cosimo de'Medici whose partly erased name is just legible in the middle of this page.

necne: tamen docere possedisse: multo iam minus que-
rit. A. cecine fundus sit necne: me tamen idipsum do
cuisse fundum esse cecine. Cum hec ita sint statuite
quid uos tempora r. p. de armatis hominibus: quid il
lius confessio de ui: quid nostra decisio de equitate: qd
ratio interdicti de iure admoneant ut iudicetis.

M. TULLII CICERONIS DE AGRARIA LEGE I
CONTRA RULLUM. TR. PL. INCIPIT. L. I.
F E L I C I T E R.

QUAE RES APERTE PETEBATUR EA
nunc occulte cuniculis oppugnatur: dicent
enī x uiri id quod & dicitur a multis & saepe
dictum est. Post eosdem consules regis alexandri testam
to regnū illud. p. r. esse factum. Dabitis igitur alexan
driā clam petentibus iis: quibus apertissime pugnantibus
restitistis. hec p deos imortales utrum esse uobis consi
lia siccoꝝ: an uinulentoꝝ somnia: & utrū cogitata sa
pientū: an optata furiosoꝝ uidentur. Videte nunc
proximo capite: ut impurus helluo turb& rem. p. ut
a maioribus nostris possessiones relictas disperdat ac dis
sip&: ut sit nō minus in. p. r. patrimonio nepos q̄ in suo

228–229 (OVERLEAF) New York, Pierpont Morgan Library M. 496, ff. 1v and 2r; Didymus of Alexandria, Opera, Florence, 1487. *This luxurious regal manuscript was written by the great scribe Sigismondo de' Sigismondi, count of Carpi (fl. 1481–1517), for Matthias Corvinus (1458–1490), king of Hungary. The right-hand page shows Matthias and his wife Beatrice of Aragon gazing up at St. Jerome who appears, like Petrarch in pl. 221, as the humanist bibliophile. In 1489 Bartolomeo Fonzio wrote from Florence that Matthias Corvinus 'intends to outshine every other monarch with his library as he does in all other points, and I think he will'.*

HAEC OPERA
CONTINENTVR IN
HOC VOLVMINE · DIDYMV
ALEXANDRINVS DE SPIRIT
S & KYRILLVS ALESADRINV
DE A POMPEO · PROCLVS
EP I NATALE · D · IOAN
SHOLASTICI GRDY

INCIPIT PRAEFATIO S HIERO
NYMI IN LIBROS S DIDYMI
GRAECI MONACHI ALEXAN
DRINI DE SPIRITU SANCTO
MA
MA
Dum in babilone uersarer et pur
purate meretricis essem colonus et
iure quiritum uiuerem uolui ali
quid garrire de spiritu sancto et

florins a twelfth-century Pliny which had been found at Lübeck, the first complete copy to reach Florence. Poggio took him exploring in Grottaferrata, Ostia, and the Alban Hills to look for Roman inscriptions. Giovanni Aretino and Antonio Mario wrote out manuscripts for him. Cosimo was enchanted with the delightful and cultivated world of the humanists. After the death of Niccolò Niccoli, Cosimo managed to come to a deal with the executors in 1441 to pay off Niccoli's debts and to acquire his library which he presented to the convent of San Marco, paying for the installation and chaining of the books. Cosimo's own library increased, and no doubt his obliging scribes and friends did not feel diffident about charging him for their services. It is difficult (and fascinating) to try to detect the moment when the passion for old texts and old books edged from the private interest of an ever-increasing group of enthusiasts into a vast business which could support the professional book trade. This probably happened in Florence about 1440, and the agent who profited most was Vespasiano da Bisticci (1422–98).

Vespasiano was a bookseller and agent for making humanist libraries. He advised collectors, employed scribes and illuminators when required, and acted as a bibliographical broker for wealthy men like Cosimo de' Medici (Pl. 230). At the end of his life Vespasiano wrote a kind of book of reminiscences, *Vite di Uomini Illustri*, which comprises short biographies of the famous men of the author's lifetime, and the implication (and often the fact) is that Vespasiano knew them and furnished them with libraries. Thus he tells us that Cosimo de' Medici had taken on the expense of building the Badia in Florence: 'and one day, when I was with him, he said, "What plan can you suggest for the formation of this library?" I replied that if the books were to be bought, it would be impossible, for the reason that they could not be found. Then he went on, "Then tell me what you would do in the matter." I said it would be necessary to have the books transcribed, whereupon he wanted to know whether I would undertake the task. I said that I would . . .'. Vespasiano goes on to say that arrangements were made for payment through the Medici bank, and claims that he then employed forty-five scribes who completed two hundred volumes in twenty-two months. This was obviously big business. The figures (if true) show that each scribe would have averaged five months to make a volume. No doubt every one of the books was written in the humanistic minuscule and decorated with the white-vine initials.

At this period, and really for the first time in the history of medieval books, we begin to know a great deal about some of the scribes who were making manuscripts. Many copyists signed and dated their volumes. Others have been identified from archival sources and their hands recognized in actual manuscripts by Dr A. C. de la Mare of Oxford. Well-known Florentine scribes of the fifteenth century include men like Antonio Mario (Pl. 238), who signed about forty surviving manuscripts between 1417 and 1456. Antonio often added cheery messages at the end of his books such as 'Good-bye, reader' ('Valeas qui legis') or the names of his clients, like Benedetto Strozzi in 1420 or Cosimo de' Medici in 1427, or notes on contemporary events such as a battle with the duke of Milan in 1425, a plague throughout Tuscany in 1437, the Council of Florence in 1440, or the republic's concern about vexation from the king of Aragon in 1448. There are about thirty manuscripts signed by Gherardo di Giovanni del Ciriago (d. 1472), dating from 1446 to the end of his life. He was the son of a Florentine silk dyer. A number of Ciriago's manuscripts were made for Cosimo de' Medici and in one he says that he wrote it out when he was a notary and scribe to the

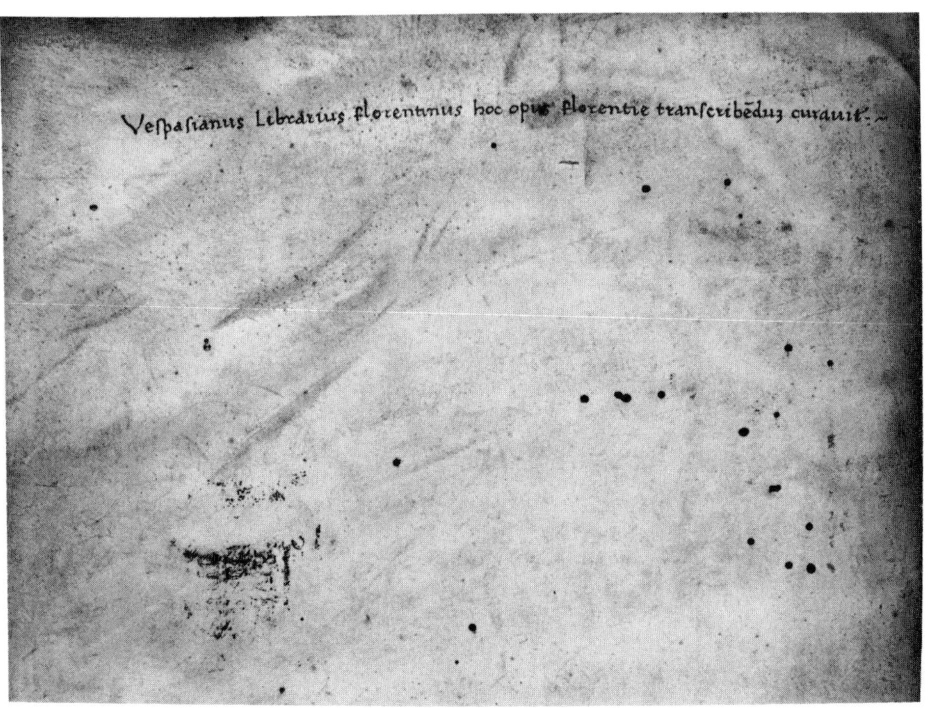

230 London, British Library, Royal MS. 15. C. XV, detail of f. 1v; Julius Caesar, Commentariorum Libri, Florence, second half of the fifteenth century.
The inscription of the flyleaf records that Vespasiano, Florentine bookseller, undertook to have this manuscript copied in Florence.

231 Florence, Biblioteca Laurenziana MS. Plut. 63. 12, f. 1r; Livy, Ab Urbe Condita, Decas Quarta, Florence, 1458.
This manuscript, illuminated for Piero de'Medici, is mentioned in a letter to Piero from Vespasiano in May 1458 when he says that Piero Strozzi has finished writing out the text and that the book has now gone to 'Pipo' (Filippo Torelli) for illumination.

lords of the municipality of Florence and that he afterwards sold it to Cosimo in 1457 (Bibl. Laur. 37. 16). One of Ciriago's last manuscripts was made for Federico da Montefeltro, 'through the agency of Vespasiano son of Filippo' (writes the scribe, fully aware of who is paying him) 'the prince of all the booksellers of Florence' (Vat. Urb. Lat. 1314).

Obviously there was money to be made in copying out manuscripts. Very many of the best scribes seem not to have been full-time professionals. They were often notaries (like Antonio Mario and Gherardo del Ciriago) or members of the Church, like Piero Strozzi who was a priest in Florence from 1447 to 1491 and (as Vespasiano tells in his book on famous men) supplemented his income by copying manuscripts so that he would not feel dependent on charity. Strozzi came from a good family and there was no shame in being a scribe (Pl. 231). One reason which turned men to scribal work was that they needed money quickly. A curiously large number of manuscripts were written in *le stinche*, the debtors' prison in Florence: Gabriele da Parma wrote a Petrarch there

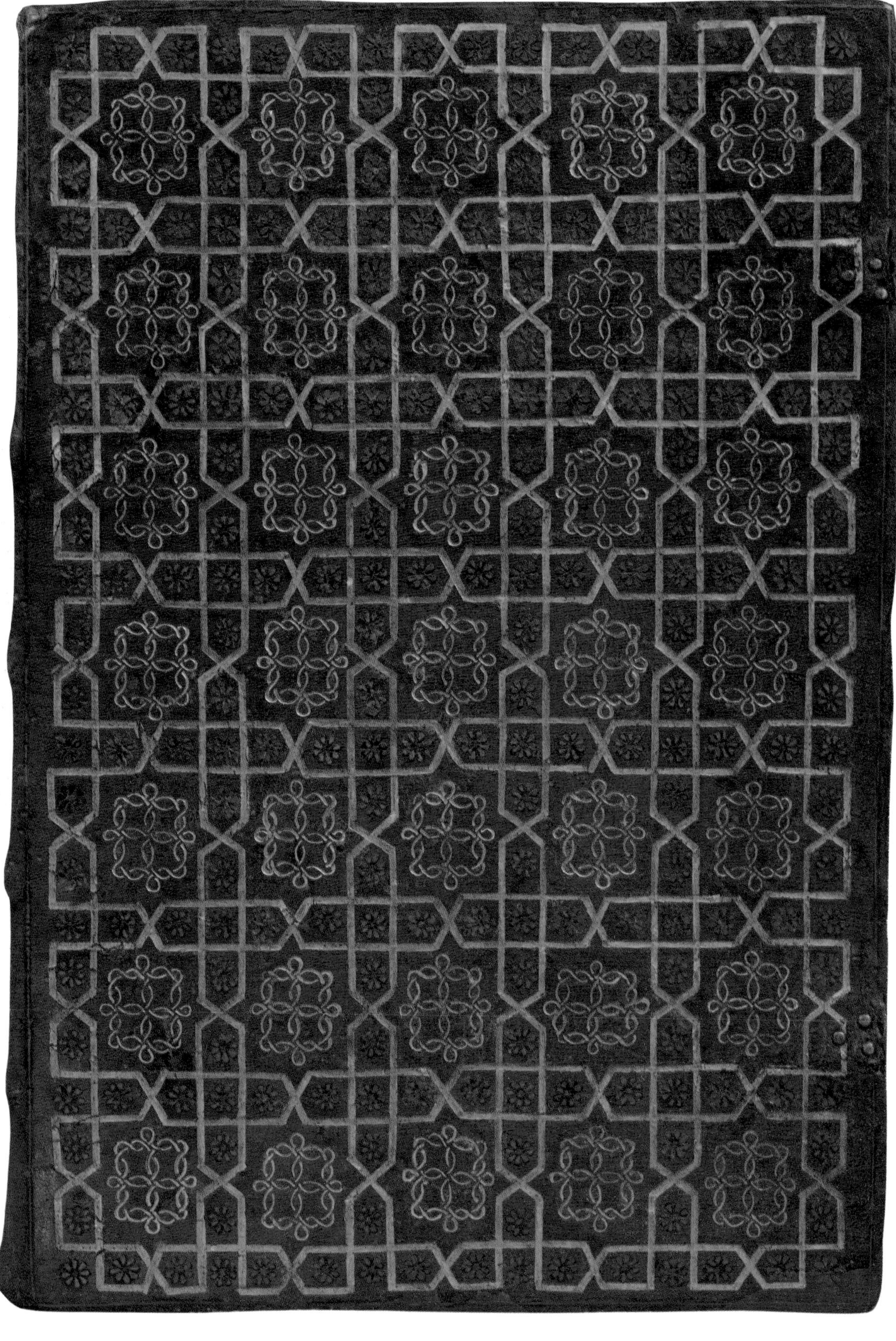

232 (LEFT) France, private collection, upper cover of binding; Thomas Aquinas, Commentary on St. John's Gospel, Naples, 1486.
The scribe of this manuscript records that he copied it at the expense of Cardinal Giovanni of Aragon (1456–85) and that he finished it in Naples on 18 November 1486 but that, while the work was in progress, the Cardinal had suddenly died in Rome in September that year. He probably fell victim to the plague and was only 29 when he died. This manuscript, in its magnificent contemporary binding inspired by Hispano-Moorish designs, passed into the Aragonese royal library.

233 (ABOVE) London, Sotheby's, 22 June 1982, lot 56, ff. 1v–2r; Ovid, De Arte Amandi, Florence, *c.* 1480–5.
This manuscript was written in Florence by Niccolò Fonzio and was illuminated by an artist known as the Master of the Hamilton Xenophon. The miniatures show Atlanta stooping to pick up the golden apples dropped by Hippomenes, and other scenes from Ovid.

234 Melbourne, State Library of Victoria *fo.96.1/Au.4, f.122v; Scriptores Historiae Augustae, Florence, 1479. *This manuscript, probably written by Neri Rinuccini for Lorenzo de'Medici, contains 81 classical portraits and survives in its contemporary binding.*

in 1427 (Sotheby's, 21 November 1972, lot 555), Agostino di Bartolo wrote B.L. Add.MS.8784 there in 1442 (and if he also wrote Vat.Pal.Lat.1607, was back inside again in 1444), and Andreas de' Medici signed six manuscripts between 1468 and 1472, two of them 'nelle stinche' in 1468. It was probably quite an agreeable way of passing one's time in prison and paying off debts at the same time.

A scribe who is being paid for his work will naturally prefer to work as quickly as possible. The beautiful round humanistic minuscule required care and precision and the pen often had to be lifted as each letter is formed of neat little strokes. Some scribes began to slope their script and join up the letters into a cursive script which must have been much faster to write. It is basically this joined-up script of the humanist scribes which has been revived by some calligraphers in the twentieth century and is known as 'italic' from its Italian Renaissance models. One scribe, Giovanni Marco Cinico of Parma, who trained in Florence but worked in Naples, 1458–98, sometimes signed himself 'velox' (speedy) and boasts in manuscripts that he was able to make them in fifty-two hours (Bibl.Laur.Strozzi.MS.109) or fifty-three hours (former Dyson Perrins MS.79). By contrast, he says in B.L. Add.MS.24895 that it was written 'tranquille', no doubt meaning that he was working at a more leisurely pace.

235 Oxford, Bodleian Library MS.Canon. Pat.Lat.159, f.1r; Cyril of Alexandria, Commentary on St.John's Gospel, Florence, *c.*1460–70.
The wreath for a coat-of-arms was left blank so that a customer could have his own arms inserted.

236 (OVERLEAF, LEFT) London, Sotheby's, 13 July 1977, lot 56, f.9r; Livy, De Bello Punico Secundo, Ferrara, 1449–50.
This copy of the third decade of Livy was illuminated for Leonello d'Este (1407–50), prince of Ferrara. It is dated 1449 by the scribe Johannes Maguntinus and the inscription around Leonello's arms, shown here, is dated 1450. The manuscript later belonged to the Vatican Library, the Dukes of Leuchtenberg, and to Sir Alfred Chester Beatty.

237 (OVERLEAF, RIGHT) Paris, Bibliothèque Nationale MS.lat.5713, f.1r; Thucydides, De Bello Peloponesium, *c.*1470.
The scribe concludes this manuscript with a note that Vespasiano the bookseller had it made in Florence. It was illuminated for Cardinal Jean Jouffrey (d.1473) to present to Louis XI of France (1461–85).

T. LIVII PATAVINI HISTORICI CLARISSIMI DE BELLO PUNI
CO SECUNDO LIBER PRIMUS FELICITER INCIPIT. LEGE :·

IN PARTE OPERIS MEI LICET MIHI
prefari q in principio summe totius p
fessi plerique sunt rerum scriptores. Bel
lum maxime omnium memorabile
quae unq gesta sunt me scripturum
quod hannibale duce carthaginienses
cum pp. Ro. gessere. Nam neque vali
diores opibus ulle interse civitates g
tesque contulere arma neque his ipsis
tm unq virium aut roboris fuit. Et
haud ignotas belli artes interse s; expertas primo punico conserebant bel
lo. & ideo varia belli fortuna ancepsque mars fuit ut propius periculo
fuerint qui vicere odiis & prope maioribus certarunt q viribus. Romanis
indignantibus q victoribus victi ultro inferrent arma penis q superbe avareque
crederent imperitatum victis. Fama etiam hannibalem annorum ferme
novem pueriliter blandientem patri hamilcari ut duceret in hispani
am cum perfecto affrico bello exercitum eo traiecturus sacrificaret altaribus
admotum tactis sacris iure iurando adactum se cum primum posset hostem
fore pp ro. Angebant ingentis spiritus virum sicilia sardiniaque amisse na
et siciliam nimis celeri desperatione rerum concessam & sardiniam inter
motum affrice fraude romanorum stipendio etiam superimposito intercep
tam. His anxius curis ita se affrico bello quod fuit sub recentem romanam
pacem pquinque annos ita deinde novem annis in hispania augendo puni
co imperio gessit ut appareret maius eum q quod gereret agitare in animo
bellum & si diutius vixisset hamilcare duce penos arma italie illa
turos fuisse qui hannibalis ductu intulerunt. Mors hamilcaris pepor
tuna & pueritia hannibalis distulere bellum. Medius hasdrubal in
ter patrem et filium octo ferme annos imperium obtinuit. Flore etatis

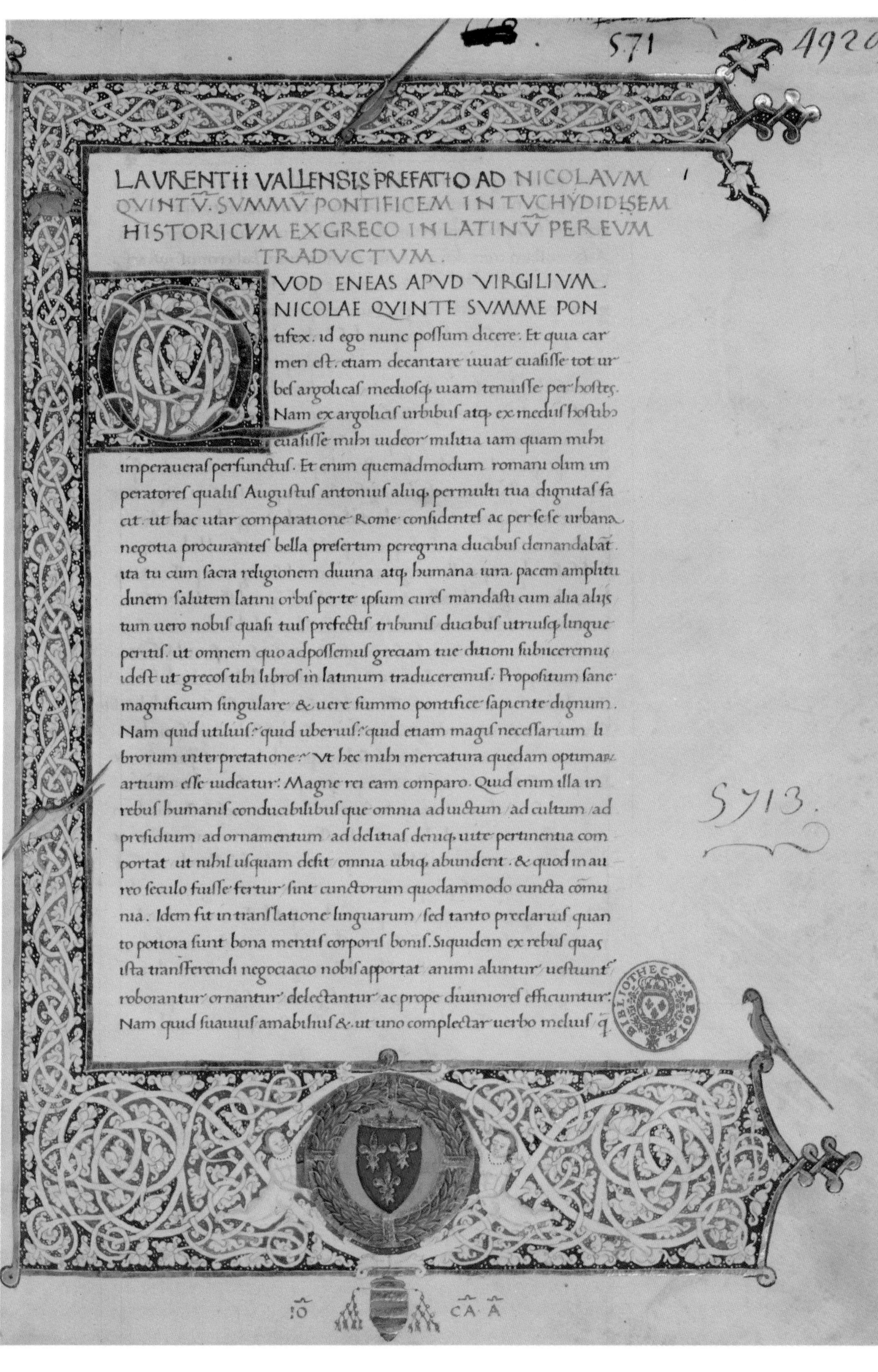

LAURENTII VALLENSIS PREFATIO AD NICOLAUM QUINTU. SUMMU PONTIFICEM IN TUCHYDIDI SEM HISTORICUM EX GRECO IN LATINU PER EUM TRADUCTUM.

QVOD ENEAS APUD VIRGILIUM NICOLAE QUINTE SUMME PONTIFEX. id ego nunc possum dicere. Et quia carmen est. etiam decantare iuuat euasisse tot urbes argolicas mediosq; uiam tenuisse per hostes. Nam ex argolicis urbibus atq; ex mediis hostib9 euasisse mihi uideor militia iam quam mihi imperaueras perfunctus. Et enim quemadmodum romani olim imperatores qualis Augustus antonius aliq; permulti tua dignitas facit. ut hac utar comparatione Rome considentes ac per se se urbana negotia procurantes bella presertim peregrina ducibus demandabat. ita tu cum sacra religionem diuina atq; humana iura pacem amplitudinem salutem latini orbis per te ipsum cures mandasti cum alia aliis tum uero nobis quasi tuis prefectis tribunis ducibus utriusq; lingue peritis. ut omnem quo ad possemus greciam tue ditioni subiceremus idest ut grecos tibi libros in latinum traduceremus. Propositum sane magnificum singulare & uere summo pontifice sapiente dignum. Nam quid utilius? quid uberius? quid etiam magis necessarium librorum interpretatione? Vt hec mihi mercatura quedam optimar[um] artium esse uideatur. Magne rei eam comparo. Quid enim illa in rebus humanis conducibilibus que omnia ad uictum ad cultum ad presidium ad ornamentum ad delitias denique uite pertinentia comportat ut nihil usquam desit omnia ubiq; abundent. & quod in aureo seculo fuisse fertur sint cunctorum quodammodo cuncta comunia. Idem fit in translatione linguarum sed tanto preclarius quanto potiora sunt bona mentis corporis bonis. Siquidem ex rebus quas ista transferendi negociacio nobis apportat animi aluntur uestiunt[ur] roborantur ornantur delectantur ac prope diuiniores efficiuntur. Nam quid suauius amabilius & ut uno complectar uerbo melius q[uam]

IO CA A

238 Oxford, Balliol College MS.78 B, f.108v; John Climacus, Spiritalis Gradatio, and other texts, Florence, 1448.
This is one of the manuscripts written by Antonio Mario for William Gray through the agency of Vespasiano in the late 1440s. It still belongs to Balliol College to which Gray bequeathed his library in 1478.

239 (OPPOSITE) Paris, Bibliothèque Nationale MS.lat.3063, upper cover of binding; Duns Scotus, Quaestiones on the second book of Peter Lombard's Sentences, Naples, 1481–2.
The manuscript was written for the Aragonese royal Library by Pietro Hippolyto da Luna, and survives in its fine Neapolitan gilt binding.

240 (RIGHT) Paris, Bibliothèque Nationale MS.lat.12946, detail of f.423r; Cardinal Bessarion, Adversus Calumniatorem Platonis, Naples, 1476.
In this circular colophon the scribe Gioacchino de Gigantibus, of Rothemburg, calls himself bookseller and illuminator to King Ferrante I of Naples and says that he wrote this book peacefully and decorated it in 1476. He is documented as working for the royal library in Naples from at least March 1471 to November 1480.

A copy of Caesar written by a scribe Stephen in 1462 (B.L.Add.MS.16982) took thirty-eight days, which works out at eleven pages a day. This must have been a much more usual kind of rate. A customer commissioning a manuscript through Vespasiano, for instance, would have to allow time for the book to be written out and illuminated.

William Gray (*c.*1413–78), from Balliol College in Oxford, is a good example of a book collector who seized the chance of a few days in Florence to place an order with Vespasiano that would take several years to fulfil. Gray was a notable English scholar and had been chancellor of Oxford University about 1440. By the end of 1442 he had left on a tour of Europe, going first to Cologne (where he acquired a number of manuscripts such as a Seneca, now Balliol College MS.130) and late in 1444 or early in the next year he travelled on to Italy, spending time in Padua, Ferrara, and Rome. However, he came first to Florence. Vespasiano includes William Gray among his lives of great men, and says that he was so rich (one can see Vespasiano's eyes flashing with approval) that he had to travel from Cologne in disguise to avoid being robbed on the journey. 'When he arrived in Florence', writes Vespasiano, 'he sent for me and told me about this adventure. He ordered many books, which were transcribed for him, and then left for Padua . . .' When Vespasiano says the books were transcribed, he means that they were specially made rather than acquired second-hand. They were still working on the order in December 1448 when Vespasiano wrote to Gray in Rome to say that a Tertullian manuscript had been sent off and that he was waiting for his instructions on the Plutarch and other texts. The scribes employed for this job included Antonio Mario and Piero Strozzi. Some of the manuscripts themselves survive, mostly still in Balliol College to which Gray bequeathed them many years later. They include a five-volume Cicero (one volume dated November 1445 and another September 1447), Sallust, Quintilian, Virgil, Pliny, and two religious texts, St. John Chrysostom and John Climacus (Pl. 238), which Antonio Mario signed in most friendly terms in August 1447 and June 1448: 'Lege feliciter, mi suavissime Ghuiglelme' ('Have a nice read, my dearest William'). Obviously the relationship between the bookseller, his scribes, and his customer, was one of cultivated cordiality. It is as if the fellowship of Florentine bibliophiles has temporarily admitted William Gray into their number. When he left Italy finally in 1453, he had much less money and some fine manuscripts. Personal contact and shared enthusiasm are the delight of all collectors, and Vespasiano was a most genial man.

Good booksellers are brought by their profession into the most exalted circles. Mr. H. P. Kraus, certainly the greatest twentieth-century vendor of medieval manuscripts, called four chapters of his autobiography (1979), 'The Collector *par Excellence*', 'In Noble Company', 'The Great Collector of Aachen', and 'The Bibliophile of Schweinfurt'. It pays to cultivate the very richest people. It is remarkable how Vespasiano's reminiscences of his clients have exactly the same theme. His four sections are on popes, kings, and cardinals; archbishops and bishops; sovereign princes; and men of state and letters. Vespasiano's most complimentary comment (and both he and Mr. Kraus use it quite often) is 'he collected a fine library, not regarding cost.' Like all republicans, the Florentines adored royalty. Vespasiano goes out of his way to praise the culture of Alfonso of Aragon (1401–58), king of Naples, but in fact the best he can really say about the king's bibliophily is that Antonio Panormita used to read Livy manuscripts out loud to him. Vespasiano had his own name written in the Thucydides manuscript intended for King Louis XI of France (B.N. MS. lat. 5713) as if he wanted it quite clearly stated where the king should apply for future manuscripts (Pl. 237). When in 1488 the Florentine scribe Antonio Sinibaldi copied out a book for Matthias Corvinus, king of Hungary (1458–90), he could not resist name-dropping in signing himself 'formerly scribe and book-agent to Ferdinand, king of Sicily' (B.N. MS. lat. 16839). The scribe and illuminator Gioacchino de Gigantibus (fl. 1448–85), who worked mainly in Rome with excursions to Siena and Naples, loved to call himself 'royal bookseller and miniaturist on vellum' (B.L. Add. MS. 15272). The massive royal and princely orders for manuscripts were certainly welcomed by the humanist scribes

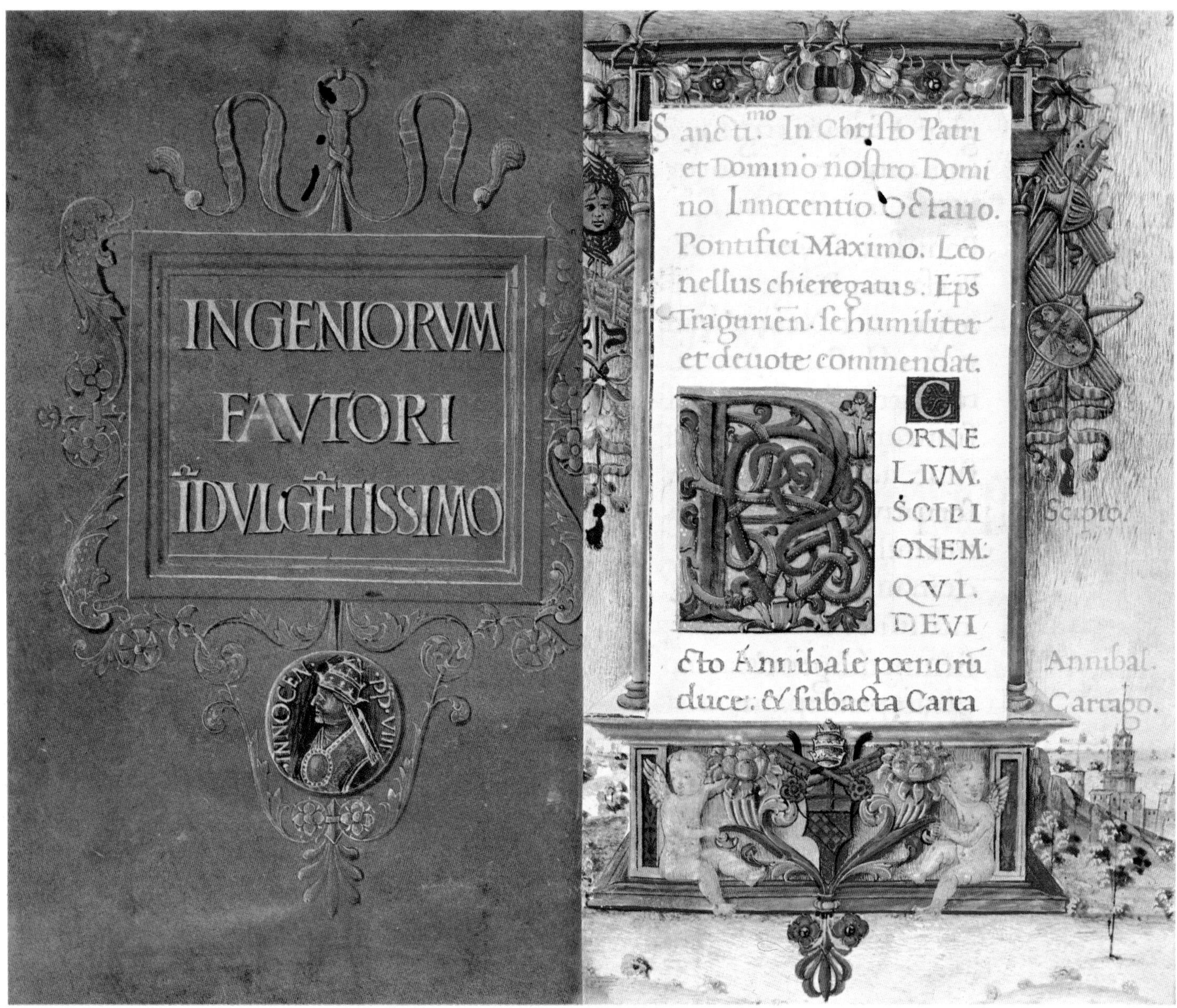

241 London, Christie's, 30 January 1980, lot 213, ff. IV–2r, Agapetus, Ad Iustinianum Imp. Adhortationes, Venice, October 1484.
This copy of St. Agapetus was illuminated for presentation by Leonello Chiericeti to Pope Innocent VIII (1484–92). The opening page is decorated in gold on purple-stained vellum in imitation of classical imperial manuscripts.

242 (RIGHT) Geneva, Bibliothèque Publique et Universitaire MS. lat. 49, Eusebius of Caesarea, De Temporibus, in the Latin translation of St. Jerome, Venice, late fifteenth century.
The illuminators of north-east Italy struggled with the problem of how to reconcile a two-dimensional text area with a three-dimensional border. The writing here is ingeniously represented as an ancient scroll being pulled tight across a monumental arch. The arms are those of Maffei of Venice.

INTERPRETATIO. EVSEBII. CAESARIENSIS. EDITA.
PER. BEATVM. HIERONYMVM. ET. IPSIVS. PROSPE
RIQ: ADDITIONES. DE. TEMPORIBVS.
PROLOGVS. BEATI. HIERONYMI.
EVSEBIVS
HIERONIMVS. VINCENTIO. ET. GALIENO. SVIS. SALVTEM
VETVS ISTE DISERTOR

NTER HAEC
ALEXANDER
AD CONDVCE-
DVM EX PELO-
PONENSO MI-
LITEM: CLEAN-
DRO CVM PE-
CVNIA MISSO:
LICIAE PAMP-

and by booksellers. Their motives were not only the financial profit to themselves but also the practical value to scholarship in promoting semi-public libraries and (very probably) the pure enjoyment of building great collections at someone else's expense. As it happened, the greatest humanist libraries were assembled for the princes of the Renaissance: the Aragonese kings of Naples and Cardinal Giovanni of Aragon, the king's brother (Pl.232), King Matthias Corvinus of Hungary (Pl.228–9 and 249), the Visconti and Sforza dukes of Milan, the Medici in Florence, the Este court in Ferrara, the Gonzaga dynasty of Mantua, Federigo da Montefeltro in Urbino, and the popes in Rome. The amount of money spent on manuscripts must have been extraordinary. Vespasiano says Federigo da Montefeltro spent 30,000 ducats on manuscripts, plus the cost of binding (Pls.243 and 244). Italian Renaissance manuscripts are very splendid things. The vellum pages are creamy white and open beautifully. The lovely humanistic script is laid out with superbly proportioned margins. Elegant white-vine initials spill over into the borders with charming little putti, insects, and butterflies. Florentine illuminators excelled in the opening pages of

243 (ABOVE, LEFT) Vatican, Biblioteca Apostolica MS. Urb. lat. 508, inside front cover; Cristoforo Landino, Disputationes Camaldulenses, Florence, *c.* 1475.
It is said that Federigo de Montefeltro (1422–82), Duke of Urbino, would allow no printed books in his library. In the dedication miniature here Federigo is holding a renaissance manuscript as he gazes benignly at a young man, presumably the author.

244 (ABOVE) Vatican, Biblioteca Apostolica MS. Urb. Lat. 427, f. 2r; Quintus Curtius Rufus, Historiae Alexandri Magni, probably Ferrara, *c.* 1480.
This manuscript was illuminated for Federigo da Montefeltro and has his arms and name on the opening leaf. It was written by Matteo de'Contugi of Volterra.

245 (OPPOSITE) Longleat, Library of the Marquess of Bath, Botfield collection, f. 1; Virgil, Opera, Florence, *c.* 1460.
The illuminated border here is probably the work of Francesco d'Antonio del Cherico (fl. 1452–84). The book belonged to the eccentric English collector Beriah Botfield (1807–63) who had his own arms inserted in the illuminated border and then presented his library to the Marquess of Bath to whom he hoped to prove kinship.

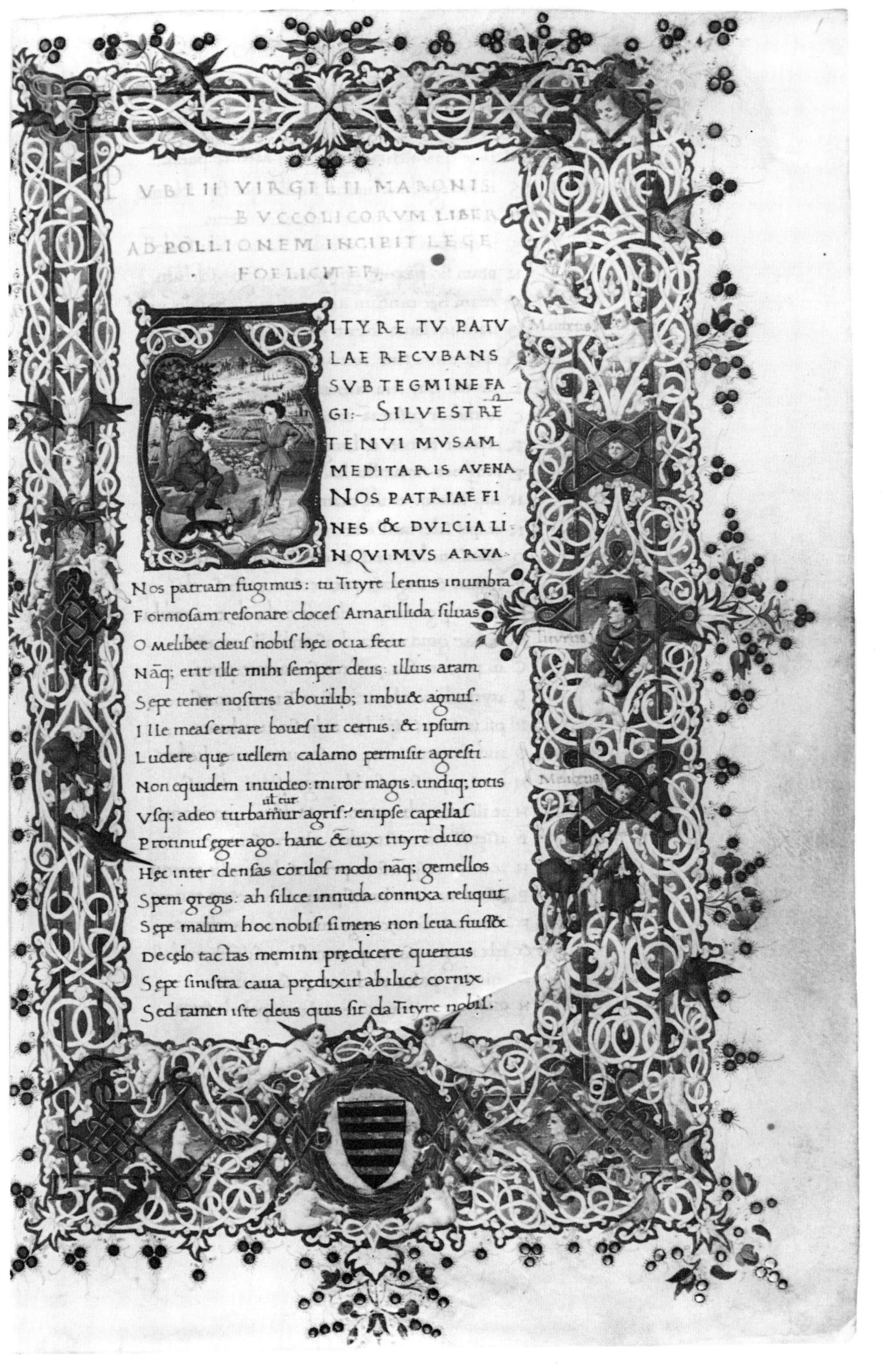

PVBLII VIRGILII MARONIS
BVCCOLICORVM LIBER
AD POLLIONEM INCIPIT LEGE
FOELICITER

TITYRE TV PATV
LAE RECVBANS
SVBTEGMINE FA
GI: SILVESTRE
TENVI MVSAM
MEDITARIS AVENA
NOS PATRIAE FI
NES & DVLCIA LI
NQVIMVS ARVA.

Nos patriam fugimus: tu Tityre lentus inumbra
Formosam resonare doces Amarillida silvas
O Melibee deus nobis hec ocia fecit
Naq; erit ille mihi semper deus: illius aram
Sepe tener nostris abouilib; imbu& agnus.
Ille meas errare boues ut cernis. & ipsum
Ludere que uellem calamo permisit agresti
Non equidem inuideo: miror magis. undiq; totis
Usq; adeo turbamur agris: en ipse capellas
Protinus eger ago. hanc & uix tityre duco
Hec inter densas corilos modo naq; gemellos
Spem gregis. ah silice innuda connixa reliquit
Sepe malum hoc nobis si mens non leua fuiss&
De celo tactas memini predicere quercus
Sepe sinistra caua predixit ab ilice cornix
Sed tamen iste deus quis sit da Tityre nobis.

LAVDES BELLICAE
ILIACAS ALII
FLAMMAS THE
BANAQVE FRA
TRVM ARMA:
ET IASONIIS
INSIGNEM HEROIBVS ARGO
A strorum cursus: & ditis inania regna.
F ictaq; pierio referant miracula cantu:
N os propriis spectanda oculis: nos inclyta dextre
F acta tue canimus: quibus aurea sydera viuis
T angis: & ætherias fama petis arduus arces:
S ed sine te nunq tenues ad carmina tanto
S ubsistant uires oneri: tu numine toto
D exter ades: da mæoniam tua facta canenti
M atthia coruine chelyn: si delphica parent
T empla tibi: sentitq; frequens tua nomina cyrrha
S i musæ si phoebus amant: hoc tempore solus
C arminibus si digna facis: quæ nulla uetustas.

246 Wolfenbüttel, Herzog August Bibliothek MS. 85.1.1. Aug. 2°, f. 3r; Alexander Cortesius, Laudes Bellicae, Rome, *c.* 1480–90.
This presentation manuscript for Matthias Corvinus is by the hand of the very great Paduan scribe Bartolomeo Sanvito. It was given to Corvinus in the hope that it would encourage his support for the pope's military campaigns.

247 (RIGHT) New York, Pierpont Morgan Library E. 2.78 B, frontispiece to second volume; Aristotle, Libri Metaphysice, printed in Venice by Nicolas Jenson in 1483.
This is a printed book illuminated in the very richest style of a Renaissance manuscript. The artist, who excelled in the north-eastern Italian style, was Girolamo da Cremona who worked first in Mantua for the Gonzaga family, and then in Siena and perhaps in Florence. By 1475 he had settled in Venice where he decorated manuscripts and printed books for nostalgic bibliophiles.

Liber primus metaphysice.

Omnes homines natu
ra scire desiderant. Si-
gnū aūt est sensuū dile
ctio: preter enī vtilitatē
ꝓpter seipsos diligūtur
⁊ maxie alioꝝ qui est
per ipsos oculos. non
enim soluz vt agamus:
sed ⁊ nihil agere deben
tes: ipꝫ videre pre oib⁹
vt dicam alijs eligim⁹. causa aūt est quia hic ma
xime sensuū cognoscere nos facit: ⁊ multas reꝝ
differētias demōstrat. Aialia quidē igitur sensuꝫ
habētia natura fiūt. ex sensibus aūt qbusdā qdē
ipsoꝝ memoria non fit: quibusdā vero fit: ⁊ ꝓpt
hoc alia qdeꝫ prudētia sunt: alia vero disciplina-
biliora non potentibus memorari. Prudentia
quidē sunt sine addiscere quecūqꝫ sonos audire
nō potētia sunt: vt apes. ⁊ vtiqꝫ si aliqd aliud ge-
nus animaliū huiusmodi est. addiscūt autē quecūqꝫ cum memoria: ⁊ hunc habēt sensum. Alia
quidē igitur imaginatiōibus ⁊ memorijs viuūt:
experimēti autē parū participāt: hominū aūt ge
nus arte ⁊ ratiōibus. Fit aūt ex memoria homi
nib⁹ experimētū: eiusdē naqꝫ rei multe memorie
vnius experiētie potentiā faciunt: ⁊ fere videt̄ sci
entie ⁊ arti simile experimētum esse. hominibus
aūt sciētia ⁊ ars per experimentū euenit. expiētia
quideꝫ enim artem fecit: vt Ptolemeus recte di
cens: sed inexpientia casum. Fit autē ars cum ex
multis experimētalibus ꝯceptōibus vna fit vni-
uersalis velut de similibus acceptio. acceptionē
enim quidē habere: q callie ⁊ socrati hac egritu
dine laborātibus hec ꝯtulit: ⁊ ita multis singula
riū experimenti est. Quod aūt oibus huiusmodi sm autē vnam speciē determinatis hac egritu
dine laborātib⁹ cōtulit: vt phlegmaticis aut cho
lericis aut estu febricitātibus artis est. Ad agere
quidē igitur expiētia nihil ab arte differre videt̄:
sed ⁊ exptos magis ꝓficere videmus sine expiētia rationē habētibus. causa aūt est quia experiē
tia qdeꝫ singulariū est cognitio: ars vero vniuer
saliū. actus aūt ⁊ oēs generatiōes circa singlare

sunt. nō enim hominē medicus sanat nisi sm ac-
cidēs: sed aut calliā aut socratē aut aliquod sic di
ctoꝝ: cui esse hominē accidit. si igitur sine experi
mēto quis ratiōeꝫ habeat: ⁊ vniuersale quidē co
gnoscat: in hoc aūt singulare ignoret: multotiēs
quidē curatiōe peccabit: singulare nanqꝫ magis
curabile est. Sed tamē scire ⁊ intelligere magis
arte qꝫ expimēto esse arbitramur: ⁊ artifices exp
tis sapientiores esse opinamur: tanqꝫ magis sm
scire sapiētia oia sequēte. hoc aūt est: quia hi qdē
causam sciūt: illi vo non. expti quidē enim sciunt
ipm quia: sed ꝓpter quid nesciūt: illi aūt ꝓpt qd
⁊ causam cognoscūt. vnde ⁊ architectores circa
quodlibet quidē huiusmodi honorabiliores ⁊
magis scire manu artificibus putamus ⁊ sapien
tiores: quia factoꝝ causas sciūt: illi vo sicut qdā
inanimatorū faciunt quidē: non scientia autem
faciunt que faciunt: ut ignis quod exurit. inaia-
ta quidem igit natura qdam vnūquodqꝫ horuꝫ
facere sed manu artifices propter consuetudinē
est tanqꝫ non sm practicos esse sapiētiores sint
sed sm q rationē habēt ipsi ⁊ causas cognoscūt
Et oio scientis signū est posse docere: ⁊ ob hoc
artem magis experimento scientiā esse existima
mus. Possunt autē hi: hi autē docere non possunt: amplius auteꝫ sensuū neqꝫ vnū sapientiam
esse ponimus cum his singuloꝝ cognitiōes ma
xime proprie sint: sed ꝓpter quid de nullo dicūt
ut propter quid ignis calidus sed quia calidus
solum sit. Primū quidem igitur conueniens est
quālibet artem inuenienteꝫ vltra cōes sensus ab
hominibus mirari non solū propter aliquaꝫ in-
uentoꝝ vtilitatē sed sicut sapientem ⁊ ab alijs dif
ferentē. pluribus autem repertis artibus ⁊ alijs
quideꝫ ad necessaria: alijs vo ad introductionē
existentibus: tales illis sapientiores esse arbitrā-
dum est propter id qd illoꝝ scientie ad vsum nō
sunt. vnde iam omnib⁹ talibus institutis que nō
ad voluptatē neqꝫ ad necessitatem scientiarū re-
perte sunt. ⁊ primū in his locis vbi vacabāt: vñ
circa egyptū mathematice artes primū consti-
tuerunt: ibi nāqꝫ gens sacerdotū vacare dimissa
est. In moralibus quidem igitur que sit artis ⁊

manuscripts with full white-vine borders enclosing vignettes, birds, and coats-of-arms within wreaths. These were the work of great painters like Filippo di Matteo Torelli (1409–68, his friends called him Pippo), Ricciardo di Nanni, and Francesco d'Antonio del Cherico. The edges of the pages are gilded. The books are bound in the smoothest goatskin stamped with arabesque designs, sometimes with gold or painted with the owner's arms. These are really treasures for the cabinets of the most refined and wealthy princely book collectors.

There is some information about how these rich collections were kept. The library which Malatesta Novello built up for the Franciscan convent in Cesena is still there, in a special upstairs room above the refectory with manuscripts arranged on twenty-nine benches and desks on either side of a central aisle. Piero de' Medici (1416–69) had his manuscripts specially bound according to the way they were to be arranged in his library (Pl. 231): theology books were bound in blue, grammar in yellow, poetry in purple, history in red, the arts in green, and philosophy in white. It must have looked wonderful. Leonello d'Este (1407–50) kept manuscripts in a room decorated with figures of the Muses, and he appears in Decembrio's dialogue *De Politia Litteraria* where he says that books are less likely to suffer from dust if they are

248 (LEFT) Paris, Bibliothèque Nationale MS. lat. 6376, lower cover of the binding; Seneca. *This book was bound for Giovanni de' Medici, son of Cosimo, and it has the Medici arms in the centre of the cover.*

249 (RIGHT) Vienna, Österreichische Nationalbibliothek MS. Lat. 22, f. 1r; Livy, Ab Urbe Condita, Decas Prima, Florence, *c.* 1460–70. *The arms and initials here are those of Matthias Corvinus. The manuscript is signed by the scribe Giovanni Francesco Martino, of San Gimignano, and another volume from the same set is in the Spencer Collection in the New York Public Library (MS. 27).*

stored in cupboards. Pope Nicholas v (the humanist Tommaso Parentucelli) had his library room painted with portraits of pagan and Christian writers by Fra Angelico in 1449. Federigo da Montefeltro's study at Urbino still has its cupboards with *trompe-l'œil* inlay work showing tantalizing heaps of manuscripts. These rooms were meeting places too for convivial evenings. 'At your place in Várad', wrote a visitor in 1463 to the collections of Johannes Vitéz (d. 1472, chancellor to Matthias Corvinus), 'we often sat together with many scholars in your magnificent library, and spent a pleasant and happy time among the innumerable volumes of illustrious men.'

We must now pause to ask a fundamental question. Were the owners true bibliophiles? How is it that the passion for long-lost classical texts among a small group of late fourteenth-century enthusiasts had moved within eighty years into the business of furnishing princes with packaged culture? It brings us to a definition of what motivates any collector. There is something fundamentally human about longing to go out in pursuit of a rarity which can be acquired and brought home. To some people this instinct is quite basic; to others (who never collected anything as children) the desire for possessions is so alien that collecting must be a total mystery. The real collector knows that, for all his careful rationalization, the actual motive is because it is fun. There is something very exciting and enjoyable about knowing that one is missing a key item to complete part of a collection and then, perhaps a long time later, triumphantly finding the longed-for piece. This is just what people like Coluccio Salutati, Niccolò Niccoli, and Poggio were doing. Their *desiderata* were the complete works of Latin authors and they sought them with the passion bordering on mania which drives on all collectors. They exchanged and weeded and upgraded their collections, like all bibliophiles, and in the 1420s Poggio began replacing his paper manuscripts with vellum copies. The script and decoration devised for these books is aesthetically very pleasing and appropriate. A well-made Florentine manuscript of the mid-fifteenth century is a thoroughly desirable artefact. The amateur but very rich princely collectors, whose needs were met by men like Vespasiano, no doubt responded in much the same way as we do in handling these beautiful books. Even the smell of a clean humanist manuscript is strangely seductive. One difficulty faced by a modern book collector is that the number of books is infinite and a new collector benefits from a classified list or catalogue of items to be sought; this is why stamps and coins are popular areas of collecting and why catalogues of them are usually published or promoted by dealers. A great twentieth-century bookseller, Dr A. S. W. Rosenbach, used to specialize in drawing up for his customers lists of (for example) the hundred best books in literature or science or American history. This is an excellent way of crystallizing the collecting instinct. It is therefore interesting to see Tommaso Parentucelli in 1439–40 compiling a list for Cosimo de' Medici of the texts he ought really to be collecting for his library in San Marco and to find Malatesta Novello using the same list in building up the library at Cesena around 1450. Vespasiano is revealing in his account of how Federigo da Montefeltro outfitted his library. 'He took the only way to make a fine library,' writes Vespasiano, who then lists a careful order of priorities according to which Montefeltro set to work: the Latin poets and commentaries first, followed by the orators and grammarians, the historians (Latin writers and Greek historians translated into Latin), philosophers, theologians, writers on the arts and medicine, and books in Greek and finally in Hebrew. This was not a random accumulation or a bulk order, as the manuscripts came from many different places. Beautiful books were acquired in an orderly way, using money and an irrational passion for the objects themselves (Montefeltro would never allow a printed book in his house, an attitude which by the 1480s was certainly eccentric), and they were finely bound and housed. This is the nearest we can get in the Middle Ages to the bibliophilia of today. It represents a natural acquisitive passion and a delight in fine objects. To be able to respond systematically to this instinct is peculiarly modern, or humanistic.

To summarize, then, the style and taste of the humanists of Florence were transmitted by personal enthusiasm and careful cultivation of collectors, and humanistic manuscripts and their white-vine initials were dispersed outwards from Florence to the libraries of Rome and Naples (in particular) and to Ferrara and Milan, and beyond Italy to collections as far distant as those of William Gray in Oxford and Johannes Vitéz in Várad in Hungary. We must, however, introduce another development which complicates the story. From the north-east of Italy there came a new style of humanistic manuscript. It is later in development but by the last quarter of the fifteenth century the two types are merging in central Italy. From Verona, Padua, and Venice there came a generation of mid-fifteenth century antiquarians with a passion for ancient Roman culture quite as lively as that of Coluccio, Niccoli, and Poggio. By the 1450s, however, there were fewer manuscripts to rediscover. Perhaps they came to realize too that even the very oldest extant volumes of classical texts were still centuries later than their authors. They therefore began to look at ancient Roman inscriptions on stone: after all, a monumental epigraph is an authentic Latin text and (though less portable) is as near to an original Roman manuscript as anyone can hope to find. They started to make collections of these inscriptions. The merchant Ciriago (1391–1452) from Ancona travelled extensively in the course of his business and took every opportunity to copy inscriptions he found. He wrote them out prettily in coloured inks. He had a remarkably eccentric young friend, Felice Feliciano (*c.* 1432–80) of Verona. The late James Wardrop describes Feliciano in *The Script of Humanism* (Oxford, 1963) as a totally madcap scribe, antiquary, doggerel poet, painter, alchemist, and immoralist, whose own brother called him a vagabond, who used to disappear into the foothills of the Alps for days at a time and would suddenly re-emerge unshaven like a tramp, a wit, a delightful, amusing, unpredictable, wild eccentric. 'It seems fairly certain there was a screw loose in Felice Feliciano,' observed Wardrop.

None the less, the passion of Feliciano and his friends for ancient monuments had a far-reaching consequence. He used

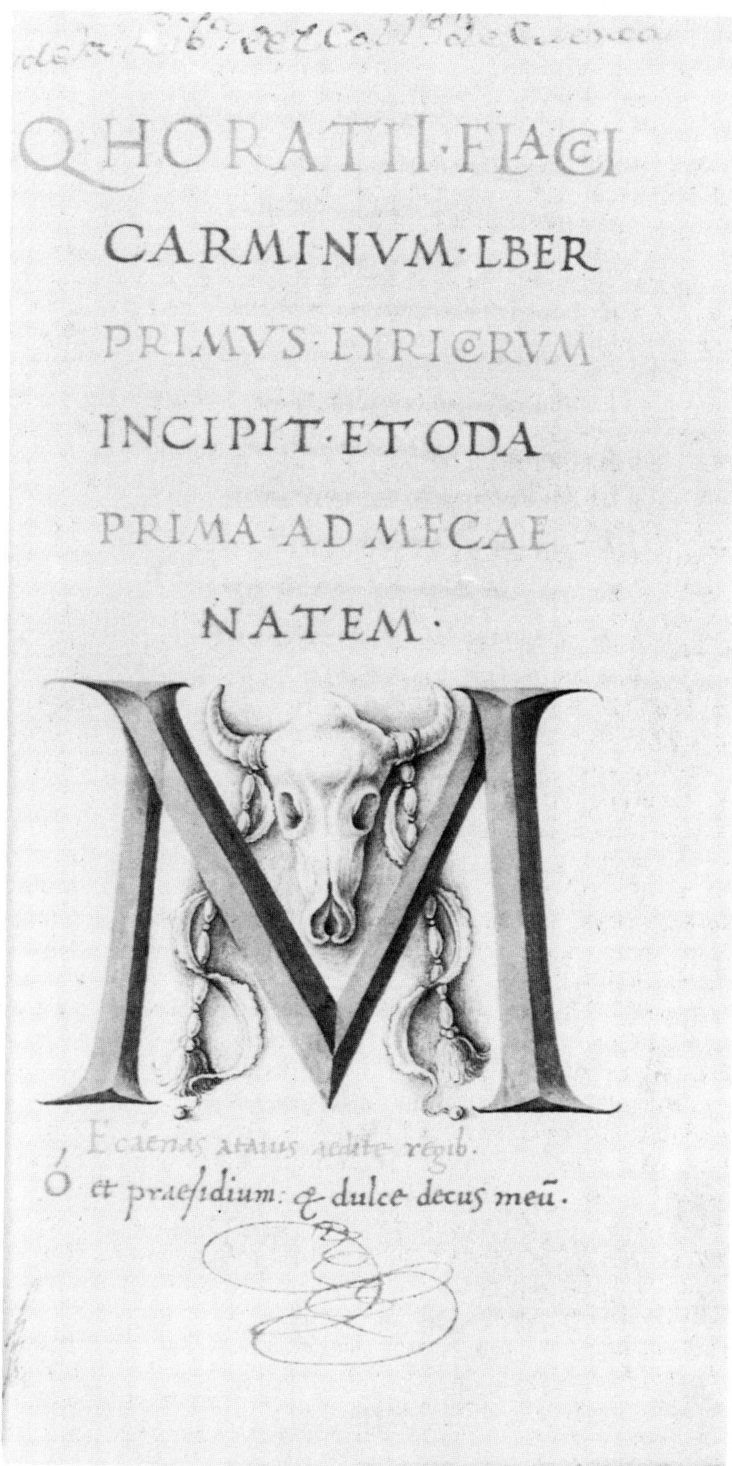

250 London, Sotheby's, 19 June 1979, lot 45, f.1; Horace, Carminum Liber, Padua or Venice, *c.* 1470.
The decorated initial here and the six lines of green and red capitals above it are modelled on the lettering and ornament of classical monuments. This manuscript belonged to King Charles IV *of Spain (1788–1808) and was one of the art works appropriated by Joseph Bonaparte whose baggage train was intercepted at the Battle of Vitoria on 21 June 1813. This book was seized during the battle and afterwards presented to the Duke of Wellington.*

to go on rambles with fellow antiquaries and with the painter Andrea Mantegna to copy out inscriptions. Artists like Mantegna and Marco Zoppo then started to work features of Roman monuments into painting and manuscripts. Illuminators began to rethink the white-vine initials which (of course) had nothing to do with ancient writing. They started to paint into manuscripts capitals copied from monuments: narrow-faceted initials shadowed to look like epigraphic letters chiselled on stone (Pl.250). They introduced a punctuation mark which resembles a little ivyleaf and which is copied from Roman tombstones. Above all, they abandoned the white-vine borders of Florence and they painted as realistically as possible the paraphernalia of Roman carvings, military standards, spears, shields, cornucopiae, funerary vases, coins, rams' heads, dolphins, candelabra, and so forth (Pl.241). They even began to paint the opening pages of manuscripts in colour so that the whole of the text looked deceptively like a Roman inscription or scroll. It was a remarkable new style and very characteristic of the north-east of Italy from about 1470.

There was one great scribe and probably illuminator too from Padua who excelled above all others in his splendid script and the *trompe-l'œil* borders based on classical monuments. This was Bartolomeo Sanvito (1435–1511 or 1512). His script is a most beautiful fluent italic and his elegant coloured capital letters are really admirable (Pl. 246). As so often with great Renaissance scribes, Sanvito was not simply a professional copyist. He was an antiquarian and scholarly collector in the circle of the humanists in Padua: Bernardo Bembo even named his illegitimate son Bartolomeo after him (*c.* 1458). Sanvito's great skill, however, brought him to the papal court in Rome where he is documented from 1469 to 1501. Through him and other north-eastern Italian illuminators, such as Gasparo Padovano, the monumental epigraphic style of manuscripts reached Rome and filtered through to Naples.

In fact this chapter ought to end in the summer of 1465 when two Germans, Conrad Sweynheym and Arnold Pannartz, brought their carts trundling down the same road south towards Rome, bringing the first printing press into Italy. The art of printing with movable type was devised in Mainz in Germany about 1450, and its tremendous advantages to publishers and booksellers were quickly realized. The first books printed in Italy were produced anonymously at the monastery of Subiaco near Rome: probably a Cicero, *De Oratore* (perhaps as early as September 1465), a Lactantius (29 October 1465) and a St. Augustine (12 June 1467). One copy of the St. Augustine, now in the Bibliothèque Nationale, has a purchase note dated November 1467 by Leonardo Dati (d. 1471), the bishop of Massa who figures briefly in Vespasiano's memoirs as a slightly ridiculous bespectacled papal secretary. It says, 'Leonardo Dati, bishop of Massa, with his nephew Giorgio, bought this book about the *City of God* for himself with his own money for 8 gold ducats and two *grossi*, from those two Germans living in Rome who are accustomed to print not write countless books like this.' Sweynheym and Pannartz moved their press into Rome itself that winter. The innumerable copies of the same book amazed Dati and many other people seeing printing for the first time. In one book of 1472, Sweynheym and Pannartz recorded the number of copies they had made of each edition they printed: the usual print run was 275 and sometimes 300. It had taken Vespasiano forty-five scribes and nearly two years to produce fewer volumes than this. The low price intrigued Leonardo Dati too. The chronicler Hartman Schedel happens to record the prices which Sweynheym and Pannartz were asking for printed books in 1470: St. Augustine (1468 edition) has dropped now to 5 ducats; Cicero, *De Oratore*, 1469, is only 19 *grossi* (there were 24 *grossi* to a ducat); Cicero, *De Officiis*, 1469, is one ducat; Caesar's *Commentaries*, 1469, are 2½ ducats; Pliny's massive *Natural History*, 1470, containing 378 leaves, is the most expensive at 8 ducats. By comparison, Cardinal Bessarion had offered his manuscript library to the city of Venice in 1468 at a valuation of 15,000 ducats for 900 volumes: this is an average of just over 16 ducats a book. Federigo da Montefeltro spent 30,000 ducats on his library in Urbino. Even a humble Valerius Maximus manuscript was sold by its scribe in 1440 for 10 ducats (B.L. Add. MS. 14095). The printers could produce books more accurately and more cheaply than any team of scribes. In the event, accuracy and price were more important than script and illumination, and we have been printing books ever since.

Of course this is not the end of making books for humanist bibliophiles. Some illuminators decorated printed books to make them resemble manuscripts. Sweynheym and Pannartz evidently employed their own illuminator if one can judge from the fine white-vine initials by the same artist in many of their books. Especially in Venice, artists who had worked on manuscripts transferred their skills to illuminating printed books, and the quality is sometimes breathtaking (Pl. 247). In Florence scribes went on copying out books for special occasions. The great scribe Antonio Sinibaldi claimed in his tax declaration in 1480 that his work had been reduced by the invention of printing but in fact most of his thirty-two signed manuscripts were made after 1480. Business was not too bad after all. Texts wanted in fewer copies than a printer found economical continued to be written by hand for generations: commemorative addresses, prayers for special occasions, commissions issued by the Doge of Venice, university degrees, unreadable poems, grants of nobility, wedding presents, maps, and, above all, books which collectors simply seemed to prefer in manuscript form. They just liked some books handwritten. Collecting books is not governed by logic. The human response distinguished Renaissance collectors from previous generations. It is enough to like a book without having to explain why. Manuscripts were fine things to collect, and they still are.

BIBLIOGRAPHY

INTRODUCTION

There are many books on medieval manuscripts, frequently out of print and sometimes more expensive than a cheap manuscript, and it is difficult to know how to guide the general reader into the literature on the writing and illumination of books in the Middle Ages. A good recent bibliography, with emphasis on script rather than on illumination, is L. E. Boyle, *Medieval Latin Palaeography, A Bibliographical Introduction* (Toronto, 1984). For the decoration of manuscripts there is L. Donati, *Bibliografia della Miniatura* (*Biblioteca di Bibliografia Italiana*, LXIX), 2 vols. (Florence, 1972). The section 'Bulletin Codicologique' in *Scriptorium*, the journal of manuscript studies published twice a year from Brussels, includes brief summaries of recent books and articles.

I think the first book I read on medieval books was a field guide to *The Oldest Manuscripts in New Zealand* by D. M. Taylor (Wellington, 1955) which includes a step by step account of how to examine the seventy-seven medieval manuscripts then in collections in New Zealand, including the Book of Hours illustrated here as Pl. 2. I visited each of the seventy-seven manuscripts and discovered one or two more. Then, as I remember, I began to look at the popular facsimiles of famous manuscripts such as the *Très Riches Heures* of the Duc de Berry, the *Belles Heures*, the *Rohan Hours* and the *Cloisters Apocalypse*. Such editions usually have introductions explaining the manuscript illustrated. I found John Plummer's *The Hours of Catherine of Cleves* (New York, 1966) particularly useful. Facsimiles like this should not be difficult to obtain and can give much pleasure. Exhibition catalogues, sale catalogues and even postcards can provide the nucleus of an inexpensive palaeographical reference library.

General surveys of medieval manuscript decoration include J. A. Herbert, *Illuminated Manuscripts* (London, 1911, reprinted in 1972), D. M. Robb, *The Art of the Illuminated Manuscript* (Cranbury, N.J., 1973), J. J. G. Alexander, *The Decorated Letter* (London, 1978), and the brief but recent *The Illuminated Manuscript* by Janet Backhouse (Oxford, 1979). I think that F. Madan's *Books in Manuscript* (London, 1893) is still the most readable general account and that D. Diringer's *The Illuminated Book* (2nd ed., London, 1967) is the most unreadable – it aims at comprehensiveness and makes up in telegraphic fact what it loses in narrative. While I was writing the present book, R. G. Calkins's *Illuminated Books of the Middle Ages* (New York and London, 1983) was published. I fell upon it suspiciously, convinced that I would find my unfinished book already superseded, and was relieved to find that it was a detailed guide to a small selection of great manuscripts, mostly liturgical; furthermore, I acknowledge gratefully the help it gave me at the last minute, especially in its early chapters.

For the history of script, E. Maunde Thompson's *An Introduction to Greek and Latin Palaeography* (Oxford, 1912, reprinted in 1975) is the best-known textbook, now old-fashioned, and S. H. Thomson, *Latin Bookhands of the Later Middle Ages, 1100–1500* (Cambridge, 1969), through criticized by professional palaeographers, is a good pictorial guide for the amateur who wants to practise dating and localizing a page of medieval script. On the mechanics of how the script was written, an eccentric and amusing book is M. Drogin, *Medieval Calligraphy, its History and Technique* (Montclair, N.J., 1980); it is compulsory reading for all forgers of medieval manuscripts. Many libraries are now involved in a vast international publishing project which goes under the name of *Manuscrits Datés*: they produce volumes or loose packages of plates from medieval books which are exactly dated by their scribes or to which almost exact dates can be assigned from internal evidence. Two English contributions so far published are by A. G. Watson, for the British Library (1979) and for Oxford (1984). Manuscripts with fixed dates are crucial for book historians who must assemble in sequence the vast majority of other medieval manuscripts which contain no explicit clues as to their date or place of origin. A less critical but monumental anthology of inscriptions and signatures by the scribes themselves in the manuscripts they wrote is the huge six-volume *Colophons des Manuscrits Occidentaux des Origines au XVIe Siècle* by the Bénédictins de Bouveret (Fribourg, Switzerland, 1965–82). I read it right through before I began to write this book, and every chapter is indebted to it.

I Books for MISSIONARIES

There are two fundamental reference books for this chapter. The first is the great twelve-volume series *Codices Latini Antiquiores, A Palaeographical Guide to Latin Manuscripts prior to the Ninth Century*, edited by E. A. Lowe (Oxford, 1934–72). This is an illustrated catalogue of all known Latin manuscripts and fragments earlier than about 800 AD. It is arranged by the countries where the manuscripts are now preserved. The most relevant to the present chapter is Volume II (1935, and a second edition in 1972) for Great Britain and Ireland, but Volumes VIII–IX (1959) include many insular manuscripts taken by the missionaries and others to Germany. The second essential source, at least for manuscripts with illumination, is J. J. G. Alexander, *Insular Manuscripts, 6th to 9th Century* (London, 1978), Volume I in the series *A Survey of Manuscripts Illuminated in the British Isles.* It briefly describes and illustrates 78 decorated English or Irish manuscripts from the period of the missionaries. Almost every manuscript mentioned in this chapter is listed in *C.L.A.* (as it is usually called) or in Dr. Alexander's book, or both, and comprehensive bibliographies are printed there. Recent discoveries include the fragment of St. Gregory's *Moralia*, now at Yale (Pl. 28), and the Bankes leaf of the Ceolfrith Bible (Pls. 11–12); these are listed in B. Bischoff and V. Brown, 'Addenda to *Codices Latini Antiquiores*', *Mediaeval Studies*, XLVII (1985), pp. 340–1 and 351–2. The relic label mentioned on pp. 29–30 is illustrated in the complementary series for documents, *Chartae Latinae Antiquiores*, edited by A. Bruckner and R. Marichal, I (Olten and Lausanne, 1954), no. 36.

The outstanding contemporary source for the period is Bede's *History of the English* which he completed in 731. The quotations in this chapter are from the Penguin Classics edition by Leo Sherley-Price (1955). Much of the historical background to the period can be found in F. M. Stenton, *Anglo-Saxon England* (Oxford, 1947, 2nd edn. 1971). My account of book production at Wearmouth and Jarrow owes much to articles by T. J. Brown and R. L. S. Bruce-Mitford in *Evangeliorum Quattuor Codex Lindisfarnensis*, ed. T. D. Kendrick (Olten and Lausanne,

II, 1960) and especially to the Jarrow Lecture by M. B. Parkes, published as *The Scriptorium of Wearmouth-Jarrow* (1982); the quotation at the top of p. 32 is from this source. I attended Dr. Parkes's classes on insular manuscripts in 1972–3 and some lines of inquiry in this chapter are derived from imperfect recollections of those excellent seminars. The Durham Cathedral fragment of Maccabees (p. 19 here, and Pl. 13) is described by R. A. B. Mynors, *Durham Cathedral Manuscripts to the End of the Twelfth Century* (Oxford, 1939), p. 14 and Pl. 1, and E. A. Lowe in his *Palaeographical Papers, 1907–1965*, ed. L. Bieler (Oxford, 1972), II, pp. 475–6. Detailed studies of individual manuscripts include F. Wormald, *The Miniatures in the Gospels of St. Augustine, Corpus Christi College, MS. 286* (Cambridge, 1954, reprinted in his *Collected Writings*, I, London and Oxford, 1984, pp. 13–35); T. J. Brown, *The Stonyhurst Gospel of St. John* (Oxford, 1969); the massive analysis of the Lindisfarne Gospels cited above and the much more accessible *The Lindisfarne Gospels* by Janet Backhouse (Oxford, 1981); D. H. Wright and A. Campbell, *The Vespasian Psalter* (*Early English Manuscripts in Facsimile*, XIV, 1967); E. H. Alton and P. Meyer, *Evangeliorum Quattuor Codex Cenannensis*, 3 vols. (Berne, 1950–1), a full facsimile of the Book of Kells, though readers will not find it as easily available as F. Henry, *The Book of Kells* (London, 1974) and P. Brown, *The Book of Kells* (London, 1980). Each one of these has an introduction as well as many plates, and I have consulted both. One of the cheapest monographs ever published on a manuscript is in the series of Pitkin Pictorial Guides and Souvenir Books, *The Lichfield Gospels* by D. Brown, based on work by Wendy Stein (London, 1982); it is excellently produced.

2 Books for EMPERORS

Except for books like C. R. Dodwell, *Painting in Europe, 800–1200* (Harmondsworth, 1971), which spans the period admirably, most of the literature on imperial manuscripts focuses either on the Carolingian or on the Ottonian period. For the former age, the classic texts include A. Boinet, *La Miniature Carolingienne* (Paris, 1913), A. Goldschmidt, *German Illumination*, I, *The Carolingian Period* (Florence and Paris, 1928), R. Hinks, *Carolingian Art* (London, 1935) and W. Köhler, *Die Karolingischen Miniaturen*, 4 vols. (Berlin, 1930–71). A short but excellent recent book is Florentine Mütherich and J. E. Gaehde, *Karolingische Buchmalerei* (Munich, 1976, published the same year in English as *Carolingian Painting*). The progress of art history in Germany owes much to vast exhibition catalogues. The huge *Karl der Grosse, Lebenswerk und Nachleben*, 4 vols. (Düsseldorf, 1965–67), forms a great synthesis of recent scholarship on manuscript studies of the period, especially volumes II, *Das Geistige Leben*, edited by B. Bischoff (including his article on the court library of Charlemagne, pp. 42–62), and III, *Karolingische Kunst*, edited by W. Braunfels and H. Schnitzler; I owe to these catalogues references both to Charlemagne's library catalogue and to his elephant. For Carolingian script, the first generation of the new minuscule is netted within Lowe's *Codices Latini Antiquiores*, and a similar project is now being extended to the ninth century by the almost legendary and immensely learned Professor Bernhard Bischoff. Earlier studies include E. K. Rand, *A Survey of the Manuscripts of Tours* (Cambridge, Mass., 1929), quoted here on p. 56, and the unusual Lyell lectures of S. Morison, *Politics and Script, Aspects of Authority and Freedom in the Development of Graeco-Latin Script*, ed. N. Barker (Oxford, 1972), selecting the Maurdramnus Bible as the first great imperial book.

At the Ottonian end of the period I have been guided by the long article by Florentine Mütherich in *Le Siècle de l'An Mil* (ed. L. Grodecki, F. Mütherich, J. Taralon and F. Wormald, Paris, 1973, pp. 87–188) and helped by A. Goldschmidt, *German Illumination*, II, *The Ottonian Period* (Florence and Paris, 1928), A. R. A. Hobson, *Great Libraries* (London, 1970, esp. pp. 36–43 on the library at Bamberg), and Calkins, *Illuminated Books*, esp. pp. 119–160. The significance of gold treasure in early Germanic culture is a theme I was taught by Professor G. S. Parsonson of Otago University but its application here is my own extension of his theory. Some of the very great imperial manuscripts are available in luxurious facsimiles, including the Dagulf Psalter, Pl. 39 here (edited by K. Holter, Graz, 1980), the Lorsch Gospels, Pl. 41 (edited by W. Braunfels, Munich, 1967), the Codex Aureus of St. Emmeram, Pl. 66 (edited by G. Leidinger, Munich, 1921–31), the Gospels of Otto III, Pls. 52–3 and 61–2 (edited by F. Dressler, F. Mütherich and H. Beumann, Frankfurt, 1978), the Gospel Pericopes of Henry II, Pl. 68 (Munich, 1914), and two of the Gospel Books of Henry III, those in Bremen (Pls. 64–5, edited by G. Knoll and others, Wiesbaden, 1980) and in the Escorial (Pl. 57, edited by A. Boeckler, Berlin, 1933). A facsimile of the Gospels of Henry the Lion is in course of preparation; in the meantime, the fullest set of plates is in the Sotheby's catalogue for 6 December 1983.

3 Books for MONKS

The writing of this chapter would have been immeasurably more difficult without N. R. Ker's *Medieval Libraries of Great Britain* (2nd edn., London, 1964; a supplement is now being edited by A. G. Watson). This is a list of every surviving manuscript which is known to have belonged to any British medieval monastery. It is a fascinating book of the kind in which one cannot look up one reference only: twenty minutes later one is still absorbed, pages from where one started. The entries for Reading Abbey are on pp. 154–8. The library catalogue for Reading, Pl. 73, was published by S. Barfield, 'Lord Fingall's Cartulary of Reading Abbey', *English Historical Review*, III (1888), pp. 117–23, and needs re-editing. The liturgical fragment at Douai Abbey, cited here on p. 81, is described in N. R. Ker, *Medieval Manuscripts in British Libraries*, II (Oxford, 1977), pp. 418–9. There is a short article by J. R. Liddell, 'Some Notes on the Library of Reading Abbey', *Bodleian Quarterly Record*, VIII (1935), pp. 47–54.

For script and scribal practices in England in the twelfth century, the seminal book is N. R. Ker, *English Manuscripts in the Century after the Norman Conquest, The Lyell Lectures, Oxford, 1952–3* (Oxford, 1960), a slim folio so concisely written that every reading reveals new facts. It is out of print and second-hand copies are expensive. Supplementing this with C. M. Kauffmann, *Romanesque Manuscripts, 1066–1190* (*A Survey of Manuscripts Illuminated in the British Isles*, III, London, 1975), one can step into romanesque book production in England with greater confidence than for elsewhere in Europe. The Arts Council exhibition catalogue *English Romanesque Art, 1066–1200* (London, 1984) includes many manuscripts in a substantial section by J. J. G. Alexander and C. M. Kauffmann, pp. 82–133, bringing bibliographies up to date. Early work on English monastic libraries owes a great deal to the antiquarian work of M. R. James, writer of ghost stories and giant among English manuscript cataloguers; it is pleasant to be able to reproduce a manuscript at Eton (Pl. 79), James's own College.

Certain centres of English romanesque book production have been studied in greater detail than others. Notable books include C. R. Dodwell, *The Canterbury School of Illumination, 1066–1200* (Cambridge, 1954), which deals primarily with the decoration and iconography of manuscripts, and R. M. Thomson, *Manuscripts from St. Albans Abbey, 1066–1235*, 2 vols. (Hobart, 1982), which follows the march of library acquisition and the work of the scribes involved in one of the greatest (and not necessarily most typical) English monasteries. Mr. Michael Gullick has recently been working on the scriptorium at Cirencester Abbey and when his work is published it may necessitate corrections to my note on Cirencester scribes on p. 96 and Pls. 83–4 and 87. The *De Diversis Artibus* of Theophilus, cited on p. 84, has been edited and translated by C. R. Dodwell, *Theophilus, The Various Arts* (London and Edinburgh, 1961). Few individual manuscripts have ever been as thoroughly studied, or as worthily, as the Winchester Bible has been by Sir Walter Oakeshott. His little book *The Artists of the Winchester Bible* (London, 1945) isolated for the first time recognizable personalities among the manuscript's illuminators and introduced painters such as the Master of the Leaping Figures into the canon of English artists. Oakeshott's *Sigena, Romanesque Paintings in Spain and the Winchester Bible Artists* (London, 1972) linked these painters with fragmentary frescoes in Spain, and his huge *The Two Winchester Bibles* (Oxford, 1981) focusses on the relationship between the Bible and a second monumental copy, Bodleian MS. Auct. E. inf. 2, which the Winchester monks made at the same time. Pls. 100–101 were first reproduced in *The Two Winchester Bibles*, Pls. 39 and 60. Articles on English book production in this period include N. R. Ker on Salisbury in *Medieval Learning and Literature, Essays presented to R. W. Hunt*, ed. J. J. G. Alexander and M. T. Gibson (Oxford, 1976), pp. 23–49; R. M. Thomson on Bury St. Edmunds in *Speculum*, XLVII (1972), pp. 617–45; J. J. G. Alexander on painted 'arabesque' initials in *Medieval Scribes, Manuscripts and Libraries, Essays presented to N. R. Ker*, ed. M. B. Parkes and A. G. Watson (London, 1978), pp. 87–116; and G. Pollard on the construction of the kind of bookbindings illustrated here in Pl. 102, *The Library*, 5 ser., XVII (1962), pp. 1–22.

4 Books for STUDENTS

For the early part of Chapter 4 I have raided my own *Glossed Books of the Bible and the Origins of the Paris Booktrade* (Woodbridge, 1984), especially for the publishing of the Gloss and the works of Peter Lombard. The fine manuscript reproduced as Pl. 106 was lent to me by Messrs. Quaritch Ltd. who owned it until it was sold in December 1985 to the Walters Art Gallery; it was previously in the Dyson Perrins collection (sale at Sotheby's, 1 December 1959, lot 54). For Parisian illumination of the early thirteenth century I am indebted to F. Avril, 'À Quand Remontent les Premiers Ateliers d'Enlumineurs laïcs à Paris?', *Les Dossiers de l'Archéologie*, XVI (1976), pp. 36–44, and to the pioneering book, which is cited on p. 120, R. Branner, *Manuscript Painting in Paris during the Reign of St. Louis, A Study of Styles* (Berkeley and Los Angeles, 1977). Like all work which breaks new ground, it will need substantial revision as research progresses, and the fact that it was published after its author's early death means that it is not always free from accidents of proofreading; none the less, it is a remarkable book. The story by Odofredo (p. 107) is taken from Branner, and the identifications of workshops on p. 120 are his. Surprisingly, considering the importance of the subject, there is no standard account of the publication of the one-volume Bible, discussed on pp. 110–17. References can be found in R. Loewe, 'The Medieval History of the Latin Vulgate' in *The Cambridge History of the Bible*, ed. G. W. H. Lampe, II (Cambridge, 1969), pp. 102–54, and in B. Smalley, *The Study of the Bible in the Middle Ages* (Oxford, 1952, reprinted in 1970). For the university of Paris and its curriculum in the thirteenth century, I have used H. Rashdall, *The Universities of Europe in the Middle Ages*, edited by F. M. Powicke and A. B. Emden, I (Oxford, 1936), P. Glorieux, *Répertoire des Maîtres en Théologie de Paris au XIIIe Siècle* (Paris, 1936) and the little Sorbonne exhibition catalogue, *La Vie Universitaire Parisienne au XIIIe Siècle* (Paris, 1974). There is a vast treasury of information on French manuscripts of all periods, including the early Parisian booktrade, in L. Delisle, *Le Cabinet des Manuscrits*, 4 vols. (Paris, 1868–81, reprinted in 1969) and it was valuable here, as always.

The practice of copying manuscripts in *peciae*, pp. 126–30, still needs a full-length definitive study by a brave historian. The classic explanation is J. Destrez, *La Pecia dans les Manuscrits Universitaires du XIIIe et du XIVe Siècle* (Paris, 1935) and there is an account of Destrez's work by his pupil G. Fink-Errera in *Scriptorium*, XI (1957), pp. 264–80. A list of surviving university *pecia* exemplars is given by Destrez and M. D. Chenu in *Scriptorium*, VII (1953), pp. 68–80. A lecture by Graham Pollard (with whom I had many discussions of the early booktrade) was printed posthumously, 'The *Pecia* System in the Medieval Universities', *Essays presented to N. R. Ker* (1978, cited above), pp. 145–61. The article by P.-M. J. Gils, mentioned on p. 129, appears as 'Pour une Étude du MS. Pamplona, Catedral 51', *Scriptorium*, XXXII (1978), pp. 221–30. Above all, however, for correcting several mistaken impressions I had on *peciae* and for the identification of the bookshop in the Rue St-Jacques, I am most grateful to M. A. and R. H. Rouse for lending me their typescript of a very important forthcoming article, 'The University Book Trade in Thirteenth-Century Paris' in *La Production des Livres Universitaire au Moyen Age: Pecia et Exemplar*, edited by L. Bataillon and R. H. Rouse. The extracts from the tax rolls, cited on p. 130, are taken from Françoise Baron, 'Enlumineurs, Peintures et Sculpteurs des XIIIe et XIVe Siècles d'après les Rôles de la Taille', *Bulletin Archéologique du Comité des Travaux Historiques et Scientifiques*, n.s., IV (1968), pp. 37–121.

This chapter has been mainly concerned with Paris. Recent works on manuscript illumination in Bologna include E. Cassee, *The Missal of Cardinal Bertrand de Deux, A Study in Fourteenth-Century Bolognese Miniature Painting* (Florence, 1980), A. Conti, *La Miniatura Bolognese, Scuole et Botteghe, 1270–1340* (Bologna, 1981), and P. M. de Winter, 'Bolognese Miniatures at the Cleveland Museum', *Bulletin of the Cleveland Museum of Art*, LXX (1983). pp. 314–51. The pioneer work on the medieval booktrade in Oxford was by G. Pollard (such as his 'William de Brailes' in the *Bodleian Library Record*, V, 1955, pp. 202–9) and I owe my reference to Reginald (p. 134) to notes Mr. Pollard kindly lent me in 1974. Eton College MS. 44, quoted here on pp. 134–5, is described by N. R. Ker in *Litterae Textuales*, I, *Varia Codicologica, Essays presented to G. I. Leiftinck*, I (Amsterdam, 1972), pp. 48–60.

5 Books for ARISTOCRATS

Probably few subjects in the humanities have produced more extensive writing than literary criticism has done. To many readers, medieval manuscripts are of value primarily as vehicles of literature. This chapter comprises a necessarily superficial survey of medieval vernacular writing, and I am aware of the dangers of trying to balance literary importance with medieval circulation judged from surviving manuscripts: *Beowulf* and Malory's *Morte D'Arthur*, for example, have come down in only one manuscript each and yet no one would doubt their significance over Petrus Riga's *Aurora*, for example, which survives in very many hundreds of copies. In compiling this chapter I looked at general books on literary history and tried to bear in mind what kind of manuscripts one might actually expect to find in a library or museum. I used R. S. Briffault, *The Troubadours* (Indiana, 1965), E. Rose, *A History of German Literature* (New York, 1960), J. H. Whitfield, *A Short History of Italian Literature* (London, 1960) and E. H. Wilkins, *A History of Italian Literature*, revised by T. G. Bergin (Cambridge, Mass., 1974). As a handbook to medieval literary manuscripts, there is still great value in H. D. Ward, *Catalogue of Romances in the Department of Manuscripts in the British Museum*, 3 vols. (London, 1883–1910, reprinted in 1961) and the historian of French manuscripts will need R. Bossuat, *Manuel Bibliographique de la Littérature Française au Moyen Age* (Melun, 1951, with supplements in 1955, 1961, etc.). A useful book, not as narrow as its title suggests, is R. Lejeune and J. Stiennon, *La Legende de Roland dans l'Art du Moyen Age*, 2 vols. (Brussels, 1966).

The thirteenth-century Canticles of Alfonso the Wise (p. 141) are discussed in J. G. Lovillo, *Las Cántigas, Estudio Arqueológico de sus Miniaturas* (Madrid, 1949), and in J. Domínguez-Bordona, *Spanish Illumination*, II (Florence and Paris, 1930), pp. 38–42. Manuscripts of the Lancelot romances (pp. 141–2) are described by Alison Stones in 'Secular Manuscript Illumination in France', *Medieval Manuscripts and Textual Studies*, ed. C. Kleinhenz (Chapel Hill, 1976), pp. 83–102, and 'The Earliest Illustrated Prose *Lancelot* Manuscript?', *Annual Proceedings of the Graduate Centre for Medieval Studies in the University of Reading*, III (1977), pp. 3–44. The edition by Elspeth Kennedy, *Lancelot de Lac, The Non-Cyclic Old French Prose Romance*, 2 vols. (Oxford, 1980), uses 44 manuscripts, listed in Vol. II, pp. 1–9. A census of manuscripts of the *Roman de la Rose*, now in need of some revision, was published by E. Langlois, *Les Manuscrits du Roman de la Rose, Description et Classement* (Lille and Paris, 1910); a fluent English edition of the *Romance of the Rose* is by C. Dahlberg (Princeton, 1961). For Dante manuscripts with miniatures (and many copies are unillustrated) there is P. Brieger, M. Meiss and C. S. Singleton, *Illuminated Manuscripts of the Divine Comedy* (New York, 1969). I am grateful to Mr H. P. Kraus and to Dr Roland Folter for the illustration which forms the frontispiece here, the fine Dante manuscript which belonged to Charles James Fox, Sir Thomas Phillipps and Dr Martin Bodmer. For Chaucer's *Canterbury Tales* a quite outstanding (if sometimes over-ingenious) list of manuscripts and references to them, such as the wills mentioned here on p. 144, is by J. M. Manly and E. Rickert, *The Text of the Canterbury Tales, Studied on the Basis of all known Manuscripts*, I, *Description of the Manuscripts* (Chicago, 1940).

The production and illumination of romances in the fourteenth century is a theme which can be found in M. Meiss, *French Painting in the Time of Jean de Berry, The Late Fourteenth Century and the Patronage of the Duke*, 2 vols. (London, 1967), F. Avril, *Manuscript Painting at the Court of France, The Fourteenth Century (1310–1380)* (London, 1978) and by Avril again in *Les Fastes du Gothique, Le Siècle de Charles V*, exhibition at the Grand Palais (Paris, 1981–2). Manuscripts of the *Bible Historiale* are described in S. Berger, *La Bible Française au Moyen Age* (Paris, 1894), pp. 157–220; Alexander romances and the *Histoire Ancienne* are in D. J. A. Ross, *Alexander Historiatus, A Guide to Medieval Illustrated Alexander Literature* (London, 1963); Anne D. Hedeman has recently worked on all the manuscripts of the *Grandes Chroniques de France* (dissertation, Johns Hopkins University, 1984); for Vincent of Beauvais, see the note by G. G. Guzman in *Scriptorium*, XXIX (1975), pp. 122–5, and on the translator Jean de Vignay by C. Knowles in *Romania*, LXXV (1954), pp. 353–77; Pl. 150 here shows the Gaston de Foix manuscript recently acquired by the Morgan Library from the estate of Miss Clara Peck – for the text, see G. Tilander, *Gaston Phébus, Livre de Chasse* (Karlshamm, 1971).

6 Books for EVERYBODY

Despite a welcome number of recent publications, there is still no standard history of Books of Hours. The classic work is the catalogue by V. Leroquais, *Les Livres d'Heures Manuscrits de la Bibliothèque Nationale*, 3 vols. (Paris, 1927, with a supplement issued in 1943) with an 85-page introduction defining and describing the contents of a Book of Hours. The first modern historian to treat Books of Hours seriously was L. M. J. Delaissé who died suddenly in 1972 before his work was complete; posthumous echoes of his teaching are in his article 'The Importance of Books of Hours for the History of the Medieval Book', *Gatherings in Honor of Dorothy Miner* (Baltimore, 1974), pp. 203–25, and in the excessively big *Illuminated Manuscripts* catalogue of Waddesdon Manor (London and Fribourg, 1977). Recent accounts of Books of Hours, all of which should be easily available, include J. Harthan, *Books of Hours and their Owners* (London, 1977), Calkins, *Illuminated Books*, pp. 243–81, and the new British Library booklet by Janet Backhouse, *Books of Hours* (London, 1985). The account here of how to identify the 'Use' of a Book of Hours, pp. 164–5, is mainly based on the extensive tables published by F. Madan, 'Hours of the Virgin Mary (Tests for Localization)', *Bodleian Quarterly Record*, III, 1920–22, pp. 40–44. Because Books of Hours have such popular appeal, as they have always done, publishers of manuscript facsimiles have often chosen this text to reproduce. Editions with especially useful introductions include J. Plummer, *The Hours of Catherine of Cleves* (New York, 1966), J. Longnon, R. Cazelles and M. Meiss, *Les Très Riches Heures du Duc de Berry* (London, 1969) and the splendid new (and admittedly exceedingly expensive) full facsimile of the *Très Riches Heures* edited by R. Cazelles (New York, 1984), Margaret Manion, *The Wharncliffe Hours* (London, 1981), D. H. Turner, *The Hastings Hours* (London, 1983) and R. Watson, *The Playfair Hours* (London, 1984); I acknowledge help from the latter, in particular for the comparison of statistics of early printed Books of Hours and for the names of those involved in the Rouen booktrade (p. 185).

Most studies of late medieval manuscript decoration include many Books of Hours. Parisian illumination in the decades around 1400 is documented massively, and not always uncontroversially, in the well-illustrated series by M. Meiss, *French Painting in the Time of Jean de Berry* (London and New York, 1967–1974), including his volume on *The Boucicaut Master* (1968) from which I computed the number of surviving Boucicaut miniatures, pp. 178–9, and learned many other facts used here. Information on the booktrade in Paris is given by P. M. de Winter, 'Copistes, Editeurs et Enlumineurs de la Fin du XIVe Siècle: La Production à Paris de Manuscrits à Miniatures', *Actes du 100e Congrès National des Sociétés Savantes*, 1975 (Paris, 1978), pp. 173–98. J. Plummer's Morgan Library catalogue *The Last Flowering, French Painting in Manuscripts, 1420–1530, from American Collections* (New York, 1982) is quite the best guide to localizing Books of Hours from towns in provincial France, supplemented by E. König, *Französische Buchmalerei um 1450, Der Jouvenel-Maler, Der Maler des Genfer Boccaccio, und die Anfänge Jean Fouquets* (Berlin, 1982) for manuscripts from the Loire valley and Brittany. In an earlier exhibition catalogue, *La Miniature Flamande, Le Mécénat de Philippe le Bon* (Brussels, 1959), L. M. J. Delaissé classified provincial Flemish illuminators of the fifteenth century, and for the great period of Ghent/Bruges art of around 1500 the textbook is still F. Winkler, *Die Flämische Buchmalerei des XV. und XVI. Jahrhunderts* (Leipzig, 1925), soon to be updated by Georges Dogaer, and there is a good summary of recent work in the section on 'Flemish Manuscript Illumination, 1475–1550' by T. Kren in the exhibition catalogue he edited, *Renaissance Painting in Manuscripts, Treasures from the British Library* (New York and London, 1983), pp. 3–85. Dutch illuminated manuscripts are described by A. W. Byvanck and G. J. Hoogenwerff, *La Miniature Hollandaise* (The Hague, 1922–6) and are now being comprehensively studied by James Marrow. With the eventual publication of Professor Marrow's book, and that of Kathleen Scott on English fifteenth-century illumination, our knowledge of localizable workshops outside France will become much clearer. On the mechanics of duplicating designs for Books of Hours, by tracing or copying from pattern sheets, an excellent account is in J. D. Farquhar, *Creation and Imitation, The Work of a Fifteenth-Century Manuscript Illuminator* (Fort Lauderdale, 1976), esp. Chapter 2, pp. 41–74.

7 Books for PRIESTS

The most thorough recent study of liturgical manuscripts is A. Hughes, *Medieval Manuscripts for Mass and Office, A Guide to their Organization and Terminology* (Toronto, 1982), and the most readable, though unashamedly parochial, is C. Wordsworth and H. Littlehales, *The Old Service-Books of the English Church* (London, 1904); I owe my references to English documents on pp. 197 and 205 to this book. A clear summary of the different classes of book is *Liturgical Manuscripts for the Mass and Divine Office*, an exhibition catalogue for the Morgan Library by John Plummer (New York, 1966). Because the Roman Catholic liturgy remained largely unchanged until recent years, the basic texts of the Missal and the Breviary should be obtainable in Latin from second-hand bookshops. The *Liber Usualis*, edited by the Benedictines of Solesmes, is a handbook of plainchant intended for choristers but is a most valuable tool for medievalists and is indexed by the opening words of antiphons and other chants; I was given a copy in 1970 by Kathryn Monteath, and have found it constantly useful ever since.

The great catalogues by V. Leroquais of liturgical manuscripts in France formed the basis of my notes here on scribes and patronage in the fifteenth century. The catalogues are *Les Sacramentaires et les Missels Manuscrits des Bibliothèques Publiques de France*, 4 vols. (Paris, 1924), *Les Bréviaires*, 6 vols. (Paris, 1934), *Les Pontificaux*, 3 vols. (Paris, 1937) and *Les Psautiers*, 2 vols. (Macon, 1940–41). The observations on Bibles in the Low Countries, pp. 209 and 213, are derived in part from L. M. J. Delaissé, *A Century of Dutch Manuscript Illumination* (Berkeley and Los Angeles, 1968), the exhibition catalogue by A. Brounts, *La Miniature Hollandaise, Le Grand Siècle de l'Enluminure du Livre dans les Pays-Bas Septentrionaux* (Brussels, 1971), and from Sandra Hindman, *Text and Image in Fifteenth-Century Dutch Bibles* (Leiden, 1977). For the illumination of Gutenberg Bibles I am indebted to E. König, 'Die Illuminierung der Gutenbergbibel', commentary volume to the facsimile *Johannes Gutenbergs 42-zeilige Bibel* (Munich, 1979), pp. 71–125, and his 'The Influence of the Invention of Printing on the Development of German Illumination', *Manuscripts in the Fifty Years after the Invention of Printing, Some Papers read at a Colloquium at the Warburg Institute on 12–13 March 1982*, ed. J. B. Trapp (London, 1983), pp. 85–94.

8 Books for COLLECTORS

Research on the script and book production of the Italian renaissance is a curiously recent development. When Sydney Cockerell and the Arts and Crafts connoisseurs began to collect and admire humanistic manuscripts in the early 1900s, their tastes must have been regarded as eccentrically English. It was in England that bibliographers began to look critically at *quattrocento* script, imitating it for their own 'italic' handwriting, and it is still from England and America that much inquiry has been undertaken into the humanists' books. A little publication as recent as the Bodleian guide *Humanistic Script of the Fifteenth and Sixteenth Centuries*, by A. J. Fairbank and R. W. Hunt (Oxford, 1960) was a pioneering work. B. L. Ullman, *The Origin and Development of Humanistic Script* (Rome, 1960) introduced by name many Florentine scribes of the early period, and J. Wardrop, *The Script of Humanism, Some Aspects of Humanistic Script, 1460–1540* (Oxford, 1963) adds some of the most human anecdote and observation ever accorded to medieval workmen; his epithet on Feliciano is quoted at the bottom of p. 242. Wardrop's book must have given delight to many people. It was he who first identified the importance of Bartolomeo Sanvito, now regarded as the greatest Italian scribe; the study of Sanvito is now safely in the hands of Dr A. C. de la Mare and Mgr José Ruysschaert.

For the early part of this chapter I have used the monumental first part of A. C. de la Mare, *Handwriting of the Italian Humanists*, Vol. 1, fasc. 1 (Oxford, 1973) and have consulted L. D. Reynolds and N. G. Wilson, *Scribes and Scholars, A Guide to the Transmission of Greek and Latin Literature* (Oxford, 1968), chapter 4, pp. 101–36, and L. D. Reynolds, ed., *Texts and Transmission, A Survey of the Latin Classics* (Oxford, 1983). The references to Bembo on p. 215 are derived from C. H. Clough, 'The Library of Bernardo and of Pietro Bembo', *The Book Collector*, XXXIII (1984), pp. 305–31. The comparison between Niccoli and Old Brown (p. 218) was first made by Nicolas Barker (*The Book Collector*, XXVII, 1978, p. 383) about John Sparrow who taught me bibliophily.

The quotations from Vespasiano on p. 224 are from the translation by W. G. and E. Waters, *The Vespasiano Memoirs, Lives of Illustrious Men of the XVth Century by Vespasiano da Bisticci, Bookseller* (London, 1926). There are accounts of the Medici Library in Hobson, *Great Libraries*, pp. 85–91, B. L. Ullman and P. A. Stadter, *The Public Library of Renaissance Florence* (Padua, 1972), and F. Ames-Lewis, *The Library and Manuscripts of Piero di Cosimo de'Medici* (London, 1984). The book acquisitions of William Grey are discussed in R. A. B. Mynors, *Catalogue of the Manuscripts of Balliol College, Oxford* (Oxford, 1963), esp. pp. xxiv–xlv, and in the Bodleian exhibition catalogue by R. W. Hunt and A. C. de la Mare, *Duke Humfrey and English Humanism in the Fifteenth Century* (Oxford, 1970), esp. pp. 24–31. The library of the kings of Aragon is presented in a luxurious edition by T. De Marinis, *La Biblioteca Napoletana dei Re d'Aragona*, 4 vols. (Milan, 1947–52, with a supplement in 1969); for the books of Matthias Corvinus, see C. Csapodi and K. Csapodi-Gárdonyi, *Biblioteca Corviniana* (Shannon, 1969); and for those of Cardinal Bessarion, L. Labowsky, *Bessarion's Library and the Biblioteca Marciana* (Rome, 1979). For some of the identifications of Florentine scribes by A. C. de la Mare, see her 'Messer Piero Strozzi, a Florentine Priest and Scribe', *Calligraphy and Palaeography, Essays presented to Alfred Fairbank*, ed. A. S. Osley (London, 1965), pp. 55–68; *The Italian Manuscripts in the Library of Major J. R. Abbey*, with J. J. G. Alexander (London, 1969); and 'The Florentine Scribes of Cardinal Giovanni of Aragon', *Il Libro e il Testo, Atti del Convegno Internazionale, Urbino, 20–23 settembre 1982*, ed. C. Questa and R. Raffaelli (Urbino, 1984), pp. 245–93. I have not yet seen her new book, published in Florence late in 1985, with Annarosa Garzelli, listing manuscripts by identifiable scribes and illuminators in fifteenth-century Florence.

The illumination of humanistic manuscripts is discussed in O. Pächt, *Italian Illuminated Manuscripts from 1400 to 1550, Catalogue of an Exhibition held in the Bodleian Library* (Oxford, 1948), and by J. J. G. Alexander, both in his share of the Abbey catalogue, cited above (esp. pp. xxxiii–xl), and in his *Italian Renaissance Illuminations* (New York, 1977). There is a good recent account in the Bibliothèque Nationale exhibition by F. Avril, *10 Siècles d'Enluminure Italienne (VIe–XVIe Siècles)* (Paris, 1984), esp. pp. 109–179. For Italian renaissance bookbindings, the magisterial catalogue of surviving examples is T. De Marinis, *La Legatura Artistica in Italia nei Secoli XV e XVI, Notizie ed Elenchi*, 3 vols. (Florence, 1960).

INDEX OF MANUSCRIPTS

Italic figures indicate plate numbers

GENERAL INDEX

Italic figures indicate plate numbers